ARTICLES ON ————————————————

COLONIALISM AND NATIONALISM IN AFRICA

A Four-Volume Anthology
of Scholarly Articles

Series Editors

GREGORY MADDOX
Texas Southern University

TIMOTHY K. WELLIVER
Bellarmine College

A GARLAND SERIES

SERIES CONTENTS

VOLUME

1

CONQUEST AND RESISTANCE TO COLONIALISM IN AFRICA

Edited with introduction by

GREGORY MADDOX

GARLAND PUBLISHING, Inc.
New York & London
1993

Library of Congress Cataloging-in-Publication Data

Conquest and resistance to colonialism in Africa / edited by Gregory
Maddox.
    p.   cm. — (Colonialism and nationalism in Africa ; v. 1)
    Includes bibliographical references.
    ISBN 0–8153–1388–8 (alk. paper)
    1. Africa—Colonization. 2. Africa—History—19th century.
3. Africa—History—1884–1960. I. Maddox, Gregory. II. Series.
DT28.C66 1993
960.3—dc20   93–19790
                                    CIP

Printed on acid-free, 250-year-life paper
Manufactured in the United States of America

CONTENTS

SERIES INTRODUCTION

The study of African history as an academic discipline is a rather new field and one that still has its detractors both within and outside academics. The eminent British historian Hugh Trevor-Roper, now Lord Dacre, is once reputed to have said that African history consisted of nothing but "the murderous gyrations of barbarous tribes," while more recently the Czech novelist Milan Kundera has written to the effect that even if it could be proved that hundreds of thousands of Africans died horrendous deaths in the Middle Ages it would all count for nothing. At the very least, such views are a matter of perspective; for the 400 million or so people living in the nations of sub-Saharan Africa today history still shapes the rhythm of their destiny.

This collection of articles highlights for students and scholars the modern era in African history. It brings together published research on the colonial era in Africa, an era relatively brief but one that saw dramatic change in African societies. It highlights the ongoing research into the struggles for independence and social transformation that continue to the present. The authors of these articles eloquently rebut the Euro-centric bias of critics like Trevor-Roper and Kundera and claim for African societies and Africans their rightful place as agents of history.

The articles collected here cover the period between the "Scramble for Africa" in the late nineteenth century, when all but two nations in Africa became colonies of European powers, and the struggles to define the meaning of independence in Africa and throw off the last vestiges of white rule in the southern part of the continent. Such a concentration by no means implies that African societies before the late nineteenth century were tradition-bound or unchanging. They developed according to their own pace and played significant roles in world affairs from the days when West Africa provided a major proportion of the Old World's gold before 1500 through the era of the Atlantic slave trade. However, the colonial era created the modern map of Africa, and Africans transformed their societies politically, economically, and socially in the face of their forced integration into the world economy as producers of raw materials.

vii

The articles in this collection chart the development of African historical studies. As the field emerged in the late 1950s and early 1960s, many historians sought to place the struggle by African peoples to liberate themselves from colonialism and racial domination within a historical tradition. Some scholars, inspired by T. O. Ranger's work, sought to link modern nationalist movements to resistance to colonial rule in the late nineteenth century. They also focused on the development of what they saw as a national consciousness that overlaid existing economic, ethnic, and religious communities.

The reaction to this approach was not long in coming within both African politics and historical scholarship. The ongoing struggles within African nations, often defined in ethnic terms, find their image reflected in early critical works such as those of Steinhart and Denoon and Kuper included here that question the development of national consciousness. More generally, as I. N. Kimambo of Tanzania has argued, there was a turn towards economic and social history that concentrated on the transformation and relative impoverishment of African societies under colonialism. Some scholars have gone so far in the search for the origins and meanings of community in Africa as to reject the modern nation state as of much use as a unit of analysis. Basil Davidson, one of the most influential pioneers in African historical research and a long time supporter of African liberation, has recently produced a volume that calls for a reconfiguration of African political life to fit the reality of African communities (*The Black Man's Burden: Africa and the Curse of the Nation State*). This collection demonstrates the competition between these views and the shifts that have occurred over the last three decades.

This collection intends to make available to students and scholars a sample of the historical scholarship on twentieth century Africa. The articles come mainly from Africanist scholarly journals, many of which had and have limited circulations. It includes some seminal works heretofore extremely difficult to locate and many works from journals published in Africa. It also includes some works collected elsewhere but shown here in the context of other scholarship.

The articles collected here represent a growing and distinguished tradition of scholarship. Some are foundation works upon which the field has built. Many pioneer methodological innovations as historians have sought ways of understanding the past. All go beyond the often abstract generalities common to basic texts. Taken together they reveal the diversity and the continuity of the African experience.

Several people have contributed greatly to this project. Leo Balk and Carole Puccino of Garland Publishing have guided it through all its stages. Cary Wintz was the catalyst for the project. I. N. Kimambo critiqued the project and made many suggestions. The library staffs of the Ralph J. Terry Library at Texas Southern University, the Fondren Library at Rice University, and the University Library of Northwestern University, and especially Dan Britz of the Africana Collection at Northwestern, provided critical help. Bernadette Pruitt did some of the leg work. Pamela Maack was always supportive, and Katie provided the diversions.

INTRODUCTION

Although the history of interaction between African peoples and those from outside that continent is old, for most of Africa colonial domination by European powers was both a relatively recent and relatively short phenomenon. In 1870 most Africans lived in independent societies; by 1915 all but two African states had been conquered by Europeans. Resistance to European domination by Africans was continuous, although the level on which it occurred varied. As the articles in this collection show, the costs of conquest to Africans were great.

The articles in this collection concentrate on African struggles to maintain their autonomy. The factors that drove Britain, France, Portugal, Germany, Spain, Italy, and Belgium to divide Africa have been the subject of much comment and debate. The intellectual debate over the "new imperialism" of the late nineteenth century stretches back to V. I. Lenin and is as current as Thomas Pakenham's recent popular history.[1] The exploits of explorers, missionaries, and military conquerors continue to capture the imagination of non-African audiences. Most of this attention, however, spins around Conrad's metaphor for, as the Nigerian novelist Chinua Achebe argues, one unimportant European's descent into madness, "the heart of darkness." This metaphor has come to symbolize both the justification for colonial conquest and a nostalgia for the colonial order. The articles in this collection powerfully rebut such Euro-centric romanticism. Conquest and "pacification" was a bloody business and destroyed more than it created.

The European context of conquest is of course important. The new imperialism of the late nineteenth century was a product of both the continuing industrial revolution and the great power rivalry between European nations. The Dutch, Portuguese, British and French had long maintained outposts along the African coast and by 1850 in the case of South Africa and Angola controlled at least some of the hinterland. However, before about 1850 European powers lacked the ability to mobilize the force necessary to actually conquer dense or well organized African populations. African states had firearms but in forest regions, in particular, firearms proved no great advantage.

Likewise, Europeans found most of Africa quite deadly due to tropical diseases; South Africa again was the exception. This equation changed after 1850. Technical innovation sped up. Europeans had firearms, particularly machine guns and improved mobile artillery, that gave them a qualitative advantage over even the best armed African forces. Perhaps more importantly medical advances increased the survival rate of Europeans in the tropics. In particular, quinine was recognized as a prophylactic against malaria.

The late nineteenth century also saw the development of a firmer ideological justification for European domination of other peoples. Scientific racism reached its height in the very decades that also included the conquest of Africa. The civilizing mission, whether justified on scientific, religious, or cultural terms, remained at the fore in the minds of colonizers and missionaries throughout the period. In one of the great ironies of the history of the scramble, colonization was often portrayed as a struggle against slavery. The structures and extent of slavery in Africa by the nineteenth century created by 400 years of European demand for slaves for the New World now became a cause for conquest.[2]

Perhaps no element of conquest has aroused more debate than the economic rationale behind it. In general, in the late nineteenth century trade between Africa and the rest of the world was small. During the nineteenth century some parts of Africa had become important producers of agricultural commodities such as groundnuts, palm oil, and cloves for world markets. Initially, trade in the late nineteenth century also included in relatively large volumes two non-cultivated resources, ivory and wild rubber. In total, however, the primary product trade of most of Africa would not seem to justify the expense of conquest, although commercial interests directly involved in the Africa trade certainly did exercise a political influence on metropolitan governments much greater than their actual economic importance. However, several factors modify this judgment. First, the discovery in South Africa, a region under British control, of the largest diamond field in the world promoted visions of mineral wealth in the rest of Africa far in advance of the actuality. Others sought to ensure that they were not left out of any bonanza in the continent. Second, strategic interests gave Africa a political and military importance far greater than its initial economic importance. The British needed to control the recently completed Suez Canal as well as the sea lanes around the Cape of Good Hope in South Africa in order to have secure communications with their holdings in India. In addition, after 1871,

Created slavery (margin annotation)

the newly unified German government under Bismark encouraged French expansion in Africa as a means of diverting French attention from revanchism, and eventually his government bowed to internal pressure to acquire colonies for Germany. The Portuguese, the weakest of European colonial powers but the nation with the most extensive contacts on the ground in Africa before 1870, sought to extend their claims; even King Leopold of Belgium, unable to convince his government to back colonial acquisition, used his personal wealth to carve a private empire out of central Africa, the Congo Free State (eventually taken over by Belgium).

In 1885 an international conference held in Berlin divided up spheres of influence between the interested powers and laid ground rules for annexation. While the image of diplomats in striped pants blithely drawing lines on blank maps with rules and compasses is appealing, spheres of influence generally recognized existing commercial or political interests and final boundaries were usually fixed later. The conference established "effective occupation" as a standard by which claims could be judged that in turn set off the final scramble to establish outposts, collect dubious treaties with presumed African rulers, and build infrastructure such as ports and railroads.

On the ground in Africa, conquest took a variety of forms. In the case of large African states, wars of conquest began in the 1870s and did not end until the late 1890s. African societies with more diffuse political structures often proved more difficult to subdue than more centralized states since conquest had to go on village by village. In either case, resistance to colonial domination, properly understood, was continuous.

During the 1960s and 1970s historians, both African and foreign, developed two important paradigms out of resistance to colonial domination. First, they made a distinction between primary resistance to conquest and secondary resistance to colonialism. The first took the form of African states and communities fighting to maintain political independence. Secondary resistance occurred when Africans sought to build new structures of unity across precolonial divisions to resist demands made by the colonial state. The second insight was the argument that especially secondary resistance proved an ideological justification for the struggle by nationalist movements for independence after World War II. In essence, colonialism and the struggle against it called forth its doom in the form of African nationalism.[3]

This analysis emphasizes the many wars and rebellions that marked the period between 1870 and 1920. Such an emphasis is valid and important but even in areas where wars of conquest were brief and no rebellions occurred, resistance was continuous. Africans fought to maintain as much autonomy as possible for their communities, sometimes by military means but sometimes with other weapons. Refusal to obey colonial orders, refusal to recognize colonially-appointed African authorities, sabotage, and flight marked African responses to colonialism.[4]

This nationalist view of resistance has come under heavy attack ever since Ranger first pulled together its various strands. Some, much as Patrick Redmon in his article in this volume, argued that the unity in secondary resistance was more apparent than real. It represented more a tactical alliance between different African peoples than a permanent ideological construction.[5] Others, for example Edward Steinhart, warned of linking historical movements with modern political movements that could fail to live up to their promise.[6] While such criticisms have a great deal of validity, as Walter Rodney said, they in no way negate the heritage of struggle that Africans could and have claimed as their own.

For African societies all over the continent, the costs of conquests were great. The population of sub-Saharan Africa fell dramatically between 1870 and 1920.[7] Part of the decline came from the warfare associated with conquest and pacification. In one particularly gruesome example, the Germans wiped out an estimated 80 percent of the Herero people of Namibia after a rebellion in 1905.[8] Other losses came as a result of the spread of new diseases, both human and animal. Famine often accompanied conquest as Africans found themselves subjected to new demands for production without provisions for increased productivity in agriculture or the ability to bring in food supplies lost as a result of diversion of resources out of food production. Helge Kjekshus in particular has argued that all of these factors led to the destruction of environmental control systems developed by African societies that allowed them to survive in what were often unfavorable environments.[9]

Such analysis moves to the heart of the colonial era in Africa. Conquest was not just a beginning but also an ending. As volumes II and III of this collection explore, though, the continuity and discord that arose out of that conjuncture shaped and continue to shape the struggles of African peoples.

NOTES

1. V. I. Lenin, *Imperialism: The Highest Stage of Capitalism* (New York, 1939, first published, 1917); Thomas Pakenham, *The Scramble for Africa, 1876-1912* (London, 1991).

2. Paul E. Lovejoy, *Transformations in Slavery: A History of Slavery in Africa* (Cambridge, 1983).

3. See in particular T. O. Ranger, "Connections Between 'Primary Resistance' Movements and Modern Mass Nationalism in East and Central Africa, I & II," *Journal of African History* 9, no. 3, 4 (1968):437-53, 631-41.

4. See G. N. Uongozi, "European Partition and Conquest of Africa: An Overview," in A. Adu Boahen, *General History of Africa, VII: Africa under Colonial Domination 1880-1935* (Berkeley, 1990), pp. 10-24; and Allen Isaacman, "Peasants and Rural Social Protest in Africa," *African Studies Review*, 33, 2 (1990), pp. 1-120.

5. Partick M. Redmon, "Maji Maji in Ungoni: A Reappraisal of Existing Historiography," *International Journal of African Historical Studies*, 8, 3 (1975), pp. 407-24.

6. Edward I. Steinhart, "The Nyangire Rebellion of 1907: Anti-colonial Protest and Nationalist Myth," *Eastern African Studies*, 12 (1973), pp. 38-69.

7. R. R. Kuczynski, *Demographic Survey of the British Colonial Empire: Vol. II, East Africa Etc.* (Oxford, 1949).

8. Jon M. Bridgman, *The Revolt of the Hereros* (Berkeley, 1981).

9. Helge Kjekshus, *Ecology Control and Economic Development in East African History: The Case of Tanganyika, 1850-1950* (London, 1977); see also Juhani Koponen, *People and Production in Late Precolonial Tanzania: History and Structures* (Uppsala, 1988).

Journal of African History, IX, 3 (1968), pp. 437–453
Printed in Great Britain

CONNEXIONS BETWEEN 'PRIMARY RESISTANCE' MOVEMENTS AND MODERN MASS NATIONALISM IN EAST AND CENTRAL AFRICA. PART I

BY T. O. RANGER

A recent authoritative review of developments in African historiography pointed to one 'kind of synthesis which has always seemed worthwhile undertaking', the attempt to trace 'an historic connexion between the last-ditch resisters, the earliest organisers of armed risings, the messianic prophets and preachers, the first strike-leaders, the promoters of the first cautious and respectful associations of the intelligentsia, and the modern political parties which (initially at least) have been the inheritors of European power'.[1]

The 'historic connexions' between prophets and preachers, trade-union leaders and rural radicals, the founders of the Native and Welfare Associations and the organizers of mass nationalism, are now beginning to emerge from the very interesting work being done on the political history of East and Central Africa. But it cannot be said that the 'last-ditch resisters' and the 'earliest organisers of armed risings' have so far been placed very satisfactorily in this general context.

On this particular question, indeed, there has been very considerable scholarly disagreement. One school of thought would emphatically differentiate these initial violent reactions from later manifestations of opposition and particularly from nationalism. Nationalist movements, they contend, are essentially modernist in outlook and directed towards the concept of a territorial loyalty. Primary resistance movements, on the other hand, were inherently backward-looking and traditional; not only tribal but emphasizing the most 'reactionary' elements in tribal life. Such movements, it is held, repudiated those within African societies who wished to come to terms with modernization and to accept education, the missionary influence, and the new commercial and technical opportunities. Resistance movements of the early colonial period, write Robinson and Gallagher, were 'romantic, reactionary struggles against the facts, the passionate protest of societies which were shocked by a new age of change and would not be comforted'. Primary resistances, so Coleman tells us, were 'impulsive negative retorts', striving vainly to recapture the past and looking in no sense to the future.[2]

Such movements are contrasted with 'the defter nationalisms' which planned 'to reform their personalities and regain their powers by operating

---

[1] 'African syntheses', *The Times Literary Supplement*, 28 July 1966.

[2] R. E. Robinson and J. Gallagher, 'The partition of Africa', in *The New Cambridge Modern History*, XI (Cambridge, 1962), chap. 23, p. 640; J. S. Coleman, *Nigeria: Background to Nationalism* (Berkeley, 1963), 172.

in the idiom of the Westernisers'. It was, so the argument continues, often the men and societies that chose not to resist at all in the first instance that provided the leaders of the 'defter nationalisms' which are the obvious parents of the modern mass movements. Such men, or such societies, through their initial acquiescence or co-operation, gained privileged access to education and economic opportunity and thus learnt the new skills of opposition. Resistant societies on the other hand are generally believed to have suffered the fate sketched by Oliver and Fage:

If African leaders...were less far-sighted, less fortunate, or less well advised, they would see their traditional enemies siding with the invader and would themselves assume an attitude of resistance, which could all too often end in military defeat, the deposition of chiefs, the loss of land to the native allies of the occupying power, possibly even to the political fragmentation of the society and state.

Societies so roughly handled fell into a sullen passivity in which meaningful political activity was impossible until the old war leader could be replaced by the man with modern skills and outlooks. There was thus, especially in resistant societies, a sharp hiatus between the primary and secondary manifestations of opposition to European rule. In any real sense 'an historic connexion' did not exist.[3]

This view is not necessarily the result of lack of sympathy for pre-colonial African societies or for African grievances in the early colonial period. In essence it is the view put forward in 1924 by the famous protagonist of the Kenyan African cause, Norman Leys.

Tribal risings ceased [wrote Leys] because they were always hopeless failures. Naked spearmen fall in swathes before machine-guns, without inflicting a single casualty in return. Meanwhile the troops burn all the huts and collect all the live-stock within reach. Resistance once at an end, the leaders of the rebellion are surrendered for imprisonment...Risings that followed such a course could hardly be repeated. A period of calm followed. And when unrest again appeared it was with other leaders...and other motives.[4]

The nationalist and anti-colonial tendency in modern African historiography has tended to dispute this view of a hiatus between primary and secondary resistance, though so far without really demonstrating a continuity. The most interesting expression of this counter-view has been the paper given by Professor A. B. Davidson of Moscow to the International Congress of African History, held in Dar es Salaam in September 1965. So far from seeing primary resistance movements as cut off from modern nationalism, Davidson holds that

it is impossible to understand the African past without the re-establishment of the truth about this resistance...and without making a study of what was the answer of one people or another to the establishment of colonial rule it is difficult to

[3] R. Oliver and J. D. Fage, *A Short History of Africa* (London, 1962), p. 203.
[4] N. Leys, *Kenya*, 1924.

understand not only the past of that people but its present as well. It is difficult to comprehend the character of the liberation movement in the recent revolutionary years. Many things in this struggle and even in its demands...were defined by long-standing traditions of resistance. An attentive study of the history of popular resistance in Africa will inevitably prove that this struggle acted as one of the most important stimuli to historical development for the African peoples... Resistance left its mark on the most important internal processes of the development of the African peoples; in the course of resistance tendencies to change developed more quickly.[5]

Recent work on West Africa, particularly Francophone West Africa, has tended to substantiate Davidson's view, or at least greatly to qualify the views expressed by Coleman or Robinson and Gallagher. Thomas Hodgkin and Ruth Schachter Morgenthau have demonstrated for Mali and Guinea the continuing importance for the modern period of the resistance offered to the French by Samory and the heirs of Al Hajj Umar; showing how an alternative prestigious leadership remained available for mass discontent, and how such discontent could be channelled by the survivors or heirs of the resisters against the 'loyalist' and collaborating African authorities set up by the French; showing how this alternative leadership succeeded to the radical and reformist traditions of the nineteenth-century Islamic movements and was able to make the transition fairly readily to the notions of modern mass nationalism; and showing how not only the memory but also the surviving structural alliances of the resistant Samory and Al Hajj Umar systems could be used as the foundation of radical mass parties in the modern period. Professor Ajayi has recently suggested that the legacy of these fighting Islamic theocracies, doomed in Robinson and Gallagher's version to 'romantic, reactionary struggles against the facts', is of immediate significance to the nationalist reformer.

The over-riding interest of the colonial regime...was the maintenance of law and order, not reform. The result has been, therefore, that many of the nationalist governments of today are finding that on a number of issues they have to pick up the threads of social and political reform from the point where the radical Muslim and Christian reformers of the nineteenth century left off at the coming of colonial rule.[6]

No such argument has yet been propounded for East and Central Africa, and probably no argument in the same sort of terms can be propounded. But it seems worth while to see if it is not possible to challenge the assumption of hiatus in East and Central Africa also, and to establish some 'historic connexions' between primary and secondary resistance. This paper is an initial exploration of such possibilities.

[5] A. B. Davidson, 'African resistance and rebellion against the imposition of colonial rule', in *Emerging Themes in African History*, ed. T. O. Ranger (Nairobi, 1968).
[6] J. F. Ajayi, 'The continuity of African institutions under colonialism', ibid.; T. Hodgkin and R. Schachter, *French-Speaking West Africa in Transition* (New York, 1960).

3

The argument for East and Central Africa has to begin, I think, by establishing what is perhaps an obvious but yet insufficiently appreciated fact; namely that the environment in which later African politics developed was shaped not only by European initiatives and policy or by African co-operation and passivity, but also by African resistance. In this sense at least there is certainly an important connexion between resistance and later political developments.

In some cases the environment of later politics was shaped by the consequences of the total defeat of attempted resistance. We have seen above the stress placed by Oliver and Fage on the inevitable defeat of primary resistance movements. Yet there has been a curious failure to appreciate the wide significance of such defeats as a psychological factor. Let us take the case of Kenya as an example. British rule was established in Kenya with few spectacular or large-scale displays of force. For this reason it was possible to write about the 'pacification' of Kenya in the terms employed by A. T. Matson in 1962: 'Except in abnormal cases... the amount of force used was minimal, with the result that the pacification of the Protectorate and the settlement of its tribes were accomplished with astonishingly little loss of life... Most of the operations were carried through by local forces acting more as police than conquerors.' But such a view overlooked the fact that, for each Kenyan African society that suffered what Matson would describe as a police action, the experience of rapid and total defeat could be traumatic. The point is well brought out by Professor Low. 'It was force and military prowess which in the main effected the critical submissions to British authority of the peoples' of the Kenya uplands, he tells us.

Any map which outlined the operational theatres of the many small British military expeditions during the first fifteen years of British rule...would exhibit few interstices...And for all the exiguousness of these expeditions in European terms, they were often vastly greater, more lethal demonstrations of force than any which the defeated tribes had experienced from any quarter in the past, since they almost invariably took the form of a wholly unequal encounter between guns upon the British side and spears upon the African.

The Embu people provide an admirable example of the long-lasting impact that could be made by one of these rapid suppressions of primary resistance. For all their intransigence and for all their war-like reputation, Embu resistance was broken within two weeks when British forces entered the area in 1906; thereafter all arms were surrendered at a place called Ngoiri, and the Embu forbidden to carry offensive weapons.

Ever since the tribe has been as law-abiding as its neighbours [an Embu historian tells us], although the memories of 1906 still remain fresh...In fact, at the feeder road leading to Ngoiri Primary School, built on the scene of the surrender of the weapons, there is a sign board on which is written the words: 'RETURN OUR SHIELDS AND OUR SPEARS'. The sign board was planted there in 1963 on Kenya's

Independence Day, and demanded the return by the Wazungu of the weapons burnt at Ngoiri in 1906.[7]

And if the memory of a two-week humiliation could dominate 'the fireside stories told by the grandmothers and grandfathers' of Embu, it goes without saying that the impact of more spectacular defeats was more profound and important. Julius Nyerere tells us that memories of the suppression of primary resistance were among the factors which

determined the strategy of Tanganyika's independence struggle...Memories of the Hehe and Maji Maji wars against the German colonialists, and of their ruthless suppression, were deeply ingrained in the minds of our people. So, too, was the fact that our conquerors had themselves been defeated in battle by the British who governed the territory. The people, particularly the elders, asked, 'How can we win without guns? How can we make sure that there is not going to be a repetition of the Hehe and Maji-Maji wars?' It was therefore necessary for TANU to start by making the people understand that peaceful methods of struggle for independence were possible and could succeed. This does not mean that the people of this country were cowardly, or particularly fond of non-violence; no, they knew fighting; they had been badly defeated and ruthlessly suppressed. As realists, therefore, they wanted to know why TANU thought we could win even without guns. [This] determined the initial emphasis on the United Nations.[8]

Yet, having made this point of the continuing significance of memories of defeat, it is at once necessary to go on to say that not all resistances were doomed to total failure and crushing suppression. Some of them preserved liberties, wrung concessions or preserved pride. In so doing they made their own very important contributions to the creation of the environment in which later politics developed. I have argued this case in more detail elsewhere and will content myself here with some illustrations.[9]

Let us take the Basuto, for example. The Basuto demonstrate the invalidity of many of the generalizations usually made about resistant societies. They were certainly not backward-looking. Their leaders desired missionary education, a fruitful economic contact with the outside world, and British protection. These were things that some co-operative African societies also desired. A co-operative society like Barotseland, for example, was able to obtain them by accommodation with the colonial power. The

---

[7] A. T. Matson, 'The pacification of Kenya', *Kenya Weekly News*, 14 Sept. 1962; D. A. Low, 'British East Africa: The establishment of British rule, 1895–1912', in *History of East Africa*, II, ed. V. Harlow and E. M. Chilver (Oxford, 1965), 31, 32; D. Namu, 'Primary resistance amongst the Embu' and 'Background to Mau Mau amongst the Embu', Research Seminar Papers (Dar es Salaam, Oct. 1965 and Nov. 1966).

[8] J. K. Nyerere, *Freedom and Unity* (Dar es Salaam, 1966), 2–3.

[9] These themes and others in this paper are treated at greater length in T. O. Ranger, 'African reaction to the imposition of colonial rule in East and Central Africa', in *History and Politics of Modern Imperialism in Africa*, ed. L. H. Gann and P. Duignan (Stanford, forthcoming). Although the two papers are distinct in theme, some parts of the argument are necessarily the same, and there is some repetition in this paper of passages also included in the Stanford chapter.

Basuto, on the other hand, resisted; not because they were less well informed or less well advised than the Lozi, but because resistance was the only way of protecting themselves from the Afrikaners or the Cape, from total disarmament and probable dispossession. They were much closer to the dynamic frontier of white expansion than Barotseland. Nor was their resistance in vain. The so-called Gun War of 1880–1 between the Basuto and the Cape ended in a solid political victory for the Basuto. They won protection against white settlement and effective retention of their guns. And the direct consequence of the war was the surrender by the Cape of all responsibility with respect to Basutoland, and the establishment of the British Protectorate in March 1884. It hardly needs to be said that this hard-won Protectorate became the essential environment for all later Basuto political activity.[10]

Not many African societies were able to gain as much as this from resistance. But even those which suffered military defeat and failed to keep out white settlement or to preserve their institutions sometimes had something to gain by resisting. An example of this which I have elaborated elsewhere is that of the Ndebele of Southern Rhodesia. Their uprising in 1896 was defeated but they came out of it with some political gains. Before 1896 the Ndebele state had been in ruins; its white rulers had broken up all its institutions; confiscated all Ndebele land and nearly all Ndebele cattle; disregarded every Ndebele political authority. The 1896 rising at least showed the whites that this had been unwise. The Ndebele were still a formidable military foe; it took many men and much money to defeat their rising; and even then it had not been convincingly defeated by the end of the 1896 dry season. Rhodes faced a long-drawn-out war of attrition in which the authority of the British South Africa Company might well have collapsed through bankruptcy or British political intervention. So he negotiated with the Ndebele. They thus won in 1896 what they had not had in 1893—a voice in the settlement. The policy of the British South Africa Company was now defined as being to restore to the Ndebele *indunas* as much of the powers they had possessed under Lobengula as was possible; they received official salaries. So was struck an alliance between the Ndebele chiefs and the Rhodesian administration which still has important political consequences today.[11]

Even a much more complete defeat than this could still leave an African people with something positive to carry into the future. The Hehe of Tanzania, for example, were shattered in war by the Germans. Here there was no question of negotiations or concessions won by resistance. But military defeat did not break up the Hehe system. Out of their long resistance to the Germans the Hehe carried self-respect. Oliver and Fage have told us that 'for the African peoples the most important factor at this stage

[10] J. Halpern, *South Africa's Hostages* (London, 1965), chap. 3; I am also indebted to Mr A. E. Atmore for my understanding of the significance of the Gun War.
[11] T. O. Ranger, *Revolt in Southern Rhodesia, 1896–7* (London, 1967), chaps. 7 and 10.

of colonial history...was the intangible psychological issue of whether any given society or group was left feeling it had turned the early colonial occupation to its own advantage, or alternatively that it had been humiliated'. Their assumption in this passage is that defeated resistances led to humiliation, and this is an assumption which had been made by a good many of the writers, for instance, on Southern Rhodesia nationalism, who frequently depict the Ndebele and the Shona as consciously 'conquered people', and hence less politically assertive than peoples in Zambia and Malawi who do not have memories of humiliation. But this is an assumption that the Hehe and other instances challenge. The Hehe did not turn the early colonial situation to their own advantage, but they retained pride. 'Today all Wahehe idealize Mkwawa', wrote a British district officer in the 1920s. 'This may be because he actually beat the white man in battle.' Alison Redmayne, who has made a detailed study of Hehe political history, sees this pride as one of its determining influences.[12]

Resistances also helped to shape the environment of later African politics because of their impact upon the thinking and action of the colonial authorities. Thus actual or potential resistance brought about the collapse of the commercial companies which were at first employed by the Germans and the British to open up their East African spheres of influence, and forced the two governments to assume direct responsibility. Moreover, both under company and colonial office rule, the possibility and actuality of resistance was a main factor in bringing about those alliances between the colonial administration and co-operating African societies which are generally agreed to have been so important to later political activity. Despite their technological superiority, the new colonial regimes were weak in men and finance and needed allies to deal with resistance or rebellion. Finally, African rebellions did much to shatter the early European attitude of masterful complacency. The thinking of administrators and settlers, especially in Tanganyika after Maji-Maji and in Rhodesia after the Ndebele and Shona risings of 1896–7, was dominated by the fear of the repetition of such outbreaks. This fear had many and complex effects, but among other things it led to certain concessions to anticipated African discontent as well as to military and police contingency-planning. If Africans in Tanganyika wanted at all costs to avoid another Maji-Maji rising, so also did administrative officers.[13]

But it was not only the attitudes of defeated African societies and those of apprehensive white settlers which were affected by resistance and rebellion. There was a complex interplay between so-called 'primary' resistance and manifestations of 'secondary' opposition. We have seen above that many scholars have employed a rather rigid periodization in

[12] A. H. Redmayne, 'The Wahehe people of Tanganyika'. Oxford University D. Phil. thesis, 1964. See also her article in this number of *J. Afr. Hist.*

[13] J. Iliffe, 'The effects of the Maji-Maji rebellion on German occupation policy in East Africa', *British and German Colonialism in Africa*, ed. P. Gifford and W. R. Louis (Yale, 1968); Ranger, *Revolt in Southern Rhodesia.*

their approach to African nationalist historiography. The period of resistance is followed by hiatus; then arises the new leadership. But we must
remember that the effective establishment of colonial rule throughout
southern, central and eastern Africa took a very long time to achieve.
'Primary' resistance to it was still going on in some areas while 'secondary'
movements were developing elsewhere. Independent churches, trade
unions, welfare associations, Pan-Africanist movements all existed at the
same time as expressions of tribal or pan-tribal resistance. This fact
was important in forming the attitudes of the more radical 'secondary'
politicians.

In another paper I have given two examples of this. One concerns the
interaction of the career of the South African leader, Tengo Jabavu, and
the fact and memories of the Ndebele rising. The second example is the
fascinating one recorded in Shepperson and Price's account of the contacts
between Nyasaland and Zululand. In 1896 Booth, the radical missionary,
travelled from Nyasaland, taking with him one Gordon Mathaka, because
the Yao wished 'to send a messenger to the other tribes in the south who
had known the white man a long time to find out what they thought'.
Mathaka heard the opinion of the Zulu Christian élite. 'No matter what the
Yao thought', they told him, 'no living white man, whether carrying
guns or not, would in the end be the friend of the black men.' And when
Booth himself gathered together some 120 African intellectuals to discuss
his projected African Christian Union, 'after a twenty six and a half hour
session they rejected his scheme on the simple grounds that no white man
was fit to be trusted, not even Booth himself...No trust or reliance at all
could be placed in any representative of "the blood-stained white men,
who had slain scores of thousands of Zulus and their Matabele relations".'
These Zulu intellectuals did not perceive as sharply as some modern
historians the gulf between primary and secondary resistance.[14]

Nor, indeed, did the men who met in London in 1900 for the first Pan-
African Conference. These Afro-Americans, West Indians, West Africans,
and so on, stated that they were meeting partly because of their concern
over the wave of violent conflict between black and white which appeared
to be sweeping Africa, instancing the Sierra Leone tax revolt and the
Ndebele rising of 1896 as examples. Partly as a result of the impact made
by the Ndebele rising, this first Conference appealed to Queen Victoria
for reforms in Rhodesia.[15]

This sort of interaction lasted into the 1920s. One example, again a
Rhodesian one which refers back to Ndebele resistance, must suffice. In
June 1929 the first militant African trade union was holding its meetings in
Bulawayo; weekend after weekend it hammered away on the theme of

[14] Ranger, 'African reaction to the imposition of colonial rule', loc. cit.; G. Shepperson
and T. Price, *Independent African* (Edinburgh, 1958), 70, 71, 76.
[15] I. Geiss, 'The development of Pan-Africanism in the twentieth century', Lauterbach
conference paper, June 1966.

African unity, appealing not only to the pan-tribal union movements of South Africa but also to successful examples of continuing armed resistance. 'If Lobengula had wanted to he could have called every nation to help him. He did not. That is why he was conquered. In Somaliland they are still fighting. That is because they are united. Let us be united.'[16]

It will be seen therefore that there is a long ancestry behind the attention currently paid by nationalist leaders to the heroic myths of primary resistance. When a man like Nelson Mandela seeks inspiration in tales 'of the wars fought by our ancestors in defence of the fatherland' and sees them not as part merely of tribal history, but 'as the pride and glory of the entire African nation', he is echoing the response of many of his predecessors.[17]

In all these ways, then, resistances formed part of the complex interaction of events which produced the environment for modern nationalist politics. I now want to turn to a more complex and interesting argument. This argument runs that during the course of the resistances, or some of them, types of political organization or inspiration emerged which looked in important ways to the future, which in some cases are directly, and in others indirectly, linked with later manifestations of African opposition.

The best way into this argument is by returning for a moment to the views of Robinson and Gallagher, and their contrast between the passionate backward-looking resistances and the defter manipulations of Western ideas which led to modern nationalist politics. As noted above, it is often argued that the leading co-operating societies played a key role in the initial stages of this process of adaptation of Westernism and in so doing looked in important ways to the nationalist future. In particular it can be argued that, in a series of so-called 'Christian Revolutions', the key collaborators sought to solve some of the weaknesses of nineteenth-century African state systems; to make their bureaucracy more efficient through literacy; to liberate the central political power from traditional sanctions and limitations and to break away from dependence on kinship or regional groupings. All this was to be done through an alliance with the missionary aspects of the colonial presence in particular. This concept of 'modernizing autocracy', of the king or the aristocracy introducing internal readjustments designed to modernize 'traditional' political systems in order to allow for modernization in other ways, can be applied with force to Buganda; to Barotseland, especially after the accession of Yeta III; to Bechuanaland, where the example of Khama was of great importance to other societies; to Ankole; and so on. The cases are not, of course, identical, but in all of them internal changes of great importance were going on which can be seen, in Low's terminology, as attempts to solve the problem of effective *scale* by making use of the Christian Great Tradition.[18]

[16] John Mphamba's speech, 29 June 1929, C.I.D. report, National Archives, Salisbury, S 84/A/300.   [17] N. Mandela, *No Easy Walk to Freedom* (London, 1965), 147.
[18] Ranger, 'African reaction to the imposition of colonial rule', loc. cit.

We can hardly doubt that these changes were indeed an important pointer to the future, even if the scale proved inadequate and there had to be a further movement to territorial nationalism with which these older nationality units were sometimes in conflict. But these movements had major weaknesses from the first. The answer and opportunity provided by these Christian Revolutions was by definition a minority one, requiring alien sanctions for a relatively long time and not able to depend upon mass commitment. The breach with traditional restraints, indeed, often involved a serious weakening of the mass sense of belonging. Now, the modern nationalist movements of East and Central Africa are certainly characterized by an attempt to create effective bureaucratic and other institutions for a territorial state; but they also have to try to modernize at a more profound level by achieving mass commitment to these new institutions. Not all nationalist parties succeed in this by any means. But there can be little doubt that the 'ideal' nationalist movement consists of bringing together the urge to centralize and modernize institutions with an upsurge of mass enthusiasm. It can be argued that if the Christian Revolutions provide a fascinating early example of *élite* innovation, some of the 'primary resistances' provide equally fascinating examples of attempted answers to the problem of how to commit the masses to an effective enlargement of scale.

Here I am thinking mainly of those primary resistances which for one reason or another were unusually protracted—like the Nandi experience— or the so-called rebellions. I distinguish these two categories from other primary resistances or wars because in these cases the problem of organization, in fact the problem of scale, becomes most urgent. In many instances the initial war was fought in terms of the traditional military system, and there was little attempt to modify it or to involve more of the people within the state or to involve other peoples outside it. But a long-drawn-out struggle or a rising is a different matter. The question then arises as to how a society can effectively resist, having been beaten the first time or having initially been incapable of putting up a resistance at all. The distinction made by Iliffe between the initial tribal wars fought by the Germans in Tanganyika and the Maji-Maji rising is of the greatest importance. Maji-Maji, he says, was a 'post-pacification revolt, quite different from the early resistance... That had been local and professional, soldiers against soldiers, whereas Maji-Maji affected almost everyone in Tanganyika. It was a great crisis of commitment.'[19]

The point can be well illustrated in the cases of the two greatest rebellions in East and Central Africa, the Ndebele–Shona risings of 1896–7 and the Maji-Maji rising of 1905. The main problem about these risings is not so much *why* they happened as *how* they happened. How was it possible for the Ndebele and their subject peoples to rise together in 1896, when

[19] J. Iliffe, 'The German administration of Tanganyika, 1906–11', Cambridge University Ph.D. thesis, 1965.

in the 1893 war the subject peoples had abandoned their overlords? How was it possible for the Ndebele and the western and central Shona to co-operate in the risings in view of their long history of hostility? How was it possible for the Shona groups to co-operate among themselves in view of their nineteenth-century history of disunity? How was it possible for the very diverse peoples of southern Tanzania to become involved in a single resistance to the Germans? Finally, how was it that these apparently odd and patch-work alliances offered to the whites a more formidable challenge than had the disciplined professional armies of 1893 or the Hehe wars?

In the Rhodesian case part of the answer certainly lies in the appeal back to traditions of past political centralization. But both in Rhodesia and in Tanzania the main answer lies in the emergence of a leadership which was charismatic and revolutionary rather than hereditary or bureaucratic.

The African societies of East and Central Africa could draw in times of emergency upon a number of traditions of such charismatic leadership. Two emerge as particularly important in connexion with the sort of large-scale resistance we are discussing. The first of these is the prophetic tradition. Many African societies of East and Central Africa had religious systems in which specialist officers played an institutionalized prophetic role, speaking with the voice of the divine either through possession or through dream or oracular interpretation. Such prophet officers have usually been regarded by scholars, in common with 'traditional religion' as a whole, as conservative and normative forces. The prophet has been thought of as the ally of the established political order and as the guardian of its customary moral norms. But, as I have argued in a recent paper, the prophetic authority could not be so confined; the claim to speak with the voice of the divine was always potentially a revolutionary one, and if the prophet could invest the ordinary operations of a society with divine sanction he could also introduce new commandments. In his brilliant Malinowski Lecture for 1966, I. M. Lewis has suggested a typology and spectrum of possession and prophetic movements which throws a good deal of light on the point I am trying to make. His spectrum ranges from hysterical possession cults on the periphery of religious practice, to fully institutionalized tribal religions at the centre, in which the Messianic revelations of moral teaching shrink into creation myths and myth charters of the establishment. Lewis goes on to discuss the complex relationship of such establishment religions, 'which celebrate an accepted code of public morality', with the Messianic tradition. Establishment religions, he suggests, may have sprung from or may precede a Messianic movement; there are nearly always within them 'undercurrents' of Messianism and nearly always also opportunities for the rise of 'revitalizing prophets'; and often, where the establishment religion itself seems incapable of revitalization, it is surrounded by peripheral cults in which the innovatory vitality of prophetism is still present. 'It seems probable', he writes, 'that such displaced and peripherally relegated cults

11

may provide the kind of institutional and inspirational continuity which, in appropriate historical circumstances, enables new messianic cults to develop.'[20]

The second tradition of charismatic innovating leadership is that of the witchcraft-eradication movements. Mary Douglas has a fascinating account of Lele religious ideas which brings out very clearly the radical potential of such movements. The 'normal' religious beliefs and activities of the Lele present a balance between a general emphasis upon order and simplicity and the insight of esoteric cults into complexity and sorrow. But death and disease create tensions within the Lele system which cannot be dealt with adequately either by the routine protective devices of popular religion, or the insights of the cults.

For the Lele, [she writes] evil is not to be included in the total system of the world, but to be expunged without compromise. All evil is caused by sorcery. They can clearly visualize what reality would be like without sorcery and they continually strive to achieve it by eliminating sorcerers. A strong millenarian tendency is implicit in the way of thinking of any people whose metaphysics push evil out of the world of reality. Among the Lele the millenarian tendency bursts into flame in their recurrent anti-sorcery cults. When a new cult arrives it burns up for the time being the whole apparatus of their traditional religion... the latest anti-sorcery cult is nothing less than an attempt to introduce the millennium at once.[21]

In the various resistances to the establishment of colonial rule, there is no question that religious leadership played an important part. The character of this leadership varied greatly, however. Sometimes the establishment religion of an existing unit committed itself to resistance alongside the established political and military system. Sometimes the established religious officers resisted the movement of the established political authorities into a 'Christian Revolution'. But sometimes, in the great movements of rebellion and resistance that we are now particularly discussing, innovating religious leadership sprang up to revitalize or to challenge the established religious structure as well as the whites and, where necessary, the African political authorities. Such innovating religious leadership sprang out of either the prophetic or the witchcraft-eradication traditions. In their different ways both called for the creation of a new order in which neither sorcery nor colonial pressures nor the tensions of small-scale society would exist; both offered protection and invulnerability to those who observed their new commandments. They thus offered solutions, on however temporary a basis, to the problem of morale, to the problem of the combination of different groups, and to the problem of co-ordination.

The operation of this sort of leadership, and its interaction, can be seen

[20] T. O. Ranger, 'Towards a historical study of traditional religion in East and Central Africa', East African Academy Symposium paper, Kampala, 1966; I. M. Lewis, 'Spirit possession and deprivation cults', *Man*, 1, no. 3, Sept. 1966.
[21] Mary Douglas, *Purity and Danger* (London, 1966), chap. 10.

in the movements we are now discussing. In the Congo, a number of scholars have described the various prophetic and witchcraft-eradication movements which stimulated primary resistance to the whites and which brought together far-flung coalitions. Such movements, in Doutreloux's analysis, sprang mainly from the weaknesses of Congolese societies, which could find no permanent solution to the problem of fragmentation and instability. What stability existed was given by religions of the ancestors or cults of the land and fertility, but these were by definition always operative on too small a scale, and they were constantly undermined, moreover, by the disintegrative effect of witchcraft belief. Prophet movements and witchcraft eradication cults arose in an attempt to remedy this situation. They assaulted witchcraft and also traditional limitations; the prophet movements proclaimed themselves as a church or creed for all Africans and imposed new regulations and prohibitions upon believers: they endeavoured to create an indigenous Great Tradition to rival that alien Great Tradition which the Christian revolutionaries used.[22]

Something of the same pattern can be seen for the most striking mass primary resistances of East and Central Africa. Certainly it seems to hold for the two great risings already discussed—the Shona–Ndebele and the Maji-Maji rebellions. I have argued at length elsewhere that what I described as the 'traditional' religious authorities were the main coordinators, and in a real sense leaders, of the risings in Matabeleland and Mashonaland, and that the priests of the Mwari cult in the first province, and the spirit mediums of the Chaminuka–Nehanda hierarchies in the second, were the main vehicles of co-operation between the various elements engaged. Perhaps in these articles I have emphasized the 'traditional' character of this religious leadership too much. Certainly it was important that they presented themselves as survivors from the imperial past of the Shona—the one cult so intimately identified with the old Rozwi empire and the other with the Mutapa dynasty and its outriders. But at the same time the emergence of these religious leaders as leaders also of a widespread rebellion constituted what Gann has described as 'a theological revolution'. Contemporary white observers stressed that the Mwari cult had previously been concerned with matters of peace and fertility and its militant, authoritarian character in 1896 took them by surprise; no doubt there was both ignorance and *naïveté* in their idea of its earlier total severance from politics, but there seems no question that the power and the nature of the authority of the Mwari priesthood underwent significant development in 1896. Nor does there seem much question that this 'theological revolution' took the form ascribed by Doutreloux to the prophet movements. The Mwari priests and the spirit mediums imposed new regulations and prohibitions upon their followers; to enter the rebellion was to enter a new society and to become subject to a new 'law'; the rebels were brought into the fellow-

[22] M. A. Doutreloux, 'Prophétisme et culture', in *African Systems of Thought*, ed. Fortes and Dieterlin (London, 1965).

13

ship of the faithful by the dispensation of 'medicine' and promised immunity from bullets; they were promised success in this world and a
return from death to enjoy it. (When the religious leaders were attempting
in 1897 to bring into being a Rozwi 'front' in all the areas of Mashonaland
as a means of co-ordinating the secular side of the rising after the withdrawal of the Ndebele aristocracy, they promised that all Rozwi who were
killed should be resurrected and participate in the coming golden age.)
The religious leaders move out of the limitations which, as well as the
advantages, were implied by their connexion with specific past political
systems, and speak to all black men. And they are to an extent successful.
For a time the charismatic leadership of the prophets brings together
Ndebele aristocrats, subject peoples, deposed Rozwi chiefs, Shona paramounts; as Gann puts it, 'the proud Matabele chieftains now agreed to
operate under the supreme direction of an ex-serf, a remarkable man who
in "normal" times would hardly have acquired much political influence'.[23]

In the case of the Maji-Maji rising, the evidence presented by Iliffe
suggests a possible combination of both the prophetic and the witchcraft-
eradication elements in the inspiration and co-ordination of the rising.
Clearly the Kolelo cult played an important part. It 'was influential over
a wide area and...provided centres to which large numbers of people
went to receive medicine and instructions which they distributed on return
...The evidence is perhaps sufficient to conclude that the Kolelo cult
provided a machinery which could reach the peoples of the Rufiji complex
and perhaps further afield'. Like the Mwari cult, the Kolelo belief involved priest-interpreters of the oracle; like the Mwari cult also, its normal
preoccupation was with fertility and the land. And, as Iliffe tells us, some
evidence suggests that 'in the period before the rebellion the Kolelo cult
was transformed from its normal preoccupation with the land to a more
radical and prophetic belief in a reversal of the existing order by direct
divine intervention'. The prophets of the new development commanded
revolt in the name of 'the new God, who would come to live in the land'.
'He will change this world and it will be new...His rule will be one of
marvels.' They provided protective medicine; prescribed a new form of
dress and imposed new prohibitions; they promised invulnerability or
resurrection. The drinking of the holy water was a sign of entry into a rebel
communion. The appeal was to all Africans. 'Be not afraid,' the message
ran, 'Kolelo spares his black children.'[24]

At the same time there seems evidence to suggest that the innovatory
potentialities of witchcraft-eradication movements were also being used.
'The Vidunda understood the *maji* in the context of an attack on sorcery',
Iliffe tells us. In southern Ubena 'a series of anti-sorcery movements had

---

[23] T. O. Ranger, 'The role of the Ndebele and Shona religious authorities in the
rebellions of 1896 and 1897', in *The Zambesian Past*, ed. E. T. Stokes and R. Brown
(Manchester, 1966) L. H. Gann, *A History of Southern Rhodesia* (London, 1965).

[24] J. Iliffe, 'The organization of the Maji-Maji Rebellion', *J. Afr. Hist.* VIII, no. 3 (1967).

entered from the east, from Ungindo and the Kilombero...Maji-Maji was also brought by Ngindo, and it seems that the pattern of Bena response followed that normal with a *mwavi* medicine, the *hongo* administering the *maji* to the assembled people in the presence of the chief'. 'It seems very probable', he concludes, 'that both the rebellion...and subsequent movements were drawing on an established pattern of indigenous millenarianism. Just as the rising in the Rufiji complex became associated with the cult of Kolelo, so its expansion appears to have taken place within the context of recurrent movements to eradicate sorcery.' My own work on subsequent witchcraft eradication cults in the Rufiji complex and in the Maji-Maji area generally, leads me to suppose that the ability of such movements to pass rapidly across clan and tribal boundaries, and to sweep people into a unity which overrides suspicions and allegations of sorcery, was indeed an important element in the 1905 rising.[25]

The Maji-Maji and the Shona–Ndebele risings were, of course, exceptional affairs, resistances on a grander scale than anything else in East and Central Africa. There were, however, other examples of attempts to come to terms with the problem of scale. There is the Nandi case, for example, where the pressures of the nineteenth century produced a steady increase in the power of the Nandi prophet figure, the *Orkoiyot*, until at last the Nandi operated for the first time as a united military power in a 'rebellion' against British rule under the prophet's command. There were somewhat similar developments among the Kipsigis and perhaps the Meru. Or there is the very interesting example of the Nyabingi movement.[26]

The Nyabingi movement presented itself as a challenge to white occupation and administration in the northern areas of Rwanda, in parts of the Congo, and in Kigezi district. During the First World War, Nyabingi forces attacked British, Belgian and German troops impartially. Especially among the much-fragmented Kiga people, the cult promised to play an important integrative role. 'Just prior to the coming of the British', so a student of the Kiga tells us, 'a spirit possession cult which might have contained the seeds of a larger-scale political organisation was breaking out all over the district.' The cult involved mediumship, promised immunity to its adherents and appeared not so much as a pan-African as a pan-Bantu movement. European observers contrasted it with the stable and conservative official religion of the Rwanda monarchy. 'It has everywhere proved itself revolutionary in method and anarchic in effect', wrote the Assistant District Commissioner, Kigezi, in 1919. 'Fanaticism and terror are everywhere inculcated...The whole appeal is to fear and to the lower instincts, to the masses, Bahutu, against the classes, Batussi...The whole aspect of the Nabingi is of a fanatic anarchic sect as

[25] Iliffe, op. cit.; T. O. Ranger, 'Witchcraft eradication movements in Central and Southern Tanzania and their connection with the Maji-Maji rising', Research Seminar Paper, Dar es Salaam, November 1966.
[26] S. Arap' Ngeny, 'Nandi Resistance to the establishment of British administration, 1893–1906', Research Seminar Paper, Dar es Salaam, November 1965.

opposed to the liberal and religious principles of the indigenous Kubandwa cult.'[27]

It would be possible to multiply these examples on a smaller scale—a list of risings or resistances allegedly led by prophets or 'witch-doctors' in East and Central Africa amounts to some forty instances, in some of which, at least, the same sort of radical religious leadership was involved.

Almost everywhere this kind of leadership was seen by the Europeans as profoundly reactionary, as endeavouring merely to preserve the tribal past and to exclude all innovation. In fact it was often revolutionary in method and in purpose and sought to transcend tribal limitations. Prophet leaders were often men able at one and the same time to appeal to past notions of unity—even the Nyabingi cult appears to have celebrated the spirit of a Bantu queen, deposed in myth by a pastoralist invader—and also to attempt to restructure society. Thus they appealed to a wider unity than had been achieved in the past and they were not afraid in its service to challenge the authority of secular leaders.[28]

There are striking examples of this challenge to reluctant secular authority both in the 1896–7 Rhodesian risings and in Maji-Maji. Thus the Mwari priesthood in 1896 dismissed Ndebele *indunas* and replaced them with more militant supporters of the rising, while the leading spirit medium in Mashonaland also announced the dismissal, and tried to procure the assassination, of 'loyalist' paramounts. Thus, as Iliffe tells us, when Chief Ngwira of Vidunda attempted to prevent his people following the *hongo*, or Maji-Maji messenger, 'Hongo appointed himself chief of the district'. On the strength of this and other instances he writes that beyond the original Rufiji complex 'Maji-Maji spread as a millenarian revolt which threatened established authority. Only the strongest could reject it.'[29]

Moreover, in addition to the implied criticism of the inadequacies in scale of tribal societies and to the explicit challenges offered to some of their political leaders, risings of this sort often gave scope for the emergence of 'new men' with some acquaintance with modernizing skills. Owners and

[27] Report by Captain J. E. T. Phillips, A.D.C., Kigezi, 31 July 1919, National Archives, Dar es Salaam, Secretariat 0910. See also M. J. Bessell, 'Nyabingi', *Uganda Journal*, 6, no. 2 (Oct 1938); P. W. T. Baxter, 'The Kiga', in *East African Chiefs*, ed. A. Richards (London, 1959); M. M. Edel, *The Chiga of Western Uganda* (Oxford, 1957). Since this article was written I have been able to read a detailed appraisal of the political implications of the Nyabingi cult by Mr F. S. Brazier of Makerere University College, 'The Nyabingi cult: religion and political scale in Kigezi, 1900–1930'. Mr Brazier finds that in Kigezi Nyabingi was, indeed, 'a cult of resistance' and suggests that 'it attained its near-monopoly status among the cults which had a Kiga following just because it answered best to the political needs of the time—a rallying point against the incursions of the Ruanda and Twa', and later of the British and their Ganda agents. He notes that Nyabingi priests were involved in a series of incidents of resistance widely scattered in time and place. But he also remarks that at any single time the Nyabingi priesthood was not able to bring about widespread and co-ordinated resistance. The cult was an important focus of resistance and covered a wide area but was itself too individualistic and loosely structured to succeed in any very extensive enlargement of scale.

[28] For specific examples of religious leaders urging wider unity see Ranger, 'African reaction to the imposition of colonial rule', loc. cit.   [29] Iliffe, op. cit.

skilled users of guns were, of course, important figures in contests of this kind, and perhaps also men who were believed to understand the enemy. At any rate, as Gann has pointed out, among the personal bodyguard of the leading Shona spirit medium in 1896 were men 'who had been in touch with Europeans and picked up some of their skills'. I have myself described elsewhere how, in the 1917 Makombe rising in Portuguese East Africa, a classic 'primary resistance' despite its late date, there was a return to the new opportunities of leadership by men who had gone to seek their fortunes in the colonial economy, producing a leadership of paramounts and spirit mediums, returned waiters and ex-policemen.[30]

Finally, one can detect in some of these resistances the same ambiguity of attitude towards the world of the whites which characterized later mass movements. Thus in Rhodesia we have the Chaminuka medium's prophecy that the Shona would be able to preserve their independence only if they could resist the temptation to acquire the goods of the whites; we have the Nehanda medium's instructions to the rebels to fight only with traditional weapons. Yet we also have the promises made by the chief Mwari priest, Mkwati, that his followers had only 'to wait until all the whites are dead or fled and then they will enjoy the good things of the town and live in palaces of corrugated iron'. 'Directly the white men are killed', a police inspector was told in 1903 during another rebellion scare, 'we will occupy all your houses; all these nice things will be ours.'[31]

Resistances of this sort, then, can hardly be adequately defined as 'reactionary' or as essentially backward-looking, however passionate and romantic they may have been. In many ways they were tackling the problems which more recent proto-nationalist and nationalist movements have faced. But there still remains a key question. The great 'primary resistance' movements may have been *similar* to later expressions of opposition to colonial rule but were they *connected*? They may not have looked to the fragmented tribal past and attempted to preserve it, but did they look to the future and provide the basis for, and tradition of, the mass political movements of the twentieth century? It is to this question that the second part of this article will be devoted.

[30] T. O. Ranger, 'Revolt in Portuguese East Africa: the Makombe rising of 1917', *St Antony's Papers*, no. 15, ed. K. Kirkwood (London, 1963).

[31] *The Daily Chronicle*, 13 July and 10 Sept. 1896; intelligence reports, Inyanga, 26 Mar. 1904, National Archives, Salisbury, A/11/2/12/12; Ranger, *Revolt in Southern Rhodesia*, chap. 10.

Journal of African History, IX, 4 (1968), pp. 631–641
Printed in Great Britain

CONNEXIONS BETWEEN 'PRIMARY RESISTANCE' MOVEMENTS AND MODERN MASS NATIONALISM IN EAST AND CENTRAL AFRICA: II

BY T. O. RANGER

IN the first part of this article a number of possible connexions between 'the last-ditch resisters' and the 'earliest organizers of armed risings', and later leaders of opposition to colonial rule in East and Central Africa, were explored. It was argued that African 'primary' resistance shaped the environment in which later politics developed; it was argued that resistance had profound effects upon white policies and attitudes; it was argued that there was a complicated interplay between manifestations of 'primary' and of 'secondary' opposition, which often overlapped with and were conscious of each other. Then the argument turned to a more ambitious proposition, namely that 'during the course of the resistances, or some of them, types of political organization or inspiration emerged which looked in important ways to the future; which in some cases are directly and in others indirectly linked with later manifestations of African opposition'.

Half of the case for this assertion was set out in the first article, and the character of the organization and aspirations of the great resistance movements was discussed. It was argued that they attempted to create a larger effective scale of action; that they endeavoured to appeal to a sense of African-ness; that they displayed an ambiguous attitude to the material aspects of white colonial society, often desiring to possess them without at the same time abandoning the values of their own communities; that they attempted to assert African ability to retain control of the world by means of a millenarian message. In all these ways, it was asserted, they were *similar* to later mass movements. But the first part of this article ended by posing, rather than answering, the key question of whether they were also *connected* with later mass movements. It is to this question that we must now turn.

It has most often been argued, of course, that 'primary' resistances were *not* connected, either directly or indirectly, with later forms of opposition. Resistances were followed, it was held, by 'a period of calm', out of which emerged 'other leaders and other motives'. And it is unquestionably true that after, say, 1920 there were very few 'tribal' risings and that different sorts of political organization were developed by new men. To that extent periodization of African nationalist history is legitimate enough. But, as I suggested in the first part of this article, we need to look for continuity in mass emotion as well as for continuity in *élite* leadership, if we are to establish a satisfactory historiography of nationalism. It is obviously important to ask whether there was any continuity in terms of mass emotion between the sort of risings I have been discussing and modern nationalism.

The first part of an answer is that there is undoubtedly a link between these resistances and later mass movements of a millenarian character. Nor is this link merely a matter of *comparing* the Shona-Ndebele or Maji-Maji risings with later prophet movements or witchcraft eradication cults. There is often a quite direct connexion. The millenarian movements of the twentieth century in East and Central Africa varied widely in character. Sometimes they remained frankly 'pagan', and are hard to distinguish from the Nyabingi type of movement. (Nyabingi itself, long enduring as it was, continued to operate into the 'secondary' opposition period, and gave the British administration in Kigezi, right up until the end of the 1920s and beyond, the same sort of bother that was being provided elsewhere by 'new' pagan cults or by semi-Christian or Christian-independent movements.) In other cases Christian elements entered to a greater or lesser degree, but this does not prevent direct or indirect connexions with primary resistance movements, as we shall see.[1]

The most direct connexions, of course, are provided by examples like that of Nyabingi, which provided the basis both of 'primary resistance' and of persistent twentieth-century millenarian manifestations. Next come movements like that of the Mumbo cult in Nyanza province, Kenya. The Mumbo cult has recently been examined in a very interesting paper by Audrey Wipper. It arose among the Gusii, apparently around 1913, after the defeat of various 'primary resistances'. It reached peaks of activity in 1919, in 1933, and to a lesser extent in 1938 and 1947; it was one of the movements banned in 1954. Thus in point of time it bridged the period between the suppression of the Gusii risings of 1904, 1908 and 1916 and the emergence of modern mass nationalism. In character it was strikingly similar to the sort of movement we have already discussed. Although arising among the Gusii, it was 'a pan-tribal pagan sect', creating its own society of true believers, whom it bound by its own codes of conduct and to whom it promised eventual triumph and reward. The colonial period, in its mythology, was merely a testing period devised by the God of Africa to sort out the true believers from the faint-hearted; before long those who remained true would enter into the wealth and power of the whites. Mumbo had the most direct links with the period of primary resistance. 'The Gusii's most venerated warriors and prophets, noted for their militant anti-British stance, were claimed by the movement,' Miss Wipper tells us. 'Zakawa, the great prophet, Bogonko, the mighty chief, and Maraa, the *laibon* responsible for the 1908 rebellion, became its symbols, infusing into the living the courage and strength of past heroes...Leaders bolstered up their own legitimacy by claiming to be the mouth-piece of these deceased prophets.'

Indeed, if Miss Wipper is right, we are close here to the idea of an 'alternative leadership', stemming from traditions of resistance and opposed

[1] Bessell, op. cit. 'Nyabingi' *Uganda Journal*, 6, no. 2 (1938).

to officially recognized authority. 'Especially successful in effecting such claims were the descendants' of the prophets and chiefs concerned. 'Thus, with the progency of the Gusii heroes supporting the sect, a physical as well as a symbolic link with the past was established. Here was a powerful symbolic group whose prestige and authority could well be used to arouse, strengthen and weld the various disunited cults into a solid anti-British opposition.' Miss Wipper makes the important point that the cult looked back only to those figures who themselves stood out from and tried to transform traditional small-scale society; 'it looks to the past for inspiration and to the future for living'. 'Its goals', she tells us, 'are Utopian and innovative rather than traditional and regressive', involving attacks upon small-scale traditional values as well as upon European values. It would seem that Professor Ogot has considerable justification for applying the word 'radical' to the cult, and in claiming that 'the history of African nationalism in the district must be traced back' to its emergence.[2]

An interesting later example of a movement in the same western district of Kenya in which the continuity with the tradition of primary resistance was 'symbolic' rather than 'physical' is provided by the Dini Ya Msambwa cult, of Elijah Masinde. Through this cult Masinde called for Bukusu and for wider African unity, meeting together with cult representatives from Uganda, Suk, North Nyanza and Kiambu to resolve 'that since they have similar traditional religions they must unite in Dini Ya Msambwa'. Masinde also made a millenarian appeal, and referred back emphatically to the heroic and traumatic experience of the resistances. Mr Welime tells us that

In September 1947 he led about 5,000 followers to Chetambe's, where in 1895 many Bukusu died in their campaign against Hobley. He wanted his followers to remember the dead in their prayers. One interesting thing about this meeting is that they were dressed as in readiness for the 1895 war. At this meeting it is alleged that he unearthed a skull in which a bullet was found buried iñ the mouth... The crowd became very emotional and destructive.[3]

Similar examples of direct 'physical' and indirect 'symbolic' connexion with primary resistances can be given for Christian independent church movements. In the first category comes, for instance, Shembe's Nazarite Church in Zululand, so vividly described by Professor Sundkler. This impressive manifestation of Zulu, rather than South African, nationalism referred back to 'one of the most dramatic occasions in the history of Zulu nationalism', the Bambata rising of 1906. It was physically linked to this rising through the person of Messen Qwabe, one of its leaders. Shembe himself proclaimed: 'I am going to revive the bones of Messen and of the people who were killed in Bambata's rebellion.' All five sons of Messen

[2] A. Wipper, 'The cult of Mumbo', East African Institute Conference paper, January 1966; B. A. Ogot, 'British administration in the Central Nyanza district of Kenya', *J. Afr. Hist.* IV, no. 2 (1963).
[3] J. D. Welime, 'Dini ya Msambwa', Research Seminar Paper, Dar es Salaam (1965).

have joined the church, which was given posthumous spiritual approval by their dead father, and it is taken for granted that all members of the Qwabe clan will be members of it. In the second category comes Matthew Zwimba's Church of the White Bird, established in 1915 in the Zwimba Reserve in Mashonaland, which appealed to the memory of the 1896–7 rising by regarding all those who died in the fighting in the Zwimba area as the saints and martyrs of the new church. It is important to note also that Zwimba regarded himself as very much a modernizer and succeeded, at least for a time, in establishing himself as the intermediary between the chiefs and people of Zwimba and representatives of the modern world.[4]

It can be shown, then, that some at least of the intermediary opposition movements of a millenarian character, which are usually by common consent given a place in the history of the emergence of nationalism, were closely linked, as well as essentially similar, to some movements of primary resistance. Can we go further than this? It would be possible to argue, after all, that whatever may be the interest of such millenarian movements in the history of African politics, they have not in fact run into the main-stream of modern nationalism and in some instances have clashed with it. A movement like Dini Ya Msambwa might be cultivated for short-term purposes by a political party—as KANU is said to have cultivated it in order to find support in an otherwise KADU area—but it can hardly be thought to have had much future within the context of modern Kenyan nationalism.

It seems to me that there are a number of things to be said at this stage. I have argued that modern nationalism, if it is to be fully successful, has to discover how to combine mass enthusiasm with central focus and organization. This does not mean that it needs to *ally* itself with movements of the sort I have been describing which succeeded, on however limited a scale, in arousing mass enthusiasm. Indeed, it will obviously be in most ways a rival to them, seeking to arouse mass enthusiasm for its own ends and not for theirs. But it would be possible to present a triple argument at this stage. In the first place, one could argue, where nationalist movements *do* succeed in achieving mass emotional commitment, they will often do it partly by use of something of the same methods, and by appealing to something of the same memories as the movements we have been discussing. In the second place, where nationalist movements are faced with strong settler regimes, as in southern Africa, they will tend to move towards a strategy of violence which is seen by them as springing out of the traditions of 'primary resistance'. And in the third place, where nationalist movements fail, either generally or in particular areas, to capture mass enthusiasm, they may find themselves opposed by movements of this old millenarian kind, some of which will still preserve symbolic connexions at least with the primary resistances.

[4] B. G. M. Sundkler, *Bantu Prophets in South Africa* (London, 1961); T. O. Ranger, 'The early history of independency in Southern Rhodesia', *Religion in Africa*, ed. W. Montgomery Watt (Edinburgh, 1964), 54–7.

Let us turn first to the question of the methods by which nationalist parties achieve mass emotional involvement. Here Dr Lonsdale's comments on the history of politics in Nyanza Province—the home of both the Mumbo cult and of Dini Ya Msambwa—are pertinent. Having described how Christian independency in the Province had its roots in pre-colonial religious phenomena, and how the first and second generations of the *élite* could not come to terms with it, he notes that 'only after the start of popular, mass nationalism did the politicians court the independents'. In a sense, he suggests, the values of the independents triumphed in mass nationalism rather than those of the *élite* welfare associations and proto-nationalist parties. 'The independents' selective approach to Western culture has triumphed over the early politician's desire to be accepted by and participate in the colonial world. It is symbolic of the victory of the mass party over the intellectual and occupational *élite* of the inter-war years.'[5]

The new mass party in East and Central Africa, as it spreads to the rural districts, comes to embody much of the attitude which has hitherto been expressed in less articulate movements of rural unrest. It often appears in a charismatic, almost millenarian role—the current phrase, 'a crisis of expectations', which politicians from Kenya to Zambia employ to describe their relations with their mass constituents, is not a bad description of the explosive force behind all the movements we have described. Often the party locally— and nationally—appeals to the memories of primary resistance, and for the same reason as the millenarian cults did; because it is the one 'traditional' memory that can be appealed to which transcends 'tribalism' and which can quite logically be appealed to at the same time as tribal authorities are being attacked and undermined. My own experience of nationalist politics in Southern Rhodesia certainly bears out these generalizations. It was the National Democratic Party of 1960–1 which first really penetrated the rural areas and began to link the radical leadership of the towns with rural discontent. As it did so, the themes and memories of the rebellions flowed back into nationalism. 'In rural areas', writes Mr Shamuyarira of this period, 'meetings became political gatherings and more . . .the past heritage was revived through prayers and traditional singing, ancestral spirits were evoked to guide and lead the new nation. Christianity and civilization took a back seat and new forms of worship and new attitudes were thrust forward dramatically...the spirit pervading the meetings was African and the desire was to put the twentieth century in an African context.' So Mr George Nyandoro, grandson of a rebel leader killed in 1897, and nephew of a chief deposed for opposition to rural regulations in the 1930s, appealed in his speeches to the memory of the great prophet Chaminuka round whom the Shona rallied in the nineteenth century; so Mr Nkomo, returning home in 1962, was met at the airport by a survivor of the rebellions of 1896–7, who presented him with a spirit axe as a symbol of the apostolic succession of

[5] J. M. Lonsdale, 'A political history of Nyanza, 1883–1945', Cambridge University Ph.D. thesis (1964), chaps. 11 and 12.

resistance; so the militant songs copied from Ghana were replaced by the old tunes belonging to spirit mediums and rebel leaders.[6]

Again there are senses in which the Tanganyika African Peoples Union appeared to the people of southern Tanzania as the direct successor of the Maji-Maji movement. 'Many people took the water', runs an oral account of the spread of Maji-Maji collected in 1966.

You know this is how the water spread very quickly. Take for example the struggle for independence in Tanganyika. If you did not buy a TANU card you were considered as an enemy to Independence by those around you...The same thing with the 'maji', although this was more serious. If your wife took the water and you did not, you were considered an enemy to your fellow Africans, so you had to be removed. For how can anyone allow the life of one man who is dangerous to hazard the lives of the whole people.[7]

At any rate the continuity between Maji-Maji and TANU is a theme of some importance in contemporary Tanzanian politics.

The people fought [so Julius Nyerere told the Fourth Committee of the United Nations in December 1956] because they did not believe in the white man's right to govern and civilize the black. They rose in a great rebellion, not through fear of a terrorist movement or a superstitious oath, but in response to a natural call, a call of the spirit, ringing in the hearts of all men, and of all times, educated and uneducated, to rebel against foreign domination. It is important to bear this in mind in order to understand the nature of a Nationalist movement like mine. Its function is not to create the spirit of rebellion but to articulate it and show it a new technique.

Today, as TANU strives to retain and to develop its character as a radical mass movement, the appeal back to Maji-Maji has become more frequent. 'On the ashes of Maji-Maji' writes the *Nationalist*, 'our new nation was founded.'[8]

A caution and clarification is perhaps in order here. Obviously the *Nationalist* writer quoted above is being very selective in his use of the pre-TANU political tradition. In this paper I am anxious to show that in some ways the radical, millenarian tradition of mass protest *does* run into modern nationalism, but I certainly do not wish to claim that it is the *only* tradition that runs into modern nationalism. TANU has as its background not only Maji-Maji and the Hehe wars, but also the centralizing *élite* associations— the Tanganyika African Civil Servants Association; the Tanganyika African Association—led by the men of what Dr Iliffe has called 'the Age of Improvement'. There is obviously a danger in the nationalist historiography which sees an exclusive line of ancestry running from one episode of violent resistance to another, excluding the accommodators and the pioneers of modern political organization. Yet the fact that today Maji-Maji is seen in

[6] N. S. Shamuyarira, *Crisis in Rhodesia* (London, 1965), 68–9.
[7] Interview between Mr G. C. K. Gwassa and Mzee Hassan Mkape, Kilwa Kivinje, June 1966.
[8] Speech by J. K. Nyerere, 20 December 1956 to the 578th meeting of the Fourth Committee of the United Nations; editorial comment, *The Nationalist*, 18 September 1967.

this way as the most significant predecessor to TANU, even if this is a myth in some respects, is in itself a fact which influences contemporary nationalist politics in Tanzania.

This brings us to the second point. It is natural that a nationalist movement which is still engaged in an increasingly violent struggle for independence will turn even more exclusively to the tradition of resistance. This has certainly happened in Southern Rhodesia, for example. The present phase of guerrilla activity in Rhodesia is called by the nationalists 'Chimurenga', the name given by the Shona to the 1896 risings. 'What course of action will lead to the liberation of Zimbabwe?' asks a Zimbabwe African National Union writer. 'It is not the path of appeasement. It is not the path of reformism. It is not the path of blocking thirds. It is the path of outright fearless defiance of the settler Smith fascist regime and fighting the current war for national liberation. It is the path of direct confrontation. It is the path of Chimurenga.' Here, within the Rhodesian movement, there is not only an attempt to stress the mass, radical characteristics of the nationalist parties as with TANU, but in many ways a repudiation of the party as an organizational form in favour of a return to the older tradition.

The nationalist movement has failed to mobilize these disparate Africans of Rhodesia into an effective revolutionary force [writes Davis Mugabe] because it has moved uncertainly from one European model to another, without ever sinking its roots deep into the African soil... For almost three decades, the nationalist leaders based their operations and their pronouncements on the myth that they spoke for an integrated political community. Although we tried to paper over the differences for the sake of appearances, no real attempt was made to build bridges between the vaShona, the amaNdebele, and the immigrant groups, or even between the city politicians and the peasant farmer. In the anger and bitterness of the past year, however, a new sense of unity can be detected. It has little connexion with the personality feuds of earlier times, for the old game of constitutional politics has run its fruitless course ... From now on the only political leaders who will matter are those who are working 24 hours a day with the people in the countryside—not those in city offices with party names on the door, or in jail, or manning governments in exile. Somewhere in Rhodesia is our Mao or our Castro. His ideology and past affiliations are unimportant; but he must be a man who can become one with the people of the village and with the guerrillas preparing for war in the mountains. Bridges will fall into place between Rhodesia's divergent peoples when they are organized to fight acre by acre for what is most important to them—'the land on the hill'.[9]

Once again it is time for a caution. Mr Mugabe is appealing back to Chimurenga, 'the first war of independence', as an example of a war fought for the things people understand—land and cattle—and as an example of how best to unite the African people of Rhodesia. I have written about the 1896–7 uprisings in terms of the attempts then made to find such a basis of action and unity. To the extent that the risings took place and presented so

[9] 'Spotlight on Zimbabwe', *The Nationalist*, 18 July 1967; Davis Mugabe, 'Rhodesia's African majority', *Africa Report*, February 1967.

formidable a challenge, this attempt was successful. But one should not forget that the success of the leaders of the 1896–7 movement did not last long. Defeat broke up unity; it remains an unproven question whether unity would have survived victory. In the event it was probably true of 1896–7, as Dr Iliffe has written of Maji-Maji, that the collapse of all the high hopes resulted immediately in greater disunity and tensions. The Ndebele and the Shona joined together for a time under the leadership of the prophets; but the Ndebele, or most of them, made a separate peace while the Shona fought on. The unity gave way to Shona attacks on surrendering Ndebele. After 1896 the whites managed Ndebele society by playing upon the triple division into 'loyalists', rebels who negotiated, and rebels who vainly opposed negotiation. After 1897 Shona society was divided in a similar way. These great movements of mass resistance are important as *attempts* at unity.

It is time to move to the third point—that these traditions of resistance can sometimes be used *against* nationalist movements as well as *by* them. Indeed the whole question of African resistance to *African* pressures is one which urgently needs investigation before we can obtain a balanced view of the significance of resistance as a whole.

A number of preliminary points, however, can already be made. In the first place, of course, the extension of the concept of resistance to include African resistance to African pressures reminds us that historical discussion of the role of resistance as a force for change cannot be restricted to the period of the Scramble and the Pacification. This is true even if we limit the idea of resistance to European–African confrontations: the Shona, for instance, had a long tradition of rebellion against the Portuguese which served as the background to their rebellion against the British. But it is even more importantly true if we consider African resistance to African pressures. During the nineteenth century, East and Central Africa were exposed to a number of powerful African intrusions which threatened the very existence of certain societies. Partly in response to these intrusions, the existing secular authorities in some African societies attempted to build up new powers; sometimes this attempt also provoked resentment and resistance within the society.

Some at least of these resistances to external African invaders or to the expansion of internal central authority took the form of the reactions to European rule which I have described above. The prophetic and witchcraft eradication traditions were as available to movements of this kind as to later movements of protest against the whites; certain features of the later movements which historians have felt to be characteristic of response to colonialism as such were almost certainly present in these earlier manifestations. Thus the Nyabingi movement, which we have seen already as a focus of integrative opposition to colonial rule and as a continuing messianic cult in the twentieth century, originated as a movement of opposition to Tutsi control of northern Rwanda and served as a rallying point for Hutu resistance from the middle years of the nineteenth century onwards. Thus the hierarchy of Shona spirit mediums, which we have seen involved in the 1896 risings, also provided a focus for Shona reactions to earlier Ndebele raids; the hero-figures of nineteenth-century central Shona history are the two great mediums of the Chaminuka spirit who rallied the western and central Shona and who were killed at Lobengula's orders.

Then again, during the colonial period itself, a good deal of what we can properly call African resistance, in the sense of movements similar to those categorized as 'primary resistance' movements, has taken the form of protest against dominance or sub-imperialism by other African peoples. A few examples may be given. The violent opposition, once more using the Nyabingi cult as its vehicle, of the Kiga clans to the control of the Ganda agents of British over-rule; the rebellion in 1916 of the Konjo people against Toro control, which is being followed up at the present time by a second rebellion of the Konjo for the same reasons; the disturbances in Balovale and elsewhere against the control of local government by the Lozi; these are all instances of resistance which clearly have to be fitted into any general discussion of the topic.

Finally there is the problem of African resistance, again in the same sense of violent 'primary' style reaction, to African governments after the attainment of territorial independence. I am thinking here of events like the clashes between the followers of Alice Lenshina and members of UNIP in Zambia; of the upheavals organized by the Parmehutu association in Rwanda; above all of the Congo rebellions, particularly of the Kwilu rising. The atmosphere of these events is very similar in many ways to that of the 'primary resistances'.[10]

Let us take the Kwilu example. The Kwilu rebellion seems to fit neatly enough into the category already mentioned, in which the nationalist movement fails to retain the confidence of the mass and is faced with a millenarian style resistance. In a recent study of the Kwilu rising, a convincing argument is stated for the thesis that the inspiration for resistance came not from alien ideas but from 'frustations profoundly Congolese'. What was being aimed at, so the authors hold, was 'an inherently Congolese social revolution' which must be seen in the long line of millenarian integrative attempts so characteristic of Congolese history in the nineteenth and twentieth centuries. The Kwilu rising must be seen in the context of preceding movements in that area: the Bapende revolt of 1931, in which, 'the Bapende reached a magico-religious belief in their own invulnerability'; The Great Serpent sect of 1932, which predicted 'the collective rising of the dead, the eclipse of the sun, and the coming of a Man, part white and part black' who would institute a new order; the Nzambi Malembe movement of 1945,

[10] Andrew Roberts, 'The Lumpa Church of Alice Lenshina and its antecedents', mimeo. (Dar es Salaam, 1967). Dr Roberts argues that the clash between the Lumpa Church and the United National Independence Party arose because both organizations were making claims to exclusive emotional commitment in the same area. The Church reacted against the loss of many of its numbers to the later secular mass movement.

which appealed to the memory of the old empire of the Kongo and which
outlawed all fetishes and witchcraft; the Dieudonne movement of the 1950s,
which again ordered the destruction of all fetishes and general baptism in
its own holy water.

Into this background modern nationalism arrived in 1959 with the
creation of the Parti Solidaire Africain, which promised in its election
campaign 'total reduction of unemployment, work for all, multiplication of
schools, free primary and secondary education, a rise in salaries for all,
improvement in housing, free medical care'. 'Independence', the tribesmen
were told, 'would be an era of leisure, plenty and happiness.' They found
it instead a time of firm government by the progressive *élite* of the moderate
P.S.A., and the authors quote what they hold to be a typical reaction. 'Before
independence we dreamed that it would bring us masses of marvellous
things. All of that was to descend from the sky...Deliverance and Salvation...But here it is, more than two years we have been waiting, and nothing
has come. On the contrary our life is more difficult, we are more poor than
before.' And so, the argument concludes, the masses turned to a 'this-
worldly-oriented messianic movement, headed by a compelling leader-
saviour', Mulele.

This analysis may be greeted with some scepticism, but it rests on more
than an easy comparison of Socialist idealism with millenarian panaceas.
Mulele, it is generally accepted, has acquired the characteristics of previous
prophet figures in the minds of his followers—he is regarded as invulnerable
to bullets; his followers hope to share his invulnerability and explain death
in battle as punishment for 'having transgressed certain norms and practices
of the movement'. Rebels take *mai Mulele*, the water of the rebellion, as a
sign of commitment and guarantee of invulnerability. Mulele lays down
new rules of conduct for his fighters as strict as, and strikingly similar to,
the prohibitions of the Shona mediums in 1896—his followers must live
communally, must not loot, must not use European goods. As the authors
comment, these rules, in addition to creating the sense of the new society,
are as essential in 1966 as they were in 1896 to preserve discipline among
irregular rebel forces. According to the authors, many of those who support
the movement draw a quite conscious parallel between the colonial rule
against which their fathers revolted in 1931 and the present regime in Kwilu
province. But the authors, also make the point that, like Miss Wipper's
followers of Mumbo, the rebels look to the past for inspiration and to the
future for living. The revolt is no rejection of modern goods and advantages,
but rather an attempt to obtain them on a 'just' basis and within a 'good'
society defined in African communalist terms. 'The new society is conceived of as a gigantic village made up of thousands of small villages in
which the people find their own authenticity.'[11]

[11] R. C. Fox, W. de Cramer and J. M. Ribeaucourt, 'The second independence: a case
study of the Kwilu Rebellion in the Congo', *Comparative Studies in Society and History*,
VIII, no. 1 (October 1965).

I should perhaps say in conclusion about the Mulelist movement something which applies to all the others discussed in this paper. I have no intention of maligning or mocking the Mulelist movement by stressing its character as a successor to other millenarian Congolese cults. However strange their mythologies and structures may appear to us, these movements require to be taken seriously and with sympathy as consistent expressions of aspirations which in the end have to be met in one way or another by the rulers of East and Central Africa, whether white or black. The aspiration to 'put the twentieth century in an African context'; the aspiration towards a new society 'conceived of as a gigantic village made up of thousands of small villages in which the people find their own authenticity'; the aspiration towards gaining control of their own world without surrendering its values; all these are still characteristic of the rural masses of East and Central Africa. It is, of course, true that these movements have not offered lasting or effective solutions; to extend the already cited description of Nyabingi to all of them, they have been 'revolutionary in method' but also 'anarchic in effect'. It is the task of the nationalist movements of East and Central Africa, therefore, to maintain mass enthusiasm for their own solutions. It is their task to demonstrate that they can institutionalize and make permanent their answers to the problem of how to increase effective scale without destroying African communalist values more successfully than the primary resistance leaders or the millenarian cults.

African Critics
of Victorian Imperialism:
An Analysis

BONIFACE I. OBICHERE

THE INTERACTION between Africans and the British in the context of Victorian imperialism was not a smooth affair. In the words of Frederick Jackson Turner, it was like a frontier mountain stream and its ecosystem. It gushed and flowed, stumbled over falls, and produced cataclysmic effects, but continued on its steady progress without following a charted course. The ingredients of Anglo-African relations and interactions were many. Prominent among them were Victorian myths of African inferiority, an active hostility towards the great independent kingdoms and states in Africa, a negation of the achievements and accomplishments of Africans, and economic and cultural competition. These elicited a variety of responses from the African in different parts of the African continent. Most important among these responses were opposition and resistance, cultural nationalism, political protest, and persistent attacks on and vehement criticism of British rule seasoned with irreverent political satire and caustic diatribe.

An attempt is made here to survey the content of African criticism of Victorian imperialism and to assess its impact and effect on the development of Anglo-African relations in the colonial context of the nineteenth century. A comparison is made of the reactions of traditional rulers and those of the educated elite. The similarities and contrasts between the views of the professionals, businessmen, ministers of religion, and traditional rulers are examined. African lawyers, doctors, pastors, engineers, and entrepreneurs were among the most vocal critics of Victorian imperialism.

Many works exist on British attitudes towards Africa in the Victorian period. Notable among these are Philip D. Curtin's *Image*

1

of Africa and *Africa and the West,* R. E. Robinson and J. A. Gallagher's *Africa and the Victorians,* and Christine Bolt's *Victorian Attitudes to Race.* These books examine Anglo-African relations in the framework of Octave Manoni's *Prospero and Caliban.* The Africans are treated as objects of British thought and action and as subjects to be ruled at will who have little or no initiative of their own. This article tries to show that nineteenth-century Africans had initiative and reacted in a variety of ways to British imperialism. British rule in Africa did not neglect these African reactions and voices in its development.

One of the most significant features of the nineteenth century, according to Arthur L. Cross, was the growth of the British Empire, which by 1914 encompassed an area of 13,153,712 square miles and about 434,286,650 or more inhabitants. This vast empire on which the sun never set included an area almost one-quarter of the land surface of the globe and a little more than one-quarter of the population of the world at that time. The imperial dominion comprised territories in Europe, Asia, Africa, America, and Oceania. These territories were grouped into two: the white self-governing colonies and dominions, and the non-white colonies and protectorates, mostly in Africa and Asia.[1]

The dynamic indigenous life, politics, and military vitality of many of the older African kingdoms and states of the nineteenth century posed a serious problem to European expansionism. Asante, Dahomey, Benin, Luba, Lunda, Shona, Zulu, Bunyoro, Buganda, Egypt, and Sokoto were either expanding or consolidating their annexations. In the process of their own expansion, the newer African states and their ambitious and capable rulers collided with the imperialist forces who were also engaged in expansionist activities and territorial acquisitions in Africa. With reference to the British, it can be said that treachery, double-dealing, military campaigns and expeditions, deportations, and treaties were effective weapons by which African rulers and their states were overcome and annexed. Unfounded charges of piracy, slave trading, uncivilized laws and customs were leveled against these states, who were unreasonably expected to practice Anglo-Saxon law and its concommitant codes of conduct. It was indeed a matter of giving a dog a bad name in order to hang it.

[1] Arthur L. Cross, *A Shorter History of England and Greater Britain* (New York, 1925), p. 761.

African rulers who refused to succumb to the exigencies of British imperialism were arrested or treacherously trapped and deported from their own countries. King Jaja of Opobo was a victim of the bad faith of the British Consul in the Bight of Benin. King Jaja demanded a full explanation and an exact and accurate definition of the word *protection* as it was used in the treaty forms presented to him for his signature. Nana Olomu and other Itsekiri chiefs categorically refused to accept the clauses dealing with the freedom of trade in the treaty forms presented to them. It was only after painstaking explanations and assurances by Consul Hewett that they consented to sign the treaty less the clauses dealing with the freedom of trade.[2] This consul invited him to dinner on board a British boat in 1887 and ordered the boat to sail away after King Jaja and his party had settled down to their dinner. King Jaja was taken to Accra, and tried and convicted on phony charges of trade monopoly. He was then deported to the West Indies where he died in 1891. Other famous African rulers who were deported to the Seychelles included King Prempeh I of Asante, Bai Bureh of Sierra Leone, and Mukama Kabarega of Bunyoro. King Prempeh, who was deported in 1896, was allowed to return to Kumasi in 1924, when the British adjudged him to be an old and broken man.[3]

Earlier efforts to secure a treaty of friendship and protection in Abeokuta had failed. Alake Osonekan, the king of the Egba people, refused to sign such a treaty even after he was assured of an annual stipend of £500 for handing over his political authority to the British. He defiantly declared: "The love of independence, which state will ever be dear to, and always be inseparable with, all who have the Egba blood in their veins, wisely restricts us from signing any document or documents of any kind or nature whatsoever with any of the European powers."[4] The educated and literate Egba opposed any treaty relations with the British. They argued that "to enter into any engagement with the British Government is to put in the small end of the wedge, which will end in cession of Abeokuta to England."[5]

[2] Foreign Office to Colonial Office, 19 December 1888, encl. Henderson to F.O., CO 147/68.

[3] Mokwugo Okoye, *African Responses: A Revaluation of History and Culture* (Ilfracombe, Devon, 1964), pp. 164–66.

[4] Alake Osonekan to Sons and Gentlemen, 16 May 1888, No. 1, Encl. 3, CO 879/28.

[5] C. O. George and others to Lagos, Egba Committee, 19 May 1888, CO 879/28; also the *Lagos Observer*, 14 September 1886, editorial. This editorial dealt with the treaties made by the Royal Niger Company.

There were several cases of African rulers who were deported to other African colonies under British control. Amoako Attah, the Okyenhene of Akim Abuakwa in Ghana, was deported to Lagos, Nigeria, in 1880 and was returned to his capital in Kibi after five years in exile.[6] Nana Olomu of Itsekiri in the Niger Delta in Nigeria was deported in 1894 to Old Calabar and then to Christiansborg Castle in the Gold Coast in 1896. Nana was allowed to return to Nigeria in 1906.[7] Asafo Adjei, the fugitive chief of Juaben, was deported to Lagos in 1877. Before he was finally deported to the Seychelles, King Prempeh I was deported from Elmina Castle to Freetown, Sierra Leone, in 1899. Oba Ovonramwen of Benin was deported to Calabar in 1897. Cetshwayo, who was taken prisoner after the Zulu War of 1879, was deported to England for some years. He was restored to his Zulu throne over a broken and divided kingdom. Defeat and exile had rendered Catshwayo powerless, and his dream of a united Black Front against the Europeans in South Africa vanished.[8]

The banishment of African rulers was resorted to by the British as a very effective method of implanting their own authority in the political vacuum which they created. In most of the cases cited above, the African ruler was restored to his home after many years in exile, when he was no longer a force to reckon with and after the divide and rule principle had deprived him of a constituency. Most of those who were permitted to return died a few years after their return. Serious efforts were made to convert these rulers to Christianity while they were in exile. Some of them became literate in the solitude in which they found themselves. For instance, King Prempeh I wrote a history of Asante while he was in the Seychelles. The children of the deported Africans were sent to school and were also converted to Christianity. It was hoped that education and Christianity would make them more amenable to British rule than their parents.

African rulers opposed the annexation of their kingdoms by Britain.[9] They made known their views on this matter in letters to

[6] National Archives of Ghana, Accra, ADM.

[7] Obaro Ikime, *Merchant Prince of the Niger Delta* (New York, 1968), pp. 50–96, 165–86. The information on Amoako Attah and Asafo Adjei is from material in the National Archives of Ghana.

[8] J. C. Anene, and G. N. Brown, *Africa in the Nineteenth and Twentieth Centuries* (Ibadan, 1968), pp. 396–99, 427–28.

[9] See Michael Crowder, *African Resistance* (London, 1971).

the British government and in discussions with British officials on the spot. Most of the rulers in question went down fighting the intruders and interlopers, whom they believed had no right to exercise political authority over them and their subjects. From the time of the discovery of diamonds in Kimberly in South Africa to the completion of the partition of Africa by 1898, British policy in Africa was characterized by active hostility towards the great independent kingdoms and states in those parts of Africa where British interests were involved. The resistance of the Africans of this period to both the conquest and occupation of their territories is the most intriguing saga of modern African history. The long period of peace in nineteenth-century Europe made Africa the cockpit for British and European armies. The continual colonial wars of the period led to the rise of the British Empire in Africa. King Khama of the Bamangwato spoke for most of the African rulers of his time when he expelled "some incorrigible, arrogant European gin merchants from his Bechuana kingdom." He asserted: "I am Black but I am king in my country. When you white men rule the country, then you can do as you like. At present I rule and you *must obey* my laws. You have not respected my laws because I am a Black man. Take all your goods and go. I want none but friends in my country."[10]

John Mensah Sarbah (June 3, 1864, to November 6, 1910) fought against the destruction of time-tested and revered customs and institutions of the Fanti by European officials and colonial administrators. He spearheaded the fight against two Land Bills in the 1890s which would have given British colonial officials the legal right to alienate and acquire Fanti land at will. It was in the relentless struggle to protect the rights of the people of Ghana that he wrote his first book, *Fanti Customary Law,* which was published in 1897. He believed that colonial rule could bring definite benefits to Africans but that the first condition for the attainment of such benefits was the respect of African institutions by Europeans.

In February 1887 he wrote the Colonial Secretary and vigorously protested against the tendency of the institutions and customs of the Africans. He requested that the authority and jurisdiction of Fanti chiefs should be restored. John Mensah Sarbah and most of the Fanti nationalists of the nineteenth and twentieth centuries re-

[10] Okoye, *African Responses,* p. 155. See also J. D. Omer-Cooper, *The Zulu Aftermath* (London, 1966); and A. J. Wills, *An Introduction to the History of Central Africa,* 3rd ed. (London, 1973), pp. 105–06.

garded the Fanti-British Bond of 1844 as an agreement between equals which in no way diminished Fanti sovereignty and pride. Unfortunately, this is a legal interpretation that is based on nationalist sentiment and not on a precise and objective analysis of the terms of the agreement. The Bond of 1844 had authorized the British to do away with any "barbarous practices" among the Fanti. It assigned to the British the responsibility of molding the Fanti country "to the general principles of British Law." African chiefs resented the intrusion of British colonial officials into their affairs. The chief of Cape Coast, King John Aggrey (1865–67) clashed with British officials when he insisted on exercising his traditional rights and roles as a natural ruler. He was quickly deported to Sierra Leone.

The Fanti Confederation, 1868, formed after the Mankessim Congress of Fanti leaders, was at the same time a search for how to contain the Victorian encroachment on Fanti political constitutional rights, as well as a mechanism for resisting the Asante. By 1871 the confederation adopted a Victorian hue by establishing a legislative assembly to which both traditional rulers and the educated elite would be elected. This Mankessim Constitution of 1871 was modelled on the thought of James Africanus Beale Horton as set forth in his *Letters on the Political Condition of the Gold Coast*, which was published in London in 1870.

British administrators in the Gold Coast harassed and imprisoned some of the Fanti leaders who framed the constitution, but the Colonial Office ordered their release. This doomed the future of the confederation, which came to a premature end in 1873. John Mensah Sarbah founded the *Gold Coast People* in 1891 and it was published till 1898. It bolstered the cultural and political nationalism of the people of the Gold Coast. Fanti names, dress, and music were extolled and compared with Roman togas and the best in music: "Let us be thankful Fantis are proud to be Fantis and are not ashamed to be known by their native names, heard speaking their liquid language, and seen arrayed in their flowing robes . . . ," declared the *Gold Coast People* on November 30, 1893.

John Mensah Sarbah carried the cultural nationalism struggle to a new level when he addressed himself to the British charge that educated Africans in the Gold Coast had deteriorated culturally because they had reverted to Fanti names and dress. Sarbah declared: "I am fully convinced that it [is] better to be called one's own name than to be known by a foreign one, that it is possible to acquire Western learning and be expert in scientific attainments without neglecting one's mother tongue, that the African's dress had a closer resemblance to the garb of the Grecian and Roman . . . and should not be thrown aside."[11]

From the foregoing, we can see that John Mensah Sarbah was a protagonist in the cultural nationalist struggle that is still continuing in the United States of America in the 1970s in the corn braids, *danshiki, buba, joromi, batakali,* and *agbada* that have come to symbolize a phase of the Afro-American revolution. Sarbah and his colleagues considered it a misfortune to wear Victorian clothes, which they described derisively as "the alien badge of coat and trousers."

The fight against imperialism's spreading tentacles reached a new phase with the formation of the Gold Coast Aborigine's Rights Protection Society (ARPS). On January 1, 1898, it launched its own newspaper, the *Gold Coast Aborigines,* whose motto was "the safety of the public and the welfare of the race." The immediate stimulus for this new militant departure was the continual effort of the colonial government to alienate Fanti land through the Land Bills of 1894 and 1897. The ARPS sent a delegation of J. W. Sey, T. E. Jones, and George Hughes to London to appeal to the Colonial Secretary, Joseph Chamberlain, to repeal the 1897 Lands Bill. After meeting with Chamberlain on August 5, 1898, their wishes were granted. This Fanti delegation to London was like bearding the lion in his own den. Victorian England was confronted with the "voices from the shadows."

An important cause of friction and conflict between Africans and British imperialist administrators in Africa was the introduction of the Native Jurisdiction Ordinances by which political and judicial powers were transferred to British officials. In Ghana the Native Jurisdiction Ordinance of 1878 and 1883 were the bases for the control of the Africans until 1927. These ordinances were opposed by educated Africans and chiefs. The imposition of direct taxation was resented and opposed. Sarbah argued that from time immemorial Fanti people had enjoyed representative government and institutions without any direct taxation of the type proposed by the British. "Today we are being ruled as if we had no indigenous in-

---

[11] John Mensah Sarbah, *Fanti National Constitution,* 2d ed. (London, 1968), p. xiii.

stitutions, no language, no national characteristics, no homes," inveighed John Mensah Sarbah. British administration was producing a total disorganization of Fanti society, and the ordinances and bills were nothing but "a monument of faulty and unsympathetic statecraft," because they deprived Africans of their right to participate in any meaningful and effective way in the administration of their own affairs. Sarbah and his colleagues berated the overbearing attitude of British imperialists as well as what they called "the demoralizing effect of certain European influences." In Sierra Leone, the introduction of the Hut Tax in 1898 resulted in the rebellion of the Mende in that year. One of the leaders of the rebellion was Bai Bureh, who was later deported to the Seychelles Islands.

John Mensah Sarbah published *Fanti Customary Law* in 1897 to demonstrate that the African social system was built up over time in response to the exigencies of African life and environment. He contended that these time-honored institutions should not be dismantled with disrespect by the British. He continued this struggle all through his life and published another book, *Comments on Some of the Ordinances of the Gold Coast,* in London in 1909. In this book, he intensified his criticism of British administration in Ghana and called for what he termed "scientific colonization." He persistently argued that Crown Colony rule was unscientific colonization "from the standpoint of the African, who feels that he has no legitimate opportunity to exercise his undoubted powers in the right direction; that once he has received a fair English education, no chance has he to rise from a condition of mere passive subjection to a capacity for the discharge of one's legitimate responsibilities, public or municipal." British imperialism as practiced in Crown Colony administration contravened "a fundamental principle of every true British institution; namely, the representation of the interests of the people who are governed, and of those who have the largest stake in the countries controlled by it." He reminded the British that the average stay of European administrators in West Africa was approximately seven years at best. This was not always the case, he rejoined, because for the ten years from 1896 to 1906 there were five governors appointed to the Gold Coast. The transitory nature of British officials militated against scientific colonization. This is the most compelling reason for the induction of Africans into the decision-making process. "The African dwells here, this is his home. His interest in its welfare is not transitory but permanent."

POLITICAL PROTEST

Most of the newspapers edited by Africans in the nineteenth century were organs of political protest. The protest that they championed was not uniform in degree, but it was identical in its subject, the oppressive nature of Victorian imperialism. Their stock in trade was "irreverent political satire." No stone was left unturned by the editors of these papers in their persistent and constant attacks on British imperialism.

The *Western Echo* of Cape Coast, Ghana, was owned and edited by Timothy Laing, J. E. Casely-Hayford, and J. H. Brew. These were well-to-do and well-educated men who resented the low political position that was assigned to them by the British administration. On November 28, 1885, they attacked the governor of the Gold Coast for ordering a boat from Birkenhead, England, with which to repress piracy on the lagoons of Lagos, Nigeria. They charged that this was a waste of the taxpayers' money, since the lagoons of Lagos were several hundred miles away from Cape Coast. They posed a sharp rhetorical question, "Would not the Colonial Office do well to check such reckless expenditure of public monies for the repression of 'things' which have no existence except in the fertile brains of some official who is hard up for a subject on which to write?" Their argument was, of course, that piracy in the lagoons of Lagos was nonexistent.

In addition to the professionals and businessmen, some ministers of religion who became editors of papers entered into the field of political polemic with surprising abandon. An example would be the Reverend Attoh Ahuma alias S.R.B. Solomon, who edited the *Gold Coast Methodist* for the English missionaries. Another newspaper, the *Gold Coast Aborigines,* was the organ of the Aborigines' Rights Protection Society. It continued the political criticism and political polemic on a nationalist and militant scale. It also added cultural nationalism to its anti-imperialism. It instituted columns on the history of the Gold Coast in Nigeria and on the achievements of ancient and early African kingdoms and states. It was quick to point out to its readers that the civilization and experience of Egypt was older and more advanced than Greek and Roman civilizations. It believed that by informing its readers about the history and achievements of their forefathers and of Africa as a whole, it would instill cultural pride in them. In this respect, the *Gold Coast Aborigines* was a veritable precursor of the black nationalism of the 1970s.

The *Gold Coast People* was established in 1891 by John Mensah Sarbah, and James Bright Davis established the *Gold Coast Independent* in 1895. These two papers were nationalistic and anti-colonialist in their stance. They supported a doctrine of cultural nationalism. James Bright Davis stated the aim of the *Gold Coast Independent* as the creation and the fostering of public opinion in Africa and to make this public opinion "racy of the soil." The *Independent* inveighed and lambasted the colonial government when one of its printers was lured away and given employment by the government as a printer in the government press. This action was calculated to bring down the *Independent,* and James Bright Davis remarked that this was just one more example of the revolting and sneaky methods of operation of the colonial government. Kwame Nkrumah, the late president of Ghana, praised the undaunted courage of these pioneer nationalists and anticolonialists. He described how they operated against the colonial government and their news-gathering techniques. Nkrumah elaborated on this in his address to the Second Congress of African Journalists in Accra in June 1963. He stated:

> In those days, there was no proper road between Cape Coast and Accra. . . . So those editors and their co-workers worked their clandestine way by canoe along the coast to the capital, Accra. There they ferreted out the latest material that could be used against the colonial Government, and then they paddled their dangerous way back to Cape Coast. All these activities were done at night. It was always a puzzle to the British administration in Accra as to how these newspapers were able to appear in Cape Coast with such "hot" news so quickly.

Administrative ineptitude was attacked and categorized as political oppression and racial discrimination and prejudice. Every mistake made by a colonial official was blamed on his prejudice against the Africans. The *Lagos Times and Gold Coast Advertiser* was first published on November 10, 1880. In some of its editorials it criticized the colonial government in Lagos for not consulting the Egba of Abeokuta in matters that affected their destiny. The Egba, it was argued, should have a voice in the discussion of their affairs. The arrogance of colonial officials was quite often attacked. The *Observer* of Liberia in its issue of July 8, 1880, attacked imperialism in an editorial entitled "The Black and the White." It singled out the evils of economic imperialism and the economics of colonization. This editorial is worth quoting in detail:

On all sides . . . the same cry is heard, all the Great Nations of Europe as well as the United States of America seem to evince a more or less ardent desire to divide Africa among themselves. The reasons for this wish are obvious, when we think of the millions of heathen who are sitting in darkness and who would serve as consumers of the refuse and surplus manufactures. Heathen who, if only civilised, would buy up a large quantity of old clothes, condemned guns, bad liquor, et hoc genus. And again we must remember that surplus population which could find in Africa congenial homes. Men who are nobodies but who as missionaries and explorers would be lions; men whose genius brings them to the treadmill when exercised at home; but if exercised in Africa would make them wealthy merchants, or great landowners. Nor must we forget the philanthropists of the Jelleby stamp who unmindful of the squalor and wretchedness around them love to spend their time and other people's money in conveying doubtful blessing to the heathen. For these and a thousand other reasons the partition of Africa is a most desirable arrangement. The Negro may have some objection, but a first class English newspaper told us some months ago that savages have no rights which civilised nations were bound to respect; so the objections of the Negroes will doubtless be treated as were those of the Zulus, and because we wear the "shadowed livery of the burnished sun," and do not regulate our costumes by the latest Paris fashions, our land is to be divided out by these soi-disant Heralds of Civilisation.[12]

It will be seen from the above passage that the editor of the *Observer* had an uncanny and perceptive insight into the economics of imperialism. Furthermore, this editorial was unique because many of the African newspapers concerned themselves with the more obvious issues of political power, racial discrimination and the exclusion of the African elite from the decision-making processes of their various countries. Since Liberia had many businessmen in the import-export business, it stands to reason that a Liberian editor would be the first to pinpoint the oppressiveness of the economic exploitation of Africa under colonial rule. It was the exclusiveness and monopolistic aspects of Victorian imperialism that ruined many Liberian merchant princes between 1830 and 1900. Among these wealthy merchants of Liberia were R. A. Sherman, Joseph Roberts, Frances Devany, and E. J. Roye, who owned seagoing vessels as well as coastal vessels for trading overseas and along the coast of West Africa, respectively. The collapse of these merchant princes between 1880 and 1900 came in the wake of the partition of Africa

[12] Quoted in Rosalynde Ainslie, *The Press in Africa: Communications Past and Present* (New York, 1967), p. 27.

and the imposition of economic barriers and constraints against African entrepreneurs by European imperialists.[13]

Many other critics of British imperialism commented on the problem of economic exploitation. John Mensah Sarbah was of the opinion that British merchants and traders in West Africa were extremely conservative in their business habits and that they were neither noted for daring initiative nor were they generally conspicuous for strenuous energy or extraordinary enterprise. He continued, "The white trader confines himself within the walls of his fort or trading factory, or inside on board a pestilential hulk moored in the offing, where he kept watch over his staple goods." On the other hand, the African trader traveled far and wide and infused new life into commerce. For instance, Faustus Amissa and other Africans started the collection, manufacture, and purchase of rubber. They developed that industry and stayed with it until the high-price policy of European competitors in Africa and the low proceeds in England of consignments from African traders forced them out of this and other commercial lines. It was the Clinton brothers who began the shipping of West African timber to Europe, but discriminatory practices by European shipping companies forced them out of this lucrative business. Tetteh Quashie (1842–1892) introduced the cocoa plant into the Akwapim and Akim regions of Ghana. Africans took to the cultivation of cocoa but were subjected to unfair and monopolistic practices by English traders. Some Africans were prominent in the gold-mining business and acquired concessions. These included Africanus B. Horton, Mr. Essien, and Joseph Dawson to name a few. These entrepreneurs were forced out of business prematurely by European economic imperialism.

It can be seen from this short survey that the monopolistic and strangling effects of European economic imperialism on African commercial initiative were disastrous. The policies of colonial rulers wiped out the efforts of Africans to participate in the economies of their countries. Their situation is not very different today. The multi-national corporations from Europe and America have monopolies over the most strategic and lucrative commodities and mineral resources of Africa such as oil, copper, bauxite, tin, uranium, and gold.

[13] Nnamdi Azikiwe, *Zik: A Selection from the Speeches of Nnamdi Azikiwe* (Cambridge, 1961), pp. 154–55.

THE PRESS IN SOUTH AFRICA VS. VICTORIAN IMPERIALISM

James Fairbairn, editor of the *South African Commercial Advertiser,* fought the governor of Cape Town over the wrongdoings of the government. He criticized and questioned the governor's policies and actions. He even carried his case to England and won the support of the Colonial Secretary, who upheld the freedom of the press by the Law of April 30, 1828. His list of grievances in 1827 were quite explicit criticisms of the government:

"From the first moment," he complained, "that public attention began to be drawn by its (the Press') means to the longer arrear of wrong, outrage and cruelty inflicted on the defenceless inhabitants of that Colony, scarcely a month has elapsed in which some attempt has not been made to baffle or crush it. . . . Are such a people to be for ever trampled under foot? Is there no moderation, no sympathy, no pride in England, that, for its own honour, will put an end to the abominable scene of oppression, insolence, and bad faith practiced so long in this settlement? What gain has England in our loss? By what have we merited such treatment? We have cost her neither blood nor treasure. We never wronged her. How, then, is it, that while she boasts of her high principles, we receive only contempt, or irreparable injury at her hands?"[14]

The problem of white settlers and Africans was a common subject of articles in all newspapers. The *Grahamstown Journal* was published in the East Cape. It detailed cattle rustling by the Africans, and the border dispute with the Xhosa was a pet subject of discussion in this paper. *De Zuid Afrikaan* supported the slavery that existed in the Cape Colony. Other important papers were the *Cape Argus* (1857) and *Cape Times* (1876). Saul Solomon, the liberal Negrophilist, was brought out in the *Cape Argus* in 1881 by Cecil John Rhodes, who furnished the money to Francis Dormer. After 1881, the *Cape Argus* served the interests of the mining and commercial barons of the Cecil Rhodes type.[15]

VICTORIAN PREJUDICE

A famous West African thinker and writer remarked a few years ago that there was "dangerous nervousness" in the European character. Nineteenth-century African leaders perceived and commented

[14] Ainslie, *The Press in Africa*, pp. 39–40.
[15] See Felix Gross, *Rhodes of Africa* (London, 1956); and W.E.G. Solomon, *Saul Solomon: The Member for Cape Town* (Cape Town, 1948).

on this appalling defect in the character of the Europeans with whom they had political or economic contact and dealings. As I pointed out in 1971, the illustrious and valiant Samori Touré, who led the Mandingo against the French and some African states, commented on this dangerous nervousness in the European character. He stated: "In everything the white man is in a terrible hurry."[16] A manifestation of a form of this dangerous nervousness in the character of Victorian imperial officials and traders in Africa can be seen in Anglo-Asante relations as well as in Anglo-Bunyoro, Anglo-Buganda, Anglo-Ndebele, Anglo-Egyptian, Anglo-Sudan, and Anglo-Boer relations.

This uneasiness and unsafe nervousness resulted in a jaundiced view of Africans and African institutions by Victorian Britain. "The official adoption, publication and indoctrination of a myth concerning the moral character of the peoples" of Africa and Asia resulted from this unfortunate situation. John Mensah Sarbah summed up the two-way consequences of this Victorian prejudice. His judgment was that "a great deal of mutual unfounded distrust and fictitious difficulties, which are the growth of years of mutual misunderstanding, have done much incalculable mischief surely."

The aims and objectives of British rule in Africa were never clearly defined in the official mind of the British government in London, as has been pointed out very cogently by Ronald E. Robinson and John A. Gallagher in their masterly book *Africa and the Victorians* (1961). The vacuum created by the lack of a policy blueprint was filled by the men on the spot, who not only improvised but who also essayed to theorize and to rationalize the *raison d'être* of the British presence in Africa.[17] For instance, there were Cecil J. Rhodes in South Africa and Mashonaland, Frederick D. Lugard in Uganda and Northern Nigeria, Harry H. Johnson in Central Africa, Charles Gordon in the Sudan, Lord Cromer in Egypt, and John Kirk in Zanzibar. Each of these men were responsible for defining and delineating British policy in the parts of Africa to which they were

[16] Boniface I. Obichere, "The African Factor in the Establishment of French Authority in West Africa, 1880–1898," in *France and Britain in Africa,* ed. Prosser Gifford and W. Roger Louis (New Haven, Conn., 1971), p. 474.

[17] F. D. Lugard, *The Dual Mandate in British Tropical Africa* (London, 1922); H.A.C. Cairns, *The Clash of Cultures: Early Race Relations in Central Africa* (New York, 1965); Earl of Cromer, *Modern Egypt* (London, 1911); C. W. de Kiewiet, *The Imperial Factor in South Africa* (Cambridge, 1937); and Roland Oliver, *Sir Harry Johnston and the Scramble for Africa* (London, 1957).

assigned. One of the governors of the British West African colonies spoke for most of these Victorian administrators when he declared the aims of British rule in Africa in these terms:

> Firstly, the treatment of native races, who are centuries behind ourselves in mental evolution, and the steps by which they may be gradually brought to a higher plane of civilization and progress; and secondly, economic development by which those tropical countries may develop a trade which shall benefit our own industrial classes by the production, on the one hand, of the raw materials—rubber, oils, cotton, hides, etc., which form the staple of our manufacturers, and by the absorption in return of our manufactured cottons, hardware, and other goods.[18]

It can be seen that little or no recognition was given to the welfare of the Africans in this statement of aims. Ruthless economic exploitation was the central theme and the main prop of British policy towards Africa.

The emergence of Darwinism, the application of Herbert Spencer's "survival of the fittest" theory to Darwin's theory of biological evolution and the application of this formula of the progress of evolution to life, mind, society, and morality affected how Anglo-Saxons looked at other races of men. Darwin showed that the different species of plants and animals, "instead of being each separately created" were evolved from lower types by means of "natural selection" in the struggle for existence. Therefore, there was what Herbert Spencer in *Principles of Psychology* (1855) called "survival of the fittest," due to a process of continuous adaptation. With the popular doctrines of Darwinism in the back of his mind, a self-appointed commentator on the future of Africa wrote in the *Spectator* of December 1895:

> Why, then, have they never risen, never developed a civilization, never learned that permanent obedience to a code which enables men to aggregate themselves into mighty, and up to a certain point improving, communities? Why—for this appears to be the truth—has their point of arrest arrived so quickly that they have been unable to remain at it, and have time after time fallen back into the jungle of life, have apparently "gone Fantee," as the whites of the West Coast phrase it, in huge masses? It is the inexplicable mystery of history, and is not solved in the least by talking of deficient brain-power; for if there is one thing clear about the

[18] Sarbah, *Fanti National Constitution*, p. xix; and Aimé Césaire, *Discours sur le colonialisme* (Paris, 1955).

45

Negro, it is that there are individuals among them with plenty of brain-force, who learn the difficult trades or acquire the abstract ideas of the whites, or even master their sciences, like medicines or mathematics.[19]

This commentator was constrained to admit that some Africans were endowed with brain power equal to the best that can be found among the Anglo-Saxons of Victorian England. There was abundant evidence for this, as was pointed out in Mr. Cole's memorial to Lord Salisbury in 1886 when Mr. Cole, a graduate of Oxford University and a lawyer, complained about British policy in his home of Freetown, Sierra Leone. The author of the *Spectator* article did not mind contradicting himself in his hasty and erroneous vituperations about African history and society. His ignorance of African statecraft was profound and startling. His lack of knowledge about Africa reflected the same degree of ignorance of African history exhibited by David Hume (1711–1776) and Thomas Carlyle (1795–1881), especially in his *Nigger Question*.

That these men did not know or refused to acknowledge the richness of African history, philosophy, and society did not mean that it did not exist. Felix N. Okoye has condemned these "acknowledged intellectual giants" of the Western world as "learned ignoramuses on the subject of Africa." He flayed David Hume, who had stated in 1754 that no black person had ever attained distinction in the arts and sciences in government or in war. Okoye asserted:

Hume did not know that Mansa Musa of Mali had dazzled fourteenth century North Africans and Europeans by an extravagant display of the wealth of his empire; nor of the administrative genius of this Black emperor. The Englishman was surely unaware of the military exploits of Sundiata, Sunni 'Ali, Askia the Great, Kotal Kanta of Kebbi, Queen Amina of Zaria, Queen Zhinga of Matamba and King Agaja of Dahomey. He was ignorant of the medieval civilizations of Ghana, Mali, Songhay and Kanem-Bornu, of the intellectual ascendancy of Timbuktu in the sixteenth century, of distinguished scholars of Sankore University such as Al-Hajj Ahmad, the theologian and Makluf ibn 'Ali, a jurisconsult and geographer. He was not familiar with the writings of 'Abd Al-Rahman Al-Sa 'di, Mahmud Kati, Dan Marina and Dan Masanih of Katsina, of the poets of fourteenth century Kanem and of Anthony William Amo. Hume had no knowledge of Osei Tutu or of the constitution which he had formulated for the Asante empire.[20]

[19] The *Spectator*, December 7, 1895, p. 816.
[20] Felix N. Okoye, *American Image of Africa* (Buffalo, New York, 1971).

The Victorians were a funny lot and contradicted themselves with amazing frequency, especially about Africa. No wonder that Pierre Charles Baudelaire, the French poet and essayist, suggested two additional rights which should form part of the Declaration of the Rights of Man. These were the right to contradict oneself and the right to walk away without false pride or the fear of being branded a coward.

The most authoritative recent study by Victorian prejudice is by Christine Bolt. In her book *Victorian Attitudes to Race* (1971), she traced how nineteenth-century England became increasingly hostile to the non-white peoples of Africa and Asia. The increasing prejudice against non-whites was worsened by the American Civil War and the emancipation and enfranchisement of blacks in the U.S., the Jamaican Revolt of 1865 led by the blacks of that island and the Indian Mutiny of 1857.[21]

Pseudo-scientists, especially ethnologists and anthropologists, wrote and published scurrilous books and pamphlets about the "inferior" races and the superiority of the white man. Adventurers, explorers, missionaries, and apostles of the anti-slavery movement contributed in various ways to the racial prejudice of Victorian England. The spiritual imperialism of Christian missionaries in Africa was to blame for the increasingly hostile and prejudiced attitude of the Victorians towards the Africans. The missionaries always represented the African as a savage pagan who must be converted, baptized, and saved even against his own will.[22]

Christianized and educated Africans such as the professionals, writers, journalists, and lawyers who have been mentioned in this article often spoke up against the revolting spiritual and cultural imperialism of the missionaries. The foremost African spokesmen and attackers of Victorian prejudice included James Africanus B. Horton (1835–1883), who reminded the Europeans that "Rome was not built in a day," and that Rome was once in a state of barbarism which far exceeded anything that could be found in Africa and Asia. Horton graduated from Edinburgh University in 1859 and

[21] Christine Bolt, *Victorian Attitudes to Race* (London, 1971); C. A. Bodelson, *Studies in Mid-Victorian Imperialism* (Copenhagen, 1924); and C. E. Black, *Victorian Culture and Society* (New York, 1973).

[22] Roland Oliver, *The Missionary Factor in East Africa*, 2d ed. (London, 1965); J. F. Ade. Ajayi, *Christian Missions in Nigeria, 1831–1881* (Evanston, Ill., 1965); and Jack Simmons, *Livingstone and Africa* (London, 1955).

joined the Army Medical Service. "He was formidably equipped to combat the arguments of those Europeans who denied African capacity for Western Christian civilization and political advancement." He attacked the racist theories of the Europeans and suggested positive alternatives to British colonial rule in his book, *West African Countries and Peoples* (1868).[23]

Edward Wilmot Blyden (1932–1912) is perhaps the best known of the nineteenth-century opponents of Victorian imperialism and British rule in Africa.[24] This is perhaps due to the fact that biographies of Blyden have been published and to the more important fact that he was a prolific writer and publisher. By 1872 he was preaching the doctrine of Africa for the Africans. He devoted much energy and dedication to the subject of African accomplishments and race pride, as well as to Africa's service to the world. The most substantial of his works is *Christianity, Islam and the Negro Race* (1887). His other books which delt with the African genius are *The Prospects of the African* (1874) and *African Life and Customs* (1908). In addition to these, he wrote profusely and was published in journals in Europe and Africa. The problem with Blyden's African assertion was that he had a commitment to Victorian culture and civilization in his own personal life-style, though he attacked Victorian racial prejudice towards Africa. Blyden is like W.E.B. DuBois, who attacked American prejudice towards black people, but who did not feel comfortable around black people and wanted little or nothing to do with black culture. They were both polemicists and radical critics who did not practice what they preached.

J. E. Casely Hayford (1866–1930) was another West African from Ghana who continued the Blyden tradition and whose *Ethiopia Unbound* (1911) not only criticized British imperialism adversely but also suggested a positive and an "acceptable patriotic role for the Western-educated elite." Like Edward Blyden, Casely Hayford was fascinated by African culture and cherished African departures from Western Christianity, as was demonstrated by the life and career of the Prophet William Wade Harris, a Grebo from Liberia.

The rigidity and cultural superiority of Christian missionaries and

---

23 Harry S. Wilson, *Origins of West African Nationalism* (New York, 1969).
24 S. O. Mezu and Ram Desai, *Black Leaders of the Centuries* (Buffalo, New York, 1970), pp. 135–49, 153–64; and Robert W. July, *The Origins of Modern African Thought* (London, 1968).

their brand of Victorian Christianity turned off m
also led to the rise of several messianic churches
Africa, Central Africa, and West Africa were regio
etism arose as a reaction against European Chr
Harris of Liberia, Prophet Elijah II of Nigeria, Jc
Malawi, Simon Kibangu of Zaire, John Msikinya
and Rev. Mpambane Mzimba of South Africa rep.____
sistance and voices from the shadows against Victorian Christianity.
South Africa is especially significant in this new departure.[25] The
earliest independent churches in South Africa were led by Rev.
Nehemiah Tile (1884), Rev. M. M. Mokoni (1892), and Rev. James
Dwane (1896), who split from the Wesleyan Methodist Church. The
success of Prophet Isaiah Shembe in Zululand was phenomenal. C.
G. Baeta has analyzed and assessed the phenomenon of Africanized
Christianity in Ghana in his seminal book entitled *Prophetism in
Ghana* (1962).

CONCLUSION

It can be seen from the foregoing survey that Africans did not
endure Victorian imperialism with placid passivity. The traditional
leaders of African societies took up arms in defense of their patri-
mony. They fought against overwhelming odds and lost in most
cases. Many of them were skilled or deported into inglorious exile.
Their children continued the struggle in a different form and in a
different medium. The educated elite spoke up against British rule
and what they considered to be the oppressive elements of colonialism. They wrote letters, pamphlets, and books to express their views
on these aspects of British imperialism.

The political facets of British colonialism elicited as much criticism and attack as the economic and cultural components of the
colonial package. Newspapers were used as vehicles for the expression and dissemination of the ideas of the African elite. Most of
them who criticized colonialism did so out of frustration. They felt
left out of the management and control of the affairs of their coun-

[25] See Bengt Sundkler, *Bantu Prophets of South Africa* (1948; reprint ed., New York, 1964); G. M. Haliburton, *Prophet Harris of Liberia* (New York, 1973); Michael Banton, "African Prophets," *Race* 5, no. 2 (1963): 42–55; and George Shepperson, "Nyasaland and the Millennium," in *Millennial Dreams in Action: Essays in Comparative Study,* supplement 2, *Comparative Studies in History and Society,* ed. Sylvia L. Thrupp (The Hague, 1962).

They condemned only selected aspects of the British connection. Some of them had become "black white men" by their training and residence in Britain. Even the Africans who had embraced Christianity and become ministers of the Christian faith expressed opposition to Victorian religious culture. The African churches were a demonstration of the rejection of what was termed bland religious worship. The criticism of Africans helped focus British attention on the harsh aspects of colonial rule and to bring about desirable reforms in the administration of most of the African colonies.

THE SURVIVAL OF ETHIOPIAN INDEPENDENCE*

K. V. RAM
University of Lagos, Lagos.

The survival of Ethiopia as an independent state through the period of the "Scramble for Africa" and colonial rule is a glorious chapter in African history. How and why Ethiopia alone of all African states managed to preserve her independence where as all the other states who shared some of her strengths and many weaknesses fell fighting European imperialism has not yet been explained. It is possible to suggest a number of reasons for Ethiopia's survival: Ethiopia's geographical position; the inherent strength and solidity of her political and religious instituions: national consciousness of her people; the quality of Ethiopian leadership and above all the determination of the Ethiopina people to preserve their independence. These facts must be considered in the context of the aims and strategies of foreign powers and foreign nationals interested and involved in Ethiopia. Moreover as relations with Europe dominated Ethiopian diplomacy in the second half of the nineteenth century as she struggled to maintain her independence a study of these relations would be vital for a knowledge of the survival of Ethiopian independence. It will take years of research and synthesis before a definitive study of the subject can emerge. however it is encouraging that a beginning is made to answer this challenging question. In his latest study *The Survival of Ethiopian Independence* Professor Sven Rubenson offers some explanations for the survival through an analysis of Ethiopia's external relations. His main thesis is that the miscalculation of Ethiopia's potential by her would-be protectors and invaders played a decisive role in the preservation of her independence.

In his five-chapter and four-hundred-thirty-seven-page study Professor Rubenson examines external relations of Ethiopia from 1805 when the first of the nineteenth century European visitors arrived in Ethiopia to 1896 when that country asserted her independence by defeating Italy at the battle of Adwa. Since the aim of

*Review article on Sven Rubenson, *The Survival of Ethiopian Independence* (London Heinemann, 1976).

the author was 'to cover all foreign contacts of any importance in order to establish where the initiatives came from and what contributions they made to a formulation of an active foreign policy' he has rightly chosen a chronological approach to the study. The titles of his chapters "Prospects and first contacts", "Increasing pressures and sporadic responses" "Unification and active foreign policy" and "Trials of strength with Egypt and Italy" are appropriate as they indicate the changing nature of Ethiopia's foreign relations and different stages in the evolution of her foreign policy.

After giving, in chapter 1, a comprehensive and critical survey of source material for the study, in chaper II the author attempts an analysis of Ethiopia's internal situation as she was called upon to respond to European initiatives in the first quarter of the nineteenth century. Here the author treads upon familiar grounds and we get a succinct account of what is already known. As Ethiopia entered the nineteenth century there was no effective central authority in the country capable of conducting foreign relations. There were at least three different centres of political authority-Tigre, Begemder and Shoa — each an autonomous constituent of an enfeebled Ethiopian state, each not disinclined to respond to foreign initiatives though non was entitled or competent to speak for the whole country. Without a tradition of active foreign relations, free from external threats to its independence and preoccupied with internal power struggles Ethiopia's ruling aristocracy had become insular and conservative. The sporadic and intermittent nature of external contacts in the preceeding centuries had not facilitated the emergence of a foreign policy. In spite of these weaknesses, the Ethiopian rulers of the *Zemene Mesafint* period showed great skill in their dealings with foreigners. Ras Welde Selassie's encounter with Henry Salt in 1809 is a case in point. Though Welde Selassie received with warmth the British mission which had arrived to open up his country for British trade and commerce he could not understand why the king of England should send gifts to some one he had not seen. This put him on guard and he remained so in spite of his cordial personal relations with Salt. While rejecting British proposals for opening up his country, Welde Selassie had special prayers offered in his church for the welfare of George III and so profusely expressed his gratitude to that monarch for regarding the welfare of Ethiopia that Salt, in spite of the failure of his mission, returned to England pleased rather than disappointed with the Ras. This encounter is highly significant since it highlights not only the European motives in Ethiopia and the latter's reactions to it but also the diplomatic skills of the Ethiopians which played an important role in Ethiopoa's survival. As the author observes "On the European side the main underlying motive is fairly clear and not surprising; the promotion of trade with as high profits as possible and preferably, no engagements." The strategic position of Ethiopia and the suitability of the country to European christian endeavours were also noted. Europe had clear motives and justifications for impinging on Ethiopia. To the Ethiopians, however, the motives of Europeans remained a problem as they began to grapple with the issues of foreign relations.

The 1830—1855 period was the seed time of European imperialism in Ethiopia. The author's illuminating analysis in chapter III tends to confirm this view though the same conclusion is not reached there. The same religious imperialism of the missionary, economic imperialism of the European governments which destroyed African independence elsewhere threatened Ethiopia at this time. What is significant is the time when this imperialism manifested and not the way it did. The author makes a very significant contribution to our knowledge of the missionary imperialism in Ethiopia through a thorough analysis and excellent interpretation of the diplomatic and missionary correspondence of the times. He brings to light the intrigues, frauds, duplicities and forgeries in which both the Roman Catholic and the C.M.S. protestant missionaries in Ethiopia indulged in their relentless efforts to introduce European political influence in the country. De Jacobis' forgeries and falsification of the Ethiopian documents and his misrepresentation of Ethiopian rulers as well as the duplicities or the d'Abbadie brothers remind one of the ignoble practices of the later day lay imperialists in Africa like Karl Peters and Lugard. If the intrigues of the C. M. S missionary Krapf led to the Harris Mission to Shoa and the conclusion of the Anglo-Shoan Treaty of Commerce and Friendship of 1841 which the missionary hoped would be the first step in the establishment of British political influence in the region, the intrigues of De Jacobis at the court of Dejaz Wubi of Tigre might have led to the establishment of a French protectorate in northern Ethiopia. The French Catholic missionaries were also responsible for the anti-Theodorean policy of the French government and the alienation of certain northern people like the Beja from their loyalty to Ethiopia in the 1860's and 1870's respectively. If these missionaries failed to introduce European political influence in the country it was largely due to the vigilance of the Ethiopian Coptic church which remained opposed to foreign missionary activity because of its determination to preserve the national faith. Because of the popular support it enjoyed the Church wielded considerable influence with the Ethiopian rulers. Not only a number of Roman Catholic and Protestant missionaries were expelled but also the magnitude and area of the European missionary activity in Ethiopia was limited and controlled at the Church's behest. Had the Coptic Church been less vigilant or less nationalistic it is possible that Ethiopia might have been forced to go through the same bitter experiences which Uganda underwent in the 1880's. The role of the Church both as a defender of Ethiopian independence and as a pressure group in the formulation of Ethiopian foreign policy are very important to an understanding of the survival of Ethiopian independence. The author's treatment of this theme in an otherwise excellent discussion of the issue leaves much to be desired.

Ethiopia also came under strong economic and strategical pressures of Europe. As the author rightly concludes "The emphasis shifted with the economic and political conditions in Europe, but generally speaking the exportable resources, the potential markets and the availability of good agricultural land were taken for granted"; so was the strategic importance of the country. "The French and British pressure to gain commercial control and political influence was almost constant from the eighteen forties through the mid-sixties." Supported by governments and business at home European speculators, 'men of ardent and daring visions' like Combes and Tamisier, Ferret and Gallinier, Lefebvre and d' Hericout arrived in Ethiopia both to profit individually and create economic bases for France in that country. Similar economic objectives motivated the British missions of 1809 and 1841 to the courts of Gonder and Shoa respectively as well as the Anglo-Shoan and the Anglo-Ethiopian commercial treaties of 1841 and 1848. The head of the British mission to Shoa Cornwaltis Harris, the C.M.S. missionary Krapf, the first British Consul in Ethiopia Walter Plowden and the British explorer and geographer Dr. Beke all spoke enthusiastically about the Selaubrious climate of Ethiopia for European settlement, the richness of Ethiopian soil, the variety of her agricultural productions and the extensiveness of her markets for European manufactures as well as the need for Britain to exploit the country. A number of plans and suggestions were made and considered for the acquisition by Britain of a seaport on the Red Sea Coast of Ethiopia to which all her external trade might be directed. Dr. Beke who was considering the matter in the light of British experience in India wanted a British factory established near Massawa or around to exploit Ethiopian commerce, and of course the factory would sooner or later become the base for the expansion of British power into the interior. These Europeans were preparing economic tentacles to bind Ethiopia.

Anglo-French rivalry, for political influence in Ethiopia was a dominant feature of European activities during this period. Boardering the Western Red Sea, Ethiopia was strategically important to Britain and she was determined that no rival power should lodge itself in Abysinia as it would prove prejudicial to British interests, more especially in the Red Sea. Britain's treaties of Commerce and Friendship with Haile Selassie in 1841 and Ras Ali in 1848 as well as the appointment of a British consul to Ethiopia in 1848 were motivated by the desire to counteract French influence and to augment British influence in the region. France was also active in Ethiopia throughout the period and the French consul at Massava visited southern Ethiopia frequently and kept a constant watch on British activities in the region. It was the establishment of European economic bases in West Africa and the strategical concerns of Britain in East Africa that ultimately led to the imposition of colonial rule on those regions. Given the obvious European interests what prevented the development of Economic and strategic bases in Ethiopia? Why did not Ethiopia succumb to European imperialism? Was it the far-sighted policy of the Ethiopian rulers or the peculiar geographic and economic situation of Ethiopia that saved her from European domination? First, in spite of their friendly attitude towards the visiting Europeans and occasional indiscretions in dealing with them, the Ethiopian rulers remained determined not to open Ethiopia to foreign economic activity. The explusion of Lefebvre and Combes by Wubi and the closure of Shoa to British and French commercial penetration by Haile Selassie even before the ink was dry on the Anglo-Shoan and the Franco-Shoan-Shoan commercial treaties of 1841 are cases in point. The same concern lead Theodores to refuse the revival of the Anglo-Ethiopian commercial treaty of 1848 not withstanding his desire to cultivate closer diplomatic relations with European. Surely Ras Ali was an exception in this regard but he did not imagine that his treaty of commerce with Britain would lead to any significant foreign economic activity in Ethiopia. Professor Rubenson's analysis of the attitudes and reactions of the Ethiopian rulers to the various European schemes for economic exploitation of Ethiopia shows that their policies were largely responsible for the non-development of European economic bases in Ethiopia. However, the author's conclusion on page 407 of the study that "the geographical features of Ethiopia played almost no role at all in the preservation of her independence" is difficult to accept. To understand its real impact on Ethiopia's independence the influence of geography must be seen in its totality and not partially. Penetration into Ethiopia from the coast was possible, but it was not 'fairly easy' as we are told by the author. It must be remembered that at this time Ethiopia was a land-locked country. The Turks controlled the coast. Ethiopia's external trade passed through either the Turkish controlled part of Massawa in the north or through the Somali ports of Zeyla and Berbera in the South. In the north the bottle-necks created by the Turks at the port of Massawa discouraged the development of any significant foreign economic activity in Ethiopia. Almost all the French and British visitors to Ethiopia, on the author's own account, had the view that no profitable commercial relations with Ethiopia could be developed unless the obstruction to Ethiopian trade at Massawa was removed or a new outlet was provided to Ethiopia, obviously under the influence or control of an European power. However, the Turkish sovereignty over the Red Sea coast of Ethiopia prevented the establishment of European economic bases there until the 1880's. It is only with the collapse of the Turkish and later Egyptian authority in the coastal region that it became possible for Italy to implant herself at Massawa and it is from then onwards that Ethiopia began to experience the full weight of European imperialism. If we move from the north-east to the south-east, even if one disembarked at Zeyla or Berbera one had to pass through about 400 kilo meters in the country of the hostile and warlike Isaas before entering Ethiopia. Moreover the enormous distance from the sources of Ethiopia's export produce to the coast as well as the difficulties of terrain must have deterred the development of foreign economic activity in Ethiopia. Had the politically aggressive and economically ambitious European powers lodged themselves on the coast earlier and developed significant economic interests within Ethiopia it is doubtful if Ethiopia could have easily extricated herself from Europe's stranglehold in the period of 'scramble for Africa.' 'In the light of these considerations it is possible to suggest that the land-locked nature of the country and the difficulties of communication with the coast aided the survival of Ethiopia and that the influence of geography cannot be dismissed as inconsequential. One can only conclude that with his greater preoccupation with the analysis of political and diplomatic aspects of Ethiopia's foreign relations the author failed to consider adequately the role of economic and geographic factors in the preservation of Ethiopian independence.

Another important factor in the Survival of Ethiopia was the attitude of European powers towards that country. That the 1830–55 period was potentially dangerous to Ethiopia's independence is evident from the author's account. However the danger arose from the unofficial European imperialists in Ethiopia and not from their governments. It is these Europeans in the field in their efforts to involve their home governments in Ethiopia "who tried to bridge the gap between the non involvement and wait and see policies of their governments and their own interests by presenting the latter as "requests" and "offers" of the Ethiopian rulers. "It is they who tried to bind the Ethiopian rulers with Europe through commitments that portended danger to Ethiopian independence. Had the British and French governments been interested in territorial acquisitions they could have used Haile Selassie's unilateral abrogation of the 1841 treaties or Wubi's request for "protection" as pretexts to impose their rule on Ethiopia. That such did not happen confirms the author's conclusion "that by and large the governments in London and Paris were not in favour of territorial acquisitions in the Red Sea coast, much less in the Ethiopian hinterland."

Nevertheless as Professor Rubenson's study shows, European intrigues and activities continued to threaten Ethiopian independence during the post *Zemane Mesafint* period. The challenges which faced Ethiopia during Theodore's time were the same as those of the preceding decades; only Theodore's approaches to them were different. Britain continued to consider th Red Sea and its hinterlands as her sphere of influence and remained anxious to open Ethiopia to British trade. A British consul in Ethiopia continued to strive to accomplish this by winning Theordore's support. The French Catholic missionaries toiled untiringly to establish catholic faith and French political influence in Ethiopia and Anglo-French rivalry for preponderance continued. Causing grave concern was also Moslem Egypt's growing pressure on Ethiopia's western and northern borders and at the port of Massawa. Theodore endeavoured to contain these pressures by unifying and restructuring Ethiopian society to be able to withstand the external pressures and by trying to cultivate closer relations with Europe while at the same time refusing it access to build imperial bases in his country. In spite of the modernity of his policy in all these areas, like his predecessors of the *Zemane Mesafint*, Theodore was both naive and simplistic in his relations with Britain and France. While seeking "aid" from those powers he refused to trade with them. He did not understand that common fellowship in the faith was inadequate to attract aid from the West. Operating in the medieval frame work of Christianity versus Islam Theodore could not understand the global diplomacy of either France or Britain which transcended religious considerations in international relations. His foreign policy which was both nationalistic and goal oriented produced for Ethiopia the very opposite of the results which Theodore had intended. His opposition to the French Catholic missionary activity had won him the enemity of France which came close to establishing a French protectorate in northern Ethiopia through supporting a rival candidate to the Ethiopian throne and his opposition to Britain led to the British expedition of 1867 and his death.

Ethiopia had come close to falling under European domination during the late 1860's than ever before. If this did not happen in the end it was as much due to the policies of the concerned European powers as to the situation within Ethiopia, and entire credit for this cannot be given to Ethiopia alone as the author does. It is difficult to accept Professor Rubenson's conclusion on page 408 "The strange case of British withdrawal "from Ethiopia "as the result of the resistance which Theodore had stubbornly maintained against the introduction of special rights and privileges for Europeans in his country". The British withdrawal has to be seen in the light of Britain's territorial aspirations in Ethiopia at the time as well as in the context of political situation within Ethiopia. Britain's easy march from the coast to Magial had been made possible by the cooperation of the Ethiopian forces who had been promised that the expeditionary force would be withdrawn after the British captives had been freed and Theodore had been punished. Having been opposed to Theodore's excesses, though almost all important Ethiopian chiefs were anxious to see him fall, they were unprepared to see British rule imposed upon Ethiopia. Had Britain violated her promise and stayed in Ethiopia she would have had to face the determined and united opposition of the Ethiopian chiefs whose armies were of considerable size even then. It would also have involved Britain in great expenses and diplomatic struggles with France. In the light of Britain's experiences with Ethiopia the national mood in Britain was opposed to further involvements in that country. Britain withdrew from Ethiopia and one wonders whether resistance which Theodore had maintained against the introduction of special rights and previleges for Europeans in his country had much to do with this.

Real threat to Ethiopia's independence arose between 1870 and 1896 during the reigns of the Emperors Yohannes and Menelek. This period saw the determined efforts of the Khedive Ismail to build an empire in East Africa, the entry of Italy into the colonial polities of Africa and her establishment of Massawa and the rise of the Mahdist Sudan on Ethiopi's western border. All these developments affected Ethiopia profoundly. Ethiopia had to face the territorial imperialism of Egypt and Italy and the religions imperialism of the Mahdist Sudan. The Ethiopians accepted the challenge and inflicted most humiliating and disastrous defeats upon Egypt at the battles of Gundet and Gura in 1875—75 and upon Italy at the battle of Adwa in 1896. How could the Ethiopians inflict such crushing defeats on the two enemies who had better fire power, more resources and superior military organization than her own?

The overwhelming numerical superiority of the Ethiopian forces a large section of which had been equipped with fire arms and the military skills of the Ethiopian generals certainly helped Ethiopia to prevail over her invaders. An equally important factor which aided Ethiopia's survival was the underestimation of Ethiopia's strength by her invaders. As the author stated on page 287 of the study:

> As the special conditions which alone could explain the easy victory of the British — two died in action — were played down and forgotten, the ease with which Ethiopia 'had been invaded and conquered', in spite of topography and climate, was remembered. If moreover, the great unifier had fallen so easily, what would his disunited successors in general and 'so poor a creature' like Yohannes in particular be able to do in the face of a new invasion? out of this distorted interpretation was born a wrong opinion about Ethiopia in political circles in Europe and Egypt. Unless one takes into account a serius underestimation of Ethiopia's basic unity and military potential, it becomes very difficult to explain why the expeditions of the following decades were so incredibly insufficient."

What was under-estimated was not so much Ethiopia's military strength. For instance at Gura the Egyptians employed about 14,000 soldiers against Ethiopia whereas at the battle of Adwa the Italians fielded about 16,000 soldiers. Both the invading armies had been well supplied with firearms and ammunition and they were among the largest armies to invade Africa and hence the question of under-estimation does not arise here.

However the author is right in suggesting that the invaders and protectors of Ethiopia under-estimated her basic unity, her will to hold together, the wide spread of not well articulated sense of nationalism of her people and the abilities and skills of her rulers. They considered Ethiopia as a politically divided, loose geographical entity that could be subjugated and held easily. Apparently there was disunity among the Ethiopian chiefs. Emperor Yohannes did not enjoy the full support of his vassals, Menelek and Yekla Haymanot. On becoming Emperor Menelek had to face the opposition of Ras Mangasla of Tigre. Both Italy and Egypt counted upon exploiting these internal divisions in imposing their rule on Ethiopia. What they failed to consider was that Ethiopia's feudal system permitted vassal princes to cultivate foreign contacts and the vassals used these contacts to strengthen their position against their masters in efforts to maintain their own autonomy. This was true of Menelek when Yohannes was the Emperor and of Mangesha when Menelek became the Emperor. But ultimately their loyalty was to their own country and not to the foreign ally of whose territorial aspirations they were never in doubt. This is why neither the Egyptians nor the Italians succeeded in spreading political disloyalty among the Ethiopian chiefs. At the battle of Gura almost all northern Ethiopian chiefs fought against the Egyptians while at Adwa all the Ethiopian chiefs of any consequence fought the Italians besides Menelek. As Professor Rubenson correctly surmises that "in spite of backwardness, feudalism and disunity Ethiopia was a more solid political unit than Egypt" and she was "one body politic aware of one common identity and there was a greater political cohesion and greater awareness of the issues involved than the enemies of Ethiopia foresaw". This basic unity played a key role in Ethiopia's survival.

Under-estimated were also the diplomatic abilities and skills of the Ethiopian rulers. While sharing Theodore's perceptions of European imperialism, both Yohannes and Menelek showed greater skills in conducting foreign relations. Both Yohannes and Menelek rejected the limitations which the European powers tried to impose upon Ethiopia's right to external relations and used diplomatic channels to protect Ethiopia's territorial integrity and independence. Diplomacy was also used to check the progress of Egyptian and Italian imperialisms in Ethiopia. Yohannes's extensive diplomatic activity both before and after the battles of Gundet and Gura and that of

Menelek's following the Italian fraud to claim protectorate over Ethiopia on the basis of the Wichale treaty are cases in point. That European prejudices weighed heavily in favour of Ethiopia's invaders did not matter. The Ethiopian rulers demonstrated that neither were they petty rulers who could be ignored with impunity nor was their country a no man's land that could be seized at will without resistance. That Menelek succeeded in acquiring the diplomatic and moral support of Russia and material support of France in his struggles against Italy was a proof of the effectiveness of the Ethiopian diplomacy. Nevertheless it must be emphasized that diplomacy played only a secondary role in the preservation of Ethiopian independence. It is equally obvious that in spite of their broad perception of European imperialism and natural caution in dealing with foreign powers the Ethiopian rulers of the nineteenth century like their counterparts in Africa, got into dangerous commitments with Europe or rather were tricked into it by the agents of European imperialism. But they succeeded in disengaging themselves from these commitments before it was late through tact where they could, and through force where they could not. However what saved Ethiopia in the end was her internal unity, military capabilities and the determination of her rulers to defend Ethiopia's independence and sovereignty. This task was greatly assisted, as the author suggests, by the underestimation of her strength by Ethiopia's invaders. While the author's conclusions up to the point are sound, he fails to consider the fact that the non development of European economic, strategic and religious bases in Ethiopia was a crucial factor in the survival of Ethiopian independence. Had such European interests developed it is doubtful if Britain would have withdrawn from Ethiopia after the sucessful military expedition to Magdala in 1867 or France would have failed to impose a protectorate on northern Ethiopia in the 1860's. It must not be forgotten that the European rivalries in the region especially in the 1880's and the 90's, favoured to some extent Ethiopia's efforts to protect her independence.

While we might disagree with the author on the role of geographical and economic factors in the preservation of Ethiopian independence and would have liked him to place more emphasis on the role of the Ethiopian church in defending the country we can only congratulate him on his timely study which is informative, interesting and scholarly. Professor Rubenson's study serves a two fold purpose. It not only adds to our knowledge of the survival of Ethiopian independence, which was the aim of the author, but also gives us a comprehensive account of Ethiopia's external relations in the 19th century, thus filling a vital need in the area.* The author has given us a study which is thorough in documentation and up-to-date and balanced in conclusions. *The survival of Ethiopian Independence* is a must to every student of Modern African History.

---

*"A number of modern scholars have contributed to our knowledge of Ethiopia's external relations, directly or indirectly, through their studies. But almost all of them deal with a particular period or phase of Ethiopia's foreign relations depending upon their chosen theme. No Comprehensive Work on Ethiopian external relations in the 19th Century was available until now. A Reference to these writing can be found in the Bibliography supplied by Professor Rubenson at the end of his study *The Survival of Ethiopian Independence**

Patterns of Igbo Resistance to British Conquest

A. E. Afigbo

Department of History,
University of Nigeria, Nsukka

Historians have not yet fully told us the story of British occupation of Igboland. Nor have they told us the full story of Igbo resistance to the British occupation. However, while we know quite a bit about the major clashes between the Igbo and the British, as in the Aro Expedition and the Ekumeku movement, Igbo resistance had not received equal attention. It has not always been realised, for instance, that if the British challenge to the numerous autonomous Igbo village-groups took a similar form, Igbo resistance to it varied from group to group, and from time to time. In this article we shall not examine British designs and ambitions in Igboland, for this has already received fairly good attention in existing works. Nor do we intend to study the various wars which the British fought against the Igbo from 1901-17 or so. Rather, we intend to look at Igbo resistance and discuss the patterns which seem to emerge. We shall also try to offer some explanation why it was that even though the threat posed by the British was the same, Igbo reaction varied from place to place.

There were three main types of Igbo resistance to the British military challenge. The first type concerns the response of those communities which were not prepared to go into any diplomatic negotiations with the British, who refused to see the messengers of the British and who from the very beginning reached out for their guns and matchets as their response to the presence of the white man in their territory.

The second type has to do with those communities which negotiated and talked with the British and their messengers, hoping to keep them away from their territories by long and tedious 'palaver', but which resorted to armed resistance only after they became convinced that the British were determined to have their way at all cost.

The third type deals with those communities which, for reasons which will be discussed later, did everything possible to avoid armed encounters with the British, relying instead on magic and the intervention of their gods to drive the British back into the sea.

First type: Let the guns talk

Our first example of this pattern of resistance comes from the response of the West Niger or Ika Igbo to the threat which the advent of the white man posed to their society. This goes back to the days of the Royal Niger Company. Between 1882 and 1883 this company, then known as the National Africa Company, had established a trading post at Asaba on the basis of a treaty with the chiefs of the

14

town. From Asaba it sought to penetrate the rest of the West Niger Igbo communities in search of trade, and at the same time tried to exercise some sovereign rights over the people. The company's attempts to rule the people of this area made them hate and resent any form of foreign control. In order to guard against such foreign control, the leagues of young men (*otu okolobia*) in the various village-groups came together and formed the *Ekumeku* secret organisation, which was an underground movement of resistance to the British trader, missionary and administrator alike. The term *Ekumeku* is untranslatable into English, but brings to mind such words as 'invisible', 'whirlwind', 'devastating', 'uncontrollable' and so on. The *Ekumeku* was able to obstruct the Niger Company's agents in the region beyond Asaba with such success that the company was forced to take the field against them in 1898 and force the *Ekumeku* to accept some kind of peace settlement, which lasted until 1900 when the company was relieved of all political and administrative duties in Nigeria.

The Southern Nigeria Protectorate, which now became responsible for the administration of Asaba and its hinterland, inherited this difficult situation in which its authority could not be readily accepted by the *Ekumeku*. The more the British tried to establish themselves firmly in this area, the more they destroyed the independence and culture of the Ika Igbo. Thus they began to establish Native Courts which took power from the traditional council of elders; they began to pick some of the local chiefs and force them to carry out their will; mission stations were built in which the Christian missionaries began to preach a new religion condemning the age-old religion of the Ika people. All of these developments annoyed the people so much that the *Ekumeku* movement became very popular indeed. Some of the youths saw in the situation a chance of showing their bravery in war against the British. As the movement became more popular, so its members became harsher in their treatment of those within the community who were opposed to the *Ekumeku*. Among those most hated were the Ika Igbo who served the British administration, the missionaries or the European traders in various capacities. Such men were regarded as traitors.

The *Ekumeku* would not negotiate or talk with the British administration or their agents partly because it was a secret organisation whose members were supposed to be faceless and anonymous, and partly because the administration represented that alien control which it was determined to root out of Ikaland. The result was that the leading members of the West Niger Igbo communities would not answer to calls from touring political officers either because they were members of the organisation, or because they feared severe punishment from the society. In the same manner Native Court writs were openly ignored, while from time to time such Native Courts, mission houses and the compounds and properties of people who showed themselves friendly towards the British were looted and destroyed.

The British, for their part, did not understand the origin and character of the movement. At one time they thought it arose from those communities not having generally recognised institutions for settling inter-town disputes. As a result they established many more Native Courts in the area. At another time they thought

15

that the movement grew because the courts were not properly supervised and that because of this there was no effective contact between the people and the government. Consequently they urged closer supervision of the courts and more frequent tours by political officers.

With this failure to understand what the movement was about, the British could not establish contact with it. The result was that peaceful negotiation never entered into the relationship between the *Ekumeku* and the Southern Nigeria Protectorate. In the event the guns had to 'talk', first in 1902 and again in 1909. Eventually the *Ekumeku* society was broken by repeated military defeats, prosecutions and imprisonment by the Native Courts, proscription under the law and the use of the Collective Punishment Ordinance to discipline whole communities which entertained the activities of the society.

Our other example comes from the large and warlike Ezza group of the North-Eastern Igbo. By 1902 the British administration was established effectively at Afikpo to the south of the Ezza, as well as in Obubra Hill further up the Cross River, and from these places were making efforts to reach some understanding with the Ukawe, Okposi Ikwo and Ezza peoples around. But from the beginning the Ezza would not hear of the white man or go into any negotiations with his messengers. In March 1905 Major Crawford Cockburn, the District Officer for the Obubra Hill District, penetrated into the territory of the Ezza and their allies, escorted by a detachment of troops. The Ezza and their Achara allies

British attack on Igbo stockade

ambushed and killed some members of the escort. Exploiting their ancient warlike reputation and the fact that they out-numbered most of the communities lying between them and Afikpo, they either persuaded or bullied these to go into an alliance with them against the British. When the administration of the Cross

16

River Division sent messengers asking their representatives to come to a parley and state Ezza's grievances against the British, they chased the messengers out.

The Ezza used these messengers to let the British know what they thought of the administration. Firstly, they asked the messengers to tell the British that the Ezza had heard how the Southern Nigeria Protectorate defeated the Aro and occupied their towns. This, they said, in no way frightened them for, they boasted, the Ezza were more powerful and more warlike than the Aro. Secondly, they asked the emissaries to tell the British that the Ezza people had never been ruled by an alien and would not be ruled by one now. In the whole wide world they recognised only the heavens above and the earth below. Midway between these two great forces the Ezza ruled supreme. Finally, they told the messengers that if the British sent any more emissaries, the Ezza would cut off their heads and return these through the hands of those towns friendly with the administration. In this situation it was impossible to negotiate.

The result was that the British administration sent a military expedition against the Ezza who met force with force. Between 15 March and 3 May troops of the Southern Nigeria administration were fighting in and around Ezza. The Ezza were beaten in various battles lasting from March 25 to May 16. They were greatly handicapped by the fact that their territory is open savanna land and so exposed them very much to the devastating fire of machine guns. Furthermore, they were armed only with matchets, their traditional weapon, and could do harm only if they came close enough. But this opportunity they never had. Still, it took days to break their resistance. As to their spirit, subsequent events showed it was not broken.

Second type: diplomacy and war

The second type of resistance by the Igbo against British conquest involved first diplomacy and then war. The best known example of this type is the case of the Aro trading oligarchy which is probably the most written about of British encounters with Igbo resistance movements. By 1896 the British had consolidated their rule in the trading states of the Oil Rivers and the immediate hinterland and by so doing reached the southern outskirts of Igbo and Ibibioland where the Aro trading interest was the most important single force to reckon with. The Aro were determined to keep British interest out of this region to preserve their dominant role in the distribution of imported goods, to ensure the continuation of the slave trade which the British were anxious to abolish, and to preserve their *Long Juju* on which so much of their influence and prosperity rested. The Aro saw British influence in three forms: firstly, the Opobo, Bonny and Efik traders who now started penetrating further and further into the interior to increase their profit and earnings which the activities of European traders in the area under effective British rule had reduced; secondly, the missionaries who preached not only salvation but also social revolution through the abolition of many traditional institutions and customs; thirdly, the British political officer with his Native Courts and all that would create conditions favourable to the Opobo, Bonny and

17

Efik traders as well as the missionaries. It was these three forms of British influence the Aro were determined to keep away from their area.

Among the Igbo the Aro are noted for sweet, prolonged double-talk. This kind of talk can be very useful in diplomacy, and the Aro used it to the fullest in their confrontation with the British from 1896 onwards. Both among the Southern Igbo (Ikwerre, Ngwa etc), and among the Annang, British officers, engaged in establishing friendly relations with various groups, met Aro traders and agents from 1896 on and held discussions with them on the subject of Anglo-Aro relations. On every occasion the Aro showed themselves prepared to talk and in this way the Protectorate Authorities were able to know the Aro objections to the extension of British influence.

But at the same time the Aro took other measures to instigate different communities to resist British advance. Where these methods failed they threatened the people that they would send their hired soldiers against them. These hired soldiers proved a useful barrier against opposition; faced with this threat, people became afraid of going against Aro wishes. On the Cross River, in particular, the Aro showed a willingness to negotiate with the British agent, Chief Coco Otu Bassey, the conditions on which a relationship between them and the British could be friendly. They were even prepared to attend, in 1897, a meeting arranged by Coco Bassey on the orders of Sir Ralph Moor, the High Commissioner, to iron out existing differences. As it turned out, Moor was unable to attend the meeting as he was preoccupied with Benin affairs. The Aro delegation stayed at Itu 'for about a fortnight during which they were entertained at the expense of Government'. In spite of what may be considered shabby treatment from the High Commissioner, they were ready to attend a similar meeting in 1898 on the initiative of the Protectorate Government.

But despite this willingness to talk, the Aro remained strongly opposed to British penetration of their country. By 1899 it had become clear to Moor that the Aro could not be brought under his administration by diplomacy. After this, the relationship between the two took a turn for the worse, and the British began planning a military expedition against the Aro.

On their side the Aro redoubled their efforts among the Annang, the peoples of the Upper Cross River and elsewhere. They did all they could to persuade those who had signed treaties with the Protectorate Government to break their friendship with the British. They tried to persuade or bully those who were yet undecided about the British to join them in their resistance to the coastal traders, the British and the missionaries. In this way they attempted to build up many allies against all alien intruders. Some of those who refused to be persuaded or bullied by the Aro were attacked and looted with the help of Abam and Ohaffia headhunters.

By mid-November 1901 the British were ready to take the field against the Aro, who appear to have been well briefed on the warlike preparations against them through their network of spies and agents. Then, just a few days before the expedition set out, the Aro led a band of Abam warriors to the town of Obegu and sacked it. They also threatened the town of Akwete, which was a sub-district

18

but were prevented from attacking it by the presence of British troops. At Obegu the raiders took time to destroy the Government rest-house and to break the water casks which District Commissioner Douglas had assembled for the use of the British soldiers. Within a few days of the Obegu raid, on 28 November 1901, the British troops started operations against the Aro whose home town was captured on 24 December the same year.

The other example is provided by the resistance of the Afikpo village-group. After the capture of Arochukwu, the British began to establish their authority in the surrounding areas. In this process some of the British troops had penetrated as far north as this village-group. The Afikpo people, who were badly frightened by the disaster that had befallen the Aro, thought it wiser to submit than to resist. In fact, while fighting was still going on around Arochukwu, they had sent emissaries to the political officer in charge of Ediba district to inform him of their loyalty and friendship to the British. Similarly, when the column that came into their territory said the Government would want to establish an administrative centre at Afikpo and asked for land for this, the people promptly gave out a piece of land.

The operations connected with the Aro Expedition ended in the first quarter of 1902. But by August the same year the Afikpo had completely changed their attitude to the Protectorate Government. They would not allow a government post to be established in their territory and would not even receive messengers sent to negotiate with them. They went so far as to attack those of their neighbours, like the village-group of Anoffia, which was pro-British, and to ambush British fact-finding parties and touring officers who visited the surrounding area. So stubborn and determined was the Afikpo resistance to the British that none of their neighbours friendly with the government would take messages from the white man to them. According to one British officer, the chiefs and the peoples of these towns had grown so frightened of possible attacks from the Afikpo that 'they were living on the roads ready to run in the case of attack'. In anticipation of British reaction, the Afikpo took measures to fortify and guard all the major approaches to their town, including the Cross River landing-place through which they suspected the British might want to send troops.

On 28 December a British military force set out from Unwana to attack the Afikpo. Making use of information collected from some frightened women of Ndibe town, the troops were able to move in such a manner that they attacked the main Afikpo fighting force from the rear while the Afikpo were expecting an attack from the front. Because the battle took place in the open grassland, the Afikpo found themselves gravely handicapped in trying to crawl through the grass to get close to the British forces who were using repeater rifles and field guns. The result was that they suffered very heavy losses. Still, said the commanding officer, they showed 'great courage'. Even after they had lost the main battle, they retreated to the defence of their homes. They were only finally defeated because the British had much heavier and bigger guns. Once again after a period of diplomatic manoeuvring, the guns had been brought in to decide the issue.

19

Third type: diplomacy and magic

Much of the information on which the reconstruction of this pattern of resistance is based comes from oral tradition collected by the author. Magic has always played an important role in African warfare, and the Igbo warriors of the first two decades of this century who had the extremely difficult duty of defending their communities against better armed British forces, had to rely on this to a large extent. The result is that magic played an important part even in the first two patterns of resistance sketched above.

There are very many stories about the efforts made by famous medicine-men in the different communities to get the local gods and ancestors to take action against the British. Some towns would not rely on local doctors alone, but would travel long distances to invite more widely famed medicine-men to strike the invading troops blind, or to scatter them with swarms of bees, to make their guns backfire or make the Igbo warriors bullet-proof. The fact is that since the gods and the ancestors were regarded as being part and parcel of the society, they were called upon to help defend it against the alien invaders.

As already mentioned, even in those communities which went to war in order to resist British conquest, there were attempts to use the forces of the supernatural powers in defence of the old order. Among the Ezza, for instance, this effort not only preceded the fighting, but went on for years after the British had consolidated their presence in the entire Abakaliki Division. This was revealed by an incident which happened in 1918 and was recorded by Robert Cudjoe, a Ghanaian (then a Gold Coaster) who worked at Abakaliki as an interpreter. On one night there was a heavy rain during which thunder struck the soldiers' camp, causing extensive damages and some casualties. According to Cudjoe, some diehard Ezza resisters who were his friends rejoiced openly before him, attributing the disaster to the work of their medicine-men and the intervention of their ancestors. They were confident, they said, the white man would eventually be driven out of Abakaliki by these supernatural forces.

But apart from the above, there were many Igbo communities whose resistance to conquest consisted of making a diplomatic surrender to the British forces while devoting all their energies and resources to getting the unseen forces of their society to do their fighting for them. The scholar working on this topic will hear from the elders of many Igbo communities how their people made a show of surrendering to the invading forces only subsequently to expel them from their communities through inflicting on the troops all kinds of epidemics. Some say the soldiers were forced to move camp because they were attacked by jiggers, or swarms of crabs and toads, or by diarrhoea and vomiting, or by some such malady.

For instance, there was the case of Uzuakoli. This village-group was visited by a military expedition towards the end of 1902 because the British said it was the den of slave-dealers. But just before the troops entered the town, the elders consulted and decided not to offer open resistance. If the British had been able to conquer the Aro, the Abam, the Ohaffia, Edda and so on, they argued, they did not see how their town could fare better than these anciently famed warrior clans

20

had done. Thus as the troops entered the town, they were met by bands of dancing women who said they were happy the white man at last thought it fit to visit them. Meanwhile the men had erected shades for the troops in the central local market and provided food and water.

This diplomatic surrender, however, did not save Uzuakoli from humiliation. The leading elders were called out, bound hand and foot and left in the sun until all the Aro and other slave-dealers in the town had been surrendered. If this were not done, they were informed, the town would be razed to the ground. To treat the elders in this brutal fashion was bad enough. But among the Igbo there is nothing more humiliating than to be forced to surrender strangers within your gates to their enemies. The stranger, *Mbimbia or obia*, was entitled to protection even at the cost of the life of his host.

All the Aro and other slave-dealers were surrendered and were subsequently led away by the troops. After this, said my informants, Uzuakoli assembled all the reputed medicine-men from the neighbourhood who prepared some medicine and buried it in the town square. This medicine proved so powerful, they say, that till today no white man can prosper at Uzuakoli. To the action of this medicine, they attribute the fact that all the British mercantile firms which early in this century established at Uzuakoli subsequently pulled out because their produce-buying and all other businesses failed. The probable reason for the removal of British firms from Uzuakoli is that Umuahia, just twelve miles away to the south, is a more convenient centre for assembling the produce of the neighbourhood and so expanded at the expense not only of Uzuakoli, but also of Bende, the divisional headquarters. However, to the Uzuakoli elders, their medicine-men did it. Many more examples of resistances like Uzuakoli's can be cited from other parts of Igboland, especially from the Onitsha, Awka and Orlu areas visited by British military forces in 1904 without any show of open resistance to the invading troops.

Comments and Conclusions

The pattern of resistance adopted by each community could be related to the structure of their society and the circumstances of the time. In communities like those of the Ika Igbo where the resistance was championed by a secret society it is understandable that negotiation played little part. Also the Ika Igbo had first to deal with the worst kind of white man before coming under the Protectorate of Southern Nigeria. The Niger Company's record of relationship with the peoples of the lower Niger is probably one of the blackest in our history. It is therefore understandable that the Asaba hinterland would have nothing to do with them and that the people carried this policy of refusal to co-operate over to their dealings with the colonial government. It was not easy to distinguish between the Niger Company's agents and the European political officers. They were all whites and at times made the same demands.

It is also pertinent to mention that these communities had a long tradition of resistance to alien rule and control from Benin. The existence of the well-organised and well co-ordinated associations of warrior young men which fought the

21

British can be accounted for in terms of this earlier resistance which had taught the people the basic lessons of how to deal with the 'alien' imperialist. The influence of Benin had thus directly and indirectly influenced the social organisation of these communities and taught them how to organise for war and such emergencies.

With regard to the Ezza the circumstances were similar. This community was always seeking for more land and this meant that for centuries they had been engaged in fighting their non-Igbo neighbours from whom they seized all the land they needed. This created a fighting tradition which not only ensured that the young men were well organised for offence and defence, but also made the people proud. With such a tradition they could not be brought to surrender their independence by a process of negotiation.

The Aro on their side could afford to indulge in endless negotiations even when they had no intention of giving in to British demands. This was because at the time the British were talking of the Aro as if Aro-Chukwu lay just beyond Akwete or Itu, it lay in fact beyond easy reach of the forces of the Protectorate. There was therefore time to talk and they talked for five years. Also, as expert traders, they were used to long and tedious haggling which did not always have to lead to the realisation of the desired goal. The Afikpo on their side first tried diplomacy when they thought the British had not come to stay. When they discovered their mistake, they organised for war, and their society, with its different grades of young men's associations accustomed to war and head-hunting and with each grade anxious to achieve some fame, was well placed to fight.

With those who tried tactical surrender while seeking the use of supernatural forces against the British, there were also good reasons. They had watched many of their neighbours make heroic stands and lose. This taught them that the white man could not be beaten militarily. The defeat of the warlike Cross River and North-Eastern Igbo communities, which were anciently famed for war and had the organisations for waging it, was sobering to many. There was also the fact that many of these other Igbo groups were not as well-organised for war as the Eastern and Ika Igbo. Young men's societies were not that cohesive, nor had they recent and proud traditions of military achievement. In the light of this, such people tended to rely more on their native doctors and the unseen forces that ruled their world.

Igbo resistance to British conquest lacked epic events like those that marked the Asante campaign, the Benin expedition and Lugard's Burmi campaign in Northern Nigeria, though that is not to say that it was lacking in heroism, resourcefulness and doggedness. The fact that there was no Igbo state comparable to Asante or Benin meant that there was no authority to organise Igbo resistance to British conquest into one mighty heroic stand. The fragmentation of authority and society meant that each autonomous unit fought its own war of independence on its own, and lost it in its own way, too.

In the long run, this fact was to be a source of strength to Igbo resistance to British conquest. It meant there was no single authority whose defeat would place all Igboland at the feet of the alien conqueror. Every bit of territory, therefore,

22

had to be fought, or bargained for, separately. This took more time and more energy and was very irritating to the British. Long after the much fancied Fulani, Kanuri and Yoruba empires had been forced to accept British rule, the British were still sending military forces round and about Igboland in pursuit of 'naked savages'.

Further Reading

IGBAFE, P. A., 'Western Igbo Society and its resistance to British rule: The Ekumeku Movement, 1898-1911', *Journal of African History*, XII, 3, 1971.

AFIGBO, A. E., 'The Aro Expedition of 1901-02 (An Episode in the British Occupation of Igboland)' *Odu* New Series No. 7 April 1972.

AFIGBO, A. E., 'Trade and Politics on the Cross River 1896-1905' *Transactions of the Historical Society of Ghana* XIII, 1 forthcoming.

AFIGBO, A. E., 'The Establishment of Colonial Rule' in Ajayi and Crowder (eds) *History of West Africa* vol. II, London, forthcoming.

ANENE, J. C., 'The Southern Nigeria Protectorate and the Aros' *Journal of the Historical Society of Nigeria*, December 1955.

ANENE, J. C., *Southern Nigeria in Transition,* Cambridge, 1966, Chapter VI.

EKECHI, F. K., *Missionary Enterprise and Rivalry in Igboland 1857-1914,* London, 1971, Chapter VI.

23

The Franco-Baoulé War, 1891-1911: The Struggle against the French Conquest of Central Ivory Coast

JOHN M. O'SULLIVAN

Introduction

I am not the first to turn my attention to the long wars fought against the French who were attempting to subjugate the people inhabiting the Ivory Coast. In the introduction to his book, *West African Resistance,* Michael Crowder calls attention to the resistance in Ivory Coast, though no chapter is devoted to it. "The peoples of the southern Ivory Coast provided some of the stiffest resistance the colonial forces of occupation experienced." Adu Boahen and J. B. Webster state in their *History of West Africa,* "Particular attention must be drawn to the unprecedented resistance of the coastal forest people of the Ivory Coast, who fought for twenty-seven years (1891–1918) to preserve their independence." Jean Suret-Canale, in his magnificent *Afrique noire,* renders homage to the long, spirited fight against French conquest. Yet none of these

Several dissertations are presently being done on the subject of these wars of resistance. Christophe Wondji of the University of Abidjan is studying the wars in the whole of southern Ivory Coast. Timothy Weiskel is studying certain aspects of the Baoulé wars of resistance, I believe. Both these studies will be of great interest to the student of Ivory Coast history. Also, since this article was prepared several years ago, I did not consult the more recent work. Because of the research priorities of the two aforementioned scholars, my own research energies were directed elsewhere. The article was originally prepared for a seminar at the University of California, Los Angeles, under the direction of Professor Boniface I. Obichere. I am indebted to him and to the other participants in the seminar—notably Professors T. O. Ranger, Robert Griffeth, Edward Alpers, Christopher Ehret, as well as Raymond Ganga, Robert Edgar, William O. Eaton, and Christopher Chamberlin. The conclusions are of course my own.

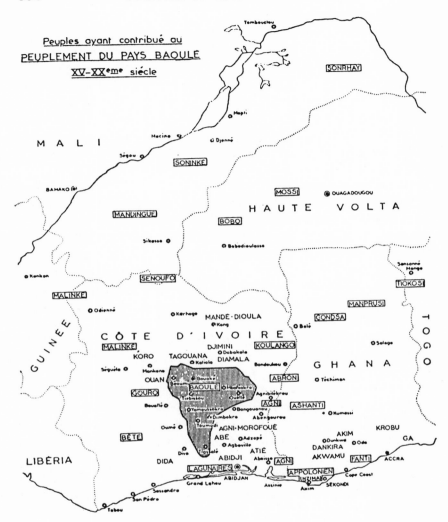

The map originally appeared in the *Etude régionale de Bouaké.*

sources, or any others for that matter, provide any real information or exposition of the wars of resistance aside from Suret-Canale, and his work seems to rely on *La Pacification de la Côte d'Ivoire,* the published report of the governor of the Colony of Ivory Coast, Gabriel Angoulvant, who directed the French operation.[1]

---

[1] Crowder, ed., *West African Resistance: The Military Response to Colonial Occupation* (New York, 1971), p. 4; Boahen and Webster with H. O. Idowa, *His-*

It must be admitted that one begins a study of resistance in West Africa already burdened with considerable intellectual baggage. The dead horse of African passivity to European conquest has been so thoroughly laid to rest that various authors strive to prove that "their" people fought the longest war or the hardest war or produced the most European casualties. In fact, it would seem that presentations of historical African resistance is in considerable vogue now. Such topicality leads one to be wary of a spacious study of African resistance and to reexamine the basic terms of resistance itself and the context in which it occurred.

The need to rethink the concept of resistance presents itself to me with particular force because of the nature of the fight the Baoulé people of present-day Ivory Coast waged against French conquest. The Baoulé lived in villages and hamlets spread throughout central Ivory Coast, roughly between the Bandama and Comoé River, with a system of political organization most often limited to the village level and a loose confederation organized at the *mé* ("clan") level when needs of defense forced such cooperation. Continuous resistance of the Baoulé delayed and hindered French conquest for nearly twenty-five years. It is not my intention to add another chapter to the growing list of studies of African resistance, but rather to suggest that such studies seem ahistorical if they do not proceed from an understanding of the historical development and situation of a resistance to European conquest. They have the further flaw of concentrating overly on the European activities, since it was usually European aggression that began the wars. Anthropology has provided additional intellectual problems with its descriptions of "stateless societies," "segmentary societies," and "tribes without rulers," expressions that lead to analytical dead ends, at least in the case I am about to discuss.

The central thesis of this article is that the war of resistance fought by the Baoulé people must be placed within the context of Baoulé military activity prior to the arrival of the French. The continuity of African social and cultural organization in the colonial era emphasizes the need to see resistance not as a unique moment in African history, but as part of the flow of the history of the region.

---

tory of West Africa: The Revolutionary Years—1815 to Independence (New York, 1967), p. 233; Suret-Canale, *Afrique noire occidentale et centrale: L'Ere coloniale (1900–1945)* (Paris, 1964); and Angoulvant, *La Pacification de la Côte d'Ivoire* (Paris, 1916).

This view will help develop the meaning of resistance so as to include the example of the Baoulé and in fact will call into question the validity of the concept. It will also allow a critical examination of the causes of the military confrontation that occurred between the French and the Baoulé.

To some extent, the attempt of the French was aimed at completely integrating the Baoulé region into their modern market economy. The military struggle that occurred, therefore, from the Baoulé point of view, in terms of previous military activities and for reasons consistant with historical developments within their own region, was the part of a much larger macrocosmic situation because of the French attempt to extend effective occupation not only in Baoulé region but throughout the Third World from Lake Chad to Tonkin Bay.

The development of the concept of resistance that this article proposes is therefore twofold. The military confrontation that occurred between the Baoulé and the French was a continuation of the flow of Baoulé history, and the military means were much the same as used previously. These means were developing within the context of needs of government and development within their region and within the context of contact with new elements, both African and European. It will be seen that the fight in the Ivory Coast was a question of sovereignty; the Baoulé people, what may be called the Baoulé nation, organized political power on a local level and defended it, each man with his own gun. This is to say that the people were sovereign, with the decision-making body an assemble of the people and the organization to effect those decisions the people themselves. The French effort was to withdraw this sovereignty by force and impose a state with power residing far away in the capital city, supported by taxes expropriated from the peasants.

Developments of Baoulé history relevant to the study of their war included not only the political system but also the economic. Trade and commerce developed within an economic system that stretched to the Dyula kingdom of Kong, to Bondoukou and Bouna, and to Marabadiassa, and that readily traded with Samori Touré when he arrived in Debakala in 1894. To the south, trade with African and European businessmen in Grand Lahou, Jacqueville, and Grand Bassam must have been brisk or the Baoulé would not have had the tens of thousands of guns with which they fought the French. The economic and political systems that were developing indigenously (of which military resistance to foreign domination was a part) were some of the means used to contest the French attempt to impose their own institutions of control and exploitation. These were institutionalized as an essential part of the history of the Baoulé and might have allowed an organic development of Baoulé society in the modern world to take place. Indigenous development and the normal social tensions that characterize this stage of historical development were brusquely stopped and reorganized by the French.

J.F.A. Ajayi wrote, "The most fundamental aspect of the European impact was the loss of sovereignty which it entailed for practically every African people. Europeans exploited their technical superiority to establish their political dominance throughout the continent."[2] This does not imply that such was the sole result of the colonial conquest. The historical complexities and the multifactoral depth of the situation are overwhelming and cannot be ignored, particularly in the light of recent Baoulé history.

It should be said that I am not concentrating on the Baoulé to show my allegiance to anthropological study, but rather to trace the historic development of warfare in one area and at the same time to maintain an article of manageable length. Study of the fight of the Bété, Dan, Gouro, Dida, Abbey, Agni, and other peoples of the Ivory Coast would give us a vast comparison of how people dealt with the French and might very well fall victim to the problem of presenting an ahistorical study whose only common denominator was the European opponent.

The scale of the fight, it must be noticed, was set by the French. They claim to have made visits along the coast as early as the fourteenth century and participated with the Portuguese, British, Dutch, Danes, and Brandenburgers in the general trade along the coast. The Compagnie de Guinée attempted to establish a trading post at Assinie between 1685 and 1701 but gave up, and it was not until Admiral Bouët-Willaumez's visit in 1838 that French presence was again felt on the coast. This lack of interest can be attributed to a lack of harbors, the very rough surf, a lack of goods for trade, and

---

[2] The reference is, of course, Ajayi's seminal article "Continuity of African Institutions under Colonialism," in *Emerging Themes in African History*, ed. T. O. Ranger (Nairobi, 1968). The theoretical point made therein is supported in the case of the Baoulé by the work of such researchers as Pierre Etienne, Vincent Guerry, and J. P. Chauveau, among others. See *Bibliographie de la Côte d'Ivoire* (Abidjan, 1973), vol. 2, for further references.

the bad reputation of the people vis-à-vis Europeans. Forts and trading centers were established after 1842 in Assinie and also Grand Bassam and Dabou. European traders in ivory, gold, and palm oil faced such stiff competition from local businessmen that one house, Victor Régis of Marseilles, gave up trying to compete. Contact was made all along the coast, though no Europeans ventured inland.[3]

After the debacle of the Franco-Prussian War, France withdrew again from Ivory Coast, leaving only Arthur Verdier, a local trader from La Rochelle, as representative. He, his family, and company controlled French interests in Ivory Coast for eighteen years. He fought British incursions from the Gold Coast Colony, and British commercial interests. He incurred the wrath of Her Majesty's represenative in Gold Coast by selling guns and powder to the Ashanti who were preparing for the Anglo-Ashanti War of 1874. He exported wood and palm oil, developed the first coffee plantation in Ivory Coast (1881), and conducted a search for gold (1880).[4] Verdier and Doctor Bayol, the French governor stationed in the Rivières du Sud (modern Guinea), wanted to put the road to Kong and Bondoukou under French control, and as a result the manager of Verdier's coffee plantation at Elima, Mr. Treich-Laplène, headed north in 1887 to sign treaties and ensure control of the Comoé Valley. In 1881 and 1889 Treich-Laplène returned north to meet Captain Louis Gustave Binger, who was traveling from Bamako. By means of the treaties signed by these two explorers, a protectorate was proclaimed from Grand Bassam to Kong. On March 10, 1893, the Ivory Coast was declared a French colony with Binger as the first governor. He attempted to set up the boundaries with Liberia and Gold Coast and to obtain treaties of protection all along the coast as far as the Cavally River. A head tax of 2.5 francs for every inhabitant over fifteen years of age was enacted in 1901. A railroad was begun in December 1903 that reached Bouaké in 1912. Attempts were also made to open a canal to the lagoon at Abidjan, but this failed. Difficulties of health were a constant problem, and repeated yellow-fever epidemics caused a transfer of the capital from Grand Bassam to Bingerville in 1900.

[3] See Paul Atger, *La France en Côte d'Ivoire de 1843 à 1893: Cinquante ans d'hésitations politiques et commerciales* (Dakar, 1962), p. 51.

[4] Arthur Verdier, *Trente-cinq années de lutte aux colonies* (Paris, 1896), chap. 1; and Amedée Bretignère, *Aux temps héroiques de la Côte d'Ivoire* (Paris, 1931).

Whatever the broader reasons for French imperialism, the French imperialism, the French contact with the Baoulé revolved around attempts to get through to the north—especially after Samori had established himself in northern Ivory Coast at Dabakala and attempts to organize effective occupation because of difficulties the local system created for the full integration of production and trade into the French colonial system. Such integration and organization required a bureaucratic state system, controlled by a colonial administration.

> All the local life is concentrated on the indigenous races, as much from the point of view political as social and economic. To educate them, to play the role with respect to them of tutors, intelligent and well meaning, but firm, to progressively establish rules of existance, and finally arrange them hierarchically (*les hierarchiser*) locally in view of a new existence, from where they can enter into the movement of the human races, such is the task which imposes itself on the intelligent wisdom of the *commandants de cercle*.

> We have underlined the word *hierarchiser,* not because it's a question of doing it one race with respect to the other race, but only of arranging hierarchically those intelligent individuals which those races can put at our disposition.[5]

As suggested by this quote, the goal of colonialism was to break the old mold, to destroy the past, traditional cultures and to create a new system built in the ways and likeness of the European system. To do so it was essential to structure the people vertically with all the exploitation, discrimination, and injustice that such structuring implies. If this meant the destruction of a comparatively egalitarian society then that was that. In response to such brutal aspirations on the part of the aggressor, there was a basic ebb and flow of coalitions of traditional political units, usually villages, depending on threats of invasions and the political size of the opponents. What has been seen as the modern African political party, such as the PDCI (Parti Démocratique du Côte d'Ivoire), would seem to fall within the same sort of model and that what has been seen as the demise of this type of party is really an ebb of the coalition in the face of the withdrawal of the perceived foe, the French. Thus, very definitely the war fought from 1891 to 1915 fits within the context of today's situation.

[5] *La Revue indigène* (December 1908), p. 518.

THE HISTORICAL DEVELOPMENT OF THE BAOULÉ

Research into the history of the Baoulé shows how the term *tribe* is a uselessly static description of a people. The people who call themselves Baoulé live in the central region of Ivory Coast roughly in an inverted triangle from where the Bandama and N'zi rivers join north to a line running east-west from the Bandama River to the Comoé River north of Bouaké. Today they number about 400,000, speak their own language, Baoulé, which is part of the Twi family, and traditionally practice a complicated sort of matrilineal descent. These people are the present result of several migrations from the Akan-Ashanti region and of interrelations with neighbors. Here as elsewhere there is no sharp line of distinction between peoples, but Baoulé speakers and people claiming Baoulé ancestors live mixed with Dida, Gouro, Attié, Tagouana, and other neighbors.

Prior to the arrival of the people specifically known as the Baoulé, Gouro hunting villages were found in the area, spreading eastward from the main Gouro territory west of the Bandama, in search of game. Tagouana, of the Sénoufo-speaking family, lived in the northern reaches of central Ivory Coast and were gradually moving southward, as cultivators. Also drifting in from the north were Mandé and Malinké families and Dyula traders, who traveled through the area. These trading families had participated in the foundation of Bondoukou in the fifteenth century, Kong in the sixteenth century, and Boron as they sought gold, kola, and slaves in the forest region and that part of the savannah that dipped into the forest between the Bandama and N'zi rivers to within ninety kilometers of the coast. While kola did not grow in the savannah region, gold was found in the hills near Toumodi. Also, ". . . from the seventeenth century, European vessels began to make regular stops before Grand Lahou, Sassandra, San Pedro, and Tabou. Without doubt this is the reason why the Koro and Ouan (Mandé families) founded a series of village reststops between Mankono and Grand Lahou."[6] Such future towns as Tiassalé were founded in this fashion.

Certain Ga and Krobu people moved into this same region from further east, near Accra. It is thought that pressures of slave raids and the wars caused by slaving caused these people to emigrate from

[6] Information in this section of the article is largely derived from *Etude régionale de Bouaké* done by B. Fride, H. L'huillier, and P. Michaud for the Ministère du Plan, 1966 (hereafter cited as *E.R.B.*).

their home region in the late sixteenth and early seventeenth centuries. Small groups of these peoples still maintain certain customs that distinguish them from later arrivals in this region.

The first Akan immigrants into this region were remnants of the Dankira Kingdom, which was destroyed by Osei Tutu in the Battle of Fyase. These Dankira (or Alankira) were able to establish themselves fairly easily because of their military organization and their probable possession of guns. They were not numerous enough, however, to take over the region in any real sense.

After the death of the Ashanti king, Osai Tutu, in the ambush on the Praa River in 1730 (?), there was a problem of succession in the Ashanti Empire and the two principal contenders, Dako and Opokou Ware, fought a civil war for the Royal Stool. Dako was killed in the fight, and his sister Abra Pokou fled west with the remnants of his party.

> She first took refuge with the Angi of Enchi for whose aid and protection she hoped. But when Opokou Ware learned of her flight, he flung himself into pursuit of her with a strong army. As he approached, panic took hold of the troops of the Queen. Their flight toward the west soon took on the aspect of the exodus of a considerable crowd. For, along the route, the populations of traversed allied villages, fearing to be pillaged by the warriors of Opokou Ware, joined the refugees, ceaselessly increasing their number.[7]

This mass of refugees was organized in a military fashion, as *akpaswa* ("a military unit with all its family members attached to it"), in spite of the haphazard nature of their flight. The royal family, the Asabou Agou, were in the center. The people of the right wing were called the Faafoue, and were under the command of the royal family. On the left were the Abe or Bessoufoue. The front was led by the Ando. The Nzipri and Ahari formed the rear guard. Other groups who came along were the Elomoue, Atoutou, Ngban, Agba, and Sa. Each *akpaswa* had its own organization of commanders, lieutenants, runners, and scouts.

This group of refugees fled west to the Comoé River. The river was in flood and blocked their further journey, while the Ashanti

---

[7] *E.R.B.*, p. 25. See also Marc Menalque, *Coutumes civiles des Baoulés de Dimbokro* (Paris, 1933), p. 6; Pierre Duprey, *Histoire des Ivoiriens: Naissance d'une nation* (Abidjan, 1962), p. 44; and Jacques Miège, "Notes de toponymie Baoulé," *Etudes Eburnéennes* 3 (Abidjan: IFAN, 1954): 133–34 (my translation).

army was closing in behind them. Oracles and diviners told the people to sacrifice a child to the spirits in the river, so that they would permit the people to cross. While the traditions differ, they insist that no one would offer a child until the queen or her sister gave her little boy. He was covered with gold ornaments and thrown into the river. Immediately the river stopped, or crocodiles or hippopotamuses formed a bridge, or a huge tree bent down to form a bridge and the people crossed. Because of this event, so central to their history, the people call themselves the Baoulé, which means "the child is dead."[8] While the folk etymology of this word is readily apparent, the importance of this legend is not to be overlooked, as an expression of unity and as a justification for the ceremonial superiority of the chief of the Asabou (also called Ouarebo), who were the descendants of Queen Pokou.

Upon crossing the Comoé, the Baoulé continued west until they reached the Bandama. There the Elomoue family remained to control Tiassalé. There they guarded the river and assured a route to the ocean. The queen and the rest of the Baoulé turned north toward the savannah region. The Agbé and Ngban stayed near the junction of the N'zi and Bandama rivers. The rest of the Baoulé proceeded north and gradually spread out along both banks of the Bandama and throughout the forest and savannah between the N'zi and Bandama. According to some traditions, Abra Pokou died, worn out by her long journey, and was buried at Niamonou, about twenty kilometers south of Bouaké.

Akoua Boni succeeded her aunt, Abra Pokou. Even at this early stage, wars broke out between the various groups of Baoulé, spelling an end to their organization. Groups and families waged war among themselves, split apart and moved to unoccupied land. The Asabou remained together long enough to found a village, Sakassou, under a Ouaré tree, from whence is derived the name of their family and the client families attached to them. They proceeded to conquer the inhabitants who, because of their lack of organization, could offer no effective resistance. A treaty of peace was signed with the Dankira in the region. With their cooperation Gouro inhabitants were driven across the Bandama or incorporated into the groups as clients or slaves. Mandé groups in the north were pushed back or conquered. With all the other groups under control, the Baoulé turned

8 Ibid.

on the Dankira, killed their chiefs, and conquered Dankira villages or forced them to flee. It is reported that Ashanti ambassadors were sent to the Baolé to arrange peace and to ask the Baoulé to return. The Baoulé refused to return and the Ashanti emissaries, under Asande Yaboua, remained with the Baoulé rather than return to Kumassi with a failure.[9]

From the central camp of Niamonou, where Abra Pokou was buried, the families of Faafoué, Ahari, Ando, Nanafoué, and Atoutou spread out and occupied the region. The Elomou and Ahua who occupied the southern-most part of the Baoulé region soon organized themselves to trade between the Baoulé and the seacoast. Markets were established by them at Daboua, Tien, Sinderesou, and Nzinoua. Besides trading, the Elomoue also engaged in raiding neighbors, especially those to the south.

In spite of the fact that on two occasions the Baoulé fought in a unified fashion in the reign of Akoua Boni and her successor, Kouakou Guie, against the Gouro and Agni severe strains made themselves felt so that in the long run Baoulé unity became less a political reality than a ceremony symbolized by the respect shown to the head of the Asabou (Ourebo). His prestige came from descent from the royal lineage of the Ashanti and from direct descent from Abra Pokou, the Queen Mother of the Baoulé. It would seem logical that the Baoulé brought many organizational ideas and principles with them from Ashanti. These broke up under the pressure of the large number of people who were incorporated into the Baoulé system. A further disruptive element was the discovery of the gold fields near Toumodi, which attracted people from all the families, thus putting pressure on the system of family treasure accumulation and matrilineal inheritance. The spread of people throughout the region disrupted close clan ties of organization. This interweaving of people occasioned countless hostilities and feuds, so that by the late nineteenth century, power, and organization center around the village.

Thus, while there was a theoretical organization, which had actually been used when they arrived, practically speaking there was a dissolution of the Baoulé hierarchy. In theory, the *auro* or *aoroba,* the family firesite, was the basic unit of society. Members of the family unit included not only freemen, *lyeoua,* but also *kanga*

[9] *E.R.B.,* p. 27.

("slaves") who were prisoners of war (*alomoué*) or in debt (*aoua*). These units were the base of the society. *Auro* were usually part of a village *kro*. (Koffikro, for example, is the village whose chief was named Koffi). Above this was a group of villages, called *Akpasoua*, which was also the military unit of defense, according to one source. Above this was the *mé,* which were clans or families with their various client families and those people who had made alliances with them. Above the *mé* was the idea of the Baoulé as a whole, represented by the head of the *Asabou.* The chief at each level was also chief at all levels below him.

As the warrior clans spread out to occupy the land or mine for gold, repeated fissures occurred not just within the structure of the Baoulé system but even within the *mé* themselves. On the one hand, there always existed a vague feeling of solidarity and allegiance to a Baoulé "nation," and on the other hand that nation was deeply split and held together by mutually exclusive confederations of *mé* or *akpasoua.*

While Abra Pokou and her three successors did in fact rule the Baoulé nation, and the Agouso family (Ouarebo) did posses the hegemony, by around 1850 this was no longer the case. The chief of the Ouarebo was respected as the representative of the historical lineage that led the conquest, but he no longer had any real power. These internal quarrels were the structural antecedents of the war with the French. The means of defense developed in these conflicts, fortified villages and ambushes, were the means used against the French.

It would seem that power was in the hands of the people at the village level. "Even within the village, the political structure took on a character more and more democratic. Practically speaking, the chief could not make a decision without his council of notables. This is not to imply that the society existed without structure or political order. In fact, aside from the chief of the village, the *kro kpingbin,* there were such figures as the *Ponafoué,* a judge who based his decisions on the rich tradition of proverbs. There was also the *Gbanfln Kpingbin,* or chief of the young men, who was responsible for civil order. He was the leader of the *milice.* During war he became the *Safonirin,* the *chef de guerre,* responsible for organizing the defense of the village. Naturally, there was also a council of notables. In any serious matter the whole village, men and women alike, would be gathered at the tree of *Palabre* to discuss the problem before a decision was reached.

Thus, there was a theoretical hierarchical system that still could be significant, depending on individual chiefs and a very real democratic village organization. While this indicates the confusion of the situation, it shows that the war waged against the French was waged by people defending their independence. There was no state as such, no army as such, no effective elite who sacrificed lives to maintain their privileges. The Baoulé war of resistance was a war of and by the people.

In order to have an accurate picture of the Baoulé situation at the time of their fight with the French, one should have some idea not only of the political system, but also of the economic situation of the people. Fortunately there is part of an economic report written by the then unknown Maurice Delafosse in 1899, before the French integrated the Baoulé system into their enterprise. At this time he was the local French administrator in Toumodi and hoped, via a peaceful system, the so-called peaceful conquest advocated by Binger and Clozel, to involve the Baoulé in the French trading system. The French were interested, therefore, in what the region was producing under Baoulé control. During this time the French were maintaining a low political profile and from 1894 to 1899 only had one administrator, three assistants, and a few *milice* in their posts at Toumodi, Ouosson, Koudiokoffikro, Tiassalé, and Bouaké. "In reality, France only had a nominal authority and the first serious attempt of administration brought a violent reaction from the people."[10]

Delafosse's report gives a picture of the Baoulé system of production and their participation in trade that indicates that the end result of colonial domination, economic integration in the world system, is only a question of degree. The Baoulé had already developed a market economy and produced surplus for trade. Some of this surplus was already oriented toward the European coastal market. This is of crucial importance. It shows, as has been recently pointed out, that the economic imbalance and Third World system of economics was already working prior to effective colonial occupation. The role of the Baoulé as producers of raw materials such as cotton

[10] *Les Armées françaises d'outre-mer: Histoire militaire de l'Afrique occidentale française* (Paris: Imprimerie Nationale, 1931) 4:601.

and rubber in exchange for manufactured goods had already been delineated. The domination that the French effected with their victory allowed them to exploit the situation more systematically via forced labor, prestation, and head tax. Yet it should be noticed in passing that at this time two-thirds of the trade done from Ivory Coast went to England, so that England was benefiting more from the French colonial effort than France was. This irony was not unique to the French effort in Ivory Coast alone.

Delafosse began by noting that various villages produced fine cattle that were sold for gunpowder. Other villages produced *ignames,* which were sold as well, though for salt, cloth, or beads rather than gunpowder. Wild rubber was being exploited by some people while others traded sheep, goats, or vegetables grown on their plantations for salt or other items. Cotton also was grown in certain regions, as was rice, peanuts, dyes, kola, and sesame. Soap was produced in the region and sold to *dyula* traders as were very highly esteemed *pagnes.* The market at Koudio-Koffi-Kro was a rendez-vous point for traders from:

> . . . Kong, Djimini, Sarakole, Markadyassa, Hausa, Anno, Mango, and even Oure or Ourie. These last bring from Attakrou and Indenie a lot of British merchandise (cloth and glassbeads) which were sold to them by the Apolleniens and Ashantis and which they go to exchange at Kofikro and especially Bouaké for gold and locally produced cloth.
>
> The *dyula* in Kofikro do not just trade but also produce goods, especially dyed cloth. Dyers are very numerous and their products are well prized as much by the *dyula* as by the Baoulé. Weavers, potters, basketweavers, cobblers, blacksmiths, carpenters, repairers of guns are very numerous. These last named repair guns in a poor state and even make replacement pieces.[11]

The use of guns and gunpower as a rate of exchange is to be remarked. Not only was the gun a means of defense but also a tool of production. It was with this tool that hunting was carried out, both for ivory and for food, and to protect the fields of *ignames,* rice, peanuts, and so on, against marauding animals. One of the essential features of the French war policy was the disarmament of the population without remuneration. This of course had a very serious effect on agriculture and hunting production.

Delafosse's view of the economic situation is certainly overly

[11] *La Quinzaine coloniale* (1899), pp. 602–03 (my translation).

rosy. Wild rubber was only a temporarily successful product, soon to be wiped out by plantation rubber from Indonesia. The internal conflicts within the Baoulé region caused frequent disruption of the commercial system. *Dyula* caravans were plundered now and again, probably for involvement in local wars, refusal to pay tolls, or false dealing. Gold obtained from the mines did not often enter the economic system but became part of the *dia,* the closely guarded treasure of the *aoro.* It is clear, furthermore, that the Baoulé had an important role as middlemen in trade between the coast and Gouro- and Sénoufo-speaking regions as well as a control of the comparatively easy route to Kong. The role of Baoulé traders as middlemen controlling the Bandama Valley was a key sore point with the French.

It must also be noted that we have given an unduly static picture of the economic situation with our concentration on the period immediately prior to the war with the French. For example, trade with the north fluctuated considerably, depending on the situation there. In the 1860s a family of Hausa created a trade center on the northern fringe of Baoulé territory at Marabadiassa, and this became a new center of trade for the region. A sizeable number of slaves were sold to the Baoulé by Samori, especially at the market of Kofikro near Bouaké on the road to Katiola, where most of the captives were Tagouana, Djimini, and Sénoufo. According to another piece by Delafosse, the chief of this market "exercised the functions of Samori's resident for Gbouéké or Bouaké."[12]

THE WAR

It must be remembered that no white man had ventured more than twenty-eight kilometers into the southern interior of Ivory Coast until 1887. It was not until after 1894 that the French went above the first rapids on the Bandama at Brou Brou near Tiassalé. The problem, of course, was the lack of an easy entrance into the interior. The rivers were blocked by rapids close to the sea and a land route had to pass through the dense rain forest.[13] It was not until the explorations of Binger and Treich Laplène that the famous mountains of Kong and the Gle Lake were proven to be the figment of some cartographer's imagination.

[12] Maurice Delafosse, "Ethnographie de la région de Bouaké," in *Dix ans à la Côte d'Ivoire,* ed. F. J. Clozel (Paris, 1906), p. 279.
[13] Clozel, *Dix ans à la Côte d'Ivoire,* p. 12.

Captain Binger only touched on Baoulé country on his first trip from Kong to Grand Bassam and described certain Ando villages along the Comoé River.[14] In 1892 he and Marcel Monnier attempted to enter Baoulé country from the north after they had participated in a futile Anglo-French mission to delineate the border between Ivory Coast and Gold Coast. They were politely received in the first Baoulé village they came to but were firmly told that if they attempted to proceed further the village would fight them.[15] It is obvious that even at this early stage in contact, even in a northern area far from the coast, the people of the first Baoulé village were not permitting strangers into the area. Was this mere xenophobia? Was it the fact that Binger and Monnier might have been seen as allies of their porters, who, it turned out, were people with whom the village was waging war? Was it because these people were seen as allies of the *Blofoué* ("whitemen") that there was a war in the first place?

About the same time another confrontation took place between the French and the Baoulé, with even more disastrous results for the French. In May 1891, Messieurs Voituret and Papillon, two explorers from Paris, from the Société d'Études de l'Ouest Africain, fell into an ambush as they mounted the Bandama River near Tiassalé and were killed.[16] It would seem that they took food from the people without paying for it. Arthur Verdier, the official French resident, remarked, "The discontent of the people of Tiassalé existed already; when they became aware of the arrival and actions of Voituret and Papillon they decided that these two unfortunates would be killed, which is what occurred."[17] Delafosse recognized that the discontent to which Verdier was referring was based on the realization that Tiassalé was the key to the southern route into the Baoulé region and because they feared for their commercial position.[18] Despite a report by Desailles pointing out the natural defenses of the region, the skill of the Baoulé in ambushes, and their willingness, if all else failed, to abandon their villages, Governor

[14] L. G. Binger, *Du Niger au Golfe de Guinée* (Paris, 1892), vol. 2.

[15] Monnier, *Mission Binger: La France noire* (Paris, 1894), pp. 249–63.

[16] *Bulletin du comité d'Afrique française* 1 (1891): 13–14 (hereafter cited as *B.C.A.F.*).

[17] Verdier, *Irente-cinq années de lutte aux colonies* (Paris, 1897), p. 126 (my translation).

[18] Gabriel Hanotaux and Alfred Martineau, *Histoire des colonies françaises et de l'expansion de la France dans le monde*, vol. 4, *Afrique occidentale française*, by Maurice Delafosse and August Terrier (Paris, 1931), pp. 277–78.

Ballay wanted to revenge the death of the two Frenchmen. Lieutenant Staub and a company of tirailleurs were sent on a punitive raid April 24. On May 10 they were attacked and hurled back. Over the next year the French were able to overcome this resistance, as much by diplomacy as by military activity, but they did not try to exploit the situation.

After Ivory Coast was declared a colony on March 10, 1893, and Binger named first governor, a renewed effort under Captain Marchand was made and it was decided to create a post at Tiassalé. This was effected after a short but fierce fight May 14, 1893. Marchand then proceeded north. He was the first white man to enter and travel through Baoulé country. In fact he did so without incident and earned the name *Kpakibo* ("Piercer of the Forest") because of his success.[19] This incident leads one to believe that a system of laissez-passer was in effect, perhaps a vestige of Ashanti heritage. In any case, once he got past Tiassalé, no shots were fired, no untoward event occurred. He set up posts in Toumodi, Kodiokofi, and Ouossou.

In March 1894, Marchand was back in Grand Bassam, reporting on the wonders of the Baoulé region (richer than America)[20] and the presence of Samori in the north.

The French government in Paris decided to send troops who originally had been earmarked for an operation in Central Africa to meet this threat. Colonel Monteil was dispatched from an operation that was to have taken place in Haut Ubangui before diplomacy solved the problem, to form a column to Kong in northern Ivory Coast.[21] After further complications in Dahomey where a short stop was made, one company was ordered to return to Congo, while another was ordered to depart from Senegal to replace it. The column of Kong arrived in Grand Bassam on September 12, 1894.[22] Against Monteil's wishes, the troops were first employed to make reprisals against various people, Akaplene, Agni, Jack Jacks who had been creating difficulties along the lagoons and coast. Despite Binger's preference for the Comoé route, under Marchand's in-

[19] Jacques Delebecque, *La Vie du Général Marchand* (Paris, 1937), chap. 4.
[20] *B.C.A.F.* 4 (1894): 24.
[21] Colonel Baratier, *Epopées africaines* (Paris, 1913); idem, *A Travers l'Afrique* (Paris, 1912), pp. 157–212; A. S. Kanya-Forstner, *The Conquest of the Western Sudan: A Study in French Military Imperialism* (Cambridge, 1969), pp. 230–31; and Yves Person, *Samori: Une révolution dyula* (Dakar, 1968–75), pp. 1637–84.
[22] Baratier, *Epopées africaines,* p. 38.

fluence the decision was made to march to Kong via the Baoulé region. The result was a disaster for Monteil. Since his mules quickly died in the forest, Monteil "had to requistion these [porters] among the quiet popuplation who, habituated to hundreds of years of complete independence suffered cruelly from this first contact with European pentration." The result of this contact—war—was to be expected. "Toward the end of December, a general insurrection broke out practically the same day, all along the route of the column, which found itself completely blocked. . . . It was war, an invisible guerilla war complicated by the absolute necessity of keeping open communications with the coast. . . ."[23] "The declared hostility of the local people who, without making common cause with Samori, took fright at the passage of our troops, so weakened the column that Moneteil could not go beyond Satama in the south of Diammna." The results of this failure were twofold. It protected Samori for another several years until the end came from the military in Soudan. Secondly, "since the column of Kong, which had another objective, did not slow down to make a methodical repression, the Baoulé could interpret the retreat of our troops in the beginning of 1896 as a success for their arms."[24] Thus it was that the second attempt by the French to impose their control on the region was decisively checked by the Baoulé.

In the years after this incident various events unfolded in Ivory Coast. Samori was captured in 1898 and his empire destroyed. A mission under Captain Houdaille arrived to prepare a study of a railroad for the Ivory Coast. In 1898 the Agni, with Ashanti assistance, besieged a French outpost for sixty-three days. Two Frenchmen were killed in a village near Bonoua.[25] In the Baoulé region, as noted above, the French only maintained posts at Tiassalé, Toumodi, Ouossou, and Kouadiokofikro with a few administrators and *milice*. Even this low profile was unacceptable, and trouble broke out in August 1859 when Delafosse, then administrator at Toumodi, tried to prevent a chief, Kouadio Okou, from interfering with trade caravans.[26] Toumodi was cut off and then the French post there was burned down. A force was hastily assembled and sent to Delafosse's aid, but it was defeated. A larger force of three columns was

[23] Hanotaux and Martineau, *Histoire des colonies françaises,* 4:212–13.
[24] Clozel, *Dix années,* pp. 272, 78.
[25] *B.C.A.F.* 8 (1898): 362, 285, 410, 347.
[26] Hanotaux and Martineau, *Histoire des colonies françaises,* 4:283–84.

sent into the region so the Baoulé withdrew and an uneasy peace settled on the region. On December 29, 1899, the post at Bouaké was attacked.[27] From then until Angoulvant finally defeated the Baoulé in 1911, there was a continual state of war between the Baoulé and the French. Villages and *mé* would fight, submit, and then, when the occasion presented itself, start the hostilities again. As Delafosse so clearly understated it, "the indigenes showed at every moment that they did not consider themselves as really subjugated."[28] One can find no obvious organization of the war on any scale. It would seem that when the French made their presence felt locally, there was a military effort made to remove them. This seems logical, given our understanding of the political system's local focus. While this disorganization and spontaneity made it difficult to drive out the French, it made the French goal of conquest very difficult too, since there was no army to destroy, no state to smash, no king to deport. It also gives the fight certain aspects that might be seen merely as resistance. The history of the Baoulé shows such a fight to be more than that, however. It was the positive expression and defense of their political system and as such it was a fight for political domination of the region. As such it was the fight of two political systems, analogous to the Franco-Prussian War.

In 1901 certain Nanafoué and Ngban as well as the Faafoué of Kokumbo fought French presence. After a fierce battle, a column under Colonna d'Istria took Kokumbo and the chief, Kouadio Okou, surrendered. Shortly thereafter, the Agba took up arms. At Toumodi, the chief, Akafou, was taken prisoner by Captain Bastard on July 8, 1902, and died in the hands of the French. With that the whole region arose and besieged the French outposts.[29] Instead of bringing peace and prosperity, the French presence brought only war and chaos. A caravan of *dyula* was attacked and pillaged. Thirty-two porters were killed in another caravan. The post at Seinzenou was burned. On September 10, Captain Privey was killed in an ambush.[30]

Prior to the last incident, the Nanafoué and Epri had demanded a French post at Salekro that was installed under Lieutenant Des-

[27] *Les Armées françaises,* 4:601.
[28] Hanotaux and Martineau, *Histoire des colonies françaises,* 4:285.
[29] *Les Armées françaises,* 4:601.
[30] August Terrier, *L'Expansion française et la formation territoriale* (Paris, 1910), p. 500.

suzes. Because of their demands for forced labor and their intervention in family quarrels, the French quickly alienated the people. On
April 8 the post was attacked and besieged until April 13, when a
larger force arrived. The people continued ambushes and even tried
to poison the Senegalese tirailleurs. Under such pressure, the French
withdrew from Salekro in October, again conceding victory to the
local Baoulé forces.

In the north among the Ouarebo of Sakassou, there was considerable unrest, so a *palabre* was arranged between the chief, notables,
and people of Salekro and the French. Kouamé Gui was the chief.
He was also the chief of all the Baoulé and a descendant of Abra
Pokou. In the course of the *palabre,* the argument became quite
heated, so Captain Lambert told the tirailleurs to shoot in the air to
force the crowd back. Kouamé Gui was shot and killed in the fusil-
lade.[31] Open war was the result.

In 1903 and 1904 hostilities and submissions continued. Submission involved a payment of reparations and the handing over to
the French of a certain number of guns. It was not until 1910 that
the sale and possession of guns in Ivory Coast was regulated and
ordinary possession of guns prohibited. This was because guns and
gunpower were such an essential part of the trade being done in
that area, and any regulation of the gun trade was vociferously denounced by the traders. Nanafoué and Ouarebo submitted; the
Nanafoué incurred the wrath of the Agba for this submission and
were attacked by them.

Because the railroad was projected to cross the N'zi River and
pass through Agba country, the French had to conquer that region.
Construction of the railroad began in December 1903 from Abidjan,
and because not even surveying had been possible in Agba country
the French did not even really know where it was going. In April
1905, therefore, a large column of 400 tirailleurs, divided into
three columns attacked and overran the Agba territory along the
N'zi from three directions.

It is important to note that not only were the Baoulé attempting
to maintain their independence, but also the Bété, Dan, Oubé,
Gouro, and other people in Ivory Coast were fighting the same fight.
The Ebrie even carried the fight into the streets of Bingerville itself.

On May 1, 1908, Gabriel Angoulvant was appointed governor

[31] Ibid., p. 501.

of the Ivory Coast Colony. He assessed the situation in the Baoulé as:

> . . . The circle of the Nzi-Comoé was run through once, from south to north by an administrator who made a summary map of his own journey, but outside the Agba region, to the west and from the north, which were part of the circles of Bondoukou and Kong, we not know anything.
>
> As for the Baoulé circle, the western part—including the annexed circle of the Gouros, the families of the Kodes, Ayaous, Nanafoues, Yaoures, Watas, Ouanfoues on both banks of the Bandama—was in a state of revolt, open or latent, depending on the season and our demands. All administration there is absolutely impossible.[32]

Criticizing the methods of the past, "peaceful conquest" and the use of columns to effect reprisals and force submissions, Angoulvant cited the lack of methodical occupation and coordinated military planning. He called for the use of a "strong method" such as Gallieni had used in Madagascar. This required a considerable number of troops, vast military operations on an expensive scale. He received support from William Ponty, the governor general of French West Africa, who agreed about the seriousness of the situation.

The method to be used was the *tache d'huile* developed by Gallieni:

> One only wins land ahead after the land behind is completely organized. It is the indigenes unsubmitting the day before who help us to beat the unsubmitting of the next day. You move ahead consistently and the latest post occupied becomes, first of all, an observation post, from where the commandant *du cercle, du secteur,* examines the situation, seeks to enter into relations with the elements in front of him, using those who have just submitted, determines new points to occupy and prepares new advances. This method never fails. It is the best way to spare the land and people and it prepares best the organization of our control over the new territories.
>
> All movement of troops forward should have as sanction the effective occupation of the conquered land. It is an absolute principle.[33]

Governor Angoulvant gave the following as his reason for such warfare: "we do not perceive any profit in these regions, listed as

[32] Angoulvant, *La Pacification*, p. 14.
[33] *Les Armées françaises*, 4:659.

unknown, hostile or doubtful. Trade there is practically nil, where there is no form of security."[34]

While the following quote applies specifically to the Abbey war against the French in 1910, the analysis certainly applies as well to the Baoulé situation:

> 1. In Bingerville, in only one month the people of the surrounding villages furnished 1,200 days of work without touching a penny.
> 2. In a peaceful *palabre,* the indigenes having made the gesture of getting up to go, fire was opened on them, without provocation on their part. [I believe this is a reference to the assassination of Kouamé Gui in 1902.]
> 3. Construction has begun throughout the colony of roads six meters wide . . . word done without pay by the people in regions where the population is sparse.[35]

From the beginning of his administration, Angoulvant continued offensive operations with large columns. Not until after he had obtained sufficient manpower could he begin his *tache d'huile* campaign (1910–1915). "Certain chiefs, discontented to see our authority tighten its grip, encouraged diverse tribes of the Morenou [southern Baoulé region] to resist."[36] A column of 200 soldiers entered the region in October and November 1908. It withdrew after the chiefs and other influential people were seized and 10,000 francs in reparations was paid.[37] In November a column was sent against the village of Gogrobo because a reconnaissance patrol had been chased out of the region, losing all its baggage, 1 policeman killed and 2 wounded. The French column of reprisal killed 75 people.

In February 1909, Angoulvant sent a column of 180 men under Captain Cohen against the Ayaou, because they had refused to pay the head tax and were also charging tolls of caravans passing through their region. This column was constantly ambushed and attacked as it passed through the region and villagers were abandoned before the invader. The column was increased to 255 men and it occupied the center of resistance, Diacoubou. The column then withdrew and one year later the region took up arms again.

The inhabitants of the region west of Yamoussoukro also fought the French effort to occupy their land. On June 24, 1909, they drove

[34] Angoulvant, *La Pacification,* p. 15.
[35] *Revue indigène* 53 (1910): 518–19.
[36] Angoulvant, *La Pacification,* p. 249.
[37] Ibid., p. 250.

the soldiers from the post at Bonzi. A column retook Bonzi July 1 and inflicted serious casualties on the people, but "the audacity of the rebels did not diminish,"[38] and the French could only just maintain themselves in the post itself. To meet this problem, a large column, under chef de bataillon Nogues, composed of the Fourth and Seventh Companies of the First Senegalese, Ninth Company of the Fourth Senegalese, First Brigade of the local guard, and 200 police invaded the country on a front twenty to twenty-five kilometers wide to sweep the region. Beginning October 23, this column methodically began moving across the region, burning villages and camps, killing many inhabitants. The Baoulé, who Angoulvant conceded were "audacious and energetic" gradually withdrew north fighting continually. By January 1, 1910, these Akou people were beaten and offered their final submission.

On January 6, 1910, the Abbey, another Akan people, living south of the Baoulé region, struck at the heart of effective French occupation of the Ivory Coast—the railroad. "The country rose together, between kilometer 40 and 120, obeying an order."[39] "The railroad and its installations were attacked, the railroad itself was cut in 25 places between kilometer 24 and 42."[40] While the Abbey fought well and hard, the French concentrated all their efforts on protecting the railroad. Because of the seriousness of the situation, Governor Ponty sent 1,400 reinforcements from Dakar. By the end of October the Abbey were beaten and disarmed. A remark in the *Dépêche de la Côte d'Ivoire* gives an indication of the method employed. "Villages which had been taken were burned. *No pity for the prisoners.* Heads which had been cut off were stuck on poles in front of the railroad stations or the houses in the villages."[41]

With an increased number of troops at his disposal, and the Abbey war in hand by late April—although operations continued for another six months—Angoulvant turned his attention to the Ngbans. "Independent, brave, tenacious, clever and tireless hunters, confident in their forests and impenetrable thickets, they have already, on many occasions, fought with our troops. They have always showed themselves formidable adversaries and have never wanted to admit to being completely beaten." They had fought

[38] Ibid., p. 265.
[39] *Revue indigène* 46 (1910): 105.
[40] Suret-Canale, *Afrique noire*, p. 131.
[41] Quoted by Suret-Canale, *Afrique noire*, p. 134.

Monteil and the small columns sent into their region in 1902–03. In 1909, when the French tried to disarm them, they chased the administrator out, threatened the people who were collaborating with the French, and got ready for war. They fortified their villages and dug trenches. In 1910 they cut the telegraph line and besieged Ouossou. A large column under Chef de Batallion Morel was prepared. It included three Senegalese companies, detachments of the local brigade, a total of 800 men, and even a piece of artillery. A three-pronged attack was launched against the Ngban on April 30, 1910. The method involved was the usual destruction of camps and villages, plantations and possible points of ambush. "Faithful to their past the Ngbans put up a strong resistance and caused us considerable losses,"[42] but they were effectively beaten and disarmed by August 1, 1910. During the same period of time the Salefoué and Belefoué were disarmed by French troops or fled into Agba territory. The Agba had fought the French in 1901 and 1902. In 1905, a large column had attacked them but in 1910 again they took up arms one more time. A column of 500 men was sent against them July 1, and they were defeated and disarmed by December 1. Similar action was continued north of Bongouanou in the Salekro and Ouelle regions.

Generally speaking, 1911 was the last year of war. After that resistance was carried out on a small scale from camps hidden in the forest. A large column under Commandant Nogues, 1,150 men strong, with one piece of artillery, took up the fight along the Bandama that the war with the Abbey had interrupted. The Baoulé people who were attacked included the Nanafoué, Kpri, Yaoure, Ayaou, and Kode. "These people, it is true to say, never completely accepted our domination. . . ."[43] The Nanafoué had been free of the French since they had driven the French from Salekro in 1902. According to Angoulvant, they had a woman chief who was particularly effective in stirring up the war against the French. In spite of energetic defense, the results were the same, the people were defeated and disarmed, and the chiefs were killed or imprisoned. The village and their way of life were destroyed.

The costs for the Baoulé of this long war, so bravely fought, were extremely heavy. How many thousands of people killed? How many plantations and flocks of animals destroyed? How much hard-earned

42 Angoulvant, *La Pacification*, pp. 284, 295.
43 Ibid., pp. 307, 308.

wealth wasted? No figures are at hand to answer these questions. The people were disarmed. Between September 1909 and April 1915, 25,125 guns were taken from the Baoulé, guns bought from French merchants at a cost of about twenty francs, guns for which a tax had been paid in some cases as required by a law of 1908, guns for which no recompense was ever made. Of a total of 220 chiefs deported or held in detention by the French in Ivory Coast between November 1908 and November 1912, 185 were Baoulé. The Baoulé were also forced to pay war reparations of 435,910 francs between June 1910 and January 1912, plus the head tax that had been instituted in 1901. To this must be added the loss and destruction of camps and villages and the whole agricultural system based on a thinly spread population. "Thus, among the conditions of submission, I included the destruction of camps and the regrouping of the people in villages. Thus it was that the Akoue, spread out in 237 small villages, are today grouped in 17 pretty villages which are easily accessible, that the Ngban have no more than 37 villages situated near the supply route instead of 312 camps in the forest."[44]

CONCLUSION

The reader has probably noticed that I have refrained from the use of the term *resistance* to a large extent. This was deliberate. What I have studied is a war between the Baoulé people and the French administration. To use *resistance* for military conflict between the African people and the foreign conquerer gives the fight an ahistoric uniqueness that historical research does not bear out. I have attempted to indicate that the military means used to fight the French were the same as had been employed before against other threatening foes.

The evidence available seems to substantiate our notion of the continuity of Baoulé military methods and goals, though the information is regrettably focused on the French efforts. This is understandable, given the sources. In a sense, it does not greatly distort the picture, since the French were the initiators of the main acts of aggression. The Baoulé were, seemingly, never to the point of trying to drive the French into the sea. They were willing to trade with them and make alliances with them, but they refused to be dominated by them. Hindsight analysis, based on an appreciation of the

---

[44] Ibid., p. 217 (guns—my computation of figures for the Baoulé); pp. 234–37 (chiefs—information on war reparations, p. 244); pp. 245–55 (quote).

macrocosmic scale of the problem, views such an attempt as inadequate.

As suggested throughout this article, the reasons for the fierce war fought by the Baoulé were manifold. It seemed that there was a tradition of guarding political independence and political power on the local level to the point where village would fight village if it felt threatened. French observers talk repeatedly about the overly independent and sensitive people of the forest region. There was also a careful attempt on the part of the Baoulé to maintain their part in the trade, that is, to maintain their control of the caravan route through the Baoulé region and their role as middlemen. This played no small part in the fight around Tiassalé and Toumodi. To these must be added the negative conditions of brutal French methods, of forced labor, reprisals, retaliation, assassination, forced taxation, forced disarmament, and the like. It must also be remembered that conditions were the same throughout the Ivory Coast as was the war. Suret-Canale has said that it was a war of "despair."[45] Because of the overwhelming weight of French heavy-handed methods, it would appear to be so. Yet historical study gives an insight that it was more than that, and that it was a careful attempt of the people to protect their right to rule themselves.

Further proof of the importance of the domination question may be seen by an analysis of the Baoulé economic situation prior to effective French occupation. Practically speaking, the Baoulé were already part of the economic system that was being set up to exploit world markets and production for the benefit of Western world profit makers. They were producing raw materials and buying manufactured goods. In fact, the dilemma of such a situation was recognized by the oracle of Keta Kratchi, who warned the Ashanti that they could not win a war against the gunpowder makers with the gunpowder makers' own gunpowder. It does not seem an overstatement to say that the way out of this situation has yet to be found, a fact the independent countries of Africa have discovered in this era of neocolonialism.

The reality of this sort of exploitation is not to be denied, whether neocolonial or precolonial, yet Amilcar Cabral's remark about the impact of colonialism in Guinea Bissau is equally true for the Ivory Coast. "We consider that when imperialism arrived in Guinea, it

[45] Suret-Canale, *Afrique noire,* p. 132.

made us leave history—our history. We agreed that history in our country is the result of class struggle, but we have our own class struggles in our own country; the moment imperialism arrived and colonialism arrived, it made us leave our history and enter another history."[46] Thus the question of sovereignty referred to by J.F.A. Ajayi as being the crux of recent African history was a matter of central importance to Amilcar Cabral also.

The reasons for the failure of the war on the part of the Baoulé are not hard to find, given the fact that they were facing a well-organized enemy with a considerable firepower advantage. One cannot help but remark on the general lack of organization and coordination on the part of the Baoulé. In fact, I would posit that there was even less organization than the French supposed at the time. The use of various names of the *mé* by Clozel and Angoulvant to indicate their opponents probably gives a picture of wider participation than was actually the case. I would think that wherever the French tried to impose their rule, each village or group of villages— what we have seen to be the functioning political unit—decided whether or not to oppose this. The war was decided on and carried on at this level.

Effective control meant to the French not just domination and control via taxes, forced labor and the like, but also the disarmament of the people, an effective alienation of political power from the hands of the people to a state organization. This was a new order of things amoung the Baoulé. Up until then, the people were sovereign, that is, they had the political power and the means of effecting their decision. This was no longer the case. Power was seized and institutionalized in a state, the colonial administration of the Ivory Coast. The administration made the decisions and then made sure, by force if necessary, that decisions were carried out. Sovereignty had been removed from the people. The legitimacy of the administration came, not from any consensus of the people nor from any divine right; it grew out of the barrel of the gun of the Senegalese tirailleur.

Perhaps it would be instructive to compare the Franco-Baoulé war with other wars of "resistance." The time has come to distinguish the nature and scope of these different wars. From the Baoulé war to the wars of Samori Touré against the French military

---

[46] Cabral, *Revolution in Guinea: Selected Texts* (New York, 1969), p. 68.

to the wars of the Ashanti and Dahomey kingdoms, is there any continuity? It would seem that the goal of all the modern western states—including Liberia—was to organize people outside the system into it. It was the goal of their opponents to participate in such a system on their own terms with their own institutions. In all cases, except Liberia and Ethiopia, not only were these wars to impose modern bourgeoisie states (except Ethiopia), but they were to impose administrations by foreign European powers, justifying their actions with theories of racial superiority.

Established states such as Dahomey fought to maintain their integrity and state institutions. Ashanti fought its enemies and the allies of its enemies. New Men in West Africa such as Samori Touré fought to establish new empires, and in so doing collided with French military ambitions. All these different African political units were therefore fighting different kinds of wars with different objectives. Yet all are subsumed under the term *resistance*. It is to point out these differences and their importance for African history that I have questioned the use of this term. It would seem that it is an oversimplification and does not do justice to the complexity of the problem.

French Colonisation and African Resistance in West Africa up to the First World War

B. Olatunji Oloruntimehin

Department of History,
University of Ibadan

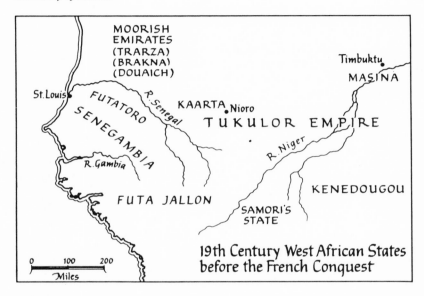

MOORISH EMIRATES (TRARZA) (BRAKNA) (DOUAICH)

Timbuktu

MASINA

St. Louis

FUTATORO

SENEGAMBIA

R. Senegal

KAARTA Nioro

TUKULOR EMPIRE

R. Niger

R. Gambia

FUTA JALLON

SAMORI'S STATE

KENEDOUGOU

19th Century West African States before the French Conquest

0   100   200
Miles

Colonisation is the imposition of foreign domination on a people. For the dominated people it means loss of independence and sovereignty. As no people ever willingly surrender their freedom and right to manage their own affairs, it is not surprising that people everywhere have resisted colonisation. The history of French colonialism and African resistance in West Africa can for convenience be divided into two broad phases. First, there was the period of penetration and conquest and, secondly, the period during which attempts were made to consolidate conquest and establish a firm colonial regime.

African reactions to the French presence were determined partly by the mode of penetration and partly by existing inter-state relations within this area of Africa during the period. It is important to bear in mind that when we talk of African reactions, we mean reactions of a number of states, and sometimes groups within the states. There was no uniformity in the responses of Africans because Africans belonged to different states. Each of these states regarded the

24

neighbouring states as foreign and dealt with them accordingly. It was thus logical that the states should react to situations, including the French presence, according to their varied interests and their understanding of the situations. One major factor that affected African reactions was the fact that French penetration and conquest took place at the same time as various movements in the Western Sudan were seeking to bring together under large empires hitherto independent states. In the process of empire-building there were groups which resisted being subjected to foreign, even though African, control. The French naturally exploited the existence of such groups. The empire-building processes began with the rise of the Tukulor empire by about the middle of the nineteenth century, and continued with the empire-building movements of Samori Ture and Tieba of Kenedougou. Each of these movements caused major revolutions in the political and social life of the areas affected as well as in relations between states. The politics of survival, and the necessity to adapt to the changing circumstances, sometimes made some African state or groups co-operate or collaborate with the advancing French imperialism, in the belief that they were thereby protecting their own interests.

French penetration dated back to the seventeenth century. A group of French commercial agents established a station at Saint Louis around 1637, and the following year they built a fort at the mouth of the River Senegal. They soon spread out to other places like Goree Island, Rufisque and Joal – places where the Portuguese had settled at one time or the other before the French came to the scene. From the seventeenth century to the nineteenth, the French, using the River Senegal, pushed into the Western Sudan from their coastal bases. Up to the middle of the nineteenth century they concentrated on a gradual, peaceful spread of commerce, in which pursuit they relied heavily on African middlemen. The spread of commerce involved building warehouses and installations to protect them and the people in charge. These warehouses were garrisoned and generally referred to as forts. They were built usually on the banks of the River Senegal and its tributaries, mainly to make access easy to boats carrying the articles of trade.

With commerce came the spread of French influence. First, those in commercial and other relations with the French gradually learnt the French language. Secondly, certain African groups became so heavily involved in French trade that common interests developed. Finally, continued stay in the area led to social and political relations. The French began, for example, to get involved in settling disputes between African groups and in succession disputes within particular states in such a way as to promote their trading interests. On the social plane, relations forged through marriage or concubinage not only linked some Frenchmen directly with some African groups but more significantly, they resulted in the emergence and growth of a distinct group of Afro-Europeans called *mulattoes* or *métis*. Though a minority, this group had, by the nineteenth century, become a dominant one in the commercial and political life of Senegal. Only the community of Frenchmen was more powerful. But then the mulattoes and these Frenchmen often shared common interests and activities.

25

In all, the early phase of French penetration was peaceful and concerned mainly with trade. However, as has been pointed out, trade led to social and political relations. In the interest of their trade, the French began to want to impose their own terms on the Africans. Because they controlled the trade in

Goree Island: major slave-trading centre

arms and ammunition they began to manipulate this trade so as to favour those groups and states which gave them better conditions of trade. Naturally, this situation began to produce conflict between those African groups who were adversely affected and the French. As such conflicts developed, so the French began to desire to control the political life of the various states. It was out of this situation that French imperialism developed from the middle of the nineteenth century onward.

Among those who began to resist the French push were certain rulers of the Senegambian states – the Tukulor of Toro, the Wolof of Jolof, the Moors of the emirates of Trarza, Brakna and Douaich in present-day Mauritania. This resistance involved military confrontations as well as the imposition of a trade embargo, especially on gum which was an important item of trade at the time. Some of the wars which were fought between these states and the French have been called trade wars because they arose from African reaction against the French attempt to dictate trade terms. The wars between the Moors of present-day Mauritania and the French between 1830 and 1854 fall into this category.

The more important resistance against French penetration came from the emergent Tukulor empire which was a product of the revolution started by al-hajj 'Umar b. Sa'id Tall. The Tukulor revolution began in Futa Toro, spreading to other parts of the Senegambia at a time when the African states in the

26

area were already in confrontation with advancing French imperialism. The Tukulor leaders were fighting to integrate all the states into a single political system that would be guided by the ideas of Islam, particularly of the Tijaniyya order. In doing this, they came into conflict with the French, whom they wanted to confine to their role as traders, paying taxes and acknowledging the authority of the Tukulor rulers, who in turn would grant the French the status of protected persons as defined in the laws of Islam. For the French the new situation created by the Tukulor revolution was unacceptable because it ran contrary to their ambition and efforts to have political control over the areas with which they had relations. It was like asking them to forget the purpose and efforts put into the trade wars from 1830 to 1854. This they could not do. Instead they fought against the emergent Tukulor empire from 1856 to 1860 for the control of the Senegambia.

One may ask: why did not the African rulers in the Senegambia cooperate with the new Tukulor rulers against the French who sought to dominate all of them? The answer is that each of the African states jealously tried to preserve its independence and sovereignty whereas French expansion and Tukulor revolution involved destroying the independence and sovereignty of the states by conquering them and absorbing them into new political systems. Much as the Tukulor leaders could be seen as standing for the African cause against the French, there was no doubt among the rulers of the states concerned that the Tukulor attempt to build a large state by merging their previously-independent states was an expression of imperialism similar to the French attempt to establish political control over them. In other words, as far as the rulers of the states were concerned, the clash between the French and the developing Tukulor empire was a confrontation between two imperialists with themselves as the target of attack and the prize to be taken by the victor.

Moreover, the Tukulor movement caused divisions within and between the states as leaders reacted differently to the ideological campaigns by al-hajj 'Umar and his supporters. Among Muslims the campaign in favour of Tijaniyya against all other brotherhoods in Islam caused division and conflict throughout the Western Sudan. Within certain states under Muslim rulers, groups accepted Tijaniyya as a means of organising opposition against the existing regimes. The opposition among non-Muslim populations, like the Bambara in Segu and Ka'arta, had a wider and deeper basis in the sense that it aimed not only at preserving their independence but also their culture, particularly religion, against the invading Tukulor forces. Against this background co-operation between the various African states against the French was out of the question.

Worse still, many African rulers considered Tukulor imperialism more dangerous than French imperialism which, by comparison, was rather distant and less overwhelming. Whereas the French had few forces at their disposal and therefore relied partly on using diplomacy, especially signing treaties, as a means of establishing their control, the Tukulor movement presented a more immediate and menacing danger with a large, well-equipped, powerful army on the frontiers of, or even within, the states concerned. In this situation the struggle to preserve

27

independence and sovereignty against the Tukulor often forced some of the African rulers to relegate the French threat to secondary importance. The search for arms and ammunition, in any case, forced some form of understanding with the French who controlled the supply. Some African rulers who found themselves in desperate situations even forgot their conflict with the French temporarily to ally with the French, who stationed troops in such states as part of the struggle against the Tukulor. In short, the conflict between the emergent Tukulor empire and the other states, and the accompanying tension within these states, not only prevented African rulers from uniting against the French, but also provided the French with the opportunity of posing as champions of some of the groups against the others and thereby penetrating and establishing control over this part of West Africa at relatively little cost.

Even when the Tukulor empire had become a reality, many groups representing the states which had been conquered and absorbed into the Tukulor empire continued to fight wars of resistance aimed at regaining their independence. By allying with the resistance movements in their wars against the Tukulor empire, the French gradually undermined the Tukulor regime until it became so weakened that it was possible to wage a short and sharp war of conquest against it between 1889 and 1894. Realising their own danger only too late, the groups that had actively collaborated with the French in the expectation that they were going to regain the independence and sovereignty lost to the Tukulor also fell victim to French imperialism in the process.

The process of French colonisation described in relation to the areas which came under the Tukulor empire was broadly the pattern followed in the colonisation of areas which were conquered to form Samori Toure's empire, the kingdom of Kenedougou with its base at Sikasso, and Dahomey. The colonisation of the Mossi states of present-day Upper Volta, the emirates of the present area of the Niger republic and the societies comprising the present Ivory Coast took the form of more brutal and speedy military expeditions in the era of the European scramble for Africa.

The earlier process of undermining and attacking African states by collaborating with resistance groups within them was repeated in the colonisation of Samori's empire and Dahomey. For example, the French supplied arms and ammunition to groups fighting to destroy Samori's state, and sometimes invaded the state in collaboration with such groups. They built and garrisoned fortresses in such places as Bamako, Bafoulabe, Niako and Niagassola not only to serve them as bases of operations against the Tukulor empire and Samori's empire, but also to serve as rallying points for the African groups operating against both empires. They signed a treaty of alliance and military assistance with the ruler of Kenedougou, Tieba, mainly as a means of combating Samori. Since in Samori's bid for the expansion of his state he had violated the territorial integrity of Tieba's Kenedougou, war broke out between them, and in this situation the French found it easy to pose as defenders of Kenedougou's independence against Samori and his forces. When Samori's state was eventually conquered by 1898, the various groups which had collaborated with the French fell with the

Emperor Samori Toure

empire. In the case of Kenedougou it became isolated and was at the mercy of the French forces which destroyed it shortly after. In the case of Dahomey the same process was evident in the French collaboration with the coastal Popo Kingdoms against the Abomey Kingdom. The exploitation of the tension between Abomey and her coastal neighbours made it relatively easy for the French forces under Colonel (later General) Dodds to conquer Behanzin's forces between 1889 and 1893.

In practically all cases, lack of political unity or existence of inter-state conflict

29

made it easy for the French to isolate and attack the states separately. The concern of each state with preserving its independence against all attack, local or external, was the main preoccupation. Each therefore confronted the French forces in uneven encounters in which the French forces benefited from their superior weapons and general military capability. The only known example of the African leaders making a serious attempt to organise a coalition against the French came too late to be successful. This was the coalition of states and groups, including the Tukulor empire, Jolof under Ali Buuri N'diaye, Samori, Tieba of Kenedougou, and the Bambara and Moorish groups in the Western Sudan, which fought gallantly against the French between 1889 and 1893. As has been indicated, the coalition was ineffective. One after the other, the states were conquered. With the conquest of the most redoubtable of all – Samori – in 1898, French colonisation became a reality in the Western Sudan. With similar results from French diplomatic and military assaults on African states in other areas, by 1900 the French empire in West African had emerged.

But although the French had succeeded in creating their empire, they still faced the problem of how to control it. Conquest and military occupation had been used to cow the population, but provided no reliable solution to the problem of how to administer the territories conquered. To maintain control by military means was too expensive and simply not feasible. Like all imperial powers, the French had created an empire mainly to be able to exploit the human and material resources of such territories for the benefit of the colonising state. They were eager to ensure that the cost of controlling or administering the empire was kept to the barest minimum so as to ensure maximum profit for France.

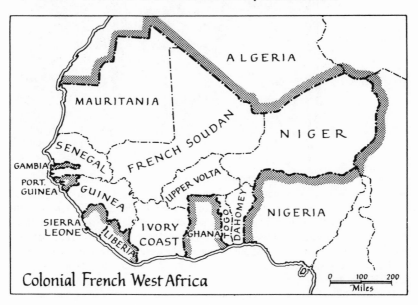

Colonial French West Africa

30

The French did not find it easy to consolidate their control over the vast area of their empire in West Africa for several reasons. First, French colonialism, being an imposed rule, did not have any concrete political and social base in the areas conquered. The peoples it set out to rule were generally against it or were at best apathetic towards it. In the circumstances, therefore, conquest and establishment of colonial rule did not mean the end of resistance against domination; it only transformed it into new forms of expression in some cases. The attempt to exploit the people and their resources for the benefit of France created new sources of discontent and bred reactions which were directed against the colonial regime. All colonialism involves the spread, to some extent, of the culture of the colonial master, who is usually eager to create among the subject people a sufficiently large number of people who accept the master's political and social institutions as well as his values. Sometimes, however, the process of spreading this imported culture led to cultural-conflict which produced violent reactions on the part of the subject people. All of these factors explain why the attempt to consolidate French colonialism in West Africa was difficult, and why the French colonial regime was haunted by fears of insecurity even after it had appeared that colonial control had been firmly established.

African reactions to the French efforts at establishing and consolidating their rule came in different forms from 1900 onwards. These differences were due to several factors. As in the period of the conquest African reactions were determined partly by the nature of inter-state relations in the pre-colonial period. There was also the fact that the mode of colonisation differed broadly between the coastal settlements in Senegal on the one hand and those which predominated in the French empire in West Africa. Local circumstances varied and therefore so did the reactions of people in such situations.

In the coastal settlements of Senegal, because of the long contact with the French, a crop of Africans had emerged with French education and some aspects of French culture. These Africans were allowed to take part in the political life of the settlements and also ultimately the political life of France. They therefore joined with the French community and the mulattoes to run the affairs of the coastal settlements. In 1914 they increased their importance when one of them – Blaise Diagne – was elected to represent Senegal in the French Chamber of Deputies in Paris.

It is possible to argue that the treatment given to the educated Africans shows evidence of the liberalism of the so-called policy of assimilation. However, there was another side to it. If this treatment were extended to all of French West Africa a very large number of Africans would have acquired political and other rights which would have made it impossible for the French to dominate them. In other words, assimilation carried to its logical conclusion would have destroyed French colonialism. The French themselves soon discovered this from the Senegal experience; consequently it was not extended to other parts of West Africa. Even in Senegal itself the local government arrangement was changed in 1920 so as to reduce the role played by the educated Africans.

31

In other areas of French West Africa the pattern of French control took a very different form. There colonialism meant a very crude repression of African liberties by autocratic French officials. African reaction to such repression naturally took a different form from what could be expected in Senegal.

In discussing African reactions in these other areas, it is necessary to bear in mind that although in some areas French military defeat had become a *fait accompli*, in some others, especially in the territories within the Sudanic belt and the Sahel region in particular, it was by no means final. In these areas, therefore, military confrontation still featured prominently in the reactions to French occupation. Up to the First World War the resistance to French rule took the form of wars in the forest states of the Ivory Coast and in Mauritania, the Timbuktu region, Upper Volta and Niger. In a sense, these areas were still being conquered. The tense military and security problem which French imperialists faced was reflected in the fact that most of these areas were put under direct military control and were designated appropriately as Military Territories. Even in areas that could be described as having recognised the fact of military defeat, reactions against French rule resulted occasionally in outbursts of armed rebellions. Examples included the Hollis Pobe region, the Bariba of Borgu and the Somba of Atacora, all in Dahomey between 1913 and 1914; of the Baoule, Akoues, Sassandra, Gouro and Lahou area in Ivory Coast from 1909 to the outbreak of the First World War, the Habe of Satadougou and the Bambara in the French Soudan, the Moors, Kounta and Tuareg of French Soudan, Mauritania and Niger from 1906 continually till the First World War. All these groups' outbursts of military confrontation against the French regime aimed at regaining their independence.

In some other areas, resistance to French rule took an ideological form. In such situations the stimulus to action was the rejection, not only of political domination, but also of the implication for the people's culture and particularly religion. Ideological movements opposing French cultural and religious domination were to be found both among the adherents of traditional religions and among Muslims. The former group was typified by the Mossi of Upper Volta, the Lobi, and the Bambara of French Soudan who were opposed to the spread among their people of both Christianity and Islam. Among the Muslims, the French administration succeeded in inducing some support. But the support which some Muslims gave the colonial regime had the effect of making the situation the more intolerable for those who sought to preserve Islam in its pure form. The desire to end the French rule – the rule of the unbeliever – led to the resurgence of Mahdism. In Islam 'Mahdi' has roughly the same meaning as the Christian 'Messiah'. It was believed that these Mahdis would rid the society of the unwanted regime and establish the government that was just and in accordance with the tenets of Islam. Expression of Mahdism was a regular feature of the anti-French reactions in the Sudanic belt of French West Africa – an area which in this respect had a good deal in common with the neighbouring British Northern Nigeria. From 1906 to the First World War, Mahdist movements were reported in several parts of the Western Sudan, Upper Guinea, Mauritania and Senegal.

Apart from Mahdism, Islam as an anti-French force was exemplified in the movements founded by Shaikh Ahmadu Bamba and Shaikh Hamallah, known as Mouridiyya and Hamalliyya respectively. The former operated mainly in Senegal, while the Hamallists covered Senegal, French Sudan, Mauritania and Niger, and were supposed to have had some influence among Muslims in Northern Nigeria.

The activities of these Islamic movements bothered the French colonial authorities to such an extent that they mobilised their intelligence service against them, using secret police usually called *Agents Politiques*, to detect the possible outbreak of resistance by any of them. Suspected leaders were often harshly treated, with punishments ranging from residential restriction, imprisonment, to banishment or deportation. With actual outbreaks of violence leaders were usually summarily tried and imprisoned, deported or in some cases shot. In normal times, the French colonial authorities tried to ensure that Islam as a political and social force was amenable to their wishes. They did this through intervening in the education of the young Muslims and their teachers by establishing or assisting in establishing schools like the one built in Jenne. Pro-French Muslims also benefitted from the patronage distributed in the form of sponsorship of pilgrimages, appointment as court judges or as village or *canton* or *cercle* chiefs. All these were to show that it paid to be pro-French. Finally a deliberate attempt was made to spread the French language at the expense of Arabic. An example of this was the ban on the use of Arabic in Native court records and its substitution by French.

As the French tried to exploit the resources of their colonies, taxation became a main instrument – particularly to raise funds to meet the cost of the colonial administration and contribute towards the cost of opening up the colonies for the exploitation of its natural resources. But excessive taxation soon became an issue which caused the people in various parts of West Africa to rebel against the colonial regime. Examples of such revolts were to be found among the Mossi in Koudougou and Fada N'Gourma in the present area of Upper Volta from 1908 to 1914, the Lobi and Dioula in the French Soudan between 1908 and 1909, in the uprising in Porto Novo in Dahomey in 1908 and in several parts of Guinea up to 1914, the Lobi and Dioula in the French Sudan between 1908 and 1909, in form of diverting trade away from French territories to neighbouring foreign colonies like the Gambia and Portuguese Guinea as was the case with the Dioula reaction against excessive levy on articles of trade. Sometimes it involved emigration as was reported from Guinea and parts of French Sudan.

One other medium of expressing anti-French reactions was the newspaper Press. This medium was only available, however, to some of the coastal societies, especially in Senegal and Dahomey, where a sufficient number of literate people existed to patronise newspapers. As education spread in the period after the First World War, the newspapers grew in number and in area covered most of French West Africa. At that stage newspapers became an important channel for spreading anti-colonial ideas and giving information on the activities of the inter-related movements involved in the resistance against French colonialism in West Africa.

33

Further Reading:

Books:

CROWDER, MICHAEL, *West Africa Under Colonial Rule,* London, 1968.

CROWDER, MICHAEL (ed.), *West African Resistance,* London, 1971.
especially 'Mali-Tukulor' by A. S. Kanya-Forstner, 'Senegambia-Mahmadou Lamine' by B. Olatunji Oloruntimehin; 'Guinea-Samori' by Yves Person and 'Dahomey' by David Ross.

HARGREAVES, JOHN D., *West Africa: The Former French States,* New Jersey, 1967.

JOHNSON, G. WESLEY, *The Emergence of Black Politics in Senegal,* Stanford, 1971.

OLORUNTIMEHIN, B. O., *The Segu Tukulor Empire,* London, 1972.

Articles:

JOHNSON, G. WESLEY, 'The Ascendancy of Blaise Diagne and the Beginning of African Politics in Senegal', *Africa,* xxxvi, 1966.

OLORUNTIMEHIN, B. O., 'Anti-French Coalition of States and Groups in the Western Sudan, 1889-93', *ODU* (New Series), No. 3, April 1970.

OLORUNTIMEHIN, B. O., 'Resistance Movements in the Tukulor Empire', *Cahiers d'Etudes Africaines,* viii, 1, 1968.

34

RESISTANCE AND COLLABORATION IN SOUTHERN AND CENTRAL AFRICA, c. 1850-1920[1]

Allen Isaacman and Barbara Isaacman

Few aspects of African history have generated as much interest or undergone as dramatic a reinterpretation as the study of resistance to colonial rule. Initially African resistance was examined from the perspective of imperial history. Passing references to it reflected the cultural arrogance and racist assumptions prevalent at the turn of the twentieth century, attitudes which subsequently were perpetuated by the colonial regimes.[2] Only in the last fifteen to twenty years has the image of Africans as passive barbarians been seriously challenged, as a more "balanced" analysis which took account of local factors began to emerge from the writings of R.E. Robinson and John Gallagher. While their identification of local pressures modified the prevailing assumptions of

[1]This paper originally was presented as the keynote address at an international conference, "African Responses to European Colonialism in Southern Africa: 1652 to the Present," held at the California State University at Northridge, 8-10 Jan. 1976. The authors are grateful to David Chanaiwa and his colleagues for the opportunity to participate in this conference. We would also like to thank James Johnson, Paul Lovejoy, Jan Vansina, Terence Ranger, Charles Van Onselen, Sue Rogers, Jeanne Penvenne, and Frederick Cooper for their penetrating criticisms of an earlier draft of this paper. We owe a special debt of gratitude to Hunt Davis for sharing both his invaluable insights and his historiographical knowledge of South Africa. We have also benefited from the criticism of our colleagues at the Centro de Estudos Africanos of the Universidade de Eduardo Mondlane, who have made us more sensitive to the role of the underclasses. We are particularly indebted to Aquino Bragança, António Noguiera de Costa, António Pacheco, Barry Munslow, Marc Wurtz, and Edward Alpers, from whom we have learned a great deal.

[2]See, for example, Harry Johnston, *A History of the Colonization of Africa by Alien Races* (London, 1899); C.P. Lucas, *A Historical Geography of the British Colonies* (London, 1894); J.S. Keltie, *The Partition of Africa* (London, 1895); Hugh Trevor Roper, "The Rise of

imperial primacy, their characterization of African resistance leaders as romantic reactionaries[3] and their "modernization bias" nevertheless were consistent with the older historiography.

John Hargreaves's article in the first issue of the *Journal of African History* represented a more substantial departure from earlier Eurocentric analysis. Hargreaves acknowledged that some African rulers were manipulated by the Europeans, but "more often they pursued clear purposes of their own—the maintenance of independence, the retention of power within their dominion, and the elimination of commercial rivals."[4] He challenged the portrayal of Africans as one-dimensional men, laying blame for this distortion on the shoulders of those who created it. "Once historians can begin to see African states not as curious museum pieces whose affairs are only intelligible to anthropologists, but as polities sharing many basic aims with governments everywhere, this whole perspective may begin to change."[5] Other contemporaries of Hargreaves acknowledged African factors, although they shared his assessment that "it is probably still desirable to give primacy in exposition to the drives and pressures which ultimately led European governments to impose their power."[6]

During the past decade a number of historians have rejected this emphasis in favor of an Afrocentric approach. Without discounting the power of the imperialists, they have argued that African initiative, adaptation, and choice played a dominant role both in the scramble and in the subsequent process of decolonization. T.O. Ranger's pioneering work raises fundamental questions about the organizational and ideological underpinnings of mass resistance movements as well as their

Christian Europe," *The Listener,* 70, 1809 (1963), 871. This premise was challenged by a number of prominent historians of Afro-American descent, most notably W.E.B. DuBois, Carter Woodson, C.L.R. James, and John Hope Franklin, and several African scholars, including C.A. Diop and K.O. Dike. Similarly, some, but not all, Marxist scholars were able to avoid the arrogance of their non-Marxist counterparts. Engels, for example, wrote sympathetically of Zulu resistance during the war of 1879. See A.B. Davidson, "African Resistance and Rebellion against the Imposition of Colonial Rule," in T.O. Ranger, ed., *Emerging Themes in African History* (Nairobi, 1968), 184.

[3] R.E. Robinson and J. Gallagher, "The Partition of Africa," in F.H. Hinsley, ed., *New Cambridge Modern History* (London, 1962), XI, 640.

[4] J.D. Hargreaves, "Toward a History of the Partition of Africa, "*Journal of African History,* I (1960), 108.

[5] *Ibid.,* 109.

[6] *Ibid.,* 113. See, for example, Roger Anstey, *Britain and the Congo in the Nineteenth Century* (London, 1962); Colin Newbury, *The Western Slave Coast and its Rulers* (London, 1962); Eric Axelson, *Portugal and the Scramble for Africa* (Johannesburg, 1967).

links to latter-day nationalist activities and the liberation struggles in southern Africa.[7] His provocative essays have influenced a number of historians, including John Illife, John Lonsdale, D.N. Beach, and ourselves, some of whom have no connection with the reputed Dar es Salaam school of nationalist historiography.[8]

Our own research on primary and early colonial resistance in Mozambique suggests that the emphasis on local initiative is fundamentally sound as long as the imperialist and capitalist context in which it occurred is made explicit. The principal deficiency of the recent resistance literature has been its emphasis on only a *select* set of reactions rather than on identifying and explaining the wide range of responses. For example, there has been a tendency to overlook the impact of African expansionist activities and collaboration on the outcome of the scramble. As a result, resistance is often depicted as the normal response to the imperialist incursions, while in reality it represented only one of several options. Furthermore, because of the emphasis on the behavior of the so-called elite, historians have failed to recognize that the decision to fight, to remain neutral, or to collaborate did not rest exclusively with the aristocracy; splits occurred not only within the ruling factions but between different social strata.[9]

---

[7]Among Ranger's most important contributions to the literature of resistance are *Revolt in Southern Rhodesia* (Evanston, 1967); *The African Voice in Southern Rhodesia* (Evanston, 1970); and "Primary Resistance Movements and Modern Mass Nationalism in East and Central Africa," *Journal of African History,* IX (1968), 437-453, 631-642.

[8]For the debate centering around the existence of such a school of historiography, see Donald Denoon and Adam Kuper, "Nationalist Historians in Search of a Nation—The New Historiography of Dar es Salaam," *African Affairs,* 69 (1970), 329-349. Ranger has written a response in *African Affairs,* 70 (1971), 50-61. Edward Steinhart has presented the most provocative criticism of the Ranger thesis in an unpublished paper, "Resistance and Nationalism: A Critique of the Ranger Hypothesis" (delivered at Syracuse University, 11 March 1971).

[9]Throughout this paper we have used the terms *social strata* or *social groupings* to indicate a socioeconomic differentiation which existed in most precolonial southern and Central African societies. Because of the absence of extensive fieldwork analyzing the organization of precapitalist economies and the related process of class formation, delineating with any certainty the actual degree of stratification in these societies is often impossible. There is no doubt that by the middle of the nineteenth century class had replaced kinship as the dominant social variable in a number of commercial societies, but in many other cases sufficient data are unavailable. The authors are currently working on a nineteenth-century social and economic history of the Zambezi Valley, examining in part the interrelationship between shifts in the dominant mode of production and class formation. The works of Catherine Coquery-Vidrovitch, Claude Meillassoux, Emmanuel Terray, and Maurice Godelier, though not in total agreement, represent an important theoretical breakthrough for an analysis of class formation. See Catherine Coquery-

To a large measure the choice of reactions which historians have studied has been determined by their implicit emphasis on racial categories, that is, the juxtaposition of European aggressors against African defenders. The resulting implication often has been that all Africans during this period were fighting to maintain or regain their independence. Such an analysis assumes *a priori* that members of a particular African society shared a common set of interests and goals, and to a lesser degree that a spirit of fraternity often linked neighboring states and chieftaincies.

Neither proposition can be sustained without explicit verification. Recent studies suggest that, even within small-scale, kinship-based societies characterized by low levels of production and generally considered to be undifferentiated, the control of the elders over the means of production often generated antagonism between generations.[10] Social heterogeneity and potential conflict were proportionately greater within the state systems of nineteenth-century Central and southern Africa where clearly differentiated social strata existed. There is no reason to accept the presumption of homogeneity within a particular African society; moreover, the success of the imperialist policy of divide and rule suggests that multi-ethnic alliances were not a common strategy among Africans.[11] This is not to argue that no African societies united with their neighbors in an effort to repel the common enemy, but rather that this strategy was only one of several options they selected.

In an effort to expand the discussion of resistance, the remainder of this essay will focus on four neglected themes: the impact of African expansionist activities on the scramble, the diversity of responses to imperialism among different strata within any given society, localized protests against the imposition of a capitalist economy, and collabora-

Vidrovitch, "Research on an African Mode of Production," in Martin Klein and G. Wesley Johnson, eds., *Perspectives on the African Past* (Boston, 1972), 33-52; Claude Meillassoux, "From Reproduction to Production—A Marxist Approach to Economic Anthropology," *Economy and Society*, I (1972), 93-105; Emmanuel Terray, "Long-Distance Exchange and the Formation of the State: The Case of the Abron Kingdom of Gyaman," *Economy and Society*, III (1974), 315-345; Emmanuel Terray, *Marxism and "Primitive" Societies*, Mary Klopper, trans. (New York, 1972); Maurice Godelier, "Modes of Production, Kinship and Demographic Structure," in Maurice Bloch, ed., *Marxist Analysis and Social Anthropology* (London, 1975), 3-29.

[10]Claude Meillassoux, *Anthropologie économique des Gouro de Côte-d'Ivoire* (Paris, 1964), 217; Georges Balandier, *Political Anthropology* (New York, 1970), 58-64.

[11]For an example of the failure to create multi-ethnic alliances in the Zambezi Valley, see Allen Isaacman, *The Tradition of Resistance in Mozambique: Anti-Colonial Activity in the Zambesi Valley, 1850-1921* (Berkeley and London, 1976), 38-39, 66-67.

tion. Although the specific case studies we have utilized will not be categorized as precolonial or colonial, the point in time in which the responses occurred limited the choices available. This essay takes in only the period before 1920. To give the discussion a degree of universality, we have selected examples from Mozambique and from other regions of southern and Central Africa.

African Expansionism and the Scramble

Although the literature on the scramble includes recurring references to conflicts between African polities, historians have generally ignored the impact of African expansionist activities on the ability and decision of affected peoples to resist. In Central and southern Africa these aggressions tended to be related to the perpetuation of preexisting territorial expansion, the rise of new conquest states dependent on European weapons and markets, or the Ngoni-Sotho diaspora.

Much of the expansionist activity which occurred on the eve of the scramble manifested territorial ambitions largely unrelated to European imperial designs. The activities of the Barue, the Bemba, and the Merina of Malagasy are but a few examples of territorial aggrandizement whose roots date back at least to the eighteenth century.[12] At the opposite extreme were the conquest states which developed as a by-product of the nineteenth-century European commercial penetration of Central Africa and the incorporation of this region into the world capitalist economy. The skyrocketing demand for ivory and slaves and the accessibility of relatively inexpensive and sophisticated firearms facilitated the creation of new conquest states such as the Chikunda-dominated polities of the Zambezi and Luangwa valleys, the Yeke state of Tippu Tib, and the Arab-Swahili enclaves of Msiri and Jumbe of Kuta.[13] These same factors enabled several existing states, including the Namarral Makua and

[12]For a discussion of Barue, Bemba, and Merina expansionism respectively, see *ibid*; Andrew Roberts, *A History of the Bemba* (Madison, 1973); and P.M. Mutibwa, *The Malagasy and the Europeans* (Atlantic Highlands, 1974).

[13]Philip Curtin has referred to these states as secondary empires because they were dependent on European firepower. For a detailed discussion of this concept, see Paul Bohannan and Philip Curtin, *Africa and Africans* (New York, 1971), 271. The differential impact of European weapons on Central African societies is discussed in A.D. Roberts, "Firearms in North-Eastern Zambia before 1900," *Transafrican Journal of History*, I (1971), 3-21.

several Yao chieftaincies, to extend their hegemony.[14] Although politically independent, these conquest states were an indirect or secondary extension of European power into the interior, justifying the term *sub-imperialist*.[15] The Ngoni-Sotho diaspora, known as the Mfecane, represents yet another nineteenth-century pattern of African conquest and absorption. In this case improvements in locally produced weapons combined with more effective infantry organization shifted the balance of power as dramatically as had the massive introduction of European arms, resulting in the conquest of a large portion of southern and Central Africa.[16]

The scale of indigenous conquests, which seems to have increased dramatically during the nineteenth century, radically altered the political map of Central and southern Africa by destroying or weakening existing states and creating new multi-ethnic polities. This transformation in turn had a profound impact on the types of African responses to European imperialism. In a number of cases expansionist activities weakened local polities; not only did they reduce their potential capacity to resist, they actually motivated several states to seek the protection of European states. The losses which the Herero repeatedly suffered at the hands of the Nama and Oorlams left them vulnerable to German occupation.[17] To the north, the predatory raids of the Chikunda, Yao, and Ngoni so incapacitated the centralized kingdoms of Undi and Kalonga that they were unable or unwilling to challenge British claims to the homelands.[18]

[14]Jan Vansina, *Kingdoms of the Savanna* (Madison, 1966), 228-242; Nancy J. Hafkin, "Trade, Society and Politics in Northern Mozambique, ca. 1753-1913" (unpublished Ph.D. dissertation, Boston University, 1973), 366-367; Edward A. Alpers, *Ivory and Slaves: Changing Patterns of International Trade in East Central Africa to the Later Nineteenth Century* (Berkeley and London, 1975), 251-252.

[15]This term was first advanced by A.D. Roberts, "The Sub-Imperialism of Buganda," *Journal of African History,* III (1962), 435-450.

[16]For a general overview of the Mfecane, see J.D. Omer-Cooper, *The Zulu Aftermath* (Evanston, 1966). Recent evidence suggesting the economic and ecological basis for different aspects of the Mfecane has been advanced by Alan Smith, "The Trade of Delagoa Bay as a Factor in Ngoni Politics," in Leonard Thompson, ed., *African Societies in Southern Africa* (New York, 1969), 171-189, and Jeff Guy, "Destruction of a Pre-Capitalist Economy: A Zulu Case Study" (unpublished paper). We are grateful to Charles Van Onselen for information about the last work.

[17]Helmut Bley, *South-West African under German Rule, 1894-1914* (London, 1971), 6; I. Goldblatt, *History of South-West Africa* (Capetown, 1971), 11.

[18]Harry Langworthy, "A History of the Undi to 1890" (unpublished Ph.D. dissertation, Boston University, 1969), 258-302; Kings Mbacazwa Phiri, "Chewa History in Central Malawi and the Use of Oral Tradition, 1600-1920" (unpublished Ph.D. dissertation, University of Wisconsin, 1975), 177-202.

Other intimidated peoples collaborated with the European forces in an effort to gain protection against future incursions by surrounding powers. The Sena, fearing renewed Barue attacks, aided the Portuguese in the 1902 war,[19] while the Yao raids motivated Chikuse and his followers to assist the British in Nyasaland in their efforts to "pacify" the Yao.[20]

The destruction of a number of Central and southern African polities as a result of inter-African rivalries had far-reaching, though by no means uniform, effects on the nature of local responses to European incursions. Predatory raids often made the central authority too weak to contain the centrifugal tendencies of their outlying provinces. The outcome was a proliferation of smaller autonomous chieftaincies with no shared allegiance who proved incapable of resisting European penetration. This political fractionation reduced the likelihood of united anticolonial campaigns, and increased the possibility that the European powers could successfully pursue a strategy of divide and rule. The destruction of the Manganja kingdom of Lundu and the Rozvi dynasty, for example, left power vacuums into which the European forces moved easily.[21] Other smaller polities, fearing outright annexation, collaborated with the various European states in the hope of maintaining their newly acquired independence. Gaza Ngoni invasions of the lower Zambezi Valley destroyed many large *prazos*, thereby freeing a number of Tonga and Sena chieftaincies who allied with the Portuguese in exchange for promises of protection.[22]

Expansionist forces also conquered existing polities and incorporated them into their burgeoning empires. Although José Fernandes Júnior has argued that the size and military capacity of these states enabled them to withstand European incursions more effectively than their predecessors, this was not always the case.[23] The critical factor appears

---

[19]Isaacman, *Tradition of Resistance*, 66-67.

[20]Anthony J. Dachs, "Politics of Collaboration: Imperialism in Practice," in B. Pachai, ed., *The Early History of Malawi* (London, 1972), 288-289.

[21]Matthew Schoeffeleers, "The History and Political Role of the M'Bona Cult among the Mang'anja," in T.O. Ranger and Isaria Kimambo, eds., *The Historical Study of African Religion* (Berkeley, 1972), 82-87; D.N. Beach, "Ndebele Raiders and Shona Power," *Journal of African History*, XV (1974), 637.

[22]Allen Isaacman, *Mozambique: The Africanization of a European Institution, the Zambesi Prazos, 1750-1902* (Madison, 1972), 22, 122-123.

[23]T.O. Ranger, "African Reactions to the Imposition of Colonial Rule in East and Central Africa," in L.H. Gann and Peter Duignan, eds., *Colonialism in Africa* (London, 1969), I, 296.

to have been not the size of the empire but the loyalty of the subject peoples. The inability or unwillingness of many conquest states to integrate the indigenous populations compelled alien rulers to govern through force. Intimidation merely intensified the level of hostility and the frequency of insurrection, however. Thus on the eve of the scramble the Gaza Ngoni faced a major uprising from the Inhambane Tonga,[24] the Taware sought to overthrow the Chikunda,[25] the Lakeside Tonga and Tumbuka challenged Mbwela Ngoni rule,[26] and a number of Shona chieftaincies were hostile toward their Ndebele overlords.[27] These manifestations compelled the aristocracy to expend much of their energies controlling the subject populations, thereby weakening their defensive ·capabilities. Furthermore, when the actual confrontations began, large numbers of the oppressed either fled or defected to the Europeans. In the first situation the conquest state was reduced in size and fighting capacity, while in the second the proportionate reduction in strength was even greater because of the influx of new allies for the Europeans. Neither outcome lent itself to the formation of broad-based anticolonial alliances necessary to counter the technological advantage of the invading colonial forces.

These expansionist activities did not always have a divisive effect, however. Several conquest states either successfully incorporated the indigenous population or created new supra-ethnic polities to replace fragmented chieftaincies. The Sotho expansion under Sekonyela, Mzilikazi's Ndebele state, the Zambezian empire of Massangano, the Makololo polity in the Shire Valley, the confederation of Yao and Malawian peoples under Makanjila, and the Bemba kingdom are examples of effective expansion.[28] Although this process did not automatically generate resistance, it enabled these societies to defend themselves more effectively or to negotiate from a position of strength.

[24]Douglas Wheeler, "Gungunyane the Negotiator: A Study in African Diplomacy," *Journal of African History,* IX (1968), 586.

[25]José Fernandes Júnior, "Narração do Districto de Tete" (unpublished manuscript, Makanga, 1955), 25-27.

[26]Keith Rennie, "The Ngoni States and European Intrusion," in Erick Stokes and Richard Brown, eds., *The Zambesian Past* (Manchester, 1966), 310-311.

[27]Beach, "Ndebele Raiders," 263.

[28]William Lye, "The Distribution of the Sotho Peoples after the Difaqane," in Thompson, *African Societies,* 192; W.H.J. Rangeley, "The Makololo of Dr. Livingstone," *Nyasaland Journal,* XVI (1963), 32-42; Isaacman, *Mozambique,* 138-147; Dachs, "Politics of Collaboration," 289.

In fact, all but the Bemba engaged in armed confrontation against European forces, and in the Bemba case the untimely death of Mwamba III probably explains their ultimate submission with only a minimal amount of resistance.[29]

Apart from these examples of effective incorporation, there were a few instances in which external threats or temporary annexation ultimately led to a strengthening of the centralized political machinery and military capabilities of particular African societies. In part the Ngoni incursions intensified the process by which power became concentrated within one Bemba royal lineage (*miti*), while the successful Lozi insurrection against the Kololo precipitated a restructuring of the kingdom.[30] To the south, Moshoeshoe capitalized on the precarious position of the fragmented Sotho chieftaincies to create a Sotho nation.[31]

Although further research is necessary, the evidence suggests that African expansionist activities were both a vital factor in the nineteenth-century political history of southern and Central Africa and profoundly altered the outcome of the scramble. Conquests affected the scale and number of polities within this region, and on balance facilitated the European expansion.

The Diversity of Internal Responses to Imperialism

To date, the study of resistance has been extremely elitist, a bias contemporary African historians share with their Eurocentric predecessors. While the latter presented Gungunyane, Cetshwayo, Lobenguela, and Moshoeshoe as blood-thirsty tyrants, it has been extremely fasionable more recently to focus on the heroic exploits of these men.[32] This shift from tyrant to hero might be more gratifying and more historically accurate, but it nevertheless creates a distorted and oversimplified picture in which all other strata of society are reduced to non-entities, a characteristic common to all so-called Great-Man views

---

[29]Roberts, *History of the Bemba*, 217.

[30]*Ibid.*, 124, 144-146, 370-376; Gerald Caplin, *The Elites of Barotseland* (Berkeley, 1970), 39-40; Mutumba M. Bull, "Lewanika's Achievement," *Journal of African History*, XIII (1972), 463-472.

[31]Lye, "Distribution," 198.

[32]Two examples of the blood-thirsty-tyrant school, both written by Peter Becker, are *Path of Blood: The Rise and Conquests of Mzilikazi, Founder of the Matabele* (London, 1962), and *Rule of Fear: The Life and Times of Dingane, King of the Zulu* (London, 1964). Among the best of the new biographies are Leonard Thompson, *Survival in Two Worlds: Moshoeshoe of Lesotho, 1786-1870* (New York, 1975), and Peter Saunders, *Moshoeshoe, Chief of the Sotho* (London, 1975).

of history.[33]

By this we do not mean to say that aristocracies were not important; rather, the assumption that they unilaterally defined the response of a particular society to the European encroachments cannot be justified by the literature. While the dominant minority perhaps possessed a monopoly of power or a shared set of interests which might have momentarily bound them and their subjects, these assumptions must be investigated on a case-by-case basis rather than being accepted uncritically. Such an investigation is complicated by the inherent bias of most historical data. Just as European accounts, whether government reports or travelogues, dealt almost exclusively with kings and chiefs, so official traditions almost invariably serve to legitimize the position of the royal family.[34]

Despite the state ideology of sacred kingship, which legitimized the position of the king, rulers in southern and Central Africa rarely enjoyed absolute power. In fact, a great range of political roles existed throughout the region. The Tswana chiefs, for example, recognized that their authority stemmed from the people,[35] a principle of government that had its antithesis among the Ngoni states. Between these two extremes were a variety of political structures and philosophies. Although differing in detail, all systems allowed their rulers to be deposed for transgressing the bounds of authority. Indeed, nineteenth-century history is replete with examples of powerful leaders who were overthrown, such as Shaka and Lewanika. While historians have described these *coups d'état* exclusively in elitist terminology by labeling them succession crises, the transfer could not have occurred without the support of at least a portion of the subject population. In addition to their emphasis on royal intrigue, these upheavals were thought to reflect religious differences and regional conflicts. Such factors were undoubtedly important, but even here historians have overemphasized the primacy of local elites in the struggle against the central authorities.

[33]As the Soviet historian A.B. Davidson has noted: "In concentrating on the personality it is possible to miss the law of social development. It must not be forgotten that in African countries and all over the world the motive force in history was the people." Davidson, "African Resistance," 186. While non-Marxist scholars may take issue with Davidson's law of social development, there can be little disagreement that the role of various strata and classes is absent from most of the resistance literature.

[34]See Jan Vansina's seminal work, *Oral Traditions* (London, 1961), for an analysis of this self-legitimating function.

[35]Harry Saker and J. Aldrige, "The Origins of the Langeberg Rebellion," *Journal of African History,* XII (1971), 303. The abstract authority of the people is a common component of sacred kingship. The ruler acquires legitimacy in part from the fiction that his authority comes from and represents the will of the people.

Conspicuously absent is a discussion of class factors, a deficiency which characterizes the historiography of precolonial Africa in general. Those who have recognized the existence of cleavages within African societies have analyzed them in terms of such vaguely defined political categories as *mass* and *elite*. The failure of most scholars, including ourselves, [36] to consider carefully the process of class formation during the nineteenth century makes it impossible to examine the role of the underclasses in the early resistance struggles. It is more fruitful, for example, to hypothesize that different social strata (peasants, slaves, caste members, merchants, and aristocrats) were motivated by their perceived self-interests rather than an abstract loyalty to the state. Only within such a framework can we begin to comprehend the complexity of responses to European imperialism and colonialism.

Marxist historians of West Africa have recently demonstrated that even precolonial "subsistence"-based economies were characterized by social hierarchies, and that the growth of long-distance trade, independently or in conjunction with slave labor, intensified these class divisions. [37] Although similar investigations analyzing precolonial social configurations in Central and southern Africa have not yet been published, the fragmentary data suggest that class structures had progressively assumed precedence over communal ones in such disparate societies as the Malagasy, Ovambo, Tswana, Kassanje, Makua, and Kuba by the middle of the nineteenth century. [38] Moreover, in South Africa, where capitalist penetration was far more advanced, agri-

[36] In an effort to remedy this deficiency in our own research, we have begun a several-year project analyzing the social and economic history of the Zambezi Valley during the nineteenth century. This work is being done collectively with other members of a research brigade of the Centro de Estudos Africanos of the Universidade de Eduardo Mondlane.

[37] See Coquery-Vidrovitch, "Research on an African Mode of Production"; Meillassoux, "From Reproduction to Production"; Terray, "Long-Distance Exchange and the Formation of the State"; Godelier, "Modes of Production, Kinship and Demographic Structure."

[38] Mutibwa, *Malagasy,* 9-11; W.G. Clarence-Smith and R. Moorsom, "Underdevelopment and Class Formation in Ovamboland, 1845-1915," *Journal of African History,* XVI (1975), 377; Saker and Aldrige, "Origins," 304; Joseph C. Miller, "Slaves, Slavers and Social Change in Nineteenth-Century Kasanje," in Franz-Wilhelm Heimer, ed., *Social Change in Angola* (Munich, 1973), 23-26. The information on the Kuba comes from personal communication with Jan Vansina (30 Sept. 1976). As in the West African example, this class development generally seems to be related to the expansion of long-distance trade, with the Kuba case an exception. For an extremely important article which treats this question in Central Africa, see J.L. Vellut, "Le Lunda et la frontière Luso-Africaine, 1708-1906," *Études d'Histoire Africaine,* III (1972), 61-116.

culturalists and cattle keepers had been transformed into peasants and proletariat before the imposition of colonial rule.[39] The migration of the Mfengu into the Ciskei in 1835, for example, marks the emergence of a substantial peasant community.[40]

Given the absence of a homogeneous society, there is no reason to assume *a priori* that the impetus for resistance came from the leaders and that the "people" followed blindly. On the contrary, scattered examples suggest that a far more complex explanation is necessary. Unfortunately, however, the present state of the literature often makes it impossible to identify all the operative social strata and the factors which motivated each segment to choose from among various options. Limitations in our data necessitate a reliance on broad political cleavages in our discussion of the early phase of resistance. After the imposition of colonial rule we can much more easily identify the economic forces which underlay both class differentiation and the decision of whether or not to challenge the colonial system.

At the highest level of generalization, the decision to resist can be seen as a result of one of the following types of internal conflict:[41] (1) where the ruling aristocracy initially refused to resist but was compelled by one or more strata within the society to adopt a more militant posture; (2) where the political leadership refused to resist and was deposed by anticolonial militants who carried on the struggle; (3) where the rulers surrendered to the colonial authorities but at least one group in the society continued to resist; and (4) where an unpopular and exploitative segment of the aristocracy opted to resist in defense of its privileged position but confronted opposition from its oppressed subjects.

For reasons ranging from self-aggrandizement to concern for their peoples' survival, many African leaders sought to avoid armed confrontations. Their willingness to cooperate with the imperialist forces often produced a crisis of authority when the decision did not reflect the desires of a part or all of their subordinates. Thus in the Zambezian state

[39]Colin Bundy, "The Emergence and Decline of a South African Peasantry," *African Affairs,* LXXI (1972), 369-388.

[40]*Ibid.,* 373.

[41]Within this general framework it is important to note that one social stratum, like merchants, might find it in their interest to support the aristocracy's decision not to resist, while the peasants, for example, could simultaneously opt to resist because of the anticipated economic impact of taxation. Other configurations were also likely to have occurred, reflecting different economic interests which often generated competition between different social strata.

of Makanga, popular concern that the ruler, Chicucuru II, would acquiesce to Lisbon's demands and provide several thousand conscripts to serve the Companhia de Mocambique precipitated a public outcry against him. At the high point of the confrontation, one respected dissident denounced Chicucuru's timidity, "declaring that he must stand ashamed a chief who lacks the respect of the elders, who is governed rather than governs, none can exempt him from responsibility for all that has occurred."[42] After this public demonstration, which contained a veiled threat that he would be removed, Chicucuru reluctantly agreed to terminate his ties with the Portuguese. A similar cleavage occurred within Tswana society. In 1878 King Moremi II decided to convert to Christianity and forge an alliance with the missionaries. Although internal opposition to his policy has been explained in terms of a popular reaction to European cultural penetration, new evidence suggests that the privileged strata, especially the aristocracy and wealthy farmers, were principally motivated by the fear "that the Christian doctrine of human equality might inspire the serfs to revolt."[43] Within a decade internal pressures compelled Moremi to abandon both Christianity and his dependence on the missionaries. His explanation to the missionaries reflected his difficult position:

> I know that your words are good words, and that it is a blessing to any town to have the people of God therein. . . . So I know that it is right to serve God, and to build the town with God's words. But, for my part, I Moremi, wish to stand in the teaching, but many of my people refuse to do so.[44]

Similarly, Cetshwayo could not possibly have met the British demands that he disband the Zulu age regiments and surrender without being ousted himself.[45]

Colonialism often exacerbated the tensions between the indigenous aristocracy, many of whom were coopted into the alien regime, and their nominal subordinates. A number of chiefs were initially reluctant to

---

[42]Arquivo Histórico de Moçambique, Maputo [hereafter AHM], Fundo do Século XIX, Tete, Governo do Distrito, Cx. 11: Augusto Fonseca de Mesquita e Solla to Governo do Distrito de Tete (15 April 1888).

[43]Thomas Tlou, "The Batawana of Northwestern Botswana and Christian Missionaries: 1877-1906," *Transafrican Journal of History,* III (1973), 119.

[44]Cited in *ibid.*

[45]Leonard Thompson, "The Subjection of the African Chiefdoms, 1870-1898," in Monica Wilson and Leonard Thompson, eds., *Oxford History of South Africa* (London, 1971), II, 265.

challenge the colonial system because they feared losing their privileged positions. Perhaps the best examples are the two Barue pretenders to the throne just prior to the 1917 rebellion. In the face of mounting opposition to Portuguese forced-labor abuses from returning workers, both Nongwe-Nongwe and Makosa reluctantly agreed to ask the Portuguese to desist from such actions. But their timidity alienated both the peasants and the conscripts, who supported the spirit medium (*svikiro*) Mbuya's call for armed insurrection. Nongwe-Nongwe ultimately joined the movement when it became clear that this was the only way he could gain the throne.[46]

The Bambatha, or Zulu, uprising of 1906 is another example of pressure from the peasants and rural workers which compelled the leadership to adopt an anticolonial posture. Bambatha initially cooperated with government requests for a higher poll tax despite the increased financial pressure which it placed on his overburdened constitutents. His decision met with substantial opposition from his younger and more militant followers, who urged him to resist the government demands. This internal pressure and the decision of European officials to replace him motivated Bambatha to lead a popular insurrection. As one participant stated afterward, "happy are those who fought and are dead."[47]

Despite the sacred character of kingship, in at least a few documented cases the leadership was deposed after it had acquiesced in the demands of the colonial forces. In 1887, for example, Chatara, ruler of Massangano, was stripped of his authority after he agreed to renounce independence. His successor, Mtontora, was selected only after he pledged to renew the military campaign against Lisbon. Although the senior spirit medium, in conjunction with a faction of the ruling aristocracy, precipitated the *coup d'etat*, the fear of Portuguese rule generated wide-ranging support for this action.[48] Fifteen years later an alliance between Maramba peasants and the spirit medium Kageo led to the removal of the local ruler when he refused to participate in the 1901

---

[46]Interviews with Makosa (12 July 1972), Dendera (18 July 1972), Samacande (21 and 27 July 1972), Sherin (31 July 1972), and Blacken Makombe (2 Aug. 1972).

[47]Shula Marks, "The Zulu Disturbance in Natal," in Robert I. Rotberg and Ali A. Mazrui, eds., *Protest and Power in Black Africa* (New York, 1970), 235-238. For a more complete analysis of the Bambatha rebellion and related forms of resistance, see Shula Marks, *Reluctant Rebellion: The 1906-1908 Disturbances in Natal* (London, 1970).

[48]Augusto de Castilho, *Relatória de Guerra da Zambézia em 1888* (Lisbon, 1891), 9-10.

Shona insurrection.[49] While both examples reflect a temporary convergence of interests between different social strata,[50] there are also examples of oppressed peasants and workers who independently took the initiative against rulers committed to the perpetuation of the colonial regime. On the eve of the 1917 pan-Zambezian rebellion, for example, several coopted Tawara and Senaland chiefs were deposed by their subjects, who had suffered from Lisbon's forced labor practices and high taxation.[51]

Despite instances where anticolonial militants succeeded, the ruling aristocracy quashed insurrections on numerous occasions. The abortive 1884 coup against Lewanika[52] and Gungunyane's ability to contain aggressive *nduna* and rival claimants illustrate the power advantage of the incumbents, which was often buttressed by their subsequent alliance with the colonial regimes.[53] The commitment and power of the nonruling strata are most dramatically illustrated where militants continued the struggle long after the leadership had capitulated. Malagasy rebels, for example, denounced Queen Ranavalona II and her aides for their token resistance to the French invaders. The insurgents moved into the countryside and organized the 1896 Menalamba rebellion, which was directed against both the French and the coopted members of the royal family.[54] The Tswana peasants who participated in the Langeberg insurrection against the orders of King Molala shared a similar commitment to be free,[55] as did their counterparts in southern Mozambique who engaged in the Maguiguane rebellion only a year after their leader, Gungunyane, had surrendered and been sent into exile.[56]

[49]Rhodesian National Archives, Salisbury [hereafter RNA], RC 334: H.M. Taberer to Sir Marshall Clarke (18 June 1901).

[50]While it might be argued that the prominent role of spirit mediums represented the substitution of a member of the religious leadership for his secular counterpart, the spirit mediums did not assume direct political authority. Moreover, the evidence clearly suggests that, rather than precipitating the confrontation, the religious mediums simply reflected the opinion of the oppressed, who were predisposed to armed insurrection. Ranger has come to a similar conclusion in his analysis of the revolutionary role of spirit mediums throughout southern and Central Africa. See Ranger, "African Reactions," 313-315.

[51]Isaacman, *Tradition of Resistance*, 163-173.

[52]Caplan, *Elites*, 28-34.

[53]Wheeler, "Gungunyane," 585-602.

[54]Mutibwa, *Malagasy*, 363-365.

[55]Saker and Aldrige, "Origins," 312.

[56]José Justino Texeira Botelho, *História Militar e Política dos Portugueses em Moçambique* (Lisbon, 1936), II, 533-547.

The tenacious four-year-long efforts of the Barue guerrillas after the 1917 rebellion against the Portuguese was officially quashed demonstrated the willingness of militant Zambezian peasants to resist at all costs, a tradition which was preserved among their descendants who supported FRELIMO.[57]

While the cooption of the ruling aristocracy and the anticolonial militancy of their subjects has more often been emphasized, the reverse pattern, although rarer, should not be ignored. In at least a few instances the aristocracy adopted an anticolonial posture in order to defend its privileged position but found itself without popular support. This fractionization is best documented in repressive slave-holding regimes, societies with large slave populations, although other forms of exploitation presumably generated similar alienation. In the Zumbo states of Matakenya and Kanyemba, the authoritarian rule of the leaders and their large-scale slave-exporting activities precipitated growing internal opposition highlighted by rebellions in 1887. These uprisings severely limited the ability of the leadership to resist the Portuguese invaders.[58] In the Congo, a number of subject peoples cooperated with the Belgians to free themselves from their Arab and Yeke slave-trading rulers.[59] The tendency of the Mbelwa, Maseko, and Mpenseni aristocracies to enslave many of their subjects and to expropriate the agricultural production of others suggests a convergence of ethnicity and class interests and helps to explain the reluctance of the local population to support them against the advancing colonial forces.[60] There are also

---

[57]Throughout the colonial period Zambezian elders defiantly transmitted accounts of African resistance, which served as a source of pride and a model for future activity. Spirit mediums and cult priests sanctified and enshrined these heroic efforts. As late as 1972 the legacy of resistance was a vital and living part of Zambezian oral traditions. Not surprisingly, therefore, well before liberation forces had entered the region, FRELIMO officials acknowledged that "many of our young people have already crossed the Zambesi and joined our forces in the Northern part." Perhaps the most fitting recognition of the contribution of the Mozambicans living in the Zambezi Valley comes from President Samora Machel, who noted that they had given FRELIMO stronger backing than any other ethnic group. See *Mozambique Revolution*, XXXXIV (1970), 4; Adrian Hastings, "Some Reflections upon the War in Mozambique," *African Affairs*, LXXIII (1974), 268. In his excellent study of the struggle in Angola, Basil Davidson notes a similar tradition of resistance. See *In the Eye of the Storm* (New York, 1974), 20.

[58]Isaacman, *Tradition of Resistance*, 22-29.

[59]Vansina, *Kingdoms*, 227-235.

[60]Phiri, "Chewa History," 154-156; Rennie, "Ngoni States," 310-311; J.A. Barnes, *Politics in Changing Society* (Manchester, 1967), 26, 87-88. Dachs has noted a similar relationship in southern Malawi: "Above all the alien administration was able to exploit

indications that similar cleavages in the slave-trading societies along the north Mozambican coast may have ultimately undercut the ability of the leaders to maintain popular support for the anti-Portuguese revolts designed to preserve their monopoly of wealth and power.[61]

Early Localized Resistance against Capitalism

Unlike precolonial resistance, whose major aim was to maintain independence, resistance by workers and peasants during the early colonial period was directly motivated by the imposition of capitalism and the related attempts by the colonial regimes to exploit the human and natural resources of Central and southern Africa.[62] The oppressed protested in a variety of ways. In some cases they organized broad-based strikes or armed insurrections. More commonly, however, they manifested their opposition through small-scale atomized actions. Because these protests were rarely perceived as a threat to the·colonial system and tended to be extremely short-lived, they have been ignored by contemporaries and historians alike.[63] Despite more than fifteen

the conflict of interests between the settled agricultural population and the military trading elements, especially among the Yao groups, where the conflict often corresponded to a large extent with the ethnic differences between immigrant Yao and the indigenous Nyanja." See Dachs, "Politics of Collaboration," 285.

[61]"The leaders of the revolts desired to preserve their monopoly on the exploitation of the African population. The rulers of the shaikhdoms, chiefdoms and sultanates were essentially parasitic in their relationship to the African land and people. Producing little themselves, they had no organic relationship with the regimes in which they were situated. The revolts were reactionary in the sense that they represented the strivings of an elite to preserve a situation in which they alone profited." Hafkin, "Trade, Society and Politics," 399.

[62]Despite differences in detail, the colonial regimes shared the same ultimate objective: acquisition of cheap exports through the exploitation of African labor and natural resources. Efforts to create and control a labor reserve were particularly extensive and repressive in Central and southern Africa because of the great mineral wealth and the rapid development of plantation agriculture. The imposition of hut and head taxes, the use of labor recruiters and police to intimidate the rural population, the dispossession of entire communities, and the implementation of vagrancy laws characterized these labor-coercive economies. While the highest priority was placed on supplying migrant labor for plantations and mines, in backwater regions lacking well-endowed natural resources or extensive European capital emphasis was simultaneously given to the exploitation of peasant production. In Mozambique, for example, the undercapitalized and highly speculative *companhias* derived their profits not only by exporting cheap labor and subletting land but by acquiring peasant agricultural production at depressed prices.

[63]The principal exceptions are the numerous articles of Van Onselen, his *Chibaro* (London, 1976), and a recent paper by Robin Cohen, "Hidden Forms of Labor Protest in Africa" (delivered at a conference on inequality in Africa, Mt. Kisko, 6-9 Oct. 1976).

peasant revolts among the Sena and Tonga between 1888 and 1905[64] and their subsequent refusal to pay taxes and obey the Portuguese authorities, the British consul, R.C.F. Maugham, nevertheless concluded in 1909 that:

> It goes without saying that the Valley of the Zambesi has entered upon a prolonged, indeed, there is every reason to believe a permanent, state of peace. It is many years since the last armed outbreak took place and as time goes on and the native comes more clearly to comprehend the advantages they derive from the European protection and teachings, any smouldering feeling of discontent, impatience or restraint will finally die away and disappear.[65]

Maugham's assessment of the situation and his predictions for the future were totally incorrect. Rather, day-to-day resistance, withdrawal, social banditry, and peasant revolts occurred with regularity and constituted an early manifestation of class conflict in the Zambezi Valley and the adjacent regions of Central and southern Africa.

Like the slaves in the American South, many oppressed workers covertly retaliated against the colonial economic system. Because both groups lacked any significant power, direct confrontation was not often a viable strategy. Instead, the African peasants and workers expressed their hostility through tax evasion, work slowdowns, and destruction of European property. The dominant European population, as in the United States, perceived these forms of day-to-day resistance as *prima facie* evidence of the docility and ignorance of their subordinates rather than as expressions of discontent.[66]

Tax evasion was a recurring form of protest throughout all of southern and Central Africa. Just before the arrival of the tax collectors, all or most of the villagers would flee into an inaccessible region and stay there until the official left. One disgruntled Rhodesian noted in 1904 that a number of Shona polities "never paid taxes and are reported to be in a very wild state." He went on to observe that "the natives invariably run away on the approach of the police or messengers and would appear to be

---

[64]Isaacman, *Tradition of Resistance,* 115-118.

[65]R.C.F. Maugham, *Zambezia* (London, 1910), 307.

[66]For the pioneering work on day-to-day resistance, see Raymond A. Bauer and Alice H. Bauer, "Day-to-Day Resistance to Slavery," *Journal of Negro History,* XXVII (1942), 388-419. Further insights on this subject can be found in John W. Blassingame's *The Slave Community* (New York, 1972), and Eugene Genovese's *Roll Jordan Roll* (New York, 1974).

ill disposed toward both the Portuguese and British administrators."[67] His concerns were echoed by a Portuguese colonial agent, who conceded that "it remains unknown how many times six or more adults will flee from their kraal leaving only ill or elderly individuals who are exempt from taxes."[68] In Northern Rhodesia the Gwembe Tonga were notoriously successful in avoiding tax payments, as were their Bisa and Unga neighbors, who annually fled into the Bangwelu swamps,[69] while the Bambatha rebellion highlights the recurring opposition in South Africa.[70] Perhaps the most extreme reaction was that of a number of peasants in Rhodesia, who slaughtered their cattle rather than allow them to be confiscated as punishment for failing to satisfy their tax obligations.[71]

Conscripted agricultural and industrial workers developed a number of techniques to avoid, minimize, or protest the abuses of forced labor. On occasion villagers took up arms and drove recruiters off their land. Although this tactic invariably produced a violent reaction from colonial officials, such incidents were reported in South Africa, Southern Rhodesia, Angola, Nyasaland, and Northern Rhodesia.[72] Fear of an insurrection in Natal in 1854, for example, compelled the government to temporarily discontinue forced labor.[73] Other laborers refused to report unless they received specific guarantees about their working conditions and salaries. A recruiter for the Cape railroad noted that "great difficulties are experienced in the procurement of native labourers and the Kaffirs throughout the country have virtually combined to demand a higher rate than the 1s 6d per day ration—the term originally contemplated."[74]

[67]RNA, LO 5/5/28, General Letter A259; Assistant Native Commissioner, North Mazoe, "Report for Month Ended 30th September 1904."

[68]Alfredo Augusto Caldas Xavier, *Estudos Coloniaes* (Nova Goa, 1889), 25-26.

[69]Robert I. Rotberg, *The Rise of Nationalism in Central Africa* (Cambridge, Mass.), 75; Henry S. Meebelo, *Reaction to Colonialism* (Manchester, 1971), 97-98.

[70]Marks, "Zulu Disturbance."

[71]Charles Van Onselen, "The Role of Collaborators in the Rhodesian Mining Industry, 1900-1935," *African Affairs*, LXXII (1973), 411.

[72]*Ibid.*, 413-414; Meebelo, *Reaction to Colonialism*, 91-93; John Marcum, *The Angolan Revolution* (Cambridge, Mass., 1969),53-54; David Welsh, *The Roots of Segregation: Native Policy in Natal (1845-1910)* (Capetown, 1971), 122-127, 271-273.

[73]Welsh, *Roots of Segregation.*

[74]Quoted in A.H. Purkis, "The Terms of Labour on the Cape Railway" (delivered at the workshop on the social and economic history of southern Africa, Oxford University, 4 Sept. 1974), 4.

On-the-job opposition took a variety of forms. A Southern Rhodesian annual report on public health acknowledged that mine workers often "refused or neglected to do work, showed gross carelessness in handling tools, were impertinent and willfully destroyed compound huts and other property."[75] Similar complaints were made of railroad and mine workers in South Africa,[76] of agricultural laborers of the Companhia de Moçambique and the Companhia de Zambezia,[77] and of conscripts employed on state projects in Northern Rhodesia.[78] Other laborers deserted *en masse*, thereby avoiding a confrontation. Of the eight thousand workers recruited by the Rhodesian labor board between October 1900 and March 1901, more than twenty-five percent fled.[79] In 1906 forty-five thousand Africans were charged with desertion under South Africa's Masters and Servants Act.[80] Nine years later, Portuguese state officials and concessionary companies were able to recruit only three hundred of the five thousand porters which the governor of Tete ordered, and all of them fled before reaching their final destination.[81] Such lack of cooperation, along with the high rate of absenteeism, was perceived by the Europeans as just another example of the inherently slothful nature of the Africans. As one Portuguese official observed:

> None of them flees on account of bad treatment, nor do they have the slightest justifiable reason.... Thus, I am left to conclude that the great reluctance which almost all of them exhibit toward work has been the sole cause of their fleeing the services in question.[82]

Conscripted laborers were not the only oppressed people who fled. Peasants often expressed their discontent by migrating in the illusory search for a more benign form of colonialism. Although the clandestine nature of the exodus precludes any accurate assessment of its scale, there are suggestions that it was substantial. Official British records indicate

[75]Quoted in Charles Van Onselen, "Worker Consciousness in Black Miners: Southern Rhodesia, 1900-1920," *Journal of African History,* XIV (1973), 250.

[76]Purkis, "Terms," 6; Marks, *Reluctant Rebellion,* 132-134; Shelia T. Van der Horst, *Native Labour in South Africa* (London, 1971), 144-147.

[77]Isaacman, *Tradition of Resistance,* ch. 5.

[78]Meebelo, *Reaction to Colonialism,* 102-103.

[79]Van Onselen, "Worker Consciousness," 245.

[80]Cited in Marks, *Reluctant Rebellion,* 133, note 4.

[81]Arquivo da Companhia de Moçambique, formerly located in Lisbon [hereafter ACM], 3705: Governor to Companhia de Moçambique (18 April 1917); RNA, RC 3/1/28, Adm. 835: Telegram from Major Spain to S.O. (4 April 1917).

[82]AHM, Fundo do Século XIX, Cx. 4-185, M. 37: António Gomes to Sub-Intendente do Governo em Macequene (18 Nov. 1916).

that more than fifty thousand Africans living in the Zambezi Valley fled into Rhodesia and Malawi between 1895 and 1907.[83] The existence of a common or related ethnic group across the frontier facilitated the withdrawal of Ovambo and Bakongo from Angola as well as Shona and Chewa from Mozambique.[84] Similarly, around the turn of the century large numbers of Lakeside Tonga and Tumbuka migrated from the Rukuru watershed in Nyasaland to areas outside the sphere of British control to avoid paying taxes.[85]

Formation of refugee communities in backwater areas represented a variant of the withdrawal strategy. Rather than crossing international boundaries, the peasants, many of whom had refused to satisfy their so-called legal responsibilities, created autonomous enclaves in the interior. This phenomenon occurred with some regularity in northeastern Zambia among *mitanda*, or bush dwellers, who "attained a kind of independence which they fiercely and jealously guarded."[86] Similar communities developed in the Gambo region of southern Angola, which became a hideout for outlaws and disenchanted, and in the rugged Gaerezi mountains separating Mozambique from Southern Rhodesia.[87] Although little is known about the internal organization of these communities, their commitment to independence and their location in harsh backwater regions is strikingly similar to the maroon communities of the Americas.[88]

Other fugitive societies, not content to remain outside the sphere of European control, adopted an aggressive posture toward the colonial regimes. They periodically returned to their homelands and attacked the specific symbols of rural oppression—the plantation overseers, labor recruiters, tax collectors, and African police—in an effort to protect their kinsmen. Like the social bandits of Sicily and northeastern Brazil, these

[83]Carlos Wiese compiled these figures from official British blue books. See Carlos Wiese, "A Labour Question em Nossa Casa," *Boletim da Sociedade de Geografia de Lisboa*, X (1891), 241.

[84]In all these cases, migration across international borders continues to the present and carries important implications for the current political situation, especially in Angola and Zimbabwe.

[85]John McCraken, "Religion and Politics in Northern Ngoniland, 1881-1904," in Pachai, *Early History of Malawi*, 227-228.

[86]Meebelo, *Reaction to Colonialism*, 102-103.

[87]René Pelissier, "Campagnes militaires au Sud-Angola (1885-1915)," *Cahiers d'Études Africaines*, XXXIII (1969), 76-77.

[88]For an important analysis of maroons, see Richard Price, *Maroon Societies* (New York, 1973), 1-30.

bands were led by individuals who were regarded as heroes by their own society, although they were branded as criminals by the colonial regime.[89]

Consider the career of Mapondera, the best-known social bandit of south central Africa. For more than a decade his band operated along the rugged Southern Rhodesian-Mozambican frontier in the Fungwe-Chioco region, protecting the local peasantry from exploitative company officials and abusive Rhodesian and Portuguese administrators. By the time of his death in 1904, Mapondera's fame had spread throughout a vast region extending from Tete to Salisbury. Traditions recount his exploits, not only against Europeans but also against authoritarian chiefs and African collaborators.[90]

A number of other social bandits operated in Mozambique. Mapondera's successor, Dambakushamba, struck repeatedly at government holdings and European concessionary companies from 1903 to 1907.[91] Twenty-five years earlier Moave had organized a band which disrupted Portuguese holdings near the town of Tete until he was finally captured in 1883.[92] A similar situation existed on Prazo Bororo in Quelimane, where two disgruntled workers fled into the interior and, joined by other peasants, attacked government agents and outposts and plundered European fields.[93] There are indications that the southern Angola-Namibia frontier was also a haven for such groups. The career of Orlog and his followers in particular should be examined from this perspec-

---

[89]For a discussion of social bandits, see the classic work of Eric Hobsbawm, *Bandits* (New York, 1969).

[90]Interview with Enoch Mapondera (10 July 1972); RNA, N/13/14/7: W.H. Milton to General Officer Commanding Rhodesian Field Force (20 July 1900); RNA, A/11/2/12/13, H.M. Taberer to Chief Native Commissioner (6 March 1901); Isaacman, *Tradition of Resistance*, 110-114. The authors are currently completing an analysis of Mapondera as a social bandit.

[91]RNA,RC 3/3/10: R.M. Lidderdale to Commandante, British South African Police (undated); RNA, LO 5/5/33, General Letter A390: W. Edwards, Acting Native Commissioner, Mtoko District, "Report for Month Ended 31 March 1907"; joint interview with Bofana, Simero, Chuva, Sainete Cachambaweto, and Pascoal Dimba at Congololo (23 July 1976); joint interview with Tomo and Bande at Chioko (20 July 1976). Both interviews were carried out by research brigade B.E. 15 of the Universidade de Eduardo Mondlane and will be on deposit there.

[92]AHM, Fundo do Século XIX, Governo Geral, Cx. 11: Joaquim Vieira Braga to Secretário Geral do Governo (29 Nov. 1883).

[93]AHM, Fundo do Século XIX, Quelimane, Governo do Distrito, Cx. 43: Francisco Manoel Correa (undated).

tive.[94] Although fragmentary, the evidence suggests that this form of underclass protest was not uncommon, and needs to be explored in other parts of Central and southern Africa as well.[95]

During the early colonial period there were a number of uprisings by members of the rural population who were unwilling to abandon their homelands. These revolts tended to be relatively localized and of short duration. Rarely did the peasants seek to solidify their initial gains or to shift their goals from an attack on the symbol of their oppression to an attack on the colonial system as a whole. As a rule, increased or more strictly enforced taxation and labor demands precipitated the insurrections. As early as 1878, peasants in Quelimane rose up to protest the census which they correctly believed was a prelude to taxation.[96] Similar reactions occurred repeatedly throughout the Portuguese colonies; the Ovambo and Bakongo regions of Angola and the Lourenço Marques (Maputo) interior and Sena hinterland of Mozambique were the principal centers of rural agitation.[97] Peasant revolts among the Ila, Gwembe Tonga, and Lunda during the first decade of this century concerned British officials in Northern Rhodesia,[98] while opposition periodically flared up among the rural masses of South Africa.[99]

Although localized resistance was generally sporadic and directed against specific grievances rather than the exploitative system which produced them, participation sometimes raised the consciousness of the peasants and workers to the point where they subsequently joined better-organized and more militant movements. To the extent that this occurred, it undercut the prevailing ethnic and regional particularism and generated a broader commitment which reflected a shared sense of oppression. When peasants living near Lourenço Marques joined

[94] Pelissier, "Campagnes," 76.

[95] It is important to differentiate politically-motivated social bandits from a wide variety of bandits and outlaws who indiscriminately attacked the most vulnerable members of the rural or urban population. For an interesting example of this type of antisocial banditry, see Charles Van Onselen, "South Africa's Lumpenproletarian Army: 'Umkosi Wa Ntaba'—The Regiments of the Hills, 1890-1920" (unpublished paper prepared for the World Employment Research Programme, International Labour Office, Geneva, 1976).

[96] M.D.D. Newitt, *Portuguese Settlement on the Zambesi* (New York, 1973), 347.

[97] Pelissier, "Campagnes"; Marcum, *Angolan Revolution*, 53-54; Botelho, *História Militar*, 433-462; Isaacman, *Tradition of Resistance*, ch. 5.

[98] Rotberg, *Nationalism*, 73-75; Meebelo, *Reaction to Colonialism*, 97-98.

[99] Christopher Saunders has argued that fear of the rural masses slowed down the Cape annexation of the Transkei. For an interesting set of essays on the patterns of interaction along this zone of contact, see Christopher Saunders and Robin Derricourt, eds., *Beyond the Cape Frontier* (London, 1974).

Gungunyane after the tax revolt of 1894 had been quashed[100] and when Sena and Tonga militants played a prominent role in the rebellion of 1917 after nearly three decades of localized resistance,[101] they were demonstrating this process of increased consciousness. At about the same time, Tulante Alavaro Buta was able to organize a mass movement of dissident Bakongo peasants who previously had individually opposed Portuguese demands for additional laborers,[102] while the anticolonial movements of Kamwana and Chilembwe benefited from rural discontent in Nyasaland.[103]

Recent studies have also suggested that industrial workers in more advanced capitalist economies, such as South Africa and Southern Rhodesia, were conscious of their exploited status,[104] as was demonstrated during the first two decades of the twentieth century by coordinated work slowdowns, a series of strikes at the mines at Wankie and Kleimfontein, and the famous Bucket Strike. This interpretation contrasts sharply with previous analyses, which have emphasized the absence of any class action among the proletariat prior to the formation of the Industrial and Commercial Union.[105] Indeed, in 1918 a Transvaal Chamber of Mines commission was appointed specifically to examine what was recognized as growing labor unrest.[106]

Before concluding this section, we feel it necessary to address critics who argue that many of these nonviolent actions constituted noncooperation rather than resistance. The distinction between noncooperation and resistance which they have advanced rests on the premise that

[100]Botelho, História Militar, 433-468.

[101]ACM, file 1633, contains numerous telegrams and reports from officials of the Companhia de Moçambique describing the so-called defection of the Sena and Tonga peasants to the Barue.

[102]Marcum, Angolan Revolution, 53-54.

[103]For a detailed discussion of the movements led by Kamwana and Chilembwe, see the outstanding work by George Shepperson and Thomas Price, Independent African (Edinburgh, 1958).

[104]Van Onselen, "Worker Consciousness"; Duncan Clarke, "The Underdevelopment of African Trade Unions and Working Class Action in Postwar Rhodesia" (delivered at the workshop on the social and economic history of southern Africa, Oxford University, 4 Sept. 1974); Van der Horst, Native Labour, 131; Francis Wilson, Labour in the South African Gold Mines, 1911-1969 (Cambridge, 1972), 9; Edward Roux, Time Longer than Rope (Madison, 1964), 130-146.

[105]For an important discussion of previous interpretations, see Clarke, "Underdevelopment," 1-6.

[106]Van der Horst, Native Labour, 131.

resistance must "aim at affecting the distribution of power."[107] They see withdrawal and day-to-day resistance as mere protests. While this distinction might be meaningful from the perspective of the individual actor, the aggregate impact of these individual actions directly affected the distribution of power within the system. Thus, any particular act of day-to-day resistance or withdrawal was insignificant, but its cumulative impact was to create a shortage of labor which to varying degrees weakened the capitalist economy.

Collaboration

To terminate a discussion of African responses to colonial rule without treating the question of collaboration would be premature.[108] Collaboration is a subject which is politically sensitive and often ignored, a selective bias which underlies the assertion that the "struggle has never ended because when oppression exists, resistance to this oppression exists as well. This resistance can change in character and form but it never ceases."[109] A similar observation about the interrelationship of imperialism and collaboration seems equally valid. How else were the Europeans able to impose and maintain their rule with so few troops and so little administration? Indeed, just as we can identify a tradition of resistance, so can we speak of recurring patterns of collaboration. Such an assertion does not diminish the commitment of most Africans to be free; it merely emphasizes the variety of responses which reflected different ethnic, religious, and growing class interests.

Without collaborators the Europeans could not have imposed their rule so thoroughly and with such a minimal cost in manpower. More than ninety percent of the Portuguese armies which pacified the strategic

[107]Christopher Lash and George Fredrickson, "Resistance to Slavery," *Civil War History,* 13 (1967), 315-329.

[108]A few scholars have treated this question within the context of a particular society or industrial setting. See D.N. Beach, "The Politics of Collaboration (Southern Mashonaland, 1896-7)," Henderson Seminar Paper. No. 9, University of Rhodesia (Salisbury, 1970); Dachs, "Politics of Collaboration"; Van Onselen, "Role of Collaborators"; Steinhart, "Resistance and Nationalism." In addition, Ronald Robinson has looked at the question of collaboration from a broader comparative perspective. See "Non-European Foundations of European Imperialism: Sketch for a Theory of Collaboration," in Roger Owen and Bob Sutcliffe, eds., *Studies in the Theory of Imperialism* (London, 1975), 117-142.

[109]Davidson, "African Resistance," 177.

Zambezi Valley, for example, consisted of African levies.[110] Except for the major campaign against the Ovambo in 1915, which took place against the backdrop of World War I and the threat of German encroachments from South West Africa, a similar, though not as extreme, pattern existed in Angola.[111] The success of Harry Johnston's policy of divide and rule is apparent from the large number of Africans who participated in the British occupation of Nyasaland and Northern Rhodesia.[112] In South Africa the defection of the Mfengu was an important factor in the defeat of the Xhosa, and half the force which conquered the Zulu were African recruits.[113]

Collaborators and mercenaries were also instrumental in maintaining European rule and ensuring its profitability during the colonial period. The Angolan *guerra pretas,* the Mozambican *sepais,* the levies of Nyasaland, and the African police of Rhodesia and South Africa all intimidated and exploited the subject peoples. While a discussion of their specific' roles falls outside the scope of this study, it is important to emphasize not only their state functions but also their prominence throughout the industrial and agricultural sectors.[114]

Despite its significance, the role of collaborators has often been overlooked; in some cases they have been transformed into astute modernizers and innovators. Neither this semantic obfuscation nor the tendency to ignore their existence deals directly with the basic question: why and under what conditions did Africans sell their services to the repressive regimes? The problem is complicated because in many cases collaboration, like resistance, was situational. As Ranger notes:

> A historian has indeed a difficult task in deciding whether a specific society should be described as resistant or as collaborative over any given period of time. Virtually all African states made some attempt to find a basis on which to collaborate with the Europeans; virtually all of them had some interests or values which they were prepared to defend, if necessary, by hopeless resistance or revolt.[115]

[110]For a detailed discussion of the composition of various colonial forces used in the wars in the Zambezi Valley in particular and in Mozambique in general, see Botelho, *História Militar.*

[111]Pelissier, "Campagnes," 119.

[112]Dachs, "Politics of Collaboration"; Meebelo, *Reaction to Colonialism,* 57.

[113]Thompson, "Subjection," 259 ff., 264; Richard A. Moyer, "The Mfengu: Self-Defense and the Cape Frontier Wars," in Saunders and Derricourt, *Beyond the Cape Frontier,* 101-126. In South Africa a tradition of relying on African mercenaries and levies dates back to the middle of the nineteenth century. See, for example, John B. Wright, *Bushman Raiders of the Drakensberg* (Pietermaritzburg, 1971).

[114]Of all aspects of collaboration, this area has been the least researched. The most notable exceptions are the fine articles by Van Onselen previously cited.

[115]Ranger, "African Reactions," 304.

Moreover, there is a tendency in the literature to assume that particular societies always acted homogeneously, reinforcing the tendency to define them exclusively as collaborators or resisters.

Nevertheless, we can identify the principal factors which motivated Africans to collaborate at a particular point in time as well as those social strata most likely to become permanent agents of the colonial regime. As in the discussion of resistance, it is important to remember that the different strata within any society often had conflicting interests and that the decision to collaborate was characterized by similar complexity. The principal incentives to collaborate were: (1) to protect one's primordial group against encroachments by a historic enemy; (2) to facilitate expansionist ambitions; (3) to enable a segment of the ruling strata to regain or reinforce its privileged position; (4) to eliminate all authoritarian regimes; and (5) to increase one's economic status within the new colonial order. These factors were not mutually exclusive, and more than one often affected the decision to collaborate. Furthermore, while the decision was ultimately made by Africans, the Europeans approached groups whom they had stereotyped as great warriors or those who appeared alienated from their neighbors. In Mozambique, Southern Rhodesia, and to a lesser degree Malawi, the intrusive Ngoni satisfied both these requirements; they played a prominent role in consolidating the power of the colonial regime.[116] Similarly, the white settler government in Southern Rhodesia recruited Zulu to work as compound policemen in the mines because of their reputed physical capabilities.[117]

Deep-seated hostilities or fear of conquest motivated a number of southern and Central African polities to collaborate with the European powers against their regional enemies. Because their neighbors were perceived as a threat to the entire society, the decision to align with the Europeans generally had the support of all strata. The Swazi, for example, joined with the British in 1879 to defeat their long-time Pedi rivals.[118] Similarly, the Mfengu-British alliance during the Xhosa war of 1877-1878[119] and Sena support of Portugal against the Barue thirty years

---

[116]Dachs, "Politics of Collaboration," 286-287; Van Onselen, "Role of Collaborators," 404; João D'Azevedo Coutinho, *A Companha do Barue, em 1902* (Lisbon, 1904), 83-84; Silvinho Ferreira da Costa, *Governo do Território da Campanhia de Moçambique* (Chemba, 1917), 17.

[117]Van Onselen, "Role of Collaborators," 403-404.

[118]K.W. Smith, "The Fall of the Bapedi of the North-Eastern Transvaal," *Journal of African History,* X (1969), 237-252.

[119]Thompson, "Subjection," 259; Moyer, "Mfengu," 101-126.

later only become intelligible when examined from this perspective of long-term animosities.[120] In other cases, the decision to aid the Europeans was a logical by-product of nineteenth-century European expansion. For the threatened and conquered, collaboration allowed them to maintain or regain their sovereignty, factors which also impelled those who resisted. Moreover, many of the collaborators initially viewed the Europeans as just another "tribe" whose presence could be used to bolster their regional position.[121] Chikuse and his followers, for example, aided the British because they feared the Yao of Mponda, while the acquiescence of the Swazi and Lozi can be explained in terms of fears generated by Zulu and Ndebele raids respectively.[122] The defection of a number of Shona chieftaincies during the 1896 rebellion was yet another expression of hostility toward their former Ndebele rulers.[123]

Conversely, the rulers of several African societies recognized that alliances with the Europeans could facilitate their own territorial aspirations. The leaders of the Zambezi conquest states of Massangano, Matekenya, and Kanyemba all initially agreed to serve as nominal agents of Portugal in return for substantial supplies of weapons, which enabled them to conquer neighboring chieftaincies and to satisfy the predatory ambitions of their large armies.[124] Ultimately, their expansionist desires came into conflict with those of the metropole. Buganda's links with the British represent yet another alliance of convenience between expansionist powers.[125] Thus, just as the Europeans used Africans to enhance their territorial domain, so indigenous societies were not averse to collaborating if it enabled them to expand their holdings and influence.

Internal opposition also motivated segments of the aristocracy to cooperate with the Europeans. As a rule, these arrangements were

[120]Coutinho, *Companha*, 26-29.

[121]Traditions in Clivero chiefdom explain their alliance with the Portuguese in the following terms: "The tribe of the VaZungu [Portuguese] who were coming with guns [and] giving [them to] the people who were living around this place, to fight the Madisiti [Ngoni]." Cited in D.N. Beach, "Resistance and Collaboration in the Shona Country, 1896-1897" (African History Seminar, School of Oriental and African Studies, March, 1974).

[122]Dachs, "Politics of Collaboration," 288; Thompson, "Subjection," 275, 282; Caplan, "Elites," 39-40.

[123]Beach, "Politics of Collaboration," 2.

[124]The size of the armies ranged from approximately three thousand to fifteen thousand men. See Newitt, *Portuguese Settlement*, 234-240; Isaacman, *Tradition of Resistance*, 22-39.

[125]Roberts, "Sub-Imperialism," 435-450; Steinhart, "Resistance and Nationalism," *passim*.

designed either to enable a section of the royal family to usurp the throne or to reinforce the position of an unpopular ruler. Throughout the 1890s the Chibudu branch of the Barue royal family cultivated ties with the Portuguese, hoping that weapons provided by Lisbon would facilitate the removal of the rival Chipapata branch.[126] Likewise, persistent feuds among the descendants of Moshoeshoe explain the cleavages within the royal family and the defection of several prominent members to the British during the Gun War.[127] Similar considerations motivated the Yao chief Kambasani to unite with the English against his rival, Makanjila.[128] A number of threatened leaders also sought to consolidate their positions through alliances with the invading forces. Molala of the Tawana gained British support through just such a strategy,[129] while other Tawana chiefs looked to Transvaal farmers and officials for aid.[130] After the Yao chief Mponda's subjects had repudiated his sovereignty and rallied around more militant leaders, Mponda turned in desperation to the British, who helped him to reimpose his rule.[131] Similarly, Samuel Maherero agreed to aid the Germans after they promised to help eliminate his rivals and appoint him paramount chief of the Herero, a position which had not existed before that time.[132] While effective in the short run, these alliances often intensified the cleavages between the ruling elite and their subordinates. When Jumbe of Kota attempted to bolster his sagging position through an association with the queen of England, for example, his subjects defected to the anticolonial forces of Chiwaura and Makanjila.[133]

Members of the aristocracy were not the only social strata to collaborate. In an effort to free themselves from the rule of authoritarian leaders, oppressed groups occasionally aided the imperialist forces. Although determining how frequently they adopted this strategy is difficult, defections from both the Zumbo states of Kanyemba and

---

[126]ACM, 3321: Governado to Administrador da Companhia de Moçambique (6 Feb. 1896).

[127]Thompson, "Subjection," 213. A similar pattern of internal fractionation and manipulation by the British plagued the Zulu. See Colin Webb, "Great Britain and the Zulu People 1879-1887," in Thompson, *African Societies,* 302-323.

[128]Dachs, "Politics of Collaboration," 288.

[129]Saker and Aldrige, "Origins," 312.

[130]Thompson, "Subjection," 272.

[131]Dachs, "Politics of Collaboration," 288.

[132]Bley, *South-West Africa,* 124.

[133]Dachs, "Politics of Collaboration," 289.

Matakenya and the regimes imposed by the Mbwela, Maseko, and Mpeseni Ngoni suggest that alienation and internal conflict must be considered important factors in any comprehensive analysis of collaboration.[134] To the south, popular opposition to the harsh rule of Gungunyane enabled Lisbon's colonial agents to make substantial inroads among the Inhambane Tonga.[135] Perhaps the best-documented example of collaboration as a strategy to eliminate repressive regimes occurred in the upper Katanga region. Within a thirty-year period, alienated Sanga and other inhabitants of upper Katanga overthrew two different authoritarian regimes by collaborating with external forces. Initially they joined with Msiri and his Yeke followers to overthrow the ruling family of Kazembe. But popular support for Msiri rapidly dissipated after he exploited the local population in much the same way as his predecessors. His abuse of power ultimately precipitated mass defections to the Belgians, against whom the defectors subsequently, though unsuccessfully, rebelled.[136]

In the final analysis, economic considerations proved to be the most important incentive to collaboration with the colonial forces. The landless Mfengu received a homeland in return for their support of the Cape Colony during the frontiers wars on the eastern Cape.[137] Likewise, in exchange for modern weapons which facilitated their slave-raiding activities, the leaders of the Zambezian conquest states agreed to conquer a number of African states who refused to acknowledge Lisbon's preeminence.[138] The willingness of individual Ngoni to serve as mercenaries in the colonial service of Mozambique, Nyasaland, Northern Rhodesia and Southern Rhodesia demonstrates their concern for self-aggrandizement. Their role in the 1917 Barue rebellion highlights their economic motivation. Prior to the insurrection the Barue had courted the Ngoni in an effort to gain their support. The attempt was unsuccessful, but the Ngoni did promise not to assist the colonial regime, a commitment which was later forgotten when Portuguese officials offered them handsome salaries and the opportunity to keep all their plunder. Noted one British official:

---

[134]Isaacman, *Tradition of Resistance,* 36-37; McCraken, "Religion and Politics in Northern Ngoniland, 1881-1904," 227-228; Barnes, *Politics in a Changing Society,* 87-88; Phiri, "Chewa History," 154-155, 191-197; Rennie, "Ngoni States," 310-311.

[135]Botelho, *História Militar,* 473.

[136]Vansina, *Kingdoms,* 227-235.

[137]Moyer, "Mfengu," 101-126.

[138]Isaacman, *Tradition of Resistance,* 22-48.

> It is common knowledge that the Angoni native auxiliaries of the Portuguese forces were promised possession of all the loot that falls into their hands and that they have made captives and carried with them a large number of women and children from the country they passed through. A European member of the force admitted this to me.[139]

While the activities of the Ngoni and the other conquest states suggest that expansionist powers were particularly receptive to financial inducements, the annals of Central and southern African history are replete with instances of individuals from a variety of different ethnic groups who joined the police or the military to improve their economic and social positions.[140] Many chiefs and other members of the ruling hierarchy were also coopted into the new colonial order with assurances that their privileged status would be enhanced and inherited by their descendants.

African labor recruiters, foremen, and compound policemen all played a critical role in the exploitation of workers in the mines and on the plantations, as well as of conscripts employed in state projects. As a vital part of the capitalist apparatus they received a variety of real benefits. Not only were they exempt from manual labor, but their wages were appreciably higher than those of the laborers. In addition, they enjoyed certain fringe benefits, including extraction of sexual favors, the sale of special dispensations, protection money from intimidated workers, and blackmail. In short, privilege and exploitation were not the exclusive prerogative of the dominating racial minority.[141]

Conclusion

This paper has suggested several aspects of resistance which need to be examined in greater depth. Given the existence of social differentiation and inter-ethnic rivalries, the indiscriminate use of the term *African resistance* throughout the literature tends to obscure more than it illuminates. In order to sharpen our analysis, we must study seriously

---

[139]RNA, A3/18/38: Telegram from High Commissioner for South Africa to Secretary of State for the Colonies (11 April 1917).

[140]Our work among the disparate peoples of the Zambezi Valley indicates that individuals from *every* ethnic group collaborated in an effort to improve their standing in the new social order.

[141]Van Onselen, "Role of Collaborators," 406-410; Isaacman, *Tradition of Resistance,* chs. 4-8.

the economic and social configuration of Central and southern African societies on the eve of the scramble. For the colonial period, we must focus on the atomized resistance of peasants and workers as well as on the protests of the urban poor. Such loaded terms as *riots, vandalism,* and *banditry* must be critically reexamined and the context, motivation, and goals of the participants carefully identified. Finally, the role of women, conspicuously absent from virtually all discussions of resistance, needs to be considered. Recent research demonstrating their central position in the 1913-1918 anti-pass campaigns in South Africa as well as the subsequent efforts of militant women to challenge the repressive system in that country[142] needs to be duplicated for other parts of the continent. Although the study of resistance has successfully challenged most of the culturally arrogant and racist assumptions perpetuated by the colonial regimes, the newer types of elitist distortions, which deny the importance of the underclasses and equate collaboration with modernization, must also be confronted.

[142]Judith Wells, "You Have Struck a Rock Once You Have Touched a Woman: African Women's Protest in South Africa" (unpublished paper, Columbia University, 1976). Research in the Mozambican and Portuguese archives has yielded a few examples of women's protest movements. In 1916, for example, the Portuguese administration of Chemba sought to compel Mozambican peasants to cultivate cotton for export. While the men agreed, the women refused, arguing that they would not be able to cultivate enough food for their families. Despite intensive pressure from Portuguese officials as well as from their husbands, the women among the Tonga peasants ultimately prevailed. Subsequently the Tonga rose up against the colonial regime. See AHM, Negocios Indigenas, Cx. 132, Processo 55: Jose Ferreira (3 Oct. 1917).

GOD, ANTI-COLONIALISM AND DANCE:
SHEEKH UWAYS AND THE
UWAYSIAYYA
by Christine Choi Ahmed

The tomb of Sheekh Uways B. Muhammad Al-Barawi in Biyooley, Somalia is visited every year by Somalis, Tanzanians, Eastern Congolese, Zanzibaris and many persons from the rest of East Africa. Historians, specializing in Somalia, dismiss Sheekh Uways as just a holy man. Yet as Arabic sources are analyzed it appears that Sheekh Uways was in fact the leader of the most effective pan-Islamic movement in East Africa. The Uwaysiyya not only revitalized East African Islam, but changed its nature from the religion of the elites to a mass-based movement, that clearly challenged European colonialism. The fact that Sheekh Uways' contribution to Somali and East African history has been ignored in both Western and Somali academic writings highlights the contradiction that recently has plunged Somalia into civil war. A narrow clan history written by the former Somali dictator and a group of northern pastoralists was forced on Somalia as a national history. This chapter on Sheekh Uways will, hopefully, be a small contribution to the writing of an objective Somali history which includes all the Somali people.

In order to properly analyze the historical contributions of Sheekh Uways and the Uwaysiyya, it is necessary to understand both the history of Islam in Somalia and the 19th century changes that occurred in the southern portions of the country.

HISTORY OF ISLAM IN SOMALI

The Somali people are for all practical purposes completely Islamized today and the vast majority observe the Shafi'i Sunnite School of Law. Zanzibar and Somalia are the two most thoroughly Islamized countries in tropical Africa.[1] This adherence to Islam has produced in the Somali people a strong relationship with the Islamic world as well as with the rest of Islamic East Africa:

> For despite their geographical presence in African as well as
> ethnic, linguistic and cultural affinity with other neighboring
> African communities, the Somalis identify through their religion,
> emotionally and culturally with Arabia and the wider world of
> Islam.[2]

Islam probably arrived on the Somali Peninsula peacefully with Arab merchants sometime in the second half of the 7th century A.D. The Horn of Africa was not invaded during the wars of Arab conquests, in part, because there was no Muslim navy and the lands of Iraq, Syria and the Byzantine provinces of Egypt were a much richer prize. Another reason might be as:

---

[1] Hersi, Ali Abdirahman. "The Arab Factor in Somali History", PhD UCLA p. 109
[2] Ibid p. 139

> . . .many Arab authors. . .claim that the Muslims, who
> because of Meccan persecution took refuge in what was then
> Abyssinia during the early years of the Prophet Muhammad's
> preaching, passed through Zaila on their way to and from
> Abyssinia, and that some of these stayed behind on the Zaila Coast.[3]

The safe passage given by the Abyssinians to the group of Muslims
reportedly entreated the Prophet to tell his followers never to attack the
Abyssinians so long as they remained nonbelligerent. The Arabs have
historically had problems distinguishing between Abyssinians (Amharic
Ethiopians) and the Cushitic people of the Horn (Somali, Oromo, Afar-
Saho, etc.) and since Zaila is a town situated along the Red Sea in an area
inhabited by Somalis, then and now, it is possible that there was Islamic
conversion among the Somalis during the life of Mohammed.

Somalis believe that they were among the first non-Arab people
converted to Islam, but in reality it appears that the total conversion of the
Somali people took about 700 years. The Muslim merchants who arrived
on the Somali coast brought Islam with them. Even if the merchant was
not inclined to preaching, he always brought along a holy teacher to
educate his children and attempt to convert the locals. There is
archaeological evidence that Islam was present in Somalia at an early
period as is shown by two inscriptions on tombstones found in the city of
Mogadishu. The tombstones are dated to A H 138 (749 A.D.) and show that
the two women buried there had Islamic names. [4]

In the mid-eighth century Shiite Zaidis arrived on the Southern
(Banaadir) coast of Somalia and dominated that area for the next two
hundred years. As previously stated the Somalis are Sunni Moslems, yet
there are indications of some Shiite influence.

> The excessive reverence with which Ali, Fatima and their Sada and
> Ashraf descendants are held among the Somalis today also reveals
> a strong Shiite influence in the past which centuries of Sunnite
> teachings could not wipe out altogether. [5]

Of course Sunni Moslems were also arriving in Somalia during this
period. Three Sunni Muslim Sheekh are remembered as having brought
Islam to Somalia. One was Sheekh Yusuf ibn Ahmad al-Kawrayia who is
best known for his system of rendering Arabic vowel function and usage
into Somali which makes the reading of the Koran much easier for
Somali speakers in around 1150 A.D.[6] Islam was introduced to the
hinterlands during the 12th and 13th centuries by learned Somali scholars

---

[3] Ibid p. 78

[4] Ibid p.113

[5] Ibid p.115

[6] Lewis, I M *Islam In Tropical Africa*, London, 1966 p.28

who had studied at Zabid in the Yemen and the Azhar University in Cairo.

In the Horn of Africa there has been a tension between the Christian Ethiopians and the Muslim populations since the introduction of Islam. First it manifested itself in competing missionary work, but in the 15th and 16th centuries the struggle became jihadic in nature. Ahmad ibn Ibrahim, popularly called Gurey [the left handed one], who was probably a Somali, led the great jihad against Christian Ethiopia and was able to at least nominally Islamize the Ethiopian empire. The soldiers of this jihad were the nomadic people of the Red Sea coast, the majority of which were Somalis. The Islamization of Ethiopia was reversed once Gurey died and his over-extended Islamic empire collapsed. But one result of this jihad was that the partially or non-Islamized Somali and Afar groups were converted wholly to Islam by the struggle.

Meanwhile in the interriverine area of Southern Somalia, between the Juba and Shebelle river (the fertile agricultural area of Somalia), the Hawiyye clan created the Ajuuran empire in the 16th century. The Ajuuran, like most of the Somali clans, claim to be descendent from an Arab sheekh who came to their territory in Somalia and married a daughter of a local clan leader. This claim of Arab ancestry is representative of the clan's conversion to Islam and the submission of traditional laws to an Islamic legal system rather than any large influx of Arab "blood" into the Somali population.[7] This same story is found among most of the Islamized people along the East African Coast. The Ajuuran centralized state may well have been groupings of Hawiyye Islamic polities; each was headed by an imam and was a theocracy--held together by clan and religious ties. Whatever the Ajuuran state was, it consolidated the Islamization of the hinterlands of the Benaadir sections of Somalia. Somali oral tradition remembers the downfall of the Ajuuran as a result of their own despotic and non-Islamic practices.

The Somali clans in both the South and the North have the same story of conversion to Islam. It involves a battle between the pagan magician and the Moslem Sheekh. The Sheekh finally wins when he invokes the might of God and imprisons the magician forever in a mountain. This story is so widespread in Somali clan lore that it might reflect one particular clan or group's conversion that was popularized by a Sheekh throughout the country.

Often clan lineage ancestors are in effect canonized as saints along with the saints of Islam. The channel of communication to God is as follows: "The ancestor [or saint] stands in the gateway of the Prophet, who in turn, stands at the door of God."[8] The religions of the saints was often associated by the people with the practices of astrology, divination and magic. In fact since the middle ages Somali Sheekh have traveled from the Benaadir coastal cities spreading Islamic learning and rainmaking

---

[7] Cassanelli, Lee . "The Benadir Past: Essays in Southern Somali History",   Phd University of Wisconsin p.24

[8] Lewis, I M. *Islam In Tropical Africa*, p. 62.

ceremonies (both of which were equally important) to the East African Islamic cities.

As the jihad in the Northwestern section of Somalia and the Ajuuran theocracy in the South indicate, by the 17th century Islam was the only religion of consequence in the territory of the Somali people. A clear indication of this was the extreme decrease in the number of slaves coming from Somalia to the Arab world.

Islam has provided a cement for the creation of a Somali consciousness. Even though Somalis are relatively ethnically and linguistically homogeneous, the various pastoral clans and sub-clans were in constant warfare with each other for the meager resources of the Somali peninsula. The agro-pastoral and agricultural clans of the south lived more cooperatively, due in part to their reliance on cultivation. While the pastoral clans relied on raiding livestock and fighting over grazing and watering areas, the southern cultivators needed to forge more cooperative relations with their neighbors, since they needed to plant their land year after year. The universal Somali adherence to Islam has helped to forge whatever unified identity there is on the Somali peninsula. But this unified identity has always been fragile as the competing Islamic movements of the nineteenth century will indicate.

The first of the nineteenth century Islamic sufi movements was the Baardheere Jihad of Southern Somalia. The Baardheere Jihad started out with a few settlements founded on the Juba river in 1819 and grew to as many as 20,000 followers by 1840. The movement was founded by Shykh Ibrahim Hassan Jeberow. Some say he was member of the Alimediya Order, others say he was member of the Qadiriya. Today the people who claim to be descendants of those involved in the jihad are Salahiyya, a branch of the Alimediya. This fact, coupled with the rather "puritanical" nature of the Baardheere Jihad, gives creedence to the claim of the Alimediya as the ideological "mother" of the movement. Whatever order Sheekh Jeberow belonged to, he was a reformer and tried to get back to the "pure" Islam. Baardheere produced the only Somali jihad in modern times except for the anti-colonial struggle of Sayyid Muhammad Abdullah Hassan.

The Baardheere Jihad outlawed the use of tobacco, popular dancing[9] and social intercourse between the sexes. Women were to be veiled. And the movement was opposed to the ivory trade, because the elephant was considered an "unclean" animal. In the middle of the 1830's the brotherhood became very militant. At this time they united with Daarood nomads from the northern areas of Somalia who were forced by drought to migrate to the South. They attacked Oromo settlements and sacked Barava in 1840.

It is important to remember that the Baardheere's Jihad occurred at a time of economic expansion in the areas affect by the jihad. The jihad

---

[9] These prohibitions plus one against drinking coffee are part of the doctrine of Sayyid Muhammad Abdullah Hassan's Alimadiya tariqa. See
Cerulli, Enrico, Somalia, Scritti Vari Editi ed Inediti, A Cura Dell'Amminsitrazione Fiduciaria Italiana Della Somalia, 1957.

was defeated by a conglomeration of southern clans. It may well be that their main reason for opposing the jihad was not religious but economic. The Baadheeres wanted to end the ivory trade, which was expanding at the time, and many of the jihad supporters were members of the northern clan, the Daarood's, whose massive migration was threatening the precarious pastoral ecology in the area. After the jihad the Daarood migrated through Southern Somalia into an area that is today part of Northern Kenya. The jihad opposed saint worship, clan affiliation and the inheritance of baraka by relatives of a sheekh. Besides threatening the economic foundations in the area, the jihad also challenged the various power structures and justifications of the local clans' leadership.

This jihad showed the diversity and sophistication of Somalia's Islam, but it failed precisely because it attempted to strike against both the economic base and social legitimacy of the local power structure. It is clear that Sheekh Uways's organization was much more compatible with the economic needs of the local Southern Somali leaders, and was less strict on the question of merging Islamic and traditional African beliefs. It appears Sheekh Uways learned a lesson from the Baadheere Jihad and understood that it was impossible to launch a movement that challenged both the economic foundation of the society and the political. This could well account for the involvement of slave traders and other Arab businessmen as well as marginalized people in the Uwaysiyya. Whether he summed up any of the above is only speculation at this time until more work is done on his writings in Arabic and Somali. But given the Jihad's historical proximity to the development of the Uwaysiyya and the fact that it was also developed in Southern Somalia, it would be impossible that Sheekh Uways was unaware of this particular movement.

HISTORY OF SOUTHERN SOMALIA IN THE 19TH CENTURY

To understand the rise of Sheekh Uways and the Uwaysiyya, it is important to look at the historical developments in the Southern Somali area. The Somali Benaadir is the only coastal district of East Africa to have for its immediate hinterland a fertile riverine plain. Agriculture was never fully developed in this region because of three very important reasons. First the pastoral elements of Somali society held and still holds that the nomadic way of life is "noble" and agricultural production is only done by lower caste persons. The nomadic way of life is very precarious in the Somali peninsula, therefore Somali nomadic clans have a relationship with those involved in agriculture in the riverine area. According to Lee Cassanelli in The Shaping of Somali Society, the agricultural groups, for both social and protection reasons, have attached themselves to a pastoral nomadic clan. This relationship, called Sheegad. Sheegad, was a term originally used when one nomadic group was forced to be the client of another nomadic group in order to be able to use good grazing land. This form of clientage was extended to the agricultural areas. Casanelli further states that Shegaad in the agricultural areas represented the subordination of the agricultural clans, but Dr. Mohamed H Mukhtar, professor of Islamic and African History at Savannah State College, Georgia and the leading expert on the history of Islam in Somalia, disagrees. Dr. Mukhtar states:

> The *Sheegad* occurs in migrant tribes from the north and south-west who because of droughts and wars move from their original places seeking protection and asylum. Southerners were used to offering that kind of refuge and cohabitation to the migrant people of the region through out their history. This doesn't negate the fact that the migrants could maintain their previous identity as well as their occupation."

Some of the Somali agriculturalist appear to be a combination of early Bantu speaking peoples and Somalis who had lost their pastoral capital and became agriculturalists, while others were Somalis who had farmed the land for many centuries. But by the beginning of the 19th century all the agriculturalists were thoroughly Somalized, in that they spoke Somali and were Moslems. The nomadic clans use their relationships with the agricultural groups as an escape valve. They sent their excess populations (old people, children, pregnant women) during a draught to live in the areas of a particular clan of agriculturalists with whom they had a relationship. In this way the herds had only to support a small population, and they were able to maintain some of their herd capital during difficult times. Yet because agriculture was considered such lowly work, the nomadic peoples return to pastoral nomadism as soon as it was possible.

A second reason for the underdevelopment of agriculture in the region was due to a lack of labor. The majority of the population was pastoral, and as stated above, status among the pastoralists in Somali society was based on the number of camels, and to a lesser degree, cattle which a family owned. Therefore those pastoralists, who during draught periods participated in agricultural production, often returned to pastoralism as soon as possible. And thirdly, there was a small market demand for the agricultural production, a demand that did not encourage increasing production of surplus. Therefore the area only had to be self-sufficient and produce some surplus for a particular pastoral Somali clan and to maintain the relatively small urban populations of the coastal cities.

Since Pharaonic Egypt, trade had existed along the southern Somali coast, but it usually involved exotic woods, hides and ivory. This all changed with the rise of Zanzibar and the accompanying increase in trade by the Busaidi Sultanate at Zanzibar in 1840; the agricultural region of Somalia was suddenly developed to fulfill the grain and crop needs of the Persian Gulf region. As the interriverine area started exporting food to the Arab peninsula, East African slaves were imported to the region and plantation slave production was started. Two of the three reasons for underutilization of agriculture had now disappeared.

Individual land ownership was not the rule in southern Somalia. Use of the land was based on often complicated clan relationships. Theoretically access to land was determined by one's membership in one's father's clan, but practically rights could be conferred through the mother's

7

clan or through forms of fictitious clan affiliations. Until the large demand
for agricultural surplus in the 1840's, control of agricultural production
was based on individual families and in time of food shortage, the clan.
But with the need for larger production and the chronic lack of labor,
slaves from East Africa were imported to do forms of plantation labor.
Cotton and sesame seeds were being grown with the use of slave labor by
the 1840's and a few Somali plantation owners became rich. It is clear,
though, that the wealthy slaveowners along the riverine area never
developed into an independent political force at the expense of traditional
clan leaders.[10]

As early as 1843 there were records of runaway slave communities
in the area. In examining the slave records, one is struck by the huge
percentage of slaves who were able to escape. This raises questions about
how effective slavery was in Southern Somalia. The manumission
records of the Italians in the late 1890's shows that many individuals
owned only a few slaves each.[11] By 1860 the British were patrolling the
Indian Ocean in any attempt to stop the slave trade. Of course, in response,
the Zanzibari slave traders just moved inland along the East African trade
routes. But the British were able to slow down the slave trade in the area
and increase the cost for each slave.

Another important aspect of the economic situation in Southern
Somalia was the non-agricultural long distance trade. It is important to
realize that even at its peak, Somalia accounted for at the most between
1/5 and 1/3 of the Zanzibar-East African trade.[12] Ivory was a big
commodity in the 19th century, but the reserves of elephants along the
coast in Somalia had been depleted; thus the need to develop the ivory
trade further inland. By the middle of the 19th century agriculture was
playing a larger role, along with increased demand for hides and exotic
animal furs. No one Somali clan was able to monopolize the long-distance
trade, and because the trade routes had long been established, no
foreigners, including only Arabs or Swahilis, were able to control it. Clans
who would usually be fighting with each found themselves working
together in certain parts of the long-distance trade. This is not to say that
some clans did not raid the caravans, but usually if they did raid--they only
took a tribute payment for protection of the caravan until the next clan's
territory. Islam was the main unifying force in this caravan trade. Often
wadaad's (Somali Sheekh or holy men) mediated any of the problems
along the routes and between clan territories. With the great increase of
trade, more and more Somali clans were forced to work with one another.
Regardless of their nomadic pastoralist ideals, no clan wanted to miss a
chance "to make a buck".

The southern section of Somalia already had the mixed economy of
agriculture and pastoralism, the greatest heterogenity of clans living in
proximity of each other, and now an upsurge in the economy of the area.

[10] Cassaneli, Lee. *Shaping of Somali Society*, Philadelphia, 1982 p.172
[11] Robecchi-Brichetti, Luigi. Lettere dal Benadir, Milan: Society Editrice "La Poligrafica,"
1904.
[12] These could be over-inflated, see *Shaping of Somali Society*, p.160

An excellent example of this increased economic activity was the textile industry along the southern Somali coast which was at first hurt by the import of British or U.S. manufactured cloth, but soon was able to compete, because it was discovered cotton could be grown in the riverine area very cheaply.

While all these changes were going on in Southern Somalia, the European colonialists were becoming dominant in East Africa. In Zanzibar the British informally occupied the area in 1843 and in 1890 they officially declared a protectorate over Zanzibar.[13] Meanwhile Zanzibar, actually the British, had ceded the Benaadir to Italy in the same year. At first the Italians were hesitant to stop the slave trade, because they did not want to stop the economic development of the riverine areas since they were having a hard time getting Italian farmers to settle the region. If Italians worked the land themselves, they were viewed as slaves by the pastoral Somalis, therefore the proper colonialist needed to own slaves in order to have any status.[14] But much pressure was placed by the British on the Italians and soon the Italians were effectively limiting slavery and the accompanying economic development of the agricultural regions of the Benaadir. Often the British and Italians competed with each other for the use of Somali ports. Each imperialist power exacerbated various clan rivalries in order to secure access to certain good harbors. Thus the Europeans, together with the invading Ethiopians, were effectively able to stop the economic development of the interriverine areas and increase the inter-clan rivalry

As European imperialism was carving up East Africa, the Somalis were faced with another danger, from Christian Ethiopia, the Somali's traditional enemy. Ethiopia under Menelik started moving into Somalia in 1886.[15] The British signed a treaty with the Ethiopians [16] and the Italians did nothing to help the Somalis resist invasion by the Ethiopians. Therefore many Somalis felt that they were being squeezed by various Christian powers in alliance against them. This summation gained much support in Islamic Somalia because of the British attack on the Mahdi in the Sudan during the same period and the general rise of pan-Islamic consciousness in the Moslem world. The Ethiopian incursions were primarily motivated by economic necessity due to the long drought in the country. The Ethiopians were not a modern imperialist army and therefore they tended to loot and pillage in order to survive. They took livestock, even camels, which they refused to eat, but which were used as negotiating tools with other Somali clans. This forced more and more Somalis to leave the areas the Ethiopians had conquered and many Somali refugees arrived in the southern part of Somalia.

On one hand the Somalis never faced the kind of persecution that the Shona of South Africa or the Kikuyu of Kenya faced by the British, but

[13] El Sheikh, M. "State, Cloves and Planters", Phd Dis., UCLA p. 62

[14] Pankhurst, Sylvia. *Ex-Italian Somaliland*, London, 1951, p.42

[15.] Touval, Saadia. *Somali Nationalism*, Cambridge, 1963, p.43.

[16.] Cassenli, Lee. *The Shaping of Somali Society*, p. 30

the fact that the colonialists were determined to cut up the Somali traditional lands into at least five pieces added fuel to anti-western sentiment. During the 1890's, especially due to the Mahdist and other jihadist movement, a pan-Islamic sentiment was in the air in Somalia. These two element plus the disruption of the economic growth in southern Somalia all added to the anger the Somali people were developing towards Christian colonialism in all forms. We see a similar scenario today in East Africa as Islamic movements are again gaining strength because they are perceived to be the only force able to effectively confront the West.

SHEEKH UWAYS

Sheekh Uways bin Muhammad al-Barawi al-Qadiri was born to a poor family of the Tunni clan in Brawa (or al-Barawa) in the spring of 1847. In Somalia various clans are divided into "noble", "not-noble" and "outcast." It is not in the context of this paper to go into the differences among these particular Somali clans, so let it suffice that Sheekh Uways lineage was less than "noble". His background has been described as being from "client agricultural communities rather than powerful nomadic clans."[17] According to oral tradition, Sheekh Uways was special even in his mother's womb. During her pregnancy she said he felt so light, she wondered if she was really pregnant. She is reported to have seen unexplained lights during her pregnancy.[18] As a young boy, Sheekh Uways was apparently a brilliant student in Koranic school in Brawa. He studied Arabic, religious subjects and Islamic sciences with two local Sheekhs. One of his teachers, Sheekh Muhammad Zayini al-Shanshi, was a member of the Qadiriyya, and he encouraged Uways to continue his sufi studies in Baghdad. In 1870 Uways arrived in Baghdad where he studied under the Qadiri master, Sayyid Mustafa ibn al-Sayyid Salaman al-Kaylani, the son of a principal sheekh of the order Salaman al-Kaylani, who was descended from the Prophet. This relationship was to be very important in Uways' development as a pan-Islamic leader.

The Qadiriyya Tariiqa was founded by Bagdadi Sait Sayyid Abd al-Qadir Jilani who died in A.D. 1166. This was the first sufi order in Islam. Being older and more established, the Qadiriyya had a larger membership in Somalia. It also tended to be less puritanical than the other sufi orders in Somalia. Records indicate that the Qadiriyya was established in Harrar before A.D. 1508. In Somalia it has long been an educational institution devoted to Islamic literacy rather than propagandist tradition. The Qadiriyya is split into two powerful branches which reflect the North/South division in Somali society. The northern branch, the Zeyli'iya, is named after Sheekh abd al Rahman az-Zewyli, who died in the Ogaden region of Somalia in 1883. Oral tradition states that Sheekh Zewyli gave Sheekh Uways complete control of the Qadiriyya in Somalia just prior to his death.[19] Sheekh Uways became the most important leader of the order

---

[17] Ibid, p.236
[18] Interview with Sheikh Haji Osman Jan. 9th 1993 in his home in Rome
[19] Ibid.

in Somalia. The sufi order transcended the contradiction between North and South.

Uways made the required Hijaz to Mecca and Medina and visited various important saints' tombs in the Hijaz and Yemen. According to oral tradition related by Sheekh Haji Osman, when Uways went to see the prophet's grave he was refused entry by the Saudis. He then started reciting poetry and the lock broke open on the gate, followed by the opening of the building of the prophet's grave. Sheekh Uways entered. Saudi soldiers brought him out, and he began reciting poetry. The locks broke open again. To this day the Saudis respect Sheekh Uways because of his powers at the Prophet's grave.

After his studies he stopped at the British enclave on Aden and then returned to Somalia in 1881. He returned to the Benaadir Coast and became the most important religious figure in Brawa and Southern Somalia. He set up settlements in the southern interior of Somalia. The main settlement was at Biyole, near Tiyogle, on the upper reaches of the Juba River. He started a Mosque school which became the most important Qadiriyya education center in Southern Somalia and possibly for all of East Africa.[20] Sheekh Uways composed many mystical poems in Arabic. Enrico Cerulli, the Italian colonial expert on Somali, discovered at least five songs written in dialect: one in Rahanwen, two in Hawiyya, one in Digil and one in Darod. But he also wrote poetry in Arabic script in the Somali language, and his Somali poetry is the first recorded Somali literature written in Arabic script.[21] Interestingly when the Somali government was trying to decide on a type of script for the Somali language in the late 60's, the pro-Arabic forces were using Sheekh Uways' poetry as an example of Somali written in Arabic script. The irony is that the current Somali script is not capable of satisfactorily writing the southern dialect of "Mai", the dialect spoken by Sheekh Uways.[22] Sheekh Uways followed a long tradition of Somali holy man, wadaad, travelling to East Africa and spreading the Islamic sciences. With the 19th century rebirth of the sufi orders, this educating role included proselytizing of Moslems for the Qadiriyya and bringing new peoples into Islam thru the Tarriqas.

From the early 1880's to his death in 1909, Sheekh Uways was involved in missionary activities in the south of Somalia and through East Africa. This was facilitated in the early period by the fact that Benaadir, Kenyan and Tanganyikan coasts were until 1892 and 1888 respectively under nominal Zanzibari control. [23]

> Two hagiographies of Shaykh Uways, the Al-Jawhar al-Nafis and the Jala al-Aynayn, list 150 of Uways' followers. The names show the varied groups among whom Uways' fame

---

20 Hersi, Ali. Op. sit. p. 291

21 Ibid, p. 251; Cerulli, Enrico. Somalia, Scritti vari Edti ed Inediti, A cura dell'aministrazione Fiduciaria Italiana della Somalia, 1957, p.200

22 Personal communication with Dr. Mohamed Mukhtar, USA

23 Martin, B. G. "Muslim Politics and Resistance to Colonial Rule: Sheik Uways b. Muhammad al-Barawi and the Qadiriyya Brotherhood in East Africa," JAH, X, 3, 1969, p.479.

had spread--in the Comoro and Bajun Islands and the Ogaden
of Somalia from Zanzibar to Hadramawt; among the clerical
families like the Aliwis of Mogadishu and Lamus; among Bantu
speakers, perhaps from inner Tanganyika; among Swahili speakers,
possibly among the coastal Yao. The missionaries of Shaykh Uways
were even found in Java.[24]

After his first trip to Zanzibar, he made his mission center outside
of Somalia in the capital.

> . . .he cemented good relations with the sovereigns of
> the island, beginning with Barghash bin Sa'id al-Bu Sa'idi
> (to 1888) and with his successors Khalifa b. Sa'id (1888-90),
> hamid (or Ahmad) b. Thuwayni b. Sa'id (1893-6) and with
> later rulers. [25]

By 1896 the Italians were well entrenched at Baanadir and made it
impossible for Sheekh Uways to maintain a permanent center there. He
was forced to move the headquarters of the Tariqa to Zanzibar. The rulers
of Zanzibar gave him food from their own table, and provided him
houses and money to continue his ministry. Both Barghash and Hamid B.
Thuwayni are listed as sufis of moderate rank in the Uwaysiyya, and this is
very surprising since both men were adherents of the Ibadiya sect and of
Umani descent. For these men to be members of a Sunni Qadiriyya order
would require very special circumstances. B. G. Martin feels the
circumstance is a political necessity. From his base in Zanzibar Uways
moved to the mainland with his missionary activity. People adhering to
the Uwaysiyya are found as far West as the Eastern Congo. German
sources state that the Uwaysiya movement penetrated the mainland areas
near Zanzibar and some of the Tanganyikan ports in the late 1880's. [26]
The German records state that:

> They frequently ended in the phase of La ilaha illa llah (there is
> no god, but God) chanted by a circle or halaqa of Qadiris sitting in
> a mosque, swaying together to the beat of a drum and singing
> the qasidas of Shaykh Uways. [27]

It is interesting that again the use of drums is found in the religious
ceremonies of the Uwaysiyya, especially in areas where drums are
essential to the Bantu culture.

THE UWAYSIYYA

The 19th century revivalist movements in the wider Islamic world
were having an impact in Somalia. As a consequence, the Qadiriyya was
being accepted by more and more Somalis even in the less religious
interior. The Qadiriyya seems to have made a transition from just being
primarily a teaching sufi order to that of converting large sections of the
East Africans to Islam.

---

24 Ibid, p. 477
25 Ibid
26 Ibid, p.474
27 Ibid

In 1880, two separate Muslim brotherhoods were making
progress in East Africa. . .. The larger and more influential
was the Uwaysi branch of the Qadiri order named for its
Somali leader, Sheekh Uways Bin Muhammad al-Barawi.
They [sufi orders] accounted for a considerable expansion
of Islam in Tanganyika, southern Somalia, eastern Zaire,
parts of Mocambique and Malawi, the Comoro Island,
and northwest Madagascar.[28]

Since the middle ages, Ulamas and sheekhs from Brawa and
Mogadishu traveled to the coastal cities of East Africa. They served in dual
roles as masters of rainmaking ceremonies and as "bush teachers",
teaching prayers, the Koran and elementary Arabic.[29] Therefore with the
increased importance of the sufi orders, it is not unexpected that the
leadership of any widespread order in Islamic East Africa would come
from Brawa or Mogadishu. The last half of the 19th century saw a change
in these holy men who historically had traveled up and down the East
African coast. They were visiting important centers of Islam, their
religious horizons had grown since most now were educated outside of
East Africa, and they were better trained in the written sciences.[30]
Meanwhile in Somalia, the power relations between the nomadic
clan leader and the wadaad (Somali holy man) were in the process of
changing. With the spread of Islamic revivalism and the changing
economic relations in the Benaadir, the power of the wadaad had
increased. The Baardarre Jihad is an excellent example of the rise to power
of the holy men. The sufi orders were preaching against clan affiliations,
labeling such loyalties as impious acts.[31] The combination of the need for
more clan cooperation, first in developing the economy of Southern
Somalia, and later, in fighting the various colonial incursions together
with the rise of pan-Islamic movements in the Islamic world all
contributed to the new power of the wadaad. It is important here to
remember that Somalis often identified with the Islamic world as much as
they did with the rest of Africa. Though in the case of the 19th century,
Islamic revivalism there was no contradiction between the two. Whereas
Sheekh Abdallah Hassan combined the warrior and the wadaad in a
traditional sense of leadership, Uways was clearly only a wadaad, but also
the leader of a multi-ethnic African religious movement.

> . . .the emergence of organized sufism allowed these religious
> men to exercise autocratic powers unknown to secular men in
> the fragmented politics of clan organization. [32]

---

[28] Martin, B. G. *Muslim Brotherhoods in Nineteenth Century Africa*, London, 1976,
p.152

[29] Pouwels, Randall L. "Islam and Islamic Leadership in the Coastal Communities of   Eastern
Africa, 1700-1914", Phd. Diss, UCLA 1979, p.462

[30] Ibid, p.461

[31] Hersi, Ali. "The Arab Factor in Somali History" Phd Diss, UCLA, 1977, p. 249

[32] Samatar, Said. "Poetry in Somali Politics", Phd Diss. Northwestern, 1979, p.192

Even though the Qadiriyya was much less hierarchical than the other orders (the Salihiya for example had a leader in the Arab world that all members of the order must obey), for the first time, the wadaad had an organization that could rival that of the clan leader. The sufi orders' struggle against clanism helped to erode the clan leaders' power base. Also the loyalty of a disciple to a sufi leader is much more intense than loyalty the anarchistic Somali would give his clan leader.

The Uwaysiyya branch of the Qadiriyya was quite successful in converting many groups in East Africa. Part of its ability to do so was because it was much more accommodating to local customs. The Qadiriyya often used banners and drums,[33] both of which are frowned upon by more orthodox Moslems.[34] Another significant reason for the increasing membership in the Qadiriyya was its appeal to both the poor, ex-slaves, the disenfranchised, and the elites who had been displaced by colonialism. In Uwaysiyya settlements in Southern Somalia, there were many ex-slaves and those considered outcast by the "noble" Somali. Remember Uways himself was a Tunni, a clan considered "less than noble". Muhammed was now seen by the poor as the prophet of the downtrodden.[35] The following oral tradition about Sheekh Uways shows his "populist" appeal:

> Sheekh Sufi was an important sheekh in Mogadishu. Sheekh Uways came to visit him at the great mosque in Mogadishu. He asked to marry Sheekh Sufi's daughter, but Sheekh Sufi refused, saying that he couldn't marry his daughter to a slave. Every day Sheekh Sufi was given three coins by the angels to buy food for the people, but after he refused Sheekh Uways the marriage of his daughter, the coins stopped. Sheekh Uways told him they would start coming again and they did. Sheekh Sufi told Sheekh Uways he would give him four of his daughters in marriage, but Sheekh Uways refused this time. At the same time Sheekh Sufi couldn't get the people from the two sections of Mogadishu to stop having dancing contests. So Sheekh Uways came and started reciting religious poetry. The people stopped their dancing and began doing dhikr, because the poetry was more beautiful than their dancing. They all became religious people.[36]

In the above story the so-called noble Sheekh Sufi was only a mortal, whereas Sheekh Uways was able to perform miracles. Sheekh Sufi's discrimination against Sheekh Uways' background was punished by God. Clearly one's genealogy was unimportant in the face of reverence for God—Islam was the equalizer in Somali society, and beyond Somali

---

[33] Sheikh Haji Osman in interview states that the only drums used were hand held ones for the chanting rhythm, which is a different kind of drum from the dancing drums, but other sources indicate that dancing drums were also used.

[34] Nimtz, August. *Islam and Politics in East Africa*, Minneapolis, 1980, p. 101

[35] Pouwels, R. Op. sit., p.595

[36] Interview Sheikh Haji Osman.

society—as exampled by the story of Sheekh Uways at the tomb of the Prophet.

For the more marginalized people of Somalia and the rest of East Africa, Islam was a way to transcend non-noble lineage, but as much as people wanted to improve their status they still needed to define themselves ethnically. The recurring image of dance in the stories about Sheekh Uways show the constant contradiction in Islamic East African society between dance for enjoyment and dance for religion. Dr. Francesca Declich, an Italian anthropologist who did her research among the people of the lower Juba river, chronicles the role of dance in the Islamic conversion of the people of Gosha:

> In order to understand this dualistic opposition [drum dancing and dhikhr, religious trance dancing and chanting] in the local understanding, a mechanism of Islamization of the Gosha area which is recounted orally is worth mentioning. Sheekhs used to attract people to "dance" their dhikhr. . .. Although the sheekhs considered dhikhr as the opposite to dances employing drum play, originally they used the tactic of persuading Gosha people to alternate daily between the two dances; those which employed drum playing and the dhikhr. In other words, the way Muslim saints caught the attention of Gosha people is establishing a competition among different kinds of dances. Having convinced people to dance a few times, the sheekhs progressively established a foothold.[37]

Dance as a metaphor for both religious and secular identity, as Dr. Declich found in Gosha oral tradition, is mirrored in the following story about Sheekh Uways and the conversion or recommitment to Islam of another group of people in Southern Somalia.

> This is the story of Sheekh Oyaaye of Jowhar. The people of Jowhar were dancing every day and the best of the dancers was a man called Oyaaye, who danced until he cried. When Sheekh Uways came to Jowhar, he knew that if he could change Oyaaye into a religious man all the others would follow. Sheekh Uways started reciting his poetry and Oyaaye stopped dancing and began to do Dhikhr. The people were surprised and then Oyaaye was called Sheekh. The people said, "He was just dancing, how can he now be a sheekh?" Sheekh Uways answered, "We will go ask the trees". Oyaaye asked the trees if he was a sheekh. They answered that he was a sheekh and that he would marry a daughter of Sheekh Uways (and they gave her name). That is how Sheekh Oyaaye and the

---

[37] Declich, F. "Identity, Dance, and Islam among People with Bantu Origins in Southern Somalia", presented at the African Studies Association Convention, Seattle, Washington November, 1992, and to soon be published in The Invention of Somalia, edited by Ali Jimale Ahmed, published by Red Sea Press.

people of Jowhar became religious, and Sheekh Uways' daughter did marry the former dancer. [38]

Europeans became more and more worried as Islam, which in many areas of East Africa had been the religion of the elites, now was clearly attracting the have-nots, especially as it took on more and more the cry "Africa for Africans."[39]

Uwaysiyya missionaries were active in large sections of Tanzania. According to German records a Sheekh Zahur B. Muhaamad, originally from Barva, and a khalif of Sheekh Uways, was responsible for many conversions to Islam by first teaching the dhihkr ritual in the Tabor region. He became increasingly popular with the African masses of the towns, especially the Manyema who had been former slaves. During a successful rainmaking ritual, he angered the Arab elites in the area and was exiled to Zanzibar by the Germans. [40] This raises the interesting question of who were the followers of the Uwaysiyya? From Somalia to the Eastern Congo many former marginalized people were Islamized by the order. While the order apparently appealed to many of the lowest members of the social order, in various parts of East Africa also the disenfranchised Arab elites joined the order as seen by Tippu Tib and the Sultans of Zanzibar. By the late 1880's various Arab ruling classes were being disenfranchised in East Africa. These people including the two famous Arab slave runners Tippu Tib and Rumaliza, who were losing their position, income and power to the encroaching British and Germans. They definitely were unwilling to capitulate:

> Between 1884 and 1888. . .the policy of the Arabs changed abruptly
> all over Central Africa. What were the connecting threads in this
> movement, and in particular what part was played in it by Sultan
> Barghash bin Said at Zanzibar will probably never exactly be known.
> The fact that the same thing happened in so many different places,
> must, I think, be taken as proof of central planning and, since there
> was no direct communications, say between the Arabs of Nyasa and
> those of Tanganyika, the planning must have taken
> place at the coast. . .the Arabs were now aiming at political power,
> and they were seeking to drive out the Europeans. [41]

A. Nimitz in his book on Islamic Tariqas in Tanzania comes to a similar conclusion but specifically points to Sheekh Uways:

> The Qadiri leader (Sheekh Uways) was invited to Zanzibar at the
> same time that European imperialism was looking covetously at
> the Busa'id empire.' Hedged in by foreigners, and under constant
> pressure from them, Sayyid Barghash was ready to use all the
> political weapons he would find as a means of rallying his old

---

[38] Interview Sheikh Haji Osman

[39] Pouwels, op cit., p. 597

[40] Nimtz, op cit., p. 30

[41] Martin, B G. *Muslim Brotherhoods in 19th Century Africa* p.167

supporters among the Sunni Safi'is of inner Tanganyika. [42]

The Uwaysiyya was the organization that connects all these regions. The incident of the Moslem coup in Buganda in 1888 is a good example. The leader of this coup was a trader who was also a leading member of the Qadiriyya in Buganda. He was a close friend of Baraghash, sultan of Zanzibar, and he was able to oppose the Europeans and their missionaries in Buganda for a couple of years. When he returned to Zanzibar he was heavily fined, but there are indications the punishment was for show only. [43]

Sultan Baraghash was also helping the Islamic insurrection against the Germans at the coast, and it is quite possible that his capitulation to the European powers was superficial. Whether the Uwaysiyya was involved can only be speculated, but it is the one organization that was found in all the areas fighting against the colonialists. And given the fact that the Zanzibari and coastal Arabs have had a long relationship with Barwa and the Somali wadaad's from there, it could well be that Sheekh Uways was not just the holy man, but the most important leader of the anti-colonial struggle in East Africa.

In German controlled Tanganyika, the Uwasiyya appears to have played an important role. From 1905 to 1907 the Maji Maji rebellion, which was an uprising in the southern regions of Tanzania, occurred. For the first time it united Africans of diverse ethnicity in opposition to colonial rule. Islam was reported to have made its greatest gains directly after the defeat of the Maji Maji, especially among the Ngindo and Pogoro people.[44] One main reason for this increase is possibly that Moslem teachers, probably of the Uwaysiyya (since they were quite active in the area) helped spread the revolt. But more important was the fact that the prevailing ideology of the Maji Maji was animist and with its defeat a new ideology was needed in order to continue the struggle against colonialism. The Germans were increasingly afraid of the spread of Islam in the area. This was in part due to the role Islam played in the Maji Maji rebellion, but more importantly Germans saw that with the Mahdi in the Sudan and the jihad against the British in Northern Somalia; Islam was becoming synonymous with a call for African nationalism in East Africa.

Sheekh Uways was constantly sending followers into the mainland across from Zanzibar which included German Tanganyika. As more and more support was being built for the sufi order, the Germans were becoming nervous about the Uwasiyya. This culminated in the incident referred to in German documents as the "letter from Mecca". The letter contained clearly anti-colonial statements and was an attempt to instigate struggle against the German colonialists.

The governor of the colony, von Rechenberg, suspected that there

---

[42] Nimtz, Op. sit, p.73
[43] Martin, B. G. JAH, 1969, p.476
[44] Nimtz Op. sit, p.12

was associated with the letter's dissemination an Islamic movement whose ritual was a 'zikri or dervish dance.' Furthermore, he thought the movement was pan-Islamic: 'The trail leads to Barawa on the Italian Somali Coast. . .. This fits in with the view that Barawa Arabs. . .are the bearers of the movement. [45]

Some German Colonial authorities did not believe the Qadiriyya was involved or that significant in the area, but the Qadiriryya was in the town of Mpapwa when the letter was circulated in 1908.[46] It appears that at least two of those accused of circulating the letter were part of the Uwaysiyya and the Germans began trying to suppress the brotherhood, which today is strong in the area. One might conclude that suppression from the colonialist was a guarantee of longevity for a sufi order.

> The Germans debated the impact of Islam in the area, but the district officer at Bagamoyo stated: Although I should not like to go so far [as] to impute to Islam a staunch anti-European and aggressive tendency as an intrinsic characteristic. . .. I am in favor of any measures suitable to impair and stop Islamic teachings which impede any healthy cultural progress, for the benefits of the Christian and Germanic Culture. [47]

In 1911 the Germans saw the Moslem reaction in Dar es Salaam to the Italian invasion of the Ottoman empire. Mass protests were staged in coastal and upcountry towns in opposition to the invasion. At Zanzibar, six to seven thousand Moslems demonstrated, and many bands of Arabs and Swahilis had holy flags with them. Flags and banners were used almost exclusively by Moslems in the Qadiriyya in East Africa.

One important link between Sheekh Uways and the pan-Islamic movement is that the father of Uways teacher, Salman B. Ali (1843-1895) was on very close terms with Abd'al Hamid II, Sultan of the Ottoman Empire. It is very possible that the Sultan used his connections with Uways to further the pan Islamic movement in East Africa. This could also explain the explosion of Islamic sentiment with the European invasion of the Ottoman Empire a few years later.

In summation the spread of the Uwaysiyya from Brawa to Zanzibar to the Tanganyikan mainland and from there to the Eastern Congo establishes the order as a major Muslim movement in East Africa. In 1883 the Uwaysiyya reached the coastal region across from Zanzibar and was responsible for massive conversions to Islam in many areas. After the death of Uways, the order continued to spread. In Rwanda and Burundi, and through the Congo Tanzanian border region, the order was called the Muridi movement. The relationship of its leaders and the Khalifas from Tanzania, Ujiji, Dar es Salaam and Zanzibari, show that they are all

---

[45] Ibid, p.73
[46] Ibid, p.76
[47] Ibid, p. 80

connected.[48] It is also clear that the Uwaysiyya was more than strictly a "religious movement," it included anti imperialist ideology and actions. In fact it seemed to grow in direct proportions to the encroachment of European colonialism. Many persons joined for various reasons, but the unifying element, besides the belief in God, appears to have been the anti-imperialist stand of the order.

It would be an oversimplification and blatantly incorrect to view the Uwaysiyya or any Islamic movement as purely political. Western scholars tend to analyze these movements as either political or religious ignoring the fact that almost any Islamic movement that includes political action as still essentially a religious movement.

> Islam is the religion which has most completely confounded and intermixed the two powers...so that all the acts of civil and political life are regulated more or less by religious law.[49]

The idea of "give unto Caesar what is Caesar's" is a Christian concept, not an Islamic one. The line between political and religious is indeed very fine in Islam. It is especially important to keep this in mind when analyzing the contributions of Sheekh Uways. He was both an important Pan-Islamic leader and a great holy man, with important theological contributions to Islam.

Many scholars feel that the Uwaysiyya was a millenarian movement lead by the charisma [baraka] of the great mystic Sheekh Uways who called himself "Friend of the Time".[50] Most of Sheekh Uways writings have not been researched by Western scholars, and until this is done, I am not sure how much of a millenarian movement it was. But there is evidence to show that this movement was revivalist among the already Islamized populations of East Africa, but it also converted to Islam large sections of people in the area. As in most of the revivalist movements of the period, the success of the colonial powers was blamed on the Moslem laxness:

> These movements tend to justify the erosion of the Muslim Position vis-a-vis the Christians on grounds of divine displeasure—Muslims were allowed to suffer under the Christian infidel because they were under divine disfavor brought by their wickedly sinful way in wandering away from the Straight Path." [51]

It is important to remember that in Somali oral tradition the downfall in the eighteenth century of the Ajuraan theocracy is blamed on the same "backsliding" of the faithful.

---

[48] Ibid, p.73
[49] Gellner, Ernest, *Muslim Society*, London, 1981 p1
[50] Samatar, Said. "Poetry in Somali Politics", p.182
[51] Ibid, p.181

The Uwaysiyya went further, as seen in the Islamic conversions after the Maji Maji Rebellion, to show those who were not Islamized or only partially that Islam practiced correctly was their only defense against the colonial powers. And given the large numbers and varied class and ethnic groups who joined the Uwaysiyya, Islam was perceived as an effective belief system that would enable the people to fight the colonialist. Islam had also once been the belief primarily of the traders and the elites in various societies of East Africa, but with the spread of the Uwaysiyya, Islam became the religion of the East African masses.

The Uwaysiyya and the Qadiriyya as a whole tended to be a less "puritanical" or "fundamentalist" than many of the other Islamic movements of the period. As previously stated certain Bantu customs, like drums and banners, were allowed within the tenets of the Uwaysiyya and undoubtedly this helped in the massive conversions to Islam. But the use of certain forms of non-Islamic Bantu culture in the conversion process is only to lead people to "the correct path" as is exemplified by the above stories concerning the battle between secular dancing and dikhir. It seemed that the Uwaysiyya was actually revivalist in that it "revitalized " all of East Africa's interest in Islam, but very innovative in that it allowed for certain cultural differences and changes among those that embraced it.

The death of Sheekh Uways at the hands of members of a rival tariqa, the Salihiya, raises some interesting questions. Sheekh Uways was preaching in an area where the Salihiya was quite strong. Some newly converted Jidle clansmen killed the Sheekh and twenty-six of his twenty-seven disciples. Those who killed this holy man "truly repented of their deeds." [52] But their remorse was not shared by Sayyid Mohammad Hassan who wrote this verse after learning of the holy man's death:

> Rejoice, rejoice and shout with gladness
> Behold, at long last, when we slew the old wizard
> the rains began to come![53]

The above poem is questioned by various religious people from Southern Somalia who say that in fact the Sayyid was very upset and scared when he found out that his followers had killed the holy man. He is reported to have said, "this is the end of us". . .and a few days later he and his followers faced defeat.[54]

Whether or not the Sayyid was overjoyed or scared by the murder of Sheekh Uways, it was symbolic both of clan warfare and the differences between the economic and social structures of north and south Somalia.

---

[52] Ibid, p, 186

[53] bid, p 187

[54] Interview with Sheikh Haj Osman, according to historical records Sheekh Uways was murdered in 1909 and the bombing of the Sayyid's headquarters occurred in 1920, but the significance of the different interpretation of the Sayyid's reaction to the holy man's death is a north/ south one. Whether the Sayyid fell two days or eleven years later, seems less important than whether his murder of Sheekh Uways caused his eventual downfall.

For centuries Somali pastoral clans have killed each other over grazing rights, water holes and camels, but this time the deadly clashes involved religious differences within Islam. But the intense hostility between the Salihiya (an off-shoot of the Ahmadiya) and the Uwaysiyya was based on much bigger issues than whether a dead saint could be an intercessionary to God. Sheekh Uways, who was able to united many different ethnic groups and classes under one sufi order, was killed by fellow Somalis.

The Salihiya was started by the northern Somali, Sayyid Mohammed Hassan, whose lineage played an important part in his rise to power. His mother was a Dulbahante, a pastoral nomadic clan that is known for its excessive warfare. [55] His father was from the Ogadeen clan. Both clans operated in a area that was to become part of British Somaliland. In 1894 Sayyid Mohammed went to Mecca and became ordained as a Salihiya khalif. The Salihiya was popular in Arabia and spreading along the Red Sea area into Northern Somalia. He returned to Somalia and starting preaching this very "puritanical" form of Islam. His main supporters were his mother's and his father's clans, and he soon launched a jihad against the British. His whole base of power was two of the major Northern Somali clans.

As the Uwaysiyya was gaining much support in Southern Somalia and East Africa; and in Northern Somalia the other branch of the Qadiryya, the Zeyli'iya still had clout among various Somali Northern clans; the Salihiya was trying to survive in its battle with British colonialism and for the hearts of the Somalis. Even though Sayyid Mohammed Hassan (dubbed the Mad Mullah, first by the Qadariyya and later by the British) fought a very successful war against the British and is considered by some as the father of Somali nationalism, in essence his jihad was based almost exclusively on clan affiliation. And this is logical because the changes economically that had occurred in Southern Somalia had only slightly affected the North. The majority of people in the very dry and inhospitable north were still nomadic pastoralists, dependent on clan relations to survive.

The different development between the northern and southern portions of the Somali territory contributed heavily to a confrontation with Sheekh Uways, who as previously stated was of less than noble lineage, from the more economically and socially integrated southern area and born in the city Brawa that has historically had strong ties with the rest of the East African Coast. This confrontation started out in poetry, a traditional Somali form of struggle.

According to Said Samatar the following is a translation of a Sheekh Uways poem to the Sayyid:

> Blessed are Muhammad and his family
> Turn to them in every calamity
> The person guided by Muhaamad's law
>   will not follow the faction of Satan
> Who deem it lawful to spill the blood of the learned

---

[55] Samatar, Said. "Poetry in Somali Politics." p. 181

who take cash and women too: they are anarchists
They hinder the study of sciences
  Like law and grammar. they are the Karramiya
To every dead Shaykh like al-Gilani
  They deny access to God, like the Janahiya
Don't follow those men with big shocks of hair
  A coiffure like the Wahhabiya!
In our land, they are a sect of dogs
  Having permission, they dally with women
Even their own mothers, which is nothing but incest
  They follow their own subjective opinions
And no book of ours!
  Their light is from the Devil
They deny god at their dhikir
  In word and action they are unbelievers
Like their game of saying "God?"
  "Lodge a complaint with Him!"
How they are glorified by the Northerners
  Great clamor they make, a moaning and groaning!
A noise like the barking of curs
  In divorce cases they augment the oath
But they abridge the religious ceremonies
  They've gone astray and make others deviate on earth
By land and sea amongst the Somalis
  Have they no reason or understanding?
Be not deceived by them
  But flee as from a disaster
From their infamy and unbelief.

And Sayyid Mohammed A. Hassan's answer was:
  A word to the barking apostates
When the holy separated from the wicked,
  As deer from gazelle
God! Pardon us! How is it that you
  absconded with Bad-eyes?
Forsaking your lawful wives
  How have you opted to cohabit with the hairy Dog?"
And it never fills you with revulsion
  that you should continue to skin the pigs
In addition to degrading, how is it
  That you earned hell?
What on earth! Since when did you turn
  A progeny of the Evil One?

Why've you gone astray
  From the Prophet way, the Straight Path?
Why is the Truth so plain

So hidden from you? [56]

It is reported that there are other "battle" poems. In the future a more in-depth study of the poetry could help shed more light on their particular struggle. But from the above it is clear that there was much antagonism between the two. Uways calls Hassan a dog among many other things and Hassan also accuses Uways of "skinning pigs and working for the devil." Hassan accuses Uways of collaborating with the British, which is most certainly untrue. As shown above, the Uwaysiyya fought the British in East Africa and Uwaysiyya was not even present in the areas controlled by the British in Somalia. Possibly the Zaili'iya was collaborating with the British (it is not clear), but most probably Hassan was just trying to stir up the anger of his followers.

The line in Hassan's poem about the gazelle and the deer comes from the Somali belief that the two never graze together. This is very possibly a criticism of Uways widely varied following, as opposed to Hassan's pure "noble" Somali one. The skinning of the pig could represent the fact that drums and banners were being used in the various Uwaysiyya rituals, something that is found to be an abhorrence to the "noble" Somali Salihiyya. But of more significance is that Sheekh Uways clearly shows the nature of the struggle in the line "How they are glorified by the Northerners." The struggle was a north/south one. This struggle was no longer just over water or grass for grazing it has been elevated to the question of political/religious power. In the murder of Sheekh Uways one finds the beginnings of the clan political struggles that were to and are plaguing the modern Somali nation. Most Somali scholars write that the Sufi movements of the Benaadir were not anti-imperialist.

> Throughout the Benaadir, however, the tariiqa's had little
> to do with the active opposition to colonialism.
> In the Benaadir, however, the tariqas for the most part had
> little to do with the active opposition to colonialism.[57]

They cite the fact that the leaders were of lowly birth, the capitulation in the case of Uways of certain Tunni clan leaders to the Italians, and the fact that a full-scale jihad against the colonialists was not launched from the South like the one led by Sheekh Hassan in the North.

The majority of the history written about turn of the century Somalia is centered around Hassan's jihad. Usually Uways' "claim to fame" is that he was killed by a follower of Hassan. This is in part due to the fact that Hassan was in the North and his struggle was chronicled by the British in English. It also behooved British imperialism to show the struggle of Hassan as a Somali national struggle, because it would have been embarrassing to admit that it took them almost 20 years to subdue a few Northern Somali clans. The most interesting information about Uways was discovered when Arabic sources were consulted. The

---

[56] Ibid, p. 185
[57] Ibid

colonialists in East Africa knew that there was some organized anti-colonial force, but were never able to concretely prove it was the Uwaysiyya. The reason for the lack of colonial records on the Uwaysiyya is that the tariqa was well organized and able to keep much from the Europeans.

An example of the Uwaysiyya's political significance is that the tariqa was important in the formation of modern Somali political parties. Many of the founding fathers of these parties were members of the Uwaysiyya. An example is Abdulqadir Sakh'uddin, the founder of S Y L, the most nationalist of the Somali parties. He is not only Uwaysi, but the grandson of Sheekh Uways.[58] Besides the lack of documentation in English on Uways, there is a tendency in Somali historiography to see all Somalis as nomadic pastoralists and negate the very different economic development that was occurring in the southern part of Somalia; a development that gave birth to a pan-Islamic movement led by Sheekh Uways.

The recent chapter written by Said Samatar entitled "Sheekh Uways Muhammad of Baraawe, 1847-1909, Mystic and Reformer in East Africa" in In the Shadow of Conquest, Islam in Colonial Northeast Africa. [59] is an example of the attempt by northern Somalis to create a national history that excludes the agricultural people and other Southern Somalis. Under the guise of supporting a place for Sheekh Uways in Somali history Samatar accuses the holy man of having a "martyr complex" (he was asking to be killed) and incapable of writing well in Somali (though Dr. Samatar freely admits that he cannot read Mai, the Somali language in which Sheekh Uways' poetry is written, a fact that does not seem to inhibit his criticism of its literary value). Dr. Samatar sets up the philosophical constraint that "The Somali nation rests on two central pillars of inestimable value: the teaching of Islam on the one hand and lyric poetry on the other." He then proceeds to lightly criticized Sheekh Muhammad Abdul Hassan's religious credentials, but dub him the Somali Shakespeare, whereas he calls Sheekh Uways "an unmitigated disaster in Somali [language]" and "a doggerel writer." This is not just an academic exercise, it is an example of an attempt to create a national history that not only excludes half the population, it denigrates one of the most important southern Somali historical figures. In light of the recent tragedy of the disintegration of the Somali state, a one-sided Somali history must be criticized and a new impartial history written which will include important Somalis such as Sheekh Uways.

---

[58] Per Dr. Mohamed Mukhtar
[59] Red Sea Press, New York, 1992.

RESISTANCE, REVENUE AND DEVELOPMENT IN NORTHERN SOMALIA, 1905–1939

By Patrick Kakwenzire

By the outbreak of World War II the small British Somali Protectorate in Northern Somalia was probably the most undeveloped British dependency in the whole of the British Empire. It was undeveloped in the sense that it lacked virtually all the criteria which are attributed to the concept of development in the modern sense. It was evidently the only British dependency which did not have any form of Western education, social services, modern industrial activity, middle entrepreneur class, organized labor, cash crops, large-scale commercial farming or any other attributes of a developed or developing society. The territory's efforts to develop an export trade in hides and skins achieved temporary success and then came to a grinding halt when America and Egypt, the major consumers of those commodities, declared a ban on all Somali-originating animal products on account of the rampant animal diseases in the country. The territory's communication system, based on murram roads, was in terrible shape; the only modern road that the Protectorate could boast of in 1939 was the Berbera-Jigjiga road which was built by the Italians in 1937 as part of Mussolini's African dream. The first Western-type secondary school was built in 1942, and the Somali language remained unwritten until an orthography was adopted in 1972.[1] When Winston Churchill, then under-secretary of state, but already a vociferous advocate of British imperialism, visited the Protectorate in 1907, he uncharacteristically recommended its total abandonment, and he made very uncomplimentary remarks about the Protectorate, one of them being that the governor's residence was unfit for a decent English dog.[2]

This paper examines British Somalia's lack of development in the context of the country's revenue-earning capacity and the people's general antipathy for British colonial rule between 1905 and 1939. It was in 1905 that Britain, having failed to defeat the anti-colonial Dervish movement of Sayyid Muhammad Abdille Hassan (known in European literature as the Mad Mullah) in four costly military expeditions, decided on retrenchment, and subsequently on stagnation, as the policies she would henceforth pursue in her Somali territory. This attitude persisted until the late 1930s when Italy defeated Haile Selassie's regime in

---

[1] The government Committee which recommended the present orthography was chaired by a distinguished Somali poet, the late Muse Galaal.

[2] For a full report of Churchill's report, see R. Hyam, *Elgin and Churchill at the Colonial Office* (London, 1968), Ch. 10.

International Journal of African Historical Studies, 19, 4 (1986) **659**

THE HORN OF AFRICA

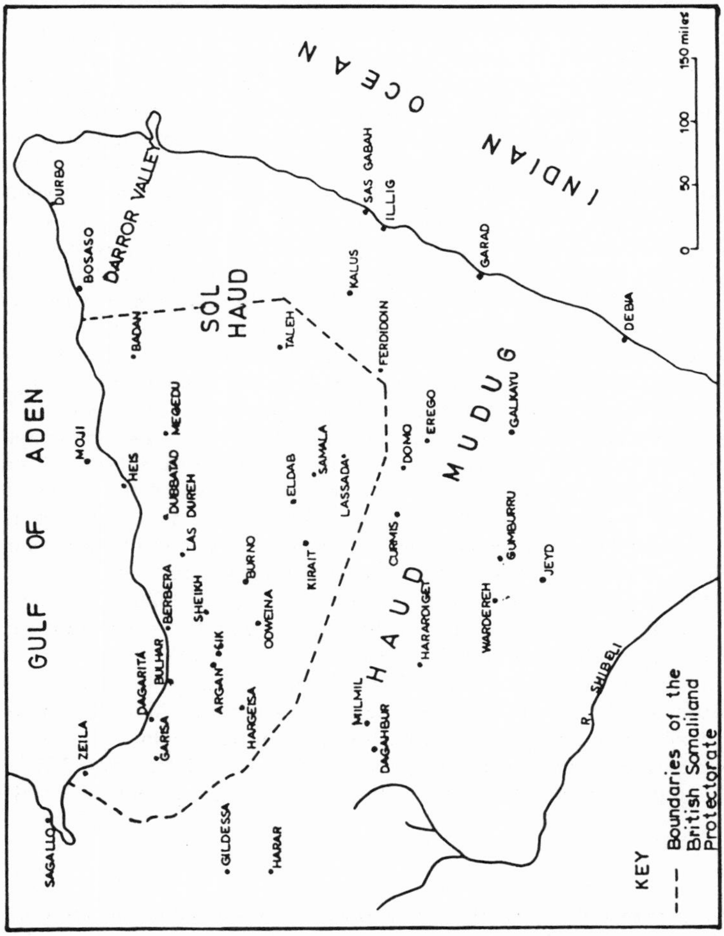

Ethiopia and thereafter embarked on a policy of massive industrialization and modernization in the new Fascist acquisition. Britain, whose backward little Somali territory shared a common border with Ethiopia, was terribly embarrassed by the glaring differences in development between Mussolini's newly acquired showpiece and their own territory, for which there was nothing to show after well over three decades of British rule. Moreover, the Italian-built road, which traversed the British Protectorate, stimulated some amount of economic prosperity, thereby encouraging the hitherto inactive British administration to make tentative efforts towards development.

Britain's initial motive in acquiring the territory was to defend her strategic interests in the Red Sea. Britain also assumed that the Protectorate would fall within the general pattern of her other dependencies, namely, that a colonial administration would be set up, missionary work would be encouraged, and, more importantly, taxation and other revenue-earning projects would be undertaken. British Somalia did not conform to this general pattern, however; the most crucial point of departure was not so much that the Somali resisted colonial rule - for this was a widespread phenomenon throughout colonial Africa - but that the territory was totally lacking in economic opportunities. Having failed to discover any exploitable resources and having failed to tax the Somali, Britain turned her back on her Somaliland Protectorate, keeping it solely for the purpose of defending her strategic interests in the Red Sea. That is why Britain's attitude towards the whole question of development in Somalia changed drastically when the Italian occupation of Ethiopia in 1935, and ultimately the eviction of Italy herself from the Horn of Africa in 1941, transformed the geopolitical situation of the region. The occupation of Ethiopia ushered in a period of economic prosperity; the expulsion of the Italians increased Britain's sphere of influence by bringing ex-Italian Somalia and the Ogaden under British administration.[3] The economic opportunities in the area now under British control improved substantially. Thus, notwithstanding the fact that the Somali had not changed their attitude towards colonial rule, Britain found it possible to initiate a number of development projects from late 1930s.

Background

"The Somali admire our rule, respect our power, comprehend our forbearance . . . and evince a gentleness of disposition and a docility which offer fair hopes of civilization in this region of barbarism."[4] Thus did Richard Burton misjudge the Somali, following his short visit on the Somali coast in 1855. Thirty-two years later, the British established a formal protectorate of 68,000 square miles on the

---

[3]The former Italian colony was returned to Italy in 1950 to be administered as a trust territory of the United Nations for ten years. In 1960 it was amalgamated with the British Protectorate, forming the present Republic of Somalia. The Ogaden was returned to Ethiopia in 1954.

[4]Burton as quoted by A.M. Brockett, "British Somaliland Protectorate to 1905" (Ph.D. thesis, Oxford University, 1969), 22.

Somali coast, directly opposite Aden. By the turn of the century, Britain found herself grappling with the anticolonial movement of Sayyid Muhammad Abdille Hassan, which challenged British authority for more than two decades.

Sayyid Muhammad was born in or about 1864 at Kirrit, in the currently disputed Ogaden. He belonged to the Bagheri section of the Dolbahanta. He was brought up in a strict religious environment, for it was his father's aim to give him a sound knowledge of the Islamic faith and law. By the age of fifteen, young Muhammad was already an acknowledged authority on Islamic law. At the age of nineteen he earned the prestigious title of shaikh.

Thus, from his childhood the Sayyid was involved with questions of religious morality and reform. His religious zeal was enhanced by his constant pilgrimages to Mecca, and his affiliation to the militant and puritanical Salihiyya brotherhood. He returned from his last pilgrimage in 1895 and settled at Berbera where, according to one Somali writer, he was appalled by the fact that "Muslims and unbelievers lived together in large numbers."[5] The Sayyid was particularly incensed by two phenomena. The first was the arrogant manner in which the small white community at Berbera carried themselves, going as far as to proselytize in the Christian tradition, in utter disregard of Muslim sensitivities. The second was the French Catholic Mission which was busy converting young Somali boys and girls to Christianity, thereby undermining Somali cultural and social foundations. Thus, Sayyid Muhammad came to the conclusion that he had no choice but to champion a cause against the British, who had become a direct threat to the three main pillars upon which Somali society was founded - their faith, their independence, and their socio-economic institutions.

The showdown came with an incident in which a European customs officer insisted that Sayyid Muhammad should pay customs duties on some goods he had brought with him from an overseas visit towards the end of 1899. Sayyid Muhammad evidently refused to pay any duty, inquiring of the customs official, "did you pay the customs duties when you landed here? Who gave you permission to enter our country?"[6] Shortly after this incident the Sayyid left Berbera for the interior and established his headquarters in the Ogaden, where he declared a jihad against the British and their collaborators.

The details of the Sayyid's resistance and of Britain's expeditions between 1900 and 1905 are, strictly speaking, beyond the scope of this study.[7] Suffice it to say that Britain despatched four military expeditions to destroy the Sayyid's Dervish movement, without success. Two problems confronted the British right from the start. The first was their inadequate knowledge of the real strength and tenacity of the Dervish movement. The second related problem was one of costs.

---

[5]Sheikh Jaamac Cumar Ciise, *Tarikh al-Sumal fi-l-'usur al-Wusta wa-l-Hadithah* (Cairo, 1965), 17.

[6]Cited in B.G. Martin, *Muslim Brotherhoods in 19th Century Africa* (Cambridge, 1976), 181.

[7]For details of the Sayyid's resistance, see I.M. Lewis, *A Modern History of Somalia* (Harlow, 1980), Ch. iv; also P.K. Kakwenzire, "Colonial Rule in the British Somaliland Protectorate 1905-1939 (Ph.D. thesis, University of London, 1976), Chs. 1-4.

Britain had certainly underestimated the Sayyid's strength when she sent the first expedition against him in April 1901. The local administration believed that the Sayyid could be defeated by a force consisting of 50 Punjabi drillers and a locally recruited levy of 1,500 Somalis. A Foreign Office proposal to send regular troops from India was turned down on the grounds that such a measure was unnecessary.

By August 1901 Britain had realized that the Sayyid's strength had been grossly underestimated. The five-month campaign against him had not only failed to check his movements, but had also left several British officers dead and Britain's reputation at stake.

Britain organized a second expedition; this time troop reinforcements were brought from various K.A.R. battalions, and more powerful guns, including three maxim guns, were added to the arsenal. In October the second expedition was called off, having fared even worse than the previous one, despite more comprehensive military preparation.

Between January 1903 and the end of 1904 Britain sent two further expeditions, organized on a more elaborate scale than the previous ones. Yet the result was the same: the Sayyid could not be defeated. The British were thoroughly alarmed not only by the extent to which they had got themselves involved in senseless wars in the deserts of Somalia, and for a cause which could neither be defended nor defined, but also by the colossal losses in revenue and personnel. The Sayyid himself was at a loss to understand what Britain was up to, fighting for so worthless a thing as Somalia; he wrote to the British officials in the Protectorate,

> We have fought for a year. I wish to rule my country and
> protect my own religion. If you wish, send me a letter saying
> whether there is to be peace or war. . . . I have no forts, no
> houses, I have no cultivated fields, silver or gold for you to
> take. If the country was cultivated or contained houses or
> property, it would be worth your while to fight, but the
> country is all jungle and that is of no use to you. If you wish
> war I am happy, if you wish peace I am also content. But if
> you wish peace go away from my country to your own. If you
> wish war stay where you are.[8]

The Aftermath of the Expeditionary Period 1905-1920

The four expeditions had failed to defeat the Sayyid's movement. However, the Sayyid had suffered heavy losses in men and equipment and that forced him to

---

[8]Cited in D.J. Jardine, *The Mad Mullah of Somaliland* (London, 1923), 122. Jardine served as chief secretary of the Protectorate administration for more than twenty years, including a good part of the period of the Sayyid's resistance. Jardine collected several of the Sayyid's letters, had them translated from their original Arabic into English, and incorporated some of them in his above-quoted book.

173

seek temporary refuge in Italian Somalia. The Italian authorities arranged a peace agreement between the subdued Sayyid and the British in 1905, in which both sides promised to observe peace. It soon transpired, however, that the Sayyid had only wanted to buy time for recuperation. Before a year was out, he had resumed his operations against the British authorities.

Britain was thoroughly vexed by the Sayyid's resumption of hostilities. The four previous expeditions had become an embarrassment to the British government; the futile adventure had cost British taxpayers 2,494,000 pounds.[9] The House of Commons took the government to task, demanding to know why so much money could be wasted on a worthless cause. The hard-pressed secretary of state for the colonies had to placate Parliament by announcing a new policy for the Protectorate:

> The wisest and most prudent policy to pursue in the future is to limit our administrative responsibility to the coast line, but there is a corollary to that policy and that is that we should arm the friendly tribes and organize them so as to be in a position to defend themselves in the event of any emergency such as that with which they have been recently confronted.[10]

An issue the secretary of state avoided was how he intended to guarantee the security of British administration on the coast, since the immediate hinterland was to be left to the tender mercies of the Sayyid and other Somali tribes over whom the British would no longer exercise any real authority. The secretary of state also failed to explain how the Sayyid, who had held his ground against the weight of Britain's imperial forces in four expeditions, was to be contained by a Somali militia, armed with British-supplied weapons but otherwise largely on their own.

Be that as it may, Britain's decision in 1905 was to diminish her responsibilities in the Somali Protectorate to a level where the territory would not continue to be a financial burden. No matter how small the British establishment became, however, expenditures would always exceed revenue, since the territory was without any exploitable resources or viable commercial activities.

At various points in the colonial history of British Somalia, Winston Churchill and other British statesmen had advocated its complete abandonment on account of its unproductivity, climatic inhospitability, and the hostility of its inhabitants. Churchill made his recommendations after undertaking an extensive tour of various British overseas territories in 1907. The tour had taken him to Malta, Cyprus, Somalia, the East Africa Protectorate and Uganda. With the exception of the British Somaliland Protectorate, Churchill supported Chamberlain's doctrine of developing Britain's "great estates" overseas. The

---

[9] The Parliamentary Debates (authorized edition) 1905, Vol. 142 (London, 1906), Column 180.

[10] *Ibid.*, Column 750.

impression he got of British Somalia was in sharp contrast to the optimistic picture he had gathered elsewhere; the British Somaliland Protectorate was barren, bankrupt and parasitical, and seemed to symbolize the irrationalities of the scramble for Africa:

> The general position in Somaliland is not satisfactory either from a financial or military point of view. The revenues of the country which are raised entirely on the coast might be sufficient to maintain a moderate civil service and military establishment for the purpose of holding seaports and patrolling the coastline. They are far from sufficient to support the forces necessary to rule the interior, and there is no likelihood of their becoming so. . . . It is scarcely possible to imagine a more uncomfortable situation. . . .[11]

Churchill then listed his objections to the idea of sending more military expeditions against the Sayyid, and concluded that the only sensible option left was for Britain to abandon, if not the whole Protectorate, at least the interior.

In both the Colonial Office and the Foreign Office, Churchill's recommendations were denounced by nearly everyone who expressed an opinion on them. Churchill's critics argued that, apart from damaging Britain's prestige in the eyes of both her colonial subjects and the other colonial powers, the loss of Somaliland would jeopardize Britain's strategic interests in the Red Sea, giving leverage to maritime rivals such as France, Italy, and Germany. Thus, the British Somaliland Protectorate was to be retained at any cost.

In 1919 Churchill's supporters urged the British government to donate the territory to Italy in return for some territorial concession in any of Italy's overseas territories. However, the Admiralty strongly denounced the advocates of such an arrangement, emphasizing "the importance of the strategic position of British Somaliland, and particularly of Berbera, in connection with the probable future sources of supply of oil. The importance of possessing ample sources of supply of oil - the fuel of the future - on British territory cannot be overestimated."[12] That settled, once and for all, Britain's position in so far as the future of the British Somaliland Protectorate was concerned.[13]

---

[11]C.O. 879/97, "A Minute on the Somaliland Protectorate," by W. Churchill, 28/11/1907.

[12]C.O. 535/57, Admiralty to F.O., 15/5/1919.

[13]Britain was really interested in the coastal strip of the Protectorate, and she would have happily donated the hinterland to either Ethiopia or Italy. In point of fact, she tried to do that on more than one occasion but Italy and Ethiopia were equally disinterested in the hinterland; they would settle for nothing less than the entire Protectorate, including the coast. That became the bone of contention, since Britain would under no circumstances cede the coast to anyone.

By 1908 the Protectorate's average annual revenue, derived mainly from the sale of hides and skins to Aden, was 38,000 pounds.[14] Yet total expenditure for the skeletal colonial establishment averaged 107,000 pounds per annum. The deficit was, therefore, made up by imperial grants-in-aid.[15] To make matters worse, the withdrawal of the expeditionary forces and their replacement with an ill equipped and frightened Somali militia augured well for the Sayyid's renewed military offensive. The militia were driven in head-long flight towards the coast where they agitated, unsuccessfully, for reinforcements. By 1908 the British administration on the coast was under serious threat from the advancing forces of the Sayyid. Britain's problems were compounded by the fact that the Sayyid insisted that Britain, and Britain alone, was responsible for whatever problem he might encounter, no matter who caused it; every one else was exonerated at the expense of Britain. Thus, he wrote to the colonial administrators in 1908:

> We also complained against the Italians who pester, incite and annoy us very much, and curse us in every way. Being cursed is harder for us to bear than having our necks cut off. They [the Italians] also captured our dhow and poisoned my son. . . . We must explain to you that we do not know the Italians, but only you, and the good or evil that they do towards or against us we attribute to you. This is the case with the Abyssinians too. We have one ear [sic] and if we want to have peace we ask it from you and not from anybody else.[16]

In 1910 Britain decided she had had enough of Somali problems. In view of the growing opposition to her colonial rule, to say nothing of the gloomy economic situation, Britain decided to withdraw completely from the interior with a view to holding the coast, which catered for Britain's strategic interests in the Red Sea.

Britain's withdrawal from the interior of her Somali Protectorate caused a row in Parliament and criticism in the press. *The Times* of London, for example, described the policy as "One of the most deplorable acts ever committed by a British Government,"[17] and one member of Parliament remarked, on the floor of the House, that "it was a most contemptible thing that, without giving Parliament the chance of discussion . . . we and the Somali should be allowed to wake up one morning and find that the Somali are going to be abandoned to the Mullah."[18] The irony was that it was these same two - the press and parliament - which were always the most outspoken critics of government expenditure on Somalia, on the grounds that the territory was of no value to Britain.

---

[14]Churchill, "A Minute on the Somaliland Protectorate."

[15]*Ibid.*

[16]Jardine, *The Mad Mullah*, 163-164.

[17]*The Times*, 8/4/1910.

[18]Parliamentary Debates (authorized edition), 1910, Vol. XV, Columns 1094 to 1100.

More serious than these criticisms was what happened in the post-withdrawal period. Withdrawal was followed by an unprecedented state of lawlessness and civil strife which spread to all corners of the Protectorate, and even beyond, eventually threatening Britain's position on the coast itself. Britain's withdrawal to the coast while the Sayyid reigned supreme in the interior could be likened to the old proverbial tactic of the ostrich which hides its head from the advancing enemy.

The administration tried in vain to get K.A.R. soldiers from various British dependencies to garrison the coast; no country was prepared to send its soldiers to the inhospitable climate of Somalia. Consequently, Aden agreed to despatch 320 Indian soldiers to defend the coast temporarily against possible Dervish invasion. After a protracted argument between the local administration and London, it was decided that complete withdrawal under those circumstances was unthinkable; an alternative security arrangement had to be devised to ensure, at least, that British personnel on the coast were not thrown into the sea.

Unfortunately, the arrangement which was finally devised turned out to be the most disastrous of all the British policies hitherto tried in that unfortunate territory. It consisted of a locally recruited camel corps 150 strong, under the command of an English officer. Its assignment was to ensure the security of the coast up to fifty miles of the hinterland. The Colonial Office was initially opposed to the whole idea, but gave in because the scheme appeared to be "cheaper than the cost of garrisoning the system in force."[19] One of the worst aspects of the Camel Corps was that it was placed under the command of a foolish young English officer by the name of Richard Corfield. He had served in Baden-Powell's Scouts movement in South Africa during the Anglo-Boer war. At the end of the war he returned to England without a job; he was generally bored by the relative absence of political turmoil in England. In November 1910 he accepted a job in northern Nigeria, thinking he would find a revolution there; on finding none, he decided to quit. Corfield was consumed by a blind craving for adventure and war.

On being appointed commander of the new Camel Corps, Corfield was warned to avoid any major collision with the Dervishes, since the Corps was not equipped or manned for that; it was meant to be a coastal constabulary and nothing more. Corfield would not obey such orders; he was obsessed with the fantasy that he would be the first man to kill or capture the Sayyid. On the 9th of August 1913, the Camel Corps - in defiance of previous instructions and numerous warnings - attacked a strong Dervish force at Dul Madoba, and was virtually wiped out, Corfield being one of the victims.[20]

Corfield's death unleashed the now-familiar uproar in the press and Parliament against what was regarded as government incompetence. Corfield acquired the status of a national martyr, and the government was left with no

---

[19] C.O. 535/27, Governor Byatt to C.O., 26/5/1912.

[20] H.F. Brovost-Baatersby, *Richard Corfield of Somaliland* (London, 1914), 245 ff.

choice but to rush reinforcements to Somalia, since further inaction would certainly have spelled disaster for the British administration on the coast. Whatever further measures Britain might have taken against the Dervishes were forestalled by the outbreak of World War I, which diverted Britain's attention and resources from the Somali problems. Thus, apart from occasional clashes, there was a general stalemate from 1914 to the end of the war in 1919.

Throughout the war period, the British government had promised the Somali administration that a full-scale assault would be undertaken against the Sayyid as soon as the War was over. At the end of the War, however, both the War Office and Foreign Office quickly dissociated themselves from the anticipated operations. It took the local administration more than ten months to persuade the two reluctant ministries to agree to a military expedition against the Sayyid who had already consolidated his position and had even acquired international recognition from the Central Powers.[21]

When the British government finally sanctioned the plans for a military expedition in December 1919, the governor, Geoffrey Archer, could not conceal his jubilation. He wrote to the Sayyid, "This letter is sent by the British Wali [representative] of the Somali to the Dervishes of the Mullah. It is carried by British Officers who, like the birds of the air, fly far and fast. The day of destruction of the Mullah and his power is at hand. He is a tyrant who has destroyed the country and this will be avenged."[22] After the Sayyid had rejected Archer's calls for unconditional surrender, the expedition was launched in earnest in January 1920. The expedition involved British air force, navy and several infantry units from different parts of the British empire.[23] Thus, the Sayyid was attacked from the air, from the sea, and on land. Towards the end of February 1920, the Sayyid's forces were routed from their strongholds, while the survivors, together with the Sayyid, vanished into the inhospitable parts of the Sogaden. Although the Sayyid had once more evaded death or capture, the operations of 1920 destroyed the Dervish movement once and for all. The Sayyid is believed to have died a natural death in the Ogaden sometime in 1921.

Stagnation, 1920 - 1931

The destruction of the Dervish movement brought relief to Britain and the local administration, as it was assumed that the Protectorate would thereafter be brought into line with the other British dependencies without further difficulty. The imperial Treasury lost no time in informing the local officials that it expected the Protectorate to generate funds through taxation and through any other schemes they might deem necessary and feasible. Quite apart from the undisclosed sums of money spent on the last expedition, the Protectorate had

---

[21]During the war the Sayyid was in constant touch with the sultan of Turkey and with the German government. They were keen to enlist his active support against the Allied Powers, especially against Britain.

[22]C.O. 535/41 Vol. 3, Archer to Mad Mullah, 30/12/1919.

[23]C.O. 535/41, Archer to C.O., 24/1/1920.

been subsidized by the Treasury since its inception, albeit with much reluctance. Besides the sale of hides and skins to Aden, the Protectorate's other sources of revenue included customs receipts, harbor dues, court fees and telegraphs. The income from those sources was not even enough to pay the salaries of the police establishment at Berbera. The following figures will give a general picture of the financial position:

Year	Revenue (£)	Expenditure (£)
1916-1917	40,000	125,000
1917-1918	42,000	115,000
1918-1919	54,498	147,328[24]

In the estimates for 1920-1921, the governor applied for an imperial grant-in-aid of 108,000 pounds. He explained, however, that "So far as can be foreseen, this request . . . constitutes the highest demand it should ever be necessary to make for this protectorate; for with the improved military situation, our commitments should be reduced, while the local revenue is capable of considerable expansion by the impending development of the Daga Shebel oil fields and other potential mineral resources, as well as by the diversion of Abyssinian trade to the Protectorate, on which it is proposed to concentrate effort next year."[25]

Without waiting for the Treasury's response to these fanciful and, quite frankly, fictitious predictions of the impending economic boom, the governor went ahead and budgeted for a number of projects, the most important one being education. On the question of immediate revenue, something on which the Treasury would not relent, the administration regarded the time as premature for initiating radical measures such as direct taxation. The omission of short-term revenue proposals prompted the Treasury to urge the Somali administration to consider the imposition of some form of direct taxation, as was the policy elsewhere in colonial Africa.

The local administration and the Colonial Office both regarded the introduction of some form of Western education as the best way of neutralizing the anticolonial legacy bequeathed by the Sayyid's resistance movement. The dominant form of education at that time consisted of memorizing a large number of Koranic verses. The need to introduce modern educational institutions in the Protectorate could, therefore, not be overemphasized. As far as the local administration was concerned, the overall advantages of starting a school outweighed whatever reservations the Treasury might have.

The governor invited E. R. J. Hussey, then inspector of schools in the Sudan, to visit the Protectorate, study the situation, and recommend a suitable educational scheme for the Protectorate. Hussey drew up a long memorandum

---

[24] Report on Somaliland Blue Book, 1918-1919 by Jardine.

[25] C.O. 535/56, Estimates of Revenue and Expenditure for 1920-1921.

which the Colonial Office commended as "astonishingly complete." Hussey's scheme was earmarked for 3,397 pounds. Without waiting for the Treasury's opinion, Hussey sent Richardson, then a teacher at Gordon College, to Somalia to become the first headmaster of the proposed school. Richardson arrived in Somalia in February 1921, equipped with books and a wide range of educational material he hoped to use. This development prompted the Colonial Office to remark that "this appointment should not have been made pending a decision on the estimates."[26] A month later the Treasury's decision came as a bombshell: there was to be no government-sponsored education, or any other development project for that matter, until the Protectorate was in a position to generate funds of its own. Thus, together with education, the Treasury slashed the other budgeted development projects.[27]

The Treasury's insistence that the Protectorate should devise its revenue-earning projects forced the local administration to experiment with unpopular revenue-earning measures, particularly direct taxation. The governor informed London in November 1921 that he was prepared to experiment with a form of direct taxation, but warned that it was likely to meet with strong opposition. Indeed, Governor Archer's attempt to tax the Somali was the first of its kind in the whole of the Somali-inhabited territory, as none of the other three occupying powers - Italy, France, or Ethiopia - had attempted it in their respective Somali-inhabited occupied territories. The other revenue-earning measures Archer proposed included an increase of customs duties by 15 percent, a compulsory registration of privately-owned rifles for which a fee would be paid, and a poll tax for the small non-Somali community on the coast. Even with all these measures, there was no prospect of the Protectorate balancing its budget within a foreseeable future; the best that was hoped was that the annual imperial grant-in-aid would reduce by half.

A month later Archer summoned the elders of the various Somali communities and informed them of his tax scheme. Although the proposals were reportedly "fairly well received," the delegates from Burao District raised objections on the grounds that, apart from the fact that the average man was too impoverished to afford it, the taxation of Muslims by non-Muslims was a blatant contravention of the Islamic law. Archer was neither swayed nor amused by the Burao dissenters, taking it for granted that the "aye" voices represented a genuine majority. He was soon to discover how mistaken he was.

On their return to the interior, the elders were heckled and in some cases stoned by angry mobs on account of their complicity in the proposed tax measures. Throughout the Protectorate anti-tax campaigns were launched by the Wadads (men of religion), who announced that any Muslim who paid the tax would pass for an infidel.

---

[26] C.O. 535/65, Minute by Machtig on the Governor's letter to C.O., 11/3/1921.

[27] C.O. 535/67, Treasury to C.O., 11/3/1921.

Archer realized that his tax scheme could be implemented only by coercion, and he duly applied for the establishment of an air force and for troop reinforcements from Aden. Both requests were turned down on the grounds that the projected punitive measures might end up costing more than whatever revenue Archer hoped to realize from his tax program. With the collapse of Archer's tax scheme, and the colonial office's instructions that he should shelve the other measures he had previously proposed, the Treasury's attitude towards development in Somalia stiffened even further. Archer was left with no choice but to cancel his plans for development and to continue begging for imperial grants-in-aid to meet the bare necessities of administration.

After everything concerning revenue and development had been laid to rest, Archer got a surprise in the form of a delegation of Somali elders in February 1922. The gist of their message was to the effect that they had thought the matter over and had decided to accept Archer's original tax proposals. They did not give him any reason for this sudden change of heart, but he surmised that the Somali were motivated by their dread of British withdrawal, reminiscent of what happened in 1910. Archer took the elders' word at face value. With conspicuous enthusiasm he started a country-wide tour, the purpose of which was to revive the issue of taxation. As part of his itinerary, he addressed an orderly rally at Burao. However, after the meeting, a group of local Wadads instigated an armed uprising in the town. The district commissioner of Burao, Captain Gibb, set out against Archer's well-considered advice, to meet and probably admonish the rioters, and was instantly shot and killed. The governor collected the local camel corps with a view to dispersing the crowd. The assembled force, however, mutinied and refused to open fire into the crowd. Recounting his experience, the Burao commanding officer of the Camel Corps wrote "I glanced down the machine gun and saw it was shooting over the tops of the high trees under which the riflemen stood. I tried to get the gun myself but could not do so. I ordered it to be depressed but the team quietly ignored my orders."[28] The Burao uprising hammered one more nail into the coffin of development plans for British Somalia.

The most crucial question was whether, in light of what had transpired, Archer was prepared to shelve his tax proposals. He was not the kind of man to concede defeat so easily. Thus in August 1922 he persuaded the sceptical Colonial Office to let him have another go, arguing that the Burao uprising was an isolated affair. No sooner did he resume his taxation campaign than a new resistance movement erupted, again in Burao. Archer ordered the arrest of the ringleaders, but the culprits escaped across the border into Ethiopian territory. Meanwhile a mob had collected in Burao to denounce Archer's tax program. The governor was in a dilemma: if he decided to disperse the mob he could not be sure of the consequences, no could he be sure that he would succeed. If he capitulated, he was bound to lose credibility; furthermore, capitulation might have encouraged the rioters to confront the administration on other occasions.

---

[28]C.O. 535/69, Capt. Rayne to Archer, 25/2/1922.

Archer found a way out of his predicament by taking advantage of a previous announcement that Gerald Summers had been earmarked to be his successor, and that he, Archer, had been transferred to Uganda. Archer, therefore, announced to the protesters that he had spared them severe punishment because he was due to leave the Protectorate for good. Having thus bequeathed the burden of dealing with the turbulent situation to Summers, Archer hastily left for Uganda in September.

In view of the failure of the tax program, the colonial administration moved to tap other possible sources of revenue for the poverty-stricken Protectorate. One strategy was to persuade private companies to invest in the Protectorate. The Abyssinian Corporation was one of the few companies which answered the call, with an interest in constructing a railway line from Berbera to Jigjiga, via Hargeisa.[29] Its other interests included trade, mineral prospecting and banking. The Corporation commenced operations in 1920 with 1,005,000 pounds capital but, unfortunately, did not go far. Mismanagement, corruption, poor planning and overambition sapped its strength and resources and forced it into liquidation in 1926, leaving no trace of its existence in the Protectorate.

The Protectorate then publicized reports about the rumored existence of oil fields at Dag Shebelli, thirty miles to the south-east of Burao. Towards the end of 1920 the D'Arcy Exploration Company applied and acquired a concession to prospect for these oil fields. The Company spent several months searching for the oil fields, and came out empty-handed. In subsequent years other companies and individuals acquired concessions to prospect for various resources; all ended up finding nothing.

By 1930 the British had more or less despaired of ever being able to find viable sources of revenue for the Protectorate. The Protectorate's financial position was not capable of supporting even the most elementary development project. On a few occasions the Treasury was talked into releasing funds for minor projects. For example, in 1927 the Treasury released 1,715 pounds for the establishment of the Department of Agriculture at Hargeisa; then in the following year the Colonial Office managed to squeeze 1,000 pounds out of the Treasury to meet the expenses of demonstrating a variety of husbandry techniques to the willing Somali, and a further 1,000 pounds for constructing a few cattle dips.[30] However, there was not a single occasion when the Treasury sanctioned expenditure for Somalia without a protracted fight with the Colonial Office and the local administration.[31]

---

[29] F.O. 371/3495, "Prospectus of Abyssinian Corporation," April 1919.

[30] Mss. AFR. S. 141 (Rhodes House, Oxford), "The Veterinary History of Somaliland Protectorate," by Edward F. Peck.

[31] The other futile revenue-earning measures included a concession granted to a Mr. Cooper in 1926 to prospect for mica, beryl, and garret, and the abortive efforts by Col. Sanford to manufacture salt at Zeila in 1928.

The only revenue-earning scheme which appeared promising was the animal husbandry improvement program. Harold Kittermaster decided in 1927 that the only hope for the Protectorate lay in boosting the livestock industry. Some of the measures introduced by Kittermaster included the launching of a compulsory inoculation program, the establishment of cattle dips, the establishment of an organized system of marketing various animal products, the digging of permanent wells, and the opening of new markets overseas for the Somali animal products. These measures impressed the Colonial Development Advisory Committee; the Committee recommended a grant of 16,000 pounds from the Colonial Development Fund in March 1930 for boosting both the water-boring program and the livestock industry.

The following figures will illustrate the gloomy financial picture of the Protectorate between 1924 and 1930:

Year	Revenue (£)	Expenditure (£)
1924-25	82,806	150,564
1925-26	89,057	167,955
1926-27	90,569	149,125
1927-28	159,478	198,628
1928-29	101,541	207,067
1929-30	105,304	199,027[32]

The exceptionally high revenue realized during the 1927-28 and 1929-30 financial years came about as a result of the severe drought, which forced the otherwise reluctant Somali to sell large numbers of their stock. Second, the high death toll of the stock added more hides and skins to the market. Thus, customs receipts for the 1927-28 and 1928-29 financial years amounted, respectively, to 121,875 pounds and 79,577 pounds, compared to 63,419 pounds and 67,716 pounds for the 1925-26 and 1926-27 financial years. By 1930 the effects of the drought were beginning to disappear and, as a result, the Somali were no longer anxious to sell their stock.

In 1928, the long-forgotten question of education for Somalia was re-opened by a half-dozen young Somali men who had just completed their studies at Gordon College in the Sudan. They were embarrassed by the backwardness of their country, and they pressured the governor to revive the question of education. However, the type of education the governor recommended seemed strange and even insulting to the Somali: he proposed to introduce schools organized along the lines of reform schools for delinquents. He wrote, "I am inclined to the opinion that a reformatory school is the best line of development . . . it might be found possible to enlarge the scope of this school by admitting

---

[32]These figures were obtained from Colonial Reports for the Somaliland Protectorate. The following volumes were consulted: Nos. 1355, 1390, 1451, 1479, 1524 and 1571.

thereto other boys who might wish to attend."[33] The governor's scheme was based on his belief that the Somali, since they had resisted other aspects of colonialism, would also oppose a government-sponsored school. In the circumstances, the governor wanted to regard the Somali as criminals and thereafter educate them by force, more or less. The governor's proposals were sent to the Colonial Office where they were rejected outright. The feeling in London was that if the governor was convinced that the Somali would not accept Western education voluntarily, then they ought to do without it, and Britain would be none the worse. The issue of education was again put to rest without even bothering the Treasury about it.

In view of Britain's failure to find a cure for Somalia's economic problems, it was decided that the whole policy for the territory should be reappraised at the highest possible level. Consequently, the Colonial Office submitted the Somali question to the Committee of Imperial Defence in 1931 for discussion. The Treasury submitted a memorandum in which it identified four alternative courses of action, namely: (a) evacuation, (b) withdrawal to the coast, (c) a policy of development, (d) continuing with the *status quo*. After lengthy deliberations on each of these alternatives, it was unanimously agreed that the best policy would have been one of development. However, the salient fact was put by the Treasury thus: "The continuance of expenditure on this scale for any inadequate return, was difficult to justify."[34] The policies of evacuation and withdrawal to the coast were ruled out on account of previous experience and possible international repercussions. The only feasible alternative, therefore, was to continue with the policy already forced upon the Protectorate by the Treasury's attitude, namely, stagnation. The Treasury noted that "the policy was obviously not an ideal one but as there was no practical alternative, it was necessary to make the best of it."[35]

To underline its determination to stagnate and reverse development, the Colonial Office ordered an immediate slashing of 30,000 pounds from the previously approved expenditure, while the rank of the officer in charge of the Protectorate was reduced from that of governor to commissioner. In fact the only project which was spared the wrath of stagnation was the water-boring scheme which had been funded by the Colonial Development Fund. However, the animal husbandry schemes which had also been allocated money by the same Fund were terminated in March 1932. The water boring program was allowed to continue because of the severe and regular drought conditions which often led to colossal losses of human and livestock lives. Thus, it was agreed that the water

---

[33]C.O. 535/85, Governor Kittermaster to C.O., 14/4/1928. By 1928 the administration was giving the coastal Koranic schools an annual subsidy totalling 30 pounds.

[34]C.O. 535/94, Minutes of the Sub-Committee of the Committee of Imperial Defence, 9/9/1931.

[35]*Ibid.*

boring program should not be affected by stagnation. The following sums of money were, for example, spent on the program: 3,838 pounds in 1932; 2,556 pounds in 1933; 7,943 pounds in 1937.[36]

A Cautious Program of Development, 1935-1939

Between 1931 and 1935 the axe of the new policy of stagnation slashed the few social and developmental services that had survived the turbulent post-Dervish period. The Protectorate's dwindling fortunes were, quite unexpectedly, revived by external factors in the form of the Italian conquest and subsequent occupation of Ethiopia in 1935. We have already noted that Mussolini was committed to a policy of massive industrialization of the hitherto feudal Ethiopian empire. By sheer coincidence of geography (British Somalia shared common borders with the rapidly changing new Italian colony of Ethiopia), British Somalia became a beneficiary of Ethiopia's misfortune. With regard to the effects of the Italian-built road, for example, the governor observed that "many who never thought of trading previously, are taking caravans over the border and doing very well. A sign of prosperity is a brisk demand for building plots in Hargeisa town."[37] Secondly, a good number of Somali ex-soldiers who had lost their jobs as a result of Britain's policy of retrenchment were recruited for either of the two fighting forces, Ethiopian or Italian. A substantial number of those who thus got recruited also took advantage of the turbulent situation to improve their lot through trade, captured booty, and several other means. And third, the effective administration which the no-nonsense Fascist soldiers established on the borders removed the earlier hazards which had discouraged trade in those parts. Drysdale writes that "In succeeding years mutual confidence between Italian and British administrators grew as practical experience of common problems was gained. For their part, the British welcomed an administration which could act promptly in the interests of the nomads concerned, and this continued until the outbreak of the war."[38] The positive effects of Italian occupation of Ethiopia were underlined by the steady increase of the Protectorate's revenues and a corresponding decrease of the imperial grants-in-aid. For the first time in the Protectorate's history no grant-in-aid was needed in 1938.

In light of the new developments, Britain decided to embark on a cautious development policy. A bold move was made in 1936 when the local administration submitted their annual budget for 1937 in which a wide range of social services were proposed. Estimated revenue for 1937 was expected to reach the record level of 164,356 pounds. The Colonial Office received Somalia's budget

---

[36] Annual Colonial Reports, British Somaliland Protectorate, No. 1613 (1932), No. 1660 (1933), and No. 1880 (1937).

[37] Annual Colonial Report, British Somaliland Protectorate, 1936, No. 1815.

[38] J. Drysdale, *The Somali Dispute* (London, 1964), 57.

with benevolent sympathy, and the Treasury, for a change, was not hostile. Nevertheless, the Colonial Office decided not to commit itself until visible changes in the economy could be confirmed. An official of the Colonial Office minuted, "I suggest we should carry on with the minimum change for the next year or two till we see how things work out."[39] The real breakthrough came in 1938 when the Colonial Office sanctioned proposed expenditure on several social and administrative services. For example, medical services were allocated 1,000 pounds, veterinary and agriculture 5,000 pounds, and education 7,350 pounds. Defending the latter, the governor explained that the "time has come when the Government of this Protectorate must provide educational facilities above that of the Koranic schools already in existence, and my very earnest wish is to start a station school at Hargeisa, Burao, Erigavo, Berbera, and Zeila."[40]

As fate would have it, no sooner had the Treasury given its belated assent than the scheme ran into trouble from unexpected quarters. The controversy this time was over the language question: the local administration wanted the language of instruction to be the Somali language, while the Somali insisted on Arabic, on the grounds that Arabic was the language of Islam. Initially, the local administration underestimated the gravity of the Somali feelings on the issue and pressed ahead with their plans. The local leaders of the anti-education campaign went so far as to claim that Ellison, the newly appointed education officer, was actually a Catholic priest disguised in civilian clothes. Thus, when Ellison went to Burao to inspect one of the Koranic schools he intended to upgrade to a full-fledged government school, word went round that he had gone to proselytize in the Christian tradition inside the buildings of the Koranic schools, which was regarded as a major insult to Islam. Thus a crowd instantly collected and stoned Ellison and his party, seriously injuring several people, including the education officer himself. The Colonial Office decided to scrap the program and, with the outbreak of World War II the following year, education plans and other projects were temporarily shelved.

Conclusion

The history of British Somalia between 1905 and 1939 revolved around the three main issues of resistance, revenue, and lack of development. Britain's problems started when her colonial rule was challenged by Sayyid Muhammad Abdille Hassan shortly after the establishment of the Protectorate. Britain's attempt to crush the resistance in a brief and cheap military operation failed. Instead, Britain found herself involved in such military ventures as she had neither expected nor budgeted for. Worse still, the Protectorate lacked any kind of economic opportunity which the British could gainfully exploit for the purpose of financing the colonial regime and deflating the costs of the military expeditions. Thus, after four futile military expeditions, the general attitude of

---

[39]C.O. 535/119, Minute by Calder on Somaliland Estimates of Revenue and Expenditure for 1937.

[40]C.O. 535/113, Governor Lawrence to C.O., 5/6/1938.

the British public was that there was no justification for further expenditure on Somalia, unless some avenues of generating local revenue could be found. The Protectorate was to be run strictly on a care-and-maintenance basis; or if you like, on the policy of no development. Yet the lack of development itself was self defeating, considering the fact that Somali resistance to colonial rule was still a factor to reckon with. Whenever the British government sent military expeditions against the resisters, the British press, public and Parliament were up in arms about the taxpayers' money and British lives being sacrificed for a worthless territory. When the British government stopped sending military expeditions, the resistance prospered and grew, thereby threatening whatever British presence there was. When, in the last resort, Britain tried to abandon the territory altogether, there was a general outcry against such a move, in the name of British prestige, philanthropy, and strategic interests.

In those strange circumstances, successive British governments tried to steer a middle course that involved neither withdrawal nor expenditure. These policies were unsatisfactory and, in some instances, disastrous, since they did not solve the basic problem - namely, how Britain was to maintain her regime in the hostile and unproductive Protectorate without spending the British taxpayers' money. The lack of development was both counter-productive and self-defeating. It created a vicious cycle in the sense that the policy left the bulk of the Somali people untouched and uninfluenced by the colonial power. There was, for example, no Westernized, educated elite to collaborate with the colonial regime; and there were no government economic and social services, such as schools, railways, hospitals, cooperatives, veterinary services, or agricultural schemes which, elsewhere in colonial Africa, tended to mitigate the otherwise harsh colonial era. In short, Somali resistance proved costly to the imperial Treasury, since it could not be suppressed or deflated from local resources and revenue. From that economic standpoint, therefore, resistance militated against normal development, although this ought not to have been the case. Consequently, Britain's ill-advised failure to develop her Somali territory - through the policies of official terror, retrenchment, and benign neglect, in that order - fertilized the ground for further resistance and, therefore, further costs.

THE PLACE IN HISTORY OF THE SUDANESE MAHDIA

by

P. M. HOLT

Described in secular terms, the Mahdia was a revolt which occurred in the Sudanese dependencies of the Khedive of Egypt, which overthrew the existing administration, and which established an indigenous territorial state, mainly in the northern part of those dependencies. The coincidence of this revolt with the establishment of British control over Egypt itself resulted in the confrontation of the Mahdist state with British military power and ultimately in its destruction, incidentally to the development of British foreign and imperial policy at the end of the nineteenth century. From these circumstances, it has resulted that current views of the Mahdia see it primarily as an episode in Egyptian or British imperial history. Writings on the movement have, with a few notable exceptions, abounded in political and propagandist overtones, and there has been little attempt to consider the Mahdia as an autonomous historical process, or to set it in the wider context of Islamic history. A further consequence of this external view of the Mahdia is that disproportionate attention has been paid to its opening and closing phases, the years 1881–85 and 1896–98, when the movement was engaged in a mortal struggle with Egyptian and British power, whereas the intervening decade, the heyday of the Mahdist state, has been almost totally neglected.

The present essay outlines some considerations germane to a reassessment of the place of the Mahdia in history. It defines first, the pattern of events and suggests some comparisons with other Islamic movements ; secondly, it suggests that the nature of the Mahdia was essentially revolutionary, and analyses the chief groups of its supporters. Thirdly, by sketching the main periods of Mahdist history, it seeks to indicate the significance of the neglected decade and to link it with the more dramatic phases which preceded and followed it.

1. The Pattern of Events and their Historical Setting.

The Sudanese Mahdia was by no means a unique development in Muslim history. It passed through three main phases, being, first, a religious movement for the revival of Islam ; secondly, a militant theocratic organisation seeking to realize the restoration of the primitive Islamic *Umma* ; thirdly, a territorial state in which the theocratic aspects gradually became obsolescent. There are several earlier movements which underwent a similar course of development. Superficially, one of the closest parallels is the Almohad movement in the Maghrib, the leader of which also claimed the Mahdiship, which originated also on the African fringe of Islam, and which established a dynastic territorial dominion. Certain developmental resemblances can also be traced between the Mahdia and the Ṣafawīya movement in north-west Persia. The Ṣafawīya, a Ṣūfī *ṭarīqa*, controlled by hereditary shaykhs, originated in the thirteenth century. In the fifteenth century it changed from a devotional and mystical brotherhood into a militant organisation, and, at the opening of the sixteenth century its third militant leader, Ismāʿīl, carved out for himself a kingdom in Iran and Iraq from which the modern Persian state has evolved. A shift from Sunnism to Shiʿism in the fifteenth century precluded the possibility of a Ṣafawī Mahdi, but the rulers of this dynasty stressed their reputed ʿAlid descent and represented themselves as vicegerents of the Concealed Imam, the Shiʿī Mahdi.

The Sudanese Mahdia, insofar as it was a religious movement, was directly linked with much more recent developments in the Muslim world. From about the middle of the eighteenth century an ideological ferment had begun, which continued throughout the nineteenth century and is by no means finished today. In its later stages, this development has appeared as a Muslim reaction against the growing pressure of Christendom on the Islamic world, a pressure which has been a solvent of the traditional political, social and cultural framework in the Middle East as elsewhere. Originally the reaction was not against Christendom, or Europe, or the West, but against the religious establishment in the eighteenth century Ottoman Empire, in which the *'ulamā'* formed a privileged and largely hereditary class ; and Ṣūfī ideas and practices, often of a primitive and un-Islamic type, deeply influenced the *'ulamā'* themselves, as they did all classes of Muslims. Beginning with the Wahhābīs in eighteenth century Najd, a series of reforming, revivalist movements occurred in the Muslim world. Current practices were confronted with the *Sunna* of the Prophet ; popular beliefs such, notably, as the veneration of saints, were denounced as innovations (*bida'*) ; the restoration of the *Sharī'a* as the actual and all-sufficient law of the Muslim community was the primary political aim. Of this general type were the Sanūsīya in Cyrenaica, the movement of Shaykh 'Uthmān dan Fodio among the Fulani, the early phase of Khatmīya activity in the Egyptian Sudan and, in a later generation, the Mahdia itself.

2. *The Mahdia as a Revolutionary Movement and its Supporters.*

Islamic reform movements are potentially revolutionary, since the confrontation of any existing political and social system with the image of an ideal Muslim society, governed by the *Sharī'a* and reproducing the traditional features of the *Umma* in its earliest phase, challenges the compromises with expediency inherent in all administration. Thus in the eighteenth century the Wahhābī movement by the nature of its tenets was fundamentally incompatible with the Ottoman state, which drew its moral sanction from a very different view of the nature of the Islamic community. Similarly in the Egyptian Sudan, Muhammad Ahmad's claim that he was the Expected Mahdi was revolutionary, not only because he thereby asserted a higher sanction for his acts than was possessed by the Khedivial administration, but also because he declared that he was sent to establish the *Sunna*, that is to establish a purely Muslim community on the primitive model. His movement was therefore directed against two groups ; first, the ruling institution of the Egyptian Sudan— the Khedive's officials and troops, who were engaged in administering a system of government that in essentials was late Ottoman in its purposes and methods, and at the same time was permeated with European influences; secondly, the Muslim institution—the cadre of *'ulamā'* associated with the administration, who gave the Khedivial system their moral support. These two groups are denoted respectively in Mahdist phraseology as *al-Turuk*, "the Turks," and *'Ulamā' al-sū'*, "the evil *'ulamā'* ".

Muhammad Ahmad's mission as a religious teacher had begun many years before he publicly announced himself to be the Expected Mahdi. After the Manifestation in Abā, his religious disciples continued to form the core of the movement and were known as *Abkār al-Mahdī*, "the firstborn of the Mahdi". Their political role was, however, insignificant; with the exception of 'Abdallāhi al-Ta'ishī none of them played a prominant part in later events. The nomination of 'Abdallāhi, at an early period in the militant phase, as *Khalīfat al-Siddīq*, the successor of the first patriarchal caliph, Abū Bakr al-Siddīq, indicated his status in relation to the Mahdi, who was *Khalīfat Rasūl Allāh*, the successor of the Prophet. Another of the *Abkār al-Mahdī*,

'Alī b. Muḥammad Ḥilū, was at the same time nominated *Khalīfat al-Fārūq*, the successor of the second patriarchal caliph, 'Umar al-Fārūq. Subsequently he exercised a moderating influence in the intestine struggles for power, but he neither sought nor achieved the political pre-eminence of 'Abdallāhi.

In the militant phase, ensuing immediately upon the Manifestation, two new classes of active supporters of the Mahdi appear. The first of these consisted of men of northern, riverain origin, particularly Danāqla and Ja'liyīn, who were dispersed among the non-Arab tribes of the upper White Nile, the Baḥr al-Ghazāl river-system and Darfur. These men formed a typical frontier society, engaged as sailors, merchants and soldiers of fortune in opening-up and exploiting these peripheral areas. Like frontiersmen elsewhere, they were impatient of government and resented the extension of Egyptian rule under Khedive Ismā'īl, although some of them ensured the continuance of their privileged position by taking administrative posts. Their loyalty was strained to breaking point by the policy, first adopted by Khedive Ismā'īl, of suppressing the slave trade—a policy which was itself a motive for the extension of Egyptian rule in the south and west. Since this policy was inspired by the European Powers, especially Britain, and since it was implemented by an influx of European Christian officials, such as Baker, Gordon and Gessi, the disaffection of the frontier-society was further inflamed by sentiments of religious hatred and xenophobia. When the Mahdia entered its militant phase, the dispersed northerners of the west and south (in marked contrast to those who remained in their original homelands in Berber and Dongola provinces) were a powerful factor in its success.

The second group which supported militant Mahdism consisted of the Baqqāra. Their support of the movement may have been due partly to the faults and venality of the Khedivial officials, partly to the personality and ability of Muḥammad Aḥmad's Ta'īshī disciple, 'Abdallāhi b. Muḥammad. Yet much must be ascribed to the inherently anarchical temperament of nomad tribes and the pitifully low standard of their existence, factors which throughout history have inclined them to warfare and the seizure of booty, and all the more easily when the raid can be viewed as a holy war. Parallels can be found in the history of the other militant movements—the Berber tribes on whom Almohad power was based, the Turcomans to whom Shah Ismā'īl owed his throne, the Arab tribesmen who, both in the early period and under 'Abd al-'Azīz in the present century, formed the physical support of the Wahhābī-Sa'ūdī polity. The Baqqāra displayed another characteristic of nomads—their adherence to the Mahdia was governed by short-term considerations; a campaign against a town or a rival tribe resulting in a rapid victory and seizure of booty was the limit of their willingness to participate in the *Jihād*.

3. *The Periods of Mahdist History*

Within the general scheme of events, the evolution from a reforming movement, through a theocracy, to a territorial kingdom, which the Mahdia shares with other movements in Islamic history, a more precise periodization is possible, in which the Mahdia discloses its individual characteristics.

A. *The creation of the Mahdist theocracy:* 1881–1885

The manifestation of Muḥammad Aḥmad b. 'Abdallāh as Mahdi (29th June 1881) marked the point at which a reforming and revivalist movement assumed a political and revolutionary significance. The inevitable reaction of the Khedivial administration initiated, almost simultaneously, the militant phase which opened with the *Hijra* to Qadir. The *Anṣār*, as the active supporters of the Mahdi were collectively known, defeated Egyptian forces in a series of skirmishes and battles, while the Mahdi's agents harrassed the administration in various parts of the Sudan. The capture of El Obeid (19th January 1883) gave the Mahdi the chief town in the western Egyptian Sudan. Egyptian hopes of overthrowing the Mahdi died when an expeditionary force under the British general, Hicks, was annihilated at Shaykān (5th November 1883). The establishment of Mahdist rule in Darfur and the Baḥr al-Ghazāl followed. The Egyptian garrison in Khartoum was isolated and the city fell to the Mahdi (26th January 1885), the British governor-general, Gordon, being among the slain. Meanwhile a simple administrative system had been organized. The Mahdi was the sole source of authority, his rulings on religious, administrative and legal matters being promulgated in personal or general letters (*manshūrāt*). His principal lieutenant was 'Abdallāhi b. Muḥammad, *Khalīfat al-Ṣiddīq*. He was represented in the provinces by agents known originally as *amīrs*, subsequently (after May 1884) as *āmils*. A central treasury (*Bayt al Māl*) received the Koranic taxes (*zakāh* and *fiṭr*) and booty (*ghanīma*). The armed forces were formed into three divisions, the Black Flag under the *Khalīfat al-Ṣiddīq* consisting of the Baqqāra tribal levies; the Green Flag under the *Khalīfat al-Fārūq*, consisting of the tribal levies of Kināna and Dighaym; and the Red Flag, consisting of the riverain Arabs and northerners of the dispersion, known collectively as *Awlād al-balad* (i.e. sedentaries, in contrast to nomads) under the Mahdi's relative, Muḥammad Sharīf b. Ḥāmid, *Khalīfat al-Karrār*. When the Mahdi died (22nd June 1885) he controlled most of the north of the former Egyptian Sudan. British and Egyptian forces held Dongola province; Emin Pasha maintained a tenuous Egyptian authority in Equatoria; the port and garrison town of Suakin never fell into Mahdist hands.

B. *The Accession-Struggle of the Khalifa 'Abdallahi* : 1885–86

The Mahdi's sovereign powers passed on his death to 'Abdallāhi b. Muḥammad, *Khalīfat al-Ṣiddīq*, who assumed the new and additional title of *Khalīfat al-Mahdī*, "the Successor of the Mahdi". His accession was unpopular with the relatives of the Mahdi (*Ashrāf*) and *Awlād al-balad*, whose nominal head was Muḥammad Sharīf b. Ḥāmid, *Khalīfat al-Karrār*. They were in touch with the powerful governor of Darfur, Muḥammad Khālid, one of their own number. He began to march on Omdurman, the Mahdist capital, with his provincial forces. A conspiracy of the *Ashrāf* in Omdurman was forestalled by the Khalifa, while the army of Darfur was intercepted and taken over in Kordofan by the loyal general, Ḥamdān Abū 'Anja. Meanwhile the Khalifa had begun to remove the Mahdi's nominees, mostly *Awlād al-balad*, from the chief offices and to substitute his own tribesmen and clients.

C. *The Militant Mahdist State* : 1886–89

The Mahdist state was committed by its ideology to the *Jihād* against other polities, whether Muslim or Christian. This policy was foreshadowed during the Mahdi's lifetime and was strenuously pursued by the Khalifa after he had established his authority. Warfare took place in three principal areas ; on the Abyssinian frontier, in Darfur and the far West, and on the Egyptian frontier. Warfare with Abyssinia was conducted by Ḥamdān Abū 'Anja, who raided the country in 1888. After his death, a battle took place on 9th March 1889, during which the Abyssinian ruler, John IV, was killed. The subsequent internal troubles of Abyssinia until the rise of Menelik ended large-scale hostilities. In the west the young general, 'Uthmān Ādam, suppressed tribal revolts against Mahdist rule and withstood a dangerous rising headed by a messianic figure known as Abū Jummayza (1887–89). Operations against Egypt were entrusted to 'Abd al-Raḥmān al-Nujūmī, who had played a prominent part in the siege of Khartoum. Al-Nujūmī, who was not a Ta'īshī, was regarded with some suspicion by the Khalifa, and Sudanese tradition suggests that he and his mainly riverain forces were deliberately sent to their deaths. They were crushingly defeated and al-Nujūmī himself killed at the battle of Ṭūshkī (Toski) by Egyptian troops under Grenfell (3rd August 1889). The Sudanese tradition is not fully warranted.

D. *The Period of Stabilization* : 1889–91

The years 1889–90 were highly critical for the Khalifa. The deaths of Abū 'Anja, al-Nujūmī and 'Uthmān Ādam deprived him of his three ablest generals. Widespread famine was followed by epidemic. The famine was made worse by the enforced migration of the Ta'āisha and neighbouring Baqqāra tribes to Omdurman where they formed a military support for the Khalifa, but one of dubious reliability. The policy of the *Jihād* was tacitly abandoned. Trade was allowed to proceed across the Egyptian frontier and with Suakin. An elaborate fiscal system was developed, worked by a bureaucracy employing Egyptian methods and largely staffed by former employees of the Egyptian administration in the Sudan. Some tentatives were made at reconciliation with the riverain tribes but the period closed with another conspiracy of the *Ashrāf* and their clients in Omdurman (November 1891). They were again outmanoeuvred by the Khalifa and reduced piecemeal. Many of their notables were exiled to the Upper Nile, while the Khalifa Muḥammad Sharīf was sentenced to an ignominious imprisonment in March 1892.

E. *The Ta'īshī Autocracy* : 1892–96

The next five years are characterised by the growing acceptance of the Khalifa's rule throughout a diminished Mahdist state ; by the tacit conversion of the Mahdist theocracy into a personal monarchy, and by the growing threat from outside, as European imperialism began to press on the Khalifa's frontiers. The failure of the revolt of the *Ashrāf* marked the end of large-scale resistance to the Mahdist state as such, or to the Khalifa personally. In effect he was a Muslim sultan with his brother, Ya'qūb, as his *wazīr* and his son, 'Uthmān Shaykh al-Dīn, as his intended successor. A large standing army, the Bodyguard (*al-Mulāzimīya*), was built up, on which, and on his less reliable Baqqāra, the Khalifa's authority ultimately rested. Imperialist pressure appeared in several directions. Anglo-Egyptian forces at Suakin, which in earlier years had failed to make headway against local *Anṣār* under 'Uthmān Diqna (Osman Digna), captured the Mahdist base of Tūkar in February 1891. The Italians captured Kassala in July 1894. Belgian expeditions began to penetrate into the Upper Nile and the Baḥr al-Ghazāl (in both of which regions Mahdist authority was exceedingly tenuous). From 1894 an advance through the Baḥr al-Ghazāl to the Nile became an objective of French policy.

F. *The Reconquest* : 1896–98

The final phase of the history of the Mahdist state was brought about, not by internal collapse, but by external pressure caused by the clash of imperialisms. The Khalifa, unlike Menelik of Abyssinia, failed to appreciate justly the European threat ; the policy of the *Jihād* had been superseded by a policy of isolation. The British realization of French aspirations to control the Upper Nile seems to have motivated the Reconquest, although the pretext for its first stages was an Italian appeal for help after Adowa. The Reconquest was carried out by Kitchener using Egyptian troops only in the early phase ; subsequently British forces also. He owed his victories to superior transport (railway construction) and armament (machine-guns). The first campaign (1896) destroyed Mahdist rule in Dongola. The advance continued towards the heart of the Mahdist state. A large army under the command of Maḥmūd Aḥmad was overwhelmed at the battle of the Atbara (8th April 1898) while the last reserves were defeated in a hard-fought battle at Kararī near Omdurman (2nd September 1898). The Khalifa escaped to maintain resistance with a shadow of his former authority until his death in the battle of Umm Diwaykarāt (24th November 1899).

FAMINE AND SOCIAL CHANGE DURING THE TRANSITION
TO COLONIAL RULE IN NORTHEASTERN TANZANIA, 1880-1896

James Giblin
University of Iowa

The Zigua-speaking cultivators of northeastern Tanzania experienced a prolonged ecological and subsistence crisis between 1880 and 1940.[1] Devastating famines which occurred in 1884-1885, 1894-1896, 1898-1900, 1907-1908, 1916-1918, 1925 and 1932-1935 punctuated this period of declining food security. Even during the years when widespread famine did not occur, localized or seasonal food deficits developed. Though the cycle of severe recursive famines was broken by increased food imports after the Second World War, its effects linger on in Tanzania's Handeni District. The population of Handeni has never truly recovered its security from food scarcity; periodic hunger and seasonal or childhood malnutrition have beset cultivating communities ever since. Indeed, because it is in large part attributable to the long-term ecological impact of the 1880-1940 crisis, the persistence of chronic hunger in Handeni may be regarded as the direct legacy of the famine period.

The famines of the 1880-1940 era are crucial events in the modern history of lowland northeastern Tanzania. They set in motion a long process of environmental deterioration which still complicates cultivators' efforts to regain subsistence security. For all of their significance, however, the historical causes of these famines are scarcely understood. Meteorological conditions in the region have long seemed to suffice as the explanation for the occurrence of famine among the Zigua. Unquestionably it is true that climatic factors, particularly variability in rainfall, have contributed to creating the threat of scarcity among the Zigua. Nevertheless, neither precipitation patterns nor other environmental factors adequately account for the frequent recurrence of major famines between 1880 and 1940.

This is not to deny that the Zigua encountered natural adversity during the famines of this period. Rainfall levels were sometimes low and there were locust plagues. Yet these misfortunes do not appear to have possessed the unparalleled degree of severity, length or geographical scope which might qualify them to be considered as the sole causes of the disasters in this period. Misfortunes such as these might have been anticipated. Hence the vital historical question concerns the reasons for Zigua unpreparedness in the face of adversity.

Since the onset of these deteriorating conditions roughly coincided with the colonial conquest, the relationship between colonialism and food scarcity obviously begs consideration. It will be seen, however, that attempts to draw a dichotomy between a secure, prosperous precolonial society and a famine-ridden, colonized people would severely distort the history of the Zigua.² In the Handeni instance, the subsistence crisis took hold some six years before the appearance of German colonialists. This does not mean, however, that colonialism had no impact on food security. To the contrary, reconstruction of the subsistence crisis which occurred between 1880 and 1900 suggests that colonial rule altered the nature of famine by rendering many individuals much more vulnerable to scarcity. Hence this study has two purposes. The first is to identify the precolonial roots of the 1880-1940 crisis, while the second is to define and account for the sharp differences in the famines which took place before and after the colonial conquest.

The Causes of Late Precolonial Famine

We have no evidence to suggest that the precolonial Zigua experienced a prolonged subsistence crisis comparable to the repeated disasters of 1880-1940. This is not to suggest, however, that precolonial society was untouched by crisis or scarcity. Famines surely struck in periods of exceptional environmental or social disruption. Indeed the prospect of these calamities exerted a formative influence on precolonial social and economic relations. But the threat of scarcity only materialized as widespread famine in rare, extraordinary circumstances. There are no signs that before 1880 Zigua society found itself in precarious circumstances for decades at a time, unable to find reliable sources of food, powerless to check environmental regression or loss of population. Yet this is what happened between 1880 and 1940. Thus the events of 1880-1940 appear to have had no identifiable precolonial precedent. Certainly none is found either in Zigua traditions or in nineteenth-century European accounts.

The evidence which we do possess on famine among the Zigua before 1880 suggests not decades-long crises, but rather rare, isolated catastrophes. The Zigua of Handeni preserve the memory of a single great famine which compelled people to consume cattle hides. But its quasi-legendary status allows the easy incorporation of its name, *Kidyakingo*, into many traditions where it provides explanation or color. Hence *Kidyakingo* would appear to be undatable in the absence of corroborating documentation.

Other evidence of large-scale slave exports from Zigua territory suggest that the Zigua may have endured serious episodes of scarcity at the turn of the nineteenth century and again during the 1820s. The earlier movement involved transportation of Zigua captives to Somalia, the later to Zanzibar. Presumably these instances of slave exports resulted from sales or pawning of dependents by Zigua as part of an effort to obtain subsistence during famines. Yet overall, the European evidence does not lead to the conclusion that scarcity was the constant condition of the Zigua in the early nineteenth century.   The earliest European information on the Zigua, gathered indirectly by Smee and Hardy in 1811, portrays a prosperous population owning many cattle and capable of sending notable quantities of produce to the coast.[3]

If the precolonial Zigua were successful in preventing frequent famines, it was not because their environment was benign.   Rather,   it   was   because   economic   and social relationships granted insurance from scarcity.   In their relatively inhospitable environment,   such   relations were necessary to maintain social and demographic stability. The Zigua inhabit a region of peneplain and low mountains which stretches from the immediate coastal hinterland to about 250 miles inland. Their territory, Uzigua, is bounded by two major rivers, the Pangani in the north and the Wami to the south. Cultivators' problems are posed primarily by the scarcity and unreliability of rainfall.   Mean annual rainfall in most of Handeni ranges between 700 and 1000mm.   The probability, moreover, that rainfall will exceed 700mm has been calculated to be only 69 percent.   Yet while statistics on mean annual precipitation do indicate that there always exists the risk of drought, they do not adequately convey a sense of the unreliability of rainfall.   The rains fall in a bimodal regime of heavier "long" rains from February through April and lighter "short" rains in November and December. Peasants in Handeni recognize that the "short" rains are not dependable as sources of crop moisture and rainfall records bear them out. Records kept since the 1920s also indicate at least partial failure of the "long" rains once in roughly every three years. The unpredictable timing of rains compounds the difficulties of cultivators.   Unexpectedly early and heavy rains may ruin young maize, while tardy rainfall means an   abbreviated growing season.[4]

Obviously the Zigua environment is dry, as its predominant *miombo* vegetation, lack of surface water, and scarcity of potable water attest.   But this does not mean that famine is inevitable in Uzigua. Since drought was expectable, even if its timing was not predictable, precolonial Zigua cultivators developed methods of preventing critical food shortfalls. Numerous aspects of Zigua society were influenced by the prospect of drought and famine. The most obvious of these was the precolonial pattern of settlements, which reflected the imperative that all sources of moisture be exploited. Habitations were established in well-watered valleys, around the lower slopes of the isolated mountain watersheds which rise from the Zigua plain, and also in serpentine patterns along winding seasonal watercourses.   These clusters of settlements and

cleared land were separated from one another by uninhabited
miombo woodland.

The pattern of cleared, settled islands scattered through
the *miombo* facilitated another vital form of environmental
control. Other than unreliable precipitation, the primary
environmental problem was trypanosomiasis, as it was throughout
the tsetse fly belt which stretches across eastern Tanzania and
Mozambique.[5] The pattern of settlement prevented constant
infection while at the same time it imposed the necessity of
occasional human activities in uninhabited wooded areas. In the
miombo, humans and domestic livestock would occasionally
encounter foci of trypanosomiasis infection, the locations where
tsetse flies transmitted trypanosomes from wildlife hosts to
humans or cattle. Infrequent infection in this manner preserved
the endemic state of trypanosomiasis.

As with settlement patterns, cropping practices were shaped
by the prospect of drought. Agriculturalists cultivated in
places where they might find varying levels of moisture in the
soil. They planted a variety of grains, legumes, tubers,
plantains, fruits and vegetables. In the second half of the
nineteenth century, both sorghum and maize were staples.
Cultivators took advantage of the complementary qualities of
these grains: relative invulnerability to birds and a shorter
growing season on the part of maize, superior resistance to
drought on the part of sorghum. Cultivators made multiple
plantings in order to reduce the possibility of drought-induced
crop failure. Missionary records from the Nguu Mountains of
western Uzigua show that in the 1880s cultivators were planting
grain in every month between November and June. Lower levels of
precipitation did not allow continuous planting over such a long
season on the Zigua plain, yet even in the lowlands repeated
plantings were made during the long rains. Gathering of roots,
leafy plants and honey supplemented cultigens. To these food
sources were also added the small number of cattle, sheep and
goats kept in tsetse-free zones.

The diversity manifested in the variety of food sources was
a major foundation of precolonial security from scarcity.
Diversity was also evident in the numerous forms of exchange and
trade carried on by the Zigua. Throughout Uzigua cultivators
devoted time and labor to the production of exchange goods, such
as tobacco, honey and livestock. These products, together with
surpluses of other crops, passed along various circuits of
exchange. Exchanges linked Zigua-speaking occupants of
different ecological niches in the Nguu Mountains, the eastern
lowlands, and the Pangani and Wami river valleys. Affinal
relationships forged among residents of various localities
opened up opportunities for such exchanges, as did claims to
shared membership in descent groups. These exchange relations
might provide access to food reserves during periods of
localized drought or crop failure.

Trade with more distant regions beyond Uzigua, especially across environmental frontiers, fulfilled the same function. Zigua communities maintained symbiotic relations with Masai pastoralists who inhabited the steppe to the west of the Zigua woodland. From the Masai, nineteenth-century Zigua cultivators obtained cattle, dairy products and hides; in exchange they provided grain, other food crops, tobacco, beer and iron wares. Similar arrangements brought together cultivators and the Ndorobo hunter-gatherers of the woodland. Trade also kept Zigua-speakers in contact with the people of the Kaguru and Usambara mountains to the southwest and north of Uzigua respectively. Of course the Zigua also looked seaward for trading opportunities. Communities situated within about fifty miles of the Indian Ocean carried on exchanges of grain with coastal towns, selling surpluses to coastal merchants and purchasing from them in the event of grain deficits. On a less frequent basis, Zigua inhabitants of the more distant hinterland brought grain, honey, clarified butter or livestock to the coast. All these relations created avenues for acquiring food during drought or famine.

The prospect of drought and famine also contributed to shaping social and political relations. Even though the nature of the Zigua social structure reflected the influence of scarcity and environmental adversity, this by no means warrants the conclusion that all Zigua individuals were integrated into a web of relations which *guaranteed* them security from food dearth. Some persons were excluded from access to food stocks by relationshps among individuals and groups, just as the same relations supported the claims of others. Political authority derived in large part from a leader's power to include or to exclude individuals from networks of redistribution. The inequalities which existed between those who possessed and those who made claims to food reserves - together with the shifting, fluid nature of Zigua kinship relations and residence patterns - combined to produce a distinctive political structure characterized above all by rivalries among patrons who competed for the loyalty and labor of clients.

Ambitious individuals tried to augment their households or settlements with dependents who might possess the status of slave, client or kin. A conscientious patron was obliged to provide protection and assistance to his dependents, and from them he or she expected to receive labor service. Varying degrees of authority over dependents were enjoyed by patrons. Indeed the main distinction between slaves and clients lay in the circumstance that a slave could find no support or refuge outside the household of his or her master, and thus was entirely under his domination. A slave, therefore, might easily be alienated from a household since he or she could make no appeal against the master's decisions. The gradations of status or subordination in a household, determined by the extent of the

patron's authority over each dependent, roughly represented the
order in which dependents might be separated from a household
and exchanged for food during a subsistence crisis.

Submission to the authority of a patron, however, might
provide an individual with tangible benefits in the form of
protection and access to food reserves. Dependents could expect
their patrons to fulfill reciprocal obligations, and not simply
because a "moral economy" enforced the norms of reciprocity.
More concretely, Zigua kinship and residence arrangements
provided most unsatisfied dependents except slaves with
opportunities to transfer their allegiance to other patrons. A
person might conceivably live with his or her parents, father's
brothers, mother's brothers, siblings, affines or unrelated
patrons. A person's choice was governed by the patron who
offered the most advantageous situation. Since both patrilineal
and matrilineal inheritance was practiced, moreover, an
individual often chose whether to maintain his primary loyalty
to his father or to his mother's brother. On the other hand,
the flexibility inherent in the system of descent was another
source of a patron's authority, since through inheritance he
could reward or punish sons and daughters, nephews and nieces.

Individuals did not remain perpetually in closed, corporate
groups, but instead participated in different bodies depending
upon the context. The membership of a communal work party, for
example, might overlap with a group which performed ancestor
propitiation rites, but the two groups would not be identical.
Thus an individual had ample opportunity to seek relationships
with patrons and to shift loyalties. The existence of multiple
opportunities and ranges of possibilities forced patrons to
compete for clients and, more importantly in the context of food
security, it compelled them to honor obligations to their
dependents. If they did not, rivals were always poised to claim
unhappy dependents. Social norms were enforced, therefore,
through competition and the struggles of people who possessed
different degrees of access to resources. The deep tensions
created by rivalries, claims and counter-claims on accumulated
resources, and exclusion of individuals from networks of
redistribution surface in the traditions of Zigua *si*, or
neighborhoods. These traditions generally hinged on the
processes of fission and amalgamation of existing groups, or the
formation of new settlements.

The great irony of Zigua history in this era is that the
very characteristics of openness and fluidity which underlay
precolonial famine insurance mechanisms undermined subsistence
security in the second half of the nineteenth century. The keen
interest of the Zigua in trade, their flexible kinship and
residence patterns, shifting political loyalties and rivalries
among their patrons all encouraged the penetration of merchant
capital after 1840. The combination of these factors led to the
emergence of a number of new leaders in Uzigua who, by acting as

the local agents of coastal merchants, were able to use commercial sources of wealth in order to extend the reach of their authority and patronage. Initially their rise may have enhanced food security, but in the 1870s their sale of food reserves began to erode subsistence security.

By 1840, Swahili traders underwritten by Indian merchants at Zanzibar were becoming active in the Zigua hinterland. As they moved inland, they were responding to two forms of market demand. One was overseas demand for ivory; the other was the growing market for slaves in Zanzibar's booming plantation sector. If they wished to conduct business in Uzigua, where no centralized government existed to organize or regulate trade, the coastal merchants needed local agents and allies. They required the services of individuals who were able to collect local supplies of ivory and slaves and who were also able to secure provisions for itinerant traders and their caravans. Traders from the coast also wished to close alliances with Zigua notables so as to avoid constant toll levies. For all these reasons, Swahili merchants were interested in fostering the emergence of individuals who, owing to their dominance in their villages or neighborhoods, were equipped to serve effectively as middlemen.

Swahili traders contributed to the creation of a new political regime in Uzigua by supplying ambitious Zigua individuals with firearms, cloth and other imports. The weapons were used by Zigua leaders to arm their followers, to take captives, and to compel the submission of weaker neighbors. Imported goods such as cloth were distributed by Zigua chieftains among their clients, subjects, and dependents as rewards for their loyalty. Zigua traditions describe these developments in terms not much different from those of the missionary J. L. Krapf, who observed in 1884 that "The Arabs from their island of Zanzibar come over here, to promise the Zigua chiefs a quantity of guns with powder and lead for a certain quantity of slaves. When a chief has reached an agreement, he suddenly attacks a hostile village, burns the houses, and drags off the inhabitants, and so fulfills the stipulations of his agreement with the Arab...."[6]

During the 1840s and 1850s, European travellers such as Krapf and Burton noted the intensive slave hunting and escalating violence engendered by exchanges of firearms for captives and ivory.[7] In this same period, as the frontier of political change and violence rolled westward across Uzigua, the regime of the Zigua middlemen expanded. Further and further from the coast, men or women inspired by political ambitions used connections with coastal traders to consolidate their authority. Eventually, alliances of these commercially-oriented Zigua chieftains grew up along the important trade routes. This proved to be a considerable convenience for coastal merchants, who could henceforth cross Uzigua by passing in safety from the

village of one middleman to the settlement of his ally. Swahili
traders probably attempted to secure control of major trade
arteries by arming the members of these alliances. Sometimes
the Zigua chieftains seem to have become involved as surrogates
in struggles among rival merchant interests. This appears to
have been the case with one of the best-remembered conflicts in
nineteenth-century Uzigua. Merchants from the rival coastal
entrepots of Pangani and Saadani apparently set competing Zigua
chieftains against each other in an effort to wrest control of a
vital trade route.[8]

The major Zigua chieftains assumed considerable regional
significance. Even the powerful sovereigns of the Kilindi
kingdom in Usambara, viewing their emergence as a threat, sought
accommodation with them. The more powerful Zigua leaders
extended their sway over wide areas; in the early 1880s, one was
reported to be taking tribute from 50 to 80 villages.[9] As their
power increased, the Zigua chieftains functioned ever more
effectively as middlemen and commercial agents. Around their
settlements were gathered considerable numbers of dependents and
subjects; thus production and consumption became more
concentrated. The seats of the dominant leaders became foci of
exchanges. Pastoralists and hunter-gatherers were attracted to
these large habitations where they could easily dispose of their
livestock, hides, honey or meat and find supplies of grain and
imports. The chieftains were also able to institutionalize and
regularize the collection of tolls.

Caravan trade and slave dealing reached their most intense
levels in the 1870s and early 1880s as plantation production
increased on the island of Pemba and along the lower Pangani
River. The seaports between Bagamoyo and Tanga, being close to
the plantation areas, became important slave markets and prime
destinations for coastward-bound caravans. Hence Uzigua was
crossed by increasing numbers of traders and caravans following
the primary routes to these coastal towns.[10] As the demand for
slave labor increased, slave traders redoubled their efforts to
obtain captives. This was the era, say Zigua informants, when
women and children dared not venture into their fields without
armed escort.

Swahili merchants also established seasonal trading camps
during this time in the Nguu Mountains. Though the camps served
a number of purposes, their primary one was to provide a place
where large contingents of slaves destined for export might be
broken up into small, scarcely detectable parties. This was
done to evade provisions of the treaty concluded between the
Omani government of Zanzibar and the British in 1876, which
prohibited the entry of slave caravans into coastal towns. In
these camps, coastal men resided for months at a time while they
collected ivory, slaves and livestock for sale in the ports.
The traders encamped in Nguu also welcomed coastward-bound
caravans as they came off the Masai steppe. Porters, who were

generally unable to procure sufficient provisions on the lightly populated steppe, were fed in the trading camps. In parts of northern Nguu they might feast on the rice which was grown in some fertile mountain valleys.

Caravans also obtained loans of imported goods in the seasonal camps which they would then use to pay tolls as they approached the seacoast. They were obliged to repay their debts to merchants affiliated with the Swahili with whom they had contracted the loans once they reached the coast. This arrangement enabled caravans coming from Unyamwezi or other western regions to avoid dissipating their precious stocks of ivory on the final leg of their journey to the sea. It also proved advantageous to the Swahili merchants in Nguu, since by extending credit in this fashion they were able to influence caravan leaders in the choice of the port town which they would select as their ultimate destination. Thus they acted as the advance agents for particular towns as they steered commercial traffic away from rival entrepots.[11]

While the northward shift of plantation production brought about an increase in commercial activity and predation among the Zigua during the 1870s, it also marked an important change in the relationship between export trade and subsistence security. Under the rule of the first generation of the trade-oriented chieftains, roughly between 1840 and 1870, much of the population probably benefitted by enhanced security from hunger. Of course the price of security was often submission to the authority of chieftains or the acceptance of servile status. The trading chieftains enjoyed greater ability to purchase food; from the 1840s, observers noted imports of grain into ports of the Mrima coast during periods of scarcity. Some of the imported grain must have come into the possession of individuals like Mhelamwana, one of the most famous and notorious Zigua leaders of the era. He moved his settlement eastward towards the coast, to a valley near the port of Saadani, where he could participate in regular exchanges of grain. Mhelamwana's people took grain to the coast in periods of abundance and brought it inland from Saadani during hungry seasons.[12]

The first-generation Zigua chieftains probably stimulated increased agricultural output. They concentrated slaves and clients in larger settlements. There, these patrons were able to coordinate closely the activities of subservient labor, particularly through employment of dependents on their extensive fields. By directing larger numbers of laborers they might have been able to widen the seasonal labor bottlenecks which constrained agricultural production. Plots were laid out contiguously to facilitate guarding the fields from pests and vermin. Larger herds of livestock might also be kept as tsetse-free clearings were extended around settlements.[13] Rulers and subjects in the larger, more powerful communities gained all these advantages, but of course they were not shared by people

who lived in smaller settlements. By contrast, residents of
weaker villages faced greater insecurity and vulnerability to
slave raiding.

In spite of all these factors which initially may have
improved subsistence security, signs of a looming crisis began
to appear from the mid-1870s. At the Catholic mission of Mhonda
in southern Nguu, food shortages were observed regularly after
1878. A circumstantial indicator of growing difficulties was
the conflict which developed between Nguu cultivators and Masai
pastoralists in the early 1880s. This fighting may have been
provoked by Masai cattle raiding as the pastoralists tried to
re-stock herds which had been reduced by an epizootic of bovine
pleuro-pneumonia. This epizootic was surely a calamity for the
Masai, but its effect may have been worsened by the fact that
reciprocal ties with Zigua cultivators which might otherwise
have alleviated the crisis were dissolving.[14]

Food shortages became more bothersome in the late 1870s
because patrons were removing food reserves from the networks of
redistribution and reciprocity which tied them to dependents and
pastoralists. Now food stocks were being sold. Reserves which
were produced by dependents or subjects and expropriated from
them through tribute-taking or the imposition of labor dues no
longer found their way back into circuits of redistribution.
Zigua chieftains exchanged food for imported goods, while
managing to retain their own famine reserves, by alienating
foodstuffs from their dependents.

Among the circumstances indicating that it was the removal
of food stocks from channels of redistribution which created a
subsistence crisis and precipitated the severe famine of 1884-
1885 are the following three. First, opportunities for sale of
grain increased markedly in the years leading up to the 1884-
1885 famine. Second, a considerable proportion of the
population depended upon patrons and possessors of accumulated
wealth in order to weather pre-harvest or prolonged hunger.
Third, the 1884-1885 famine, called *lugala* by the Zigua, struck
unevenly: for some Zigua it was a catastrophe which culminated
in their enslavement, but for the fortunate few it provided an
opportunity to increase political power.

The larger market for foodstuffs was created by the
expansion of export trade. Caravans frequently crossed Uzigua
moving eastward or westward. Whether they approached from the
western interior, or whether they had departed from coastal
entrepots only shortly before, caravaneers were eager to
purchase provisions in Uzigua. Trading parties moving into the
interior wished to buy stocks of food before entering the
inhospitable Masai steppeland. Similarly, caravans heading for
the coast had to replenish their food supplies in Uzigua after
an arduous trek of several weeks across the arid steppe. The
seasonal camps of the Swahili traders also required provisions.
Their demand for food from neighboring Nguu communities swelled

as the camps gained importance following the treaty of 1876 which placed restrictions upon the movement of slave caravans. The towns of the Mrima were themselves growing; their populations constituted another market for grain and other food produced in the Zigua hinterland. In short, as export commerce expanded in northeastern Tanzania during the 1870s, opportunities for the profitable sale of foodstuffs increased correspondingly.

Transfers of food out of redistributive networks and into markets threatened the people who depended upon patrons in periods of scarcity. That many Zigua found themselves in these vulnerable circumstances during the early 1880s is shown by the experiences of the Catholic missionaries in Uzigua. The Spiritan missionaries who established permanent stations in the late 1870s found themselves assimilated into Zigua society as influential patrons. They became firmly situated in the hierarchy, but not as overlords. The Zigua regarded them as patrons of intermediate standing. To the major patrons they were obliged to pay tribute, just as Zigua village leaders had to subordinate themselves to stronger rivals. But more pertinent than their status as clients in the context of subsistence production is the evidence of relations which developed between the mission and their own Zigua dependents.

The European missionaries, in a multitude of ways, learned to conduct themselves as would any ambitious Zigua patron. They engaged in warfare, dealt in ivory and slaves, provided their neighbors with access to imports, sought to influence supernatural forces, and arbitrated disputes. In their relations with dependents they also replicated the relationships found in Zigua communities between patrons and dependents. Always short of labor and lacking influence over their Zigua-speaking neighbors, the missionaries had little choice but to allow the Zigua to shape the manner in which the missionaries interacted with them. Hence the Zigua treated the missionaries as they would other Zigua notables. Powerful Zigua viewed the missionaries as rivals. Weaker people saw them as potential sources of patronage.

As did any Zigua chieftain, the missionaries acquired a following of people who were, in varying degrees, subordinated to them. Individuals who were purchased or, as the missionaries preferred to term it, "redeemed" from slave traders fell under the exclusive control of the Catholic fathers. Their position paralleled the status of a Zigua chieftain's slaves. The missions also attracted clients. Unlike the "redeemed" individuals, clients were not entirely dependent upon the Europeans, but they sought missionary patronage by pledging their loyalty. To the mission they looked for protection in the event of war as well as for supplies of cloth and other imports. During crises they might pawn themselves to the missions, thus

accepting a much more servile position. Such desperate actions
were often taken in times of food scarcity.

Zigua clients did not seek assistance from the missionaries
only in the event of severe distress. Many persons living in
proximity to the missions came to depend upon the Europeans'
granaries for food during pre-harvest seasons. They received
aid either in return for work performed on a temporary basis in
the mission fields, or on credit, with the promise that they
would make repayment following their next harvest. The
Spiritans obtained much of the labor which they needed in this
way. When they lacked food reserves, Zigua neighbors would work
briefly for the missionaries in order to earn payment in
staples. Some of them, particularly those who became dependent
upon the missions for long periods, fell permanently into the
debt of the missionaries.

There is no doubt that similar relations existed among
patrons and clients within Zigua communities. They provided a
model for interaction between Europeans and the Zigua. In
particular, they provided notions of reciprocal rights and
duties which regulated the arrangements made between Zigua
clients and their Spiritan patrons. Moreover, direct references
to relations of this kind within the settlements of chieftains
do exist outside mission records.[15]

The great value of the mission journals is that they
illustrate how individuals commonly depended upon patron-client
relationships for insurance against food scarcity. The Spiritan
records demonstrate that many Zigua relied upon redistribution
and reciprocal ties during pre-harvest months or during other
periods of scarcity. As merchant capital penetrated Uzigua and
induced more crop sales, however, these relations atrophied.
The many people who relied upon local patronage were left in a
highly vulnerable state when Zigua notables chose to market
grain reserves rather than to place them in circuits of
redistribution. Increased crop sales deprived clients,
dependents and tribute-paying producers of the reserves which
they were accustomed to receiving. Since grain stocks were
being alienated, the dependents and subjects of trading
chieftains must have come to rely more heavily on non-grain food
sources. It appears significant, therefore, that according to
one informant from Nguu, the famine of 1884-1885 began when
pumpkins, not maize or sorghum, were killed by drought.[16]

Brought on as it was by the collapse of redistributive
networks, the *lugala* famine of 1884-1885 had contradictory
effects. For dependents who had been deprived of entitlement to
reserves, and who were therefore hard pressed by food deficits,
it was a disaster. Many people had no recourse other than to
pawn themselves or members of their households to wealthier
individuals; submission to the authority of chieftains or
patrons who retained reserves or the ability to acquire imported
staples was their sole means of survival. One Zigua informant

described the predatory reaction of chieftains during 1884-1885 in this way: "If you went travelling on the road with your wife and your possessions you could be robbed of everything.... If you were weak you would be robbed.... That's the way the *lugala* famine was.... The locust famine [of 1894-1895] did not cause this same type of chaos....   The number of slaves increased [during 1884-1885]."[17]   Persons who wished to find refuge with the powerful chieftains had to be willing to move into their spheres of influence.   Thus the major change in settlement patterns during 1884-1885 involved increased concentration of population around the major seats of political power.

If for the weak and poor the *lugala* famine meant hunger, loss of autonomy and decline of social status, for wealthy patrons the famine was an opportunity to achieve increased power. Not only did wealthy notables attract more dependents; at the same time patrons acquired a greater degree of dominance over them as former clients or neighbors accepted a more subservient status as pawns.   Patrons who enjoyed access to imported goods were evidently able to use their wealth in order to obtain food during the drought and famine of 1884-1885. If they did not import grain, they may have utilized stock which they were unwilling to dispense to clients, but which they would distribute to persons who decided to surrender their personal autonomy.   Certainly there was no sign that the fortunes of Zigua chieftains declined during 1884-1885.

Famine in the Early Colonial Years

Tumultuous developments which would alter the nature of famine in Uzigua occurred between the *lugala* episode of 1884-1885 and the next major subsistence crisis of 1894-1896. During this period the Germans undertook the colonial occupation of Tanzania. The ability of the Zigua to resist the colonial invasion was diminished by another catastrophic occurrence which would play its own part in reducing subsistence security, the great rinderpest panzootic.

As the German conquest proceeded, it destroyed the precolonial political order. Following their victory over the Swahili towns of the Mrima in the Abushiri War of 1888-1889, the Germans gradually extended their control over the Zigua hinterland.   In a series of bloody and destructive pacification campaigns, German military forces compelled the submission of the Zigua chieftains.   One of the immediate effects of these actions was to reduce food reserves since the Germans commonly destroyed or expropriated the crops and stock of Zigua communities deemed to be recalcitrant.   Some of the Zigua-speaking leaders were left in place as the colonialists patched together a loose, indirect administrative structure.   But even though the Germans tried to turn some Zigua leaders into

administrative functionaries, the net effect of colonial
economic and political policies was to undermine the authority
of all the precolonial notables.

The German suppression of slave raiding, slave trading and
eventually slave holding struck directly at the basis of the
chieftains' power. It deprived them at once of an important
form of export trade as well as a means of labor control, while
the imposed colonial peace eliminated the need for Zigua
dependents to continue their reliance on the protection of their
patrons. Partly as a result of the suppression of slave
dealing, caravan traffic and export commerce shifted away from
the central area of Uzigua to its margins, northward to Tanga
and the Pangani Valley, southward to Bagamoyo and the Wami
Valley. For Zigua chieftains and patrons, therefore, the 1890s
were years of decline and dislocation as they lost wealth,
commercial connections and political authority. Their ability
to maintain reciprocal obligations to dependents and clients was
eroded; henceforth their responsibilities as patrons were as
much a burden as a source of authority and prestige. Seen in
this context, the manner in which slave emancipation proceeded
during the German period is understandable. It resulted as much
from the desire of Zigua patrons to shed unwanted dependents as
it did from the demands of slaves for independence.[18]

The rinderpest panzootic, which reached Uzigua in 1891 or
1892, also contributed to the collapse of redistributive
networks. Rinderpest swiftly destroyed the cattle holdings of
the Masai and of the Zigua as well. The sudden decline of
cattle populations in both woodland and steppe cost Zigua
notables a crucial reserve of wealth and at the same time
prevented them from compensating for those losses through
exchanges with the Masai. Thus it crippled famine insurance
mechanisms by ruining the basis of reciprocal exchanges between
pastoralists and cultivators.

Rinderpest, occurring in conjunction with both the colonial
assault on the independent authority of Zigua chieftains and the
re-orientation of export trade, left patrons incapable of
maintaining redistributive and reciprocal relationships during
the famine of 1894-1896. When drought and locust plagues ruined
successive plantings from early 1894 through mid-1896,
dependents found that they could no longer rely upon village or
neighborhood leaders. The Catholic missionaries, themselves
integrated into networks of reciprocal obligations as both
patrons of their own dependents and, in turn, as clients of the
more powerful Zigua chieftains, received an indication of the
failing capacity of the Zigua-speaking patrons to provide
assistance shortly after the onset of famine conditions. When
the Spiritans at Mandera asked their local patron, a formerly
powerful Zigua leader, for help, they received only a derisory
amount of grain. Evidently, patrons no longer possessed the
reserves of wealth needed to sustain their communities during

times of dearth.   Nor were they able to import food from the
coast, as chieftains of Mhelamwana's generation had done.   Now
imports would be provided either by the colonial government or
by private merchants; imported staples would be distributed not
through networks of kinship, clientage and dependency, but
rather through markets.[19]
     Other signposts pointed towards the increasing importance
of food marketing. Both indebtedness and crop sales became more
prevalent in the midst of famine. Creditors pressured those who
took loans of food to make rapid repayment of their debts. This
again indicates the degree to which precolonial famine insurance
mechanisms had been disrupted. Formerly, the redistributive or
reciprocal relationships which were aspects of long-standing
relations such as kinship or clientage had not imposed the
necessity of immediate repayment.   Instead they had involved
persons in cycles of post-harvest payments or seasonal labor
service. By 1894, however, these relationships were no longer
guarantees of security. Needy individuals now had little choice
but to take food from missionaries, traders or wealthy neighbors
who had no interest in creating the kind of relationships which
imposed permanent mutual obligations.   In 1894 patrons were
extending short-term credit.   Indebted Zigua were obliged,
therefore, to sell at least a portion of their harvests, even in
conditions of persisting scarcity.
     Again   the   Spiritan   mission   records describe these
developments. Many Zigua individuals became heavily indebted as
they accepted food from the Catholic missions. Some eventually
pawned children to the missionaries; others had to bring crops
to the missions immediately after harvests in order to retire
debts.   One of the noteworthy aspects of the 1894-1896 famine in
Uzigua was the extent to which grain and legumes were marketed
after any harvest, no matter how meagre. In June 1894, even as
famine conditions deepened, people brought maize or beans to the
mission stations.   Cultivators who obtained their first grain
harvest in more than two years during mid-1896 hastened to the
missions intent on disposing of their crops.   This attests to
the extent of indebtedness among Zigua cultivators who could no
longer find assistance from their customary patrons.[20]
     Realizing that local sources of patronage were no longer
available, many Zigua hoped to find food in other environmental
zones. The Zigua who searched for food reserves in the Nguu
Mountains, however, found that this option had been foreclosed
also. Together with the rinderpest panzootic, the political and
social disruption caused by German military activities in the
early 1890s left the usually well-provisioned Nguu people
without reserves. Indeed famine conditions were observed in the
Nguu Mountains several months before they were reported in the
drier eastern Zigua lowlands.[21]
     Because famine insurance systems no longer functioned as
they had before the colonial conquest, the famine of 1894-1896

had a much different and much more deleterious impact than its
1884-1885 predecessor. The collapse of patronage provoked the
flight of large numbers of people, many of whom headed for the
coastal towns. Not only emigration, but numerous instances of
starvation were observed by the missionaries; these reports
create a vivid contrast with the *lugala* famine, when such
occurrences had not been noted. After 1896, the demographic
impact of the famine was described in detail by the Spiritans.
In the wake of the 1894-1896 disaster, Zigua settlements were
much smaller than they had been before the famine. The
population was also much more dispersed after 1896. Evidently
the formerly large villages of the chieftains and patrons no
longer held attraction for dependents who were now denied the
benefits of patronage. The missionaries complained constantly
that their efforts to proselytize among the Zigua had been made
much more difficult by the disperal of population.[22]

In terms of both Zigua responses and ecological
consequences, the 1894-1896 famine established a pattern of
events which would reoccur during famine episodes over the next
forty years. The ways in which individuals were excluded from
or protected by patronage would again reappear in 1898-1900 and
during subsequent subsistence crises. But 1894-1896 did not
simply set a precedent. It also initiated long-term
developments which would reduce human control over the natural
environment, increase vulnerability to ecological adversity and,
overall, deepen and perpetuate the subsistence crisis. In
particular, the famine of the mid-1890s set in motion a process
which weakened defenses against human and bovine diseases. The
smallpox epidemic which accompanied the 1894-1896 famine was an
early and telling manifestation of worsening disease
environments. Large-scale movements of population which
occurred as people emigrated or dispersed from major settlements
provided the social context required to produce an epidemic.
The displacement of many people allowed frequent transmission of
and intensive exposure to smallpox infection.[23]

The reduction and dispersal of the human population in
Uzigua, coming soon after the rinderpest panzootic, led to
increased incidence of cattle disease as well. Epizootics of
trypanosomiasis and theileriosis occurred often from the late
1890s. In consequence, by 1910 Zigua cultivators were left with
very few livestock. The decline of human settlement and
cultivation allowed bush to regenerate in formerly cleared
areas. As village populations shrank, vegetation encroached and
brought tsetse and ticks (the vector of theileriosis) into close
contact with cattle. When cattle-keepers attempted to rebuild
herds which had been reduced by rinderpest or by sale and
consumption during famines, they learned that their livestock
could not tolerate constant exposure to infection. This process
of population decline during famine, followed by regeneration of
bush and outbreaks of epizootic, was recorded in detail by

concerned Spiritan missionaries. They had good reason to take careful note of changes in bovine disease environments since their own herds were dying off.

Loss of control over bovine diseases was part of a degenerative environmental cycle. The virtual elimination of cattle-keeping in Zigua communities increased the likelihood of famine. It heightened both the problem of malnutrition and vulnerability to scarcity since cultivators lost a food source and a crucial form of reserve wealth. With each successive famine, the human population was further reduced, tsetse flies and ticks colonized wider areas and the recovery of cattle-herding became ever more difficult. This process would continue unchecked into the 1940s. Epidemics and epizootics, initially the results of social and political changes which increased vulnerability to famine, subsequently became the causes of further demographic and environmental decline.

Conclusion

The famine of 1894-1896 was succeeded by a much more disruptive crisis two years later. The gradual disintegration of social relationships which had provided precolonial famine insurance deprived Zigua cultivators of their ability to weather the locust plagues and drought of 1898-1900. In 1898-1900, however, Zigua vulnerability to environmental adversity was exacerbated by the colonial obligations of taxation and compulsory cultivation which were imposed in 1898. In this regard the situation of the Zigua was of course hardly unique; devastating famine conditions developed throughout East Africa at this time.

These colonial impositions are the causes of Tanganyikan famine emphasized by Kjekshus. Certainly once they were introduced, they became crucially important factors. Indeed similar colonial initiatives would contribute to perpetuating Zigua susceptibility to famine through the end of the Second World War. But in 1894-1896 these policies had not yet come into play. Thus they were evidently not entirely responsible for creating a new, distinctive kind of colonial famine.

It was the colonial destruction of the Zigua political and social order which brought into existence novel famine conditions in 1894-1896. Because this famine broke out in a society where redistributive relations had been severely disrupted and where many individuals had lost access to food reserves, the famine caused depopulation, emigration, dispersal and eventually erosion of human control over vegetation communities and disease environments. These were the characteristics of a new kind of subsistence crisis. They had not been observed following the *lugala* episode, the last notable famine of the late precolonial era, but they would resurface in increasingly virulent form with each colonial famine of the pre-Second World War period. The novel aspects of the first colonial famine in 1894-1896 should not be taken as an indication, however, that it was the first subsistence crisis provoked by relative scarcity. Its predecessor, the *lugala* famine of 1884-1885, also occurred in circumstances which denied many people entitlement to reserves. The *lugala* famine developed as the influence of external merchant capital shifted grain stocks from channels of redistribution and reciprocity into markets.

A study of social and political relations which granted insurance against famine provides several important perspectives. First, it enables us to develop a balanced view of famine in precolonial Zigua society. Precolonial famine may not have occurred often, and certainly not with the frequency with which subsistence crises arose in the early colonial period, but it was nevertheless a threat which heavily influenced the nature of political, social and economic relationships. Second, it reveals that in the Zigua instance the mechanisms which provided protection against famine ironically facilitated the penetration of external merchant capital. Thus the *lugala* crisis of the mid-1880s must be regarded as having been caused not merely by the intrusion of merchant capital, but also by the course of nineteenth-century political development in Uzigua. Third, the focus on social famine-insurance mechanisms indicates that the colonial destruction of the Zigua political and social structure, which took place prior to the imposition of taxation and compulsory cultivation, was the fundamental cause of the subsistence crisis characteristic of the colonial period. Here lies the significance of the colonial pacification campaigns. It was not simply that they caused expropriation of reserves and destruction of crops. More importantly, they were the direct means by which the colonial state brought down the regime of the Zigua chieftains, and with it the foundations of precolonial security from food scarcity.

NOTES

1. The research on which this paper is based was supported in part by the Social Science Research Council.
2. Such an approach would be similar to that developed in Helge Kjekshus, *Ecology Control and Economic Development in East African History* (London, 1977).
3. "Report of Thomas Smee" (September 25, 1811) and "Report of Lt. Hardy with Accompaniements," India Office Marine Records, Misc. v. 586 [this source was generously provided

to me   by Professor   A.M.H. Sheriff]; Smee,   Hardy and Wingham,   "Observations During   a   Voyage   of   Research," *Transactions of   the Bombay   Geographical Society* 6 (1844), 23-61.

4. United Republic of Tanzania, Ministry of   Water, Energy and Minerals, *Tanga   Water Master Plan*, Vol. 2, 5 and 6 (Essen, 1976); Tanzania   National Archives,   Handeni District Book, V. 4; J. D. Acland, *East African Crops* (London, 1971), 125-126.

5. John Ford, "Distribution of   *Glossina* and Epidemiological Patterns   in   the   African Trypanosomiases," *The Journal of Tropical Medicine and Hygiene* 68 (1965), 211-225.

6. Johann Ludwig Krapf, *Reisen   in   Ostafrika*, (Stuttgart, 1858), I, 184-185. A lengthy account of nineteenth-century political and economic developments in Uzigua,   which draws upon written   and oral sources, is contained in my "Famine, Authority and the   Impact   of   Foreign Capital   in Handeni District, Tanzania, 1840-1940" (Ph.d. thesis, University of Wisconsin-Madison, 1986), Chs. 1-2.

7. Krapf, *Reisen*, II, 289, 299, 307, 309-310; Richard F. Burton, *Zanzibar: City, Island   and Coast*, (London, 1872), II, 145, 148, 159-173.

8. "Historia ya Wazigua," Handeni District Book, Tanzania National Archives,   Vol. 1; R. S. Kilango, S. M. Mbwana and L. Abdallah, "Historia   ya   Ufalme"   (August 15,   1951), Tanzania   National   Archives   4/6/5,   Vol. II;   Ibrahimu Mohamedi Mkwayu,   Rajabu Sefu   Mwenkumba, Ramadhani Maingwa (interview at Kwa Mkono Village, December 21, 1982); Yusufu Kaberwa (interview at Mswaki   Village,   May 28-29, 1983); Elders   of   Mgera   (interview   at Mgera Village, August 19, 1982); Salimu Kisailo (interview   at   Kwa   Maligwa Village, May 19, 1983).

9. Franz Stuhlmann,   "Bericht über eine Reise durch Usegua und Unguu," *Mitteilungen   der   Geographischen   Gesellschaft in Hamburg* 10 (1887-1888), 163-167.

10. On the   developments of   the 1870s,   see: Steven Feierman, *The   Shambaa   Kingdom* (Madison,   1974),   Ch. 7;   Frederick Cooper, *Plantation Slavery on the East Coast of Africa* (New Haven, 1977),   Ch. 4;   John Iliffe,   *A   Modern History of Tanganyika* (Cambridge,   1979), 49-50;   Marcia Wright, "East Africa, 1870-1905" in J. D. Fage   and Roland   Oliver, eds., *The Cambridge   History of Africa*, 6 (Cambridge, 1985), 539-591.

11. Nyangasi Mohamedi Munga (interview   at   Kilwa Village, September 12,   1983); Abdala   Hamani   Msede   and Ali Omali Kipande (interview   at   Kwa Dundwa Village, September 12, 1983); Omali   Maligwa Kidiza (interview at Gombero Village, September 20, 1983); Richard F. Burton,   "The Lakes Regions of   Central   Equatorial Africa," *Journal   of   the   Royal Geographical Society* 29 (1859)   57; J. T. Last,   "A Journey

into the Nguu Country from Mamboia, East Central Africa,"
Proceedings of the Royal Geographical Society N.S. 4, 3
(1882), 153-154; Fritz Ferdinand Müller, *Deutschland-
Zanzibar-Ostafrika* (Berlin, 1959), 129; Paul Reichard,
Deutsch-Ostafrika: Das Land Und Seine Bewohner (Leipzig,
1891), 438-439.

12. Abedi Juma (interview at Manga Village, October 10, 1983);
Burton, "The Lakes Regions," 398; Charles Guillain,
*Documents sur l'histoire, la géographie et le commerce de
la côte orientale d'Afrique*, III (Paris, 1856), 312-313.

13. Numerous Zigua informants described agricultural practices
which had existed in their parents' generation during the
late precolonial period. The most informative was Nyangasi
Mohamedi Munga (interview at Kilwa Village, September 12,
1983).

14. Journal de la Communauté du Sacre-Coeur à Mhonda, 1879-1884
[hereafter Mhonda Journal], which is held at the Spiritan
mission at Bagamoyo [Frs. F. Versteijnen and H. Tullemans
made this journal available to me]; Dr. G. A. Fischer,
"Vorlaüfigen Bericht über die Expedition zur Auffindung
Dr. Junkers," *Petermanns Mitteilungen* 32 (1886), 364; Last,
"A Journey," 150; J. T. Last, "A Visit to the Masai People
Living Beyond the Borders of the Nguru Country,"
Proceedings of the Royal Geographical Society N.S. 5
(1883), 521.

15. P. Baur and P. Leroy, *A Travers le Zanguebar* (Tours, 1893),
84-88; J. Kohler, "Beantwortung des Fragebogens über die
Rechte der Eingeborenen in der deutsche Kolonien," Rhodes
House, Micr. Afr. 480.

16. Sources for Spiritan mission relations with the Zigua and
also the famine of 1884-1885 are: Mhonda Journal, 1879-
1886; Journal de la communauté de St. Francais Xavier à
Mandera [hereafter Mandera Journal], 1883-1886 (this is
held at the Residence of the Bishop of Morogoro; I am
grateful to the Rt. Rev. A. Mkoba for allowing me to
examine the journal); and *Bulletin de la Congrégation de
Saint-Esprit* [hereafter BC], Vol. 14 (1887/1888). The
Bulletin was made available to me by the Rev. Richard
Wersing, Dorsey Archivist, Duquesne University. Other
sources on the 1884-1885 famine are: "Letter from Bishop
Parker," *Church Missionary Intelligencer and Record* 12
(1887), 693; letter of Ch. Ledoulx, *Compte Rendu des
séances de la Société de géographie* (1885), 104; and
Mohamedi Lusingo (interview at Mafisa Village, July 1,
1983). The informant who related the onset of the famine
to the failure of the pumpkin crop was Omali Maligwa Kidiza
(interview at Gombero Village, September 20, 1983).

17. Mzee Ndege (interview at Mafisa Village, July 1, 1983).

18. The German period in Uzigua is treated in my "Famine,
Authority and the Impact of Foreign Capital," Chs. 3-4.

19. Evidence of the collapse of redistribution in eastern Uzigua is found in Mandera Journal, 1894-1895, and BC 17 (1893-1896), 724.
20. Indebtedness and crop sales during 1894-1896 are described in Mandera Journal, 1895-1896; BC 18 (1896-1897), 785-786; and *Koloniales Jahrbuch* (1895), 114.
21. Mhonda Journal, 1892-1896; BC 17 (1893-1896), 686-687.
22. BC 18 (1896-1897), 783-785 and 19 (1898-1899), 501. Other evidence of the famine's impact on settlement patterns is found in Oscar Baumann, *Usambara und Seine Nachbargebiete* (Berlin, 1891), 276, and Dr. Max Schoeller, *Mitteilungen über meine reise nach Aequatorial-Ost-Afrika und Uganda, 1896-1897*, I (Berlin, 1901), 59, 61 and 75.
23. BC 19 (1898-1899), 501; on the epidemiology of smallpox in this period, see Marc Dawson, "Smallpox in Kenya, 1880-1920," *Social Science and Medicine* 13B, 4 (1979), 245-250.

Journal of African History, VIII, 3 (1967), pp. 495–512

THE ORGANIZATION OF THE
MAJI MAJI REBELLION

BY JOHN ILIFFE

THIS article[1] analyses the limited documentation relating to the organization of the Maji Maji rebellion of 1905–7 in the south and east of German East Africa. Perhaps a million people lived in the rebel area. The official guess was that 75,000 Africans died, mostly from famine and disease. An estimated 8,000 Pogoro and Mbunga assaulted Mahenge on 30 August 1905. Given these numbers, in an area without prior political unity, a crucial problem is to discover how the people were mobilized and organized for action. Three organizational principles require examination. First, the rebels may have organized according to prior political and cultural· groupings, perhaps forming alliances between groups as often in past emergencies. Although the word has little meaning in the ethnic confusion of southern Tanzania, this method of organization may be called the 'tribal' principle. Second, the rebels may have utilized a sense of common grievance arising from the economic pressures of German rule. For reasons which must be explained, the economic status of some rebel peoples was moving towards that of a peasantry. The use of this common economic status may be called the peasant principle of organization. Third, an attempt to mobilize the southern peoples on a basis wider than the tribe might employ a religious principle of organization. It is probable that all three organizational principles were invoked at various times and places during the rising. As more evidence becomes available, a simple chronological sequence from one principle to another may become untenable, and any remaining pattern may be extremely complex, with wide regional variation. Yet, as a working hypothesis, it is perhaps worth while to set out a relatively simple pattern which is supported by much of the evidence now available.

It is therefore the thesis of this article that Maji Maji, as a mass movement, originated in peasant grievances, was then sanctified and extended by prophetic religion, and finally crumbled as crisis compelled reliance on fundamental loyalties to kin and tribe. Implicit in this thesis is the belief that the central historical problem of the rebellion is a conflict, common perhaps to all mass movements, between the ideology of revolt and economic, political and cultural realities.

The sequence of organizational principles may be correlated with the geographical expansion of the movement. If the rebellion is dated from the death of its first victims, it began on the night of 31 July 1905, in the Ma-

---

[1] This article draws widely on the work of Professor T. O. Ranger, to whose generosity I am much indebted. The conclusions are naturally my own responsibility.

tumbi Hills, and simultaneously (or even slightly earlier) in Madaba. From this nucleus, violence spread north to Uzaramo (before 15 August), south to Liwale (somewhat earlier), and north-west to Kilosa, Morogoro, and Kisaki (by late August). This complex, centring on the middle and lower Rufiji, was the first unit of revolt. The second was the Lukuledi Valley, whither the rebellion expanded, via Liwale, during the last days of August.

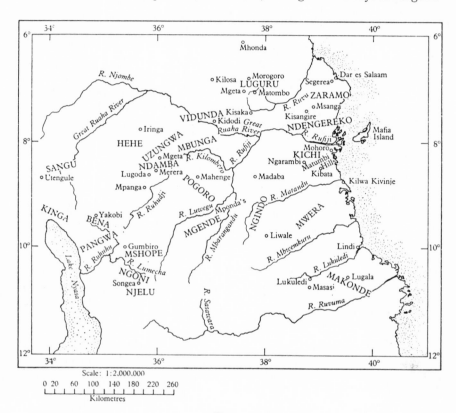

Fig. 1

Simultaneously, the movement spread to the Kilombero Valley, the Mahenge Plateau, and Uzungwa, probably carried by the Ngindo and Pogoro. Finally, it was taken by the Ngindo to Ungoni early in September, whence it spread to Upangwa and southern Ubena. The Bena, who attacked Yakobi mission on 19 September, were the last to join.

It is useful to distinguish between the first area—the Rufiji complex—and the three other major areas of revolt. In the Rufiji complex, the rebellion began as a peasant movement. It expanded elsewhere through its acquired religious content. In the later areas, the tribal principle of organization quickly predominated. This article considers successively the peasant origins of the movement, the religious beliefs through which it spread, and its acceptance and transformation by the peoples outside the original nucleus.

An analysis of the origins of Maji Maji must explain why it happened in that particular area at that precise moment. It is sometimes argued that post-pacification revolts are in reality delayed resistances, initiated by decentralized groups unable either to offer effective resistance to the first European invasion or fully to comprehend its implications. Only after internal reorganization and experience of colonial rule, it is said, are such peoples convinced of their need and ability to resist. Maji Maji cannot be explained in this way. Several rebel peoples had previously offered quite severe resistance to the Germans. The Mbunga clashed with German forces several times between 1891 and 1893. Many groups in the Kilwa hinterland had participated in Hassan bin Omari's resistance of 1894–95. The Makonde of the Lugala area, the only Makonde to rebel, had formed the core of the Yao warlord Machemba's followers, who had defied the Germans until 1899. Again, although the Ngoni were more aware of the implications of colonial rule in 1905 than at first contact in 1897, they were also in a less effective position to resist.[2] 'Delayed resistance' is too simple a concept to explain the particularity of the rising. Nor can it easily be explained by general grievances against German rule—an explanation then common among left-wing groups in Germany. The imposition of taxation and brutal methods of collection, forced labour on road construction or European plantations, the replacement of indigenous leaders by alien agents (akidas)—all these were given as explanations. These were undoubtedly grievances, but they were shared widely in German East Africa, and were experienced much more profoundly elsewhere in the colony, especially in the north. More important, they were not new grievances in July 1905, nor were they perhaps sufficiently burdensome to threaten the whole economy of the rebel peoples. If the initial stage of the rising is to be explained as a reaction to grievances, then the grievances must have been both more specific in time and place and also more destructive in their impact.

Such grievances existed in this particular area at precisely this moment. In 1902 a new governor decided to initiate large-scale African cotton-growing. Since cotton had failed on the northern coast, the experiment was confined to the south. Against much official advice, the governor doubted whether individual cultivation could be adequately supervised or produce worth-while results. He therefore ordered that a cotton plot be established in each neighbourhood of the experimental area, under the control of the local headman. Each of the headman's subjects would work for a fixed number of days on this communal plot. The Kommunalverband, the Euro-

[2] Ernst Nigmann, Geschichte der kaiserlichen Schutztruppe für Deutsch-Ostafrika (Berlin, 1909), 20–61; G. P. Mpangara, 'Songea Mbano', research seminar paper, University College, Dar es Salaam, Sept. 1966.

pean-controlled district development committee, would supply seed and supervise cultivation and marketing. As originally planned, the headman, the workers, and the *Kommunalverband* would each receive one-third of the market price.[3] The scheme began in Dar es Salaam district, whose administrator was the main advocate of 'communalization' and who introduced it to produce other cash crops and food before the plots were converted to cotton. The first plots were laid out in September and October 1902. The land was chosen by agricultural inspectors in consultation with the headmen. The normal plot was $2\frac{1}{2}$ acres for each 30–50 of the headman's adult male subjects. There were reckoned to be 25,000 of these in the district in 1902–3, and some 2,000 acres were laid out in plots of between $2\frac{1}{2}$ and 35 acres. The number of days to be worked is uncertain; twenty-eight per year, or two per month, were figures often quoted. No cotton was planted in 1902–3. The main crops were maize, millet, simsim, and rice. The total receipts were Rs. 19,185. Headmen and workers received their portions in October 1903. Each headman received Rs. 35 and 46 pesa; each worker received 17 pesa. In 1903–4 the plots were enlarged and the acreage estimated at 3,200, of which 640 were devoted to cotton. The total proceeds for 28,186 workers and 178 headmen were Rs. 13,146. These were never distributed. In the the third year only cotton was sown. This was expected to require 50–100% extra labour for the same acreage. And since cotton was more difficult to grow, control was tightened. The headman was made personally responsible for his plot, trainee agricultural assistants were sent to inspect, and a European official toured the whole area.[4]

The people of the Dar es Salaam district, the Zaramo, refused the 35 cents they were each offered for their first year's work. Refusal to work on the plots became fairly general during 1905, and headmen either reported their loss of control or conscripted women and children as labourers. Headman Pazi Kitoweo of Msanga, interviewed in Dar es Salaam gaol, replied that his people 'would pay hut tax and also clear roads, but they would not work on communal plots'. The Commission of Enquiry into the causes of the rebellion in the district noted that the scheme had disrupted the family economy of the Zaramo, and, while providing 'a welcome bonus' for the headmen, had convinced the ordinary cultivator 'that government had devised a new means of obliging him to carry out a hated task for nothing'.[5]

Communal cultivation was introduced into Kilwa district (including Ungindo) in 1903, when some 1,000 acres of cotton were laid out. On average the crop brought in Shs. 33/- per acre gross; the amount received by the workers is uncertain. The area was estimated at between 2,500 and 5,000 acres in 1904–5. European buyers offered between 4 and 7 cents a pound

[3] 'Gouvernementsrat beim Gouvernement von Deutsch-Ostafrika. Dritte Sitzung,' Dar es Salaam, 15/16 May 1905, Deutsches Zentralarchiv, Potsdam, Reichskolonialamt [RKA] 812/41–58; Stuhlmann to Dernburg, and encl., 3 Oct. 1907, RKA 775/73–74.
[4] Haber and Vincenti, 'Betr. Ursachen des Aufstandes im Bezirk Daressalam,' 17 Jan. 1906, RKA 726/109–25.   [5] Ibid.

before ginning.[6] In Lindi district (south of the Mbwemkuru and east of the Sasawara), the scheme was inaugurated during the 1904–5 season, when some 1,950 acres were planted. None was picked. A fortnight after the outbreak of the rebellion, the district officer recalled his persistent opposition to the the scheme as 'inadvisable' and 'a restriction of native freedom'. During a recent tour, he had in effect promised that it would be abandoned.[7] Of the other rebel districts, the scheme operated in Kilosa and Rufiji, but not, it appears, in Mahenge or Iringa. In Songea district, a settler organized share-cropping of cotton together with local headmen. In northern Uzaramo, where the scheme did operate, there was no rebellion. The programme was abandoned on the orders of the Colonial Secretary in February 1906.[8]

The mere coincidence of time and place between cotton scheme and rebellion does not itself demonstrate that the former caused and delimited the latter. Yet the scheme probably was the major reason for the outbreak in the Rufiji complex in July and August 1905. It is worth summarizing the evidence which supports such a view. First, of course, although the cotton scheme was not in operation throughout the rebel area, the rising began where the scheme did operate. Second, it is surely significant that the revolt began early in the cotton picking season. Third, R. M. Bell's evidence suggests that the first outbreaks in Matumbi and Madaba were directly connected with orders to begin cotton picking. Fourth, several rebel leaders had suffered from the scheme. Of the Mwera and Matumbi leaders, Selemani Mamba, Chekenje, and Abdallah Kitambi appear on a list of headmen involved in the programme. Digalu Kibasila, the leader in Kisangire, was imprisoned during June 1905 for failing to require his people to cultivate cotton, and joined the rebellion almost immediately after release.[9] Fifth, cotton was everywhere an object of attack. In Kilosa the rebels burned the crop in the fields. 'The missionaries were hunted', reported the superior of the devastated Lukuledi mission, 'because they were Europeans and all Europeans are the same, all *friends of taxes and cotton.*' Mr Gwassa was told recently by Yusuf bin Issa: 'The origin of Maji Maji is cotton. Men and women were made to work together on government plantations contrary to accepted social practice and under the most harsh conditions. The natives of up-country resented this idea of forced labour even at the pain of war.'[10] Although scarcely conclusive, this

[6] Haber to Götzen, 9 Sept. 1905, RKA 726/81–90.
[7] Ewerbeck to Government, 15 Sept. 1905, RKA 723/59–62.
[8] Report by Albinus in *Deutsches Kolonialblatt*, 1 June 1905; Hohenlohe to Government, 17 Feb. 1906, RKA 726/68–76.
[9] R. M. Bell, 'The Maji-Maji rebellion in the Liwale district', *Tanganyika Notes and Records*, XXVIII (Jan. 1950), 39; list by Lergen, 28 Dec. 1904, Tanzania National Archives, Dar es Salaam [TNA] IV/G/2/I; Haber and Vincenti, 'Betr. Ursachen...', 17 Jan. 1906, RKA 726/109–25.
[10] Paul Fuchs, *Wirtschaftliche Eisenbahn-Erkundungen im mittleren und nördlichen Deutsch-Ostafrikas* (Berlin, 1907), 9; Thomas Spreiter, 'Bericht über die Zerstörung der Kath. Missionsstation Lukuledi', 9 Sept. 1905, RKA 723/43–47; G. C. K. Gwassa, 'A report on a research project in Kilwa district', typescript, Dar es Salaam, Aug. 1966.

evidence does perhaps point to the cotton scheme as an explanation of the particularity of the outbreak. Yet the rebellion was not simply a protest against the introduction of commercial agriculture. Soon after the rising, to German surprise, cotton was widely grown by individuals in the Rufiji Valley.[11] The protest had presumably been directed against obviously unacceptable methods of cultivation, against the consequent damage to the subsistence economy, and especially against the sheer unprofitability of the experiment.

Such grievances with the functioning of the commercial sector of the economy are the grievances of peasants. To speak of the peasant origins of the rising is not merely to give it a fashionable label, but is necessary if its changing character is to be understood, and if relevant comparisons are to be made. Maji Maji was not a 'peasant revolt', if this implies that it was wholly the action of peasants for peasant ends. Indeed, as Dr AlRoy has suggested,[12] the concept of a peasant revolt as a distinct form of internal war is perhaps unfruitful. It is more useful to seek the degree and character of peasant involvement in the various stages of a mass movement. Peasant involvement predominated in the early stages of Maji Maji. Apart from the grievances specific to the outbreak area, there are two reasons for believing this. First any analysis of peasant involvement elsewhere suggests its amorphous, kaleidoscopic, essentially parochial character. The men of a locality hear that rebellion has broken out elsewhere. They congregate into a 'band', leaders and spokesmen emerge, the property of notable local enemies is destroyed and the enemies, if available, are killed. If they escape the area, they are rarely pursued. The band may coalesce with another and march jointly on a more prominent provincial centre, where the same process is repeated. Often the coalition dissolves and the men return home. Wider action is likely only if charismatic leadership has emerged, or if some millennial belief has been evoked.[13] The early phases of Maji Maji seem to follow this kaleidoscopic pattern, although the impression of formlessness may derive chiefly from the inadequacy of the evidence. This planless, local character emerges clearly from Bell's account of events in Liwale and from Abdul Karim bin Jamaliddini's *Utenzi wa Vita vya Maji-Maji*.[14] Having cleared their hills and sacked Samanga, the Matumbi returned to their homes, to mobilize again only when troops reached the area. The neighbouring Kichi dispersed once the headquarters of the local *akidas* were destroyed. Kimbasila's men remained in Kisangire, defying the government, but making no move beyond their homes. Such tactics clearly differed from the disciplined activity of the Ngoni, which will be described later. It is more diffi-

[11] Grass to Government, 18 Jan. 1909, RKA 8181/215-24.

[12] Gil Carl AlRoy, *The Involvement of Peasants in Internal Wars* (Center of International Studies, Princeton University, Research Monograph no. 24, 1966), passim. I owe this reference to Mr J. S. Saul.

[13] AlRoy, op. cit. pp. 35–6. See, for example, George Rudé, *The Crowd in History, 1730–1848* (New York, 1964), chs. 1 and 2.

[14] Trans. W. H. Whiteley, Kampala, 1957.

cult to decide whether this represents the difference between the actions of peasants and of tribesmen, or between those of ill-organized and of well-organized tribesmen. To show that the former distinction holds, it is necessary to consider the second reason for believing that peasant involvement predominated in early rebel actions.

If, on one level, the great African rebellions against early colonial rule can be traced to administrative abuses, equal or greater abuses existed in other areas where only small-scale unrest occurred. To explain a rebellion the causes alone are insufficient; the organizational possibility must also be demonstrated. This is peculiarly difficult for Maji Maji. As Professor Ranger has shown, other movements of rebellion and resistance in East and Central Africa occurred amongst peoples—the Shona and Ndebele, Nandi, Kiga, Barwe—where a historical appeal was possible.[15] It may prove that the Maji Maji rebels do have some historical unity, but this seems extremely unlikely. They lack even close linguistic affinity.[16] It remains possible, of course, that they have a historic religious unity, conceivably based on a religious system established before the movements and coalescence which formed the recognizable rebel groups. Since the Ngindo-Mwera group are probably recent immigrants from the south, they may have moved into an area already under the religious authority of the Pogoro and Luguru. The Pogoro, at least, claim long settlement. This possibility is attractive, but there is at present no evidence whatever to support it, nor is there evidence in the rising of any historical appeal. An explanation of the possibility of organizing so widespread a movement must therefore concentrate on the then existing connexions among the rebels. The peoples within the Rufiji complex were distinguished from later rebels precisely by their closer approximation to peasant status. As normally defined, this has a dual meaning. First, peasants are rural producers whose surpluses are not devoted to 'equivalent and direct exchange of goods and services between one group and another; rather, goods and services are first furnished to a centre and only later redirected'.[17] Second, peasants possess a culture (perhaps a 'folk-culture') distinct from a literary, esoteric, and normally urban version of the same culture within the same economic and political unit.[18] The peoples of the Rufiji complex approached this status through their long relationship with the East African coast. Their 'folk-culture'

[15] T. O. Ranger, 'The role of Ndebele and Shona religious authorities in the rebellions of 1896 and 1897', in Eric Stokes and Richard Brown (eds.), *The Zambesian Past* (Manchester, 1966), esp. 96; idem, 'Connections between "primary resistance" movements and modern mass nationalism in East and Central Africa', University of East Africa Social Science Conference Paper, Dec. 1966; idem, 'Revolt in Portuguese East Africa', in *St Anthony's Papers, no. 15* (ed. K. Kirkwood, London, 1963), 54–80.

[16] Dr Bryan distinguishes between a Zaramo–Luguru–Vidunda group and the Nden-gereko, Ngindo, and Mbunga languages. Kipogoro may either belong to a Hehe linguistic group or be considered separately. Kimatumbi, similarly, may belong to the Hehe or Ngindo groups. M. A. Bryan, *The Bantu Languages of Africa* (London, 1959), 123–36.

[17] Eric R. Wolf, *Peasants* (Englewood Cliffs, N.J., 1966), 3.

[18] Robert Redfield, *Peasant Society and Culture* (Chicago, 1956), ch. 2.

was distinct from the literary subculture of the coast, while their economy stood in an unequal relationship to the coastal trading area, recently supplemented by German political and economic authority. This relationship was demonstrably conscious and central to them—among the Zaramo, for example, the sense of situation between coast and 'interior' had found religious expression.[19] The prestige of the coastal subculture probably aided the expansion of the rising inland. The high degree of mobility and intercommunication among the early rebels may have been possible only because of these shared economic and cultural circumstances.

If the origins and early character of the rising are to be found in peasant grievances and peasant action, its subsequent development falls more clearly into a general pattern. In recent papers,[20] Professor Ranger has argued that several rebellions and resistance movements in East and Central Africa sought new methods of organizing effective mass action. Their integrating principles were often ideological, and the agents of reorganization were religious leaders. Further, since the object was to organize anew, it was not sufficient merely to revitalize structures and beliefs which often reflected those divisions which had previously hindered effective action. Rather, it was necessary to enlarge the scale both of resistance and of religious allegiance. The central figure in such an enlargement was the prophet, proclaiming a new religious order to supersede the old, a new loyalty to transcend old loyalties of tribe and kinship. German observers saw in Maji Maji the signs of such a transformation. The *maji*—the water-medicine accepted by each rebel—united in common action peoples with no known prior unity. Its power was believed to be religious, or in German terms was due to witchcraft. And it inspired its recipients with a passionate courage of which the Germans had believed their subjects incapable. An early analysis by the Chief Secretary, Eduard Haber, explained:

The leaders have attempted to work systematically on the broad mass of commonly indolent and apathetic natives through the use of so-called witchcraft... The stronghold of witchcraft seems to lie near Ngarambi on the Rufiji. There a family of witchdoctors trains subordinates. They receive water which, as they pass through the land, they sprinkle over the *washenzi* to make them immune to any mishap and to European weapons. Associated with the use of the water, it appears, is a revival [*Wiederaufleben*] of a cult of the snake-god Koleo among the Wazaramo and Waluguru.

The witchcraft was undoubtedly able to achieve such resounding success only because the broad mass of the natives believed they had grounds for profound dissatisfaction with the German administration. One may perhaps discern a reciprocal action [*Wechselwirkung*], in the sense that the natives, in their...

[19] Martin Klamroth, 'Beiträge zum Verständnis der religiösen Vorstellungen der Saramo im Bezirk Daressalam (Deutsch-Ostafrika)', *Zeitschrift für Kolonialsprachen*, 1 (1910–11), 148–51.

[20] Ranger, works cited, and 'African reaction and resistance to the imposition of colonial rule in East and Central Africa', in L. H. Gann and P. Duignan (eds.), *History and Politics of Modern Imperialism in Africa* (Stanford, forthcoming).

bitterness against administrative demands, resorted of their own accord to the witchdoctors, while the leaders and fomenters of the rising skilfully used native discontent to effect their purposes. For the upheaval is too well planned to be the product of sudden decisions, while use of the water-witchcraft apparently cannot be traced before the middle of June this year.[21]

Thus Haber visualized the conjunction of two elements of equal importance: the grievances which brought the people to the ministers of the Kolelo cult, and the plans of these ministers utilizing popular distress. The common German view, however, detected a conspiracy imposed on the ignorant masses. This explanation originated with Moritz Merker, who commanded the reprisals in the Matumbi Hills. He believed that a group of chiefs and religious leaders secretly planned a revolt, distributing water as a panacea while insinuating that it would also give immunity. Large groups travelled openly to fetch the water from Ngarambi. 'The true incitement was to follow at the last moment before the outbreak of hostilities. These were to be started simultaneously by each of the committed chiefs at an agreed moment, which was to be a few months after the first of August. Fortunately... this did not happen, but they began in Kibata at the end of July, apparently owing to a private quarrel between two Matumbi headmen.'[22] If Merker had evidence of prior planning, it does not survive. The conspiracy theory was later challenged by Bell, in whose account the initiative was taken by the Matumbi, who sought assistance from Kolelo's minister, Bokero, at Ngarambi, and returned to attack their *akida*. Farther west, according to Bell, the people of Madaba were given *maji* by Bokero's brother-in-law, Ngameya. At first they accepted it as a panacea, with fertility as its main element, but later visitors were told that it was effective against Europeans. When news of war reached Madaba, Ngameya was rumoured to be its leader, and he sent deputies (*hongo*) to distribute *maji* and direct operations.[23]

These accounts stress the role of the ministers of Kolelo. If the religious authorities who co-ordinated the Rhodesian risings of 1896–97 had counterparts in Maji Maji, these are the most likely. Kolelo is first mentioned by Burton:

[The Luguru] have a place visited even by distant Wazaramo pilgrims. It is described as a cave where a P'hepo or the disembodied spirit of a man, in fact a ghost, produces a terrible subterranean sound, called by the people Kurero or Bokero; it arises probably from the flow of water underground. In a pool in the cave women bathe for the blessing of issue, and men sacrifice sheep and goats to obtain fruitful seasons and success in war.[24]

[21] Haber to Götzen, 9 Sept. 1905, RKA 726/81–90.
[22] Moritz Merker, 'Über die Aufstandsbewegung in Deutsch-Ostafrika', *Militär-Wochenblatt*, XCI (1906), 1023–30.
[23] Bell, loc. cit., passim. *Hongo* is a title of unknown origin and meaning. The identity of the many *hongo* active during the rebellion is an important topic for future research.
[24] Richard F. Burton, *The Lake Regions of Central Africa*, (2 vols, New York, 1961) I, 88–9. See also A. R. W. Crosse-Upcott, 'The origin of the Majimaji revolt', *Man*, LX (1960), art. 98.

A more detailed account is given by Martin Klamroth, an informed
Lutheran missionary who served in Maneromango shortly before and
after the rising. According to Klamroth, the Zaramo believed that the
creator, Mungu, had sent Kolelo (a great snake) 'to restore order to all
that is corrupted here on earth'. On arrival, Kolelo had taken to wife a
woman of the Mlali clan, and ordered that 'your people of the Mlali clan
shall be my people and serve me here forever in this cave in the Uluguru
mountains'. Both Klamroth and recent accounts state that Kolelo was
visited at regular intervals by his hereditary representatives (*wazagila*) from
various parts of Uzaramo. On reaching the spot (known as Kolelo, near
Matombo) the *mzagila* was taken to a place above a cave where Kolelo's
words could be heard. The minister of the cult informed Kolelo of the
mzagila's mission. In Klamroth's account, Kolelo *brummt* (boomed or
grunted) unintelligibly, and the minister interpreted an order, which might,
for example, be to return to Uzaramo and carry out certain rites. Klamroth suggests that the phenomenon was an underground waterfall. Other
accounts state that any individual who followed the necessary observances
might approach Kolelo. In particular, those accused of witchcraft were
taken to be judged by Kolelo, or could appeal to Kolelo for judgement.[25]
Burton's statement that the spirit was called 'Bokero' suggests a link with
the cult-centre at Ngarambi on the Rufiji, whose chief attendant, entitled
Bokero, was believed by the Germans to have first distributed the *maji*.
Others have confirmed that there is such a link, and that there are further
cult-centres in the Rufiji area, although that in Uluguru remains the senior
branch. The cult apparently flourishes, and people travel from many parts
of southern and eastern Tanzania to seek medicines for rain and fertility.[26]

Three points emerge from these accounts. First, the Kolelo cult was
influential over a wide area, and operated as German and other accounts of
Maji Maji suggest. It provided centres to which large numbers of people
went to receive medicine and instructions which they distributed on return.
Second, the cult was chiefly concerned with the crops and the land. One of
Klamroth's informants commented: 'If the crops prosper, the Zaramo do
not think of Kolelo'.[27] It is tempting to link the resurgence of the cult to
German interference with the crops and the land. Third, the cult may have
possessed specifically supernatural elements—mediumship, possession, and
command over death. According to Hemedi bin Saidi:

Bokero was a demon [*Shitwani*]. He was not the name of a man. A man was
possessed by the spirit Bokero [*Ila mtu alikuwa alipagawa na pepo Bokera*] and
was simply used by Bokero. He was not a person, but the spirits [*mizuka*] which
had entered a person. And indeed those Unbelievers believed him without understanding because he was like a god to them.[28]

  [25] Klamroth, loc. cit., 139–52; information from Miss J. Ritchie, Dar es Salaam,
April 1966.
  [26] Information from Chief G. P. Kunambi, Dar es Salaam, July 1966, and others.
  [27] Klamroth, loc. cit., 146.
  [28] Notes of an interview by Mr Gwassa, Kilwa Kivinje, July 1966.

The evidence is perhaps sufficient to conclude that the Kolelo cult provided a machinery which could reach the peoples of the Rufiji complex. Yet there is no indication that it had political functions. It is curious and perhaps significant that the only area of Uluguru to join the rebellion— Mgeta—is on the opposite side of the mountains from Kolelo, and that for both the Luguru and Zaramo the source of medicine was the junior branch of the cult at Ngarambi.[29] Nor do the accounts suggest that the cult had any role in warfare—until Maji Maji. Here the evidence is slight, and comes largely from Klamroth. It suggests that in the period before the rebellion the cult was transformed from its normal preoccupation with the land to a more radical and prophetic belief in a reversal of the existing order by direct divine intervention. Klamroth writes:

In the year 1905...Kolelo also concerned himself with politics. He (i.e. naturally the Zaramo who honour him) clearly decided that there were other needs to satisfy besides famine, and so the xenophobic movement of that year at first simply associated itself closely with Kolelo's name. Kolelo had forbidden the further payment of taxes to the white foreigners; in mid-July a great flood would come and destroy all whites and their followers. Later it was said that the earth would open and swallow them, that no bullets but only water would come from the soldiers' guns, seven lions would come and destroy the enemy, 'be not afraid, Kolelo spares his black children'.

Soon, however, other voices intervened. Now it was not Kolelo who looked after his children, but God himself, who had previously sent Kolelo. Kolelo, however, had not adequately fulfilled his task, so that God himself now appeared.

Clearly linked to this new situation was everything said at the time about the resurrection of the dead, since according to Zaramo conceptions only God himself, and not Kolelo, has unlimited power over life and death. It was later said that, before the rising, chief Kibasila of Kisangire, subsequently the main ringleader in Uzaramo, was won for their cause by the discontented spirits in the Matumbi Hills by a sham resurrection. He was said to have first become fully convinced of the rightness of the rebel cause when they showed him a man who had seen a remarkable likeness to his dead father.[30]

According to Klamroth, God was known as Kalava Dikono, which he translates as 'he has stretched forth his hand'. His prophets (mitume— Klamroth's translation) told Kibasila that they had seen his dead father. They promised that Kibasila might also see him if he offered 'the head of a white man, a European or an Arab'.[31] According to Bell, Bokero had told Abdallah Mapanda precisely the same. A further account, headed simply *Majimaji ao Kalava Dikono*, bears out the general lines of this story. The prophets told Kibasila that they had been sent by his father to instruct him to defy the government in the name of the new god, who would come to live in the land: 'He will change this world and it will be new....His rule will be one of marvels. When Kibasila replied that the government's

[29] Klamroth, loc. cit., passim; Morogoro District Book (Area Office, Morogoro); Albert Prüsse, *Zwanzig Jahre Ansiedler in Deutsch-Ostafrika* (Stuttgart, 1929), 95.
[30] Klamroth, loc. cit., 140–1.   [31] Klamroth, loc. cit., 141–3.

weapons were strong, the prophets sold him *maji* and told him to sell it for two pesa, secretly, and give the money to them for the *mungu wa pesa mbili*. Delighted, Kibasila did this and defied the government. The writer does not directly identify Kalava Dikono, and although at one point Kibasila's father shows himself by stretching out his hand from a swamp, at another point it is the god who does this.[32]

Where such confusion exists, little can be based on the evidence. Clearly, the Ngarambi branch of the cult was deeply involved in Maji Maji. Very probably its ministers were the first to distribute the *maji*, and certainly its commitment to the rebellion became clear during the first days of violence. It remains, however, to discover whether the ministers were planning a rebellion before violence began, whether they 'embodied and set the seal of ritual approval on the decision of the community as a whole',[33] or whether they gave retrospective sanctification to violence already committed. On the present evidence, it seems more likely, as Haber first suggested, that there was a 'reciprocal action' between mass discontent and potentially prophetic leadership, their growing confidence in the *maji* impelling the people towards violence, and the increasing resolution of the people encouraging the religious leaders to expand their claims and objectives. The only indication of prior planning is that the *maji* was distributed for some weeks before violence began. Against this is the lack of evidence of any 'decision of the community as a whole', the very loose co-ordination of actions within the Rufiji complex, the complete absence of preparatory organization elsewhere, and the fact that the precipitant of violence in many areas was the unexpected news of war in the Matumbi Hills. Both Kibasila and Abdallah Mapanda, for example, received the *maji* and were told some of its powers before the rebellion began, but acted on it only after news of war arrived. The ministers of Kolelo had certainly taken a new initiative, but there is little sign that it was designed as an initiative for war.

To this point, the argument has concentrated on the first area of revolt, where the cotton scheme provided a new and critical grievance, economic and cultural circumstances offered the possibility of intercommunication, and where the cult of Kolelo held authority. Yet the rising rapidly expanded far beyond this nucleus, among tribes whose economic and political systems were relatively little affected by German rule, and where—to judge from the silence of the accounts—Kolelo's name carried less weight. Here the normal precipitant of violence was the arrival of a *hongo* from the east with news and *maji*. To understand the sequence of events which followed, it is important to stress that by no means all the peoples within the area of rebellion joined. Even among those who did, there were invariably groups which either remained passive or actively joined the German

[32] Tuheri Abraham Beho, 'Majimaji ao Kalava Dikono', manuscript, Lutheran Mission, Maneromango, Nov. 1965. I owe this reference to Miss Ritchie. See also Ramadhani Mwaruka, *Masimulizi Juu ya Uzaramo* (London, 1965), 108–9.

[33] Ranger in Stokes and Brown, 96

side. Some explanation of these different responses is suggested by analysing the actions of those peoples beyond the Rufiji complex for whom the
evidence is most extensive. Those chosen are the Vidunda and Sangu, the
Kibena-speaking peoples ruled by the Wakinamanga (Ubena of the Rivers),
the Ndamba, the Mbeyela chiefdom in the south of highland Ubena, the
Pangwa, and the Ngoni.

The factors which determined a decision to rebel are best illustrated by
Fr. Schaegelen's account of the rising in Uvidunda.[34] Maji Maji was brought
to this area by a *hongo* whose identity is uncertain. He first approached a
number of headmen and urged resistance. When they pointed to the
power of European weapons, he sold them *maji*, with which he anointed
them on face, chest, and legs. Although his claims and promises, as
recorded, were remarkably similar to those made to Kibasila and others,
three features of the Vidunda experience deserve special attention.
First, the Vidunda understood the *maji* in the context of an attack on
sorcery.

Hongo gave orders that every man must anoint himself with his Usinga medicine
[i.e. the *maji*]; anyone who refused was to be caught and killed. People began to
fear that they would be called witches and...went to Hongo to receive his
medicine...No white magic or witchcraft was to be performed, no charms or
medicines of any kind must be kept in their houses but all destroyed by fire.

Second, the movement was denounced by the Vidunda chief, Ngwira. The
chieftainship was a relatively recent institution which had emerged from
nineteenth-century defensive measures. Schaegelen writes:

All the Jumbes and old men went to Ngwira to tell him that a great witch-doctor
Hongo had come to free them from the yoke of the Europeans...Ngwira was
very angry when he heard these words for he realised that he was [an] impostor
seeking to destroy the country...Hongo must be driven right away...But the
Jumbes and old men paid no attention to his wise words.

With Ngwira discredited, 'Hongo appointed himself chief of the district...
When Hongo saw that his strength was increasing...he gathered them
together to go and take Kilosa.' The attack was a disaster. Several Vidunda
were shot. 'Hongo had nothing to say.' Now began a third phase, the
'tribalization' of the movement in its later stages. 'After this they returned
to their houses with their spoils. On arriving home they began to break the
taboos of Hongo, they killed cattle, goats and sheep and brewed beer, for
they knew that revenge was at hand.' At this point the *hongo* disappears
from the story. Instead, the Vidunda turned to guerrilla warfare in their
mountains, as so often in their history. Simultaneously, Ngwira's authority
revived.

[34] Theobald Schaegelen, 'The ethnology of the Vidunda tribe', manuscript, 1945, in
Kilosa District Book (Area Office, Kilosa). See also T. O. Beidelman, 'Notes on the
Vidunda of eastern Tanganyika', *Tanganyika Notes and Records*, LXV (March 1966),
63–80.

In recent years, social anthropologists have described a number of popular movements designed to eradicate sorcery[35] from African societies. Dr Douglas has shown[36] that among the Lele such periodic and short-lived movements are sharply opposed to routine measures to detect sorcerers and secure protection against them. Rather, they aim to rid the society of the possibility of sorcery by rendering its members unable either to practice or to suffer from it.

For the Lele [Dr Douglas writes] evil is not to be included in the total system of the world, but to be expunged without compromise. All evil is caused by sorcery. They can clearly visualize what reality would be like without sorcery and they continually strive to achieve it by eliminating sorcerers. A strong millennial tendency is implicit in the way of thinking of any people whose metaphysics push evil out of the world of reality. Among the Lele the millennial tendency bursts into flame in their recurrent anti-sorcery cults. When a new cult arrives it burns up for the time being the whole apparatus of their traditional religion...the latest anti-sorcery cult...is nothing less than an attempt to introduce the millennium at once.[37]

This analysis makes it conceivable that the Maji Maji rebellion, in its expansion beyond the borders of the Rufiji complex, was also a millenarian movement of this type. Schaegelen's narrative of events in Uvidunda supports such a description. Further evidence comes from the Mbeyela chiefdom of southern Ubena. Here, while the established cult of the ancestors, led by the chief, centred on Ukinga to the west, a series of anti-sorcery movements had entered from the east, from Ungindo and the Kilombero. Their apparent use of the *mwavi* ordeal may imply witch-finding rather than eradication, but Maji Maji was also brought by Ngindo, and it seems that the pattern of Bena response followed that normal with a *mwavi* medicine, the *hongo* administering the *maji* to the assembled people in the presence of the chief.[38] Yet the most persuasive reason for linking Maji Maji with a millennial assault on sorcery is the evidence of subsequent eradication movements within the same area. The greatest, in 1926–29, were inspired by Ngoja bin Kimeta, a Ngindo who lived in Segerea village near Dar es Salaam. Partly through his own travels, and partly through his licensed agents, Ngoja's water medicines were administered to thousands of Africans from the coast to Ungoni and Kilosa. As with Maji Maji, the main nuclei were Ungindo and the Matumbi Hills, and expansion across tribal borders was astonishingly swift. There were close similarities in methods of distribution, in the response of tribal authorities, and in as-

[35] I use this term to include also witchcraft. The primary sources do not permit a distinction.

[36] Mary Douglas, *The Lele of the Kasai* (London, 1963), ch. 13; idem, 'Techniques of sorcery control in Central Africa', in J. Middleton and E. H. Winter (eds.), *Witchcraft and Sorcery in East Africa* (London, 1963), 123–41.

[37] Mary Douglas, *Purity and Danger* (London, 1966), 171.

[38] Information from Mr M. S. Ndikwege, Dar es Salaam, July 1966. See also E. A. Mwenda, 'Historia na Maendeleo ya Ubena', *Swahili*, XXXIII, no. 2 (1963), 113–17.

sociated beliefs. Ngoja was a respected Muslim, which accords with the undoubted participation of many Muslims in Maji Maji and the coastal prestige which seems to have aided the inland expansion of both movements.[39] This is difficult evidence to evaluate. There is at present no indication of an eradication movement prior to 1905,[40] and Ngoja's activities may have been modelled on Maji Maji. Yet it seems very probable that both the rebellion and the subsequent movements were drawing on an established pattern of indigenous millenarianism. Just as the rising in the Rufiji complex became associated with the cult of Kolelo, so its expansion appears to have taken place within the context of recurrent movements to eradicate sorcery.

The second notable aspect of the Vidunda experience is the conflict between established political authority and prophetic leadership. Whether or not a people chose to rebel probably depended largely on this struggle for power. Established leaders responded in very different ways. Some, like Ngwira, opposed the movement and were swept aside. Others opposed the movement successfully. Yet others put themselves at its head and sought to control and direct it. For example, of all the peoples within the rebel area, the Sangu had the most powerful and successful political leadership. After long conflict with the Hehe, the Merere dynasty had welcomed and allied with the Germans and had won back its homeland. Then came Maji Maji. On two occasions, it appears, the Sangu decision lay in the balance. During September, Merere refused to receive a missionary, fortified his capital, and failed to send the auxiliary warriors demanded by the local German officer. Only the appearance of a military force brought him to the German side. Again, in late January, he seems to have been in contact with the Ngoni leader Chabruma. Missionaries reported a second crisis, but again a German force raced to Utengule, and Merere once more provided auxiliaries. It seems likely that a conflict took place within the Sangu leadership, and it is tempting to ascribe the subsequent decline of the dynasty to this. Merere IV died in 1906—allegedly from poison—and his successor was exiled to Mafia in 1910 for misgovernment.[41] A comparable situation existed in lowland Ubena. Although most of his people were anxious to rebel, the powerful and pro-German Kiwanga dealt with the threat by rallying immediately to the German side. 'Kiwanga', reported a missionary, 'simply cut the throat of every medicine-man.' Less dramati-

[39] This account is based on T. O. Ranger, 'Witchcraft eradication movements in central and southern Tanzania and their connection with the Maji Maji rising', research seminar paper, University College, Dar es Salaam, Nov. 1966.

[40] The earliest Tanzanian example known to me occurred in Usambara in 1906. See the correspondence in TNA IX/A/16/I.

[41] Kleist, 'Bericht über die Tätigkeit der 8 Feld-Kompagnie', 4 May 1906, RKA 700/232–41; report by Johannes in Deutsches Kolonialblatt, 15 Sept. 1906; Anlage A zum Jahresbericht über die Entwicklung der deutschen Schutzgebieten in Afrika und der Südsee im Jahre 1905/1906 (Berlin, 1907), 34; Ernst Nigmann, Die Wahehe (Berlin, 1908), 6, 11; Rechenberg to RKA, 7 Jan. 1911, RKA 702/130–31; G. A. von Götzen, Deutsch-Ostafrika im Aufstand 1905–6 (Berlin, 1909), 116–17, 212.

cally, the chief's son and ultimate successor recalled how his father, rejecting the *hongo's* message, 'was ordered to follow this man Hongo who had deceived the people and the elders, and to turn the hearts of the people back from their faith in his medicine'. The *hongo*, however, 'refused to go before Kiwanga, and the elders who followed Hongo refused also. They would pretend to agree to follow Kiwanga, but they never meant it. They delayed and delayed and in the end never appeared.'[42] Early in October the Mbunga and Pogoro rebels in the area renewed their resistance by specifically attacking Kiwanga and Kalimoto, a loyalist Mbunga subchief, 'since they love the Germans more'. Kiwanga was eventually shot dead by the rebels. Here, as in Usangu, a disruption of the chiefdom followed the rebellion.[43]

Particularly clear evidence of conflict caused by the arrival of the *maji* is available for the obscure Ndamba people of the Kilombero Valley, whose political organization was weak and most of whom were subject to Kiwanga. The leading family in this area was headed by Undole, who lived in Merera. The *hongo* first brought water to the neighbouring Mgeta area. Undole sent an agent to investigate. Although the agent was persuaded, 'drank' the *maji* and returned full of enthusiasm, Undole summoned the elders of the neighbourhood and told them: 'I do not want to hear that my people in my country are drinking *maji*. Similarly, I do not wish to welcome these people with *maji* into my country. *Majimaji* is a false medicine brought by the Ngindo from Mponda's.' The elders departed, but the movement was too strong:

Even Mtwa Makuwa in Lugoda and Masalika in Mkaja tried to prevent their people from drinking the *maji ya Hongohongo*...[Nevertheless] the *waganga wa maji* deceived Masalika and caused him and his people to drink the *maji ya uzima*, although Undole had strongly opposed it. They moved on to Makuwa at Lugoda and there they employed the same methods as with Masalika. He also was given the *maji*, and he drank.

When Undole heard that the elders had joined the rebels, he summoned them. They came and listened, but his authority over them was slight. The elders returned to join the rising; Undole sent messengers to Mahenge, who fought alongside the Germans. Undole's people were spared, but the remainder of the Ndamba suffered the normal fate.[44] Thus the pattern suggested by Schaegelen's account is supported by evidence from other areas. Maji Maji spread as a millenarian revolt which threatened established authority. Only the strongest could reject it.

[42] Berliner Missionsgesellschaft report in *Deutsches Kolonialblatt*, 1 March 1906; Mtema Towegale Kiwanga in A.T. and G. M. Culwick, *Ubena of the Rivers* (London, 1935), 55.

[43] P. *Aquilin Engelbergers Wapogoro-Tagebuch* (ed. J. Henninger, Micro-Bibliotheca Anthropos no. 13, Freiburg, 1954), 387–427; Culwick, 90; *Militärisches Orientierungsheft für Deutsch-Ostafrika* (Daressalam, 1911), section 4.

[44] Blasius Undole, 'Habari za Wandamba', typescript, 1965 (copy in the present writer's possession). This account may be distorted by its family origin.

The Vidunda evidence also describes a third phase, in which the failure of the *maji* obliged the rebels to return to customary methods of tribal warfare. This was one means by which the movement was tribalized in its later stages. Alternatively, a different process could take place. Dr Douglas has shown that movements to eradicate sorcery are able to adapt to local beliefs and circumstances until their original form is obscured.[45] As Maji Maji expanded further south and west, it entered areas of strong political authority. In consequence, the revolutionary character of the movement declined while the element of tribal warfare grew. It has been seen that the Bena chief, Mbeyela, was willing and able to patronize and control the movement.[46] Among the neighbouring Pangwa, whose chief also sided with the rebels, Maji Maji was not brought by alien *hongo* but by Pangwa resident in Ungoni.[47] In the south-east, it appears, the movement operated from the beginning within a tribal framework. The most convincing evidence comes from Ungoni.

Zwangendaba's Ngoni[48] had divided in the nineteenth century into northern and southern sections (Mshope and Njelu), although these united in crises, as during the Hehe wars of 1878–82. After these wars fissiparation continued, especially in the more settled south, where *nkosi* Mputa was considered illegitimate by many *ndunas*, and where the great warrior Songea established a power rivalling Mputa's. The decision to accept the *maji* was taken in the north by *nkosi* Chabruma, perhaps under pressure from his *ndunas*, but in the south by the individual *ndunas*, some of whom, including Songea, took the *maji* before Mputa. During the first phase of rebellion, each unit operated independently. Owing perhaps to the lay character of Ngoni chieftainship, it appears that none of the Ngoni leaders saw the *maji* as a threat to his position, any more than their successors were to fear Ngoja's activities twenty years later. Yet many were sceptical. Songea is alleged to have said: 'Let us "drink" the *majimaji* medicine so that we may all perish.'[49] Chabruma first consulted his diviners, and only then instructed his people to 'drink'. This suggests that the Ngoni did not see the *maji* as a revolutionary and self-legitimizing creed, although the Ngindo *hongo* commanded that all other medicines be burned. For Njelu, Mr Mpangara implies that the established war-diviner, Chikusi, was not consulted. There the *hongo* administered *maji* to a great assembly of warriors at the River Lumecha, presided over by Mputa and Chabruma. This

---

[45] Douglas, *The Lele*, 245.

[46] This point is made in M. J. Swartz, 'Continuities in the Bena political system', *South-Western Journal of Anthropology*, xx (1964), 249.

[47] Information from Fr. J. Stirnimann, Dar es Salaam, Nov. 1966.

[48] This account is based on the following sources: Elzear Ebner, *History of the Wangoni* (mimeographed, Peramiho, 1959), 165–84; P. H. Gulliver, 'An administrative survey of the Ngoni and Ndendeuli of Songea district', typescript, 1954, Cory Papers, University College Library, Dar es Salaam; Mpangara, op. cit.; O. B. Mapunda, 'Nkosi Mputa Gama', research seminar paper, University College, Dar es Salaam, Sept. 1966; entry by O. Guise Williams in Songea District Book (Area Office, Songea).

[49] Mpangara, op. cit.

assembly appears to have replaced the ceremony led by Chikusi which normally preceded Ngoni warfare. Apparently the Ngoni saw the *maji* not as a prophetic anti-sorcery medicine, as had the Vidunda, but as a new and uniquely powerful war medicine, superseding Chikusi's normal ministrations. This interpretation suggests the basically tribal nature of the Ngoni rebellion—perhaps more accurately described as a delayed resistance— whose organization and leadership drew on a functioning military system. What is significant about the impact of the *maji* is that during the Lumecha ceremony it provided a means for the reunification of the Ngoni people, whose last concerted action had taken place in 1882.

Thus the paradox of later nationalist movements, the need to use old loyalties in order to popularize an effort to transcend them, also characterized this earlier attempt to enlarge political scale. The Maji Maji rebellion originated in peasant grievances, expanded through the dynamism of a millennial belief which challenged the old order, and finally came to reflect the cultural and political divisions of the past. Its changing organization demonstrates the tension within a mass movement between ideology and reality.

SUMMARY

This article examines the organization of the Maji Maji rebellion of 1905–7 in German East Africa, utilizing Professor T. O. Ranger's analyses of other rebellions in East and Central Africa. The rising began in the Rufiji Valley as a peasant protest against a scheme, imposed by the German authorities, for communal cotton growing. But like other African rebellions against early colonial rule, the movement acquired an ideological content from prophetic religious leaders. This ideology enabled the rising to spread far beyond the Rufiji Valley and gave a degree of unity to diverse peoples. Two religious systems were involved. In the Rufiji Valley, the first rebels received a water-medicine from the ministers of the spirit Kolelo. This *maji* became the symbol of unity and commitment. The expansion of the movement beyond the nuclear area probably followed a pattern of recurrent millenarian movements whose chief object was to eradicate sorcery. Such a movement implied a challenge to established tribal authorities, and was seen by them as such a threat. As the rising spread, it entered areas of stronger tribal organization and also lost something of its revolutionary character. In consequence, the later rebels utilized tribal organization. This development, it is argued, conflicted with the original purpose of overcoming past political and cultural divisions in order to achieve more effective resistance to European rule. Thus, it is suggested, the rebellion demonstrated a tension between ideology and political and cultural reality which is characteristic of mass movements, including later nationalist movements.

MAJI MAJI IN UNGONI: A REAPPRAISAL OF EXISTING HISTORIOGRAPHY[1]

Patrick M. Redmond

The Maji Maji rebellion of 1905-1906 was Tanzania's most spectacular manifestation of the rejection of colonial rule. It joined numerous peoples of very diverse political, economic, and social backgrounds in a struggle to oust the German power which had recently subjugated them. Of those who participated, the Ngoni of Songea district were among the most determined, some continuing the fight till mid-1906, and most suffering heavily from massive reprisals at German hands.

While the largely independent nature of the Songea rebellion has been acknowledged elsewhere,[2] in general scholars have held that the Ngoni had the same reason for participating as had others who fought: the belief that the *maji* (Swahili, *water*) which their prophets were dispensing would protect their warriors from bullets, enabling them to throw off cruel and repressive German rule and regain their independence.[3] The reappraisal of this interpretation which follows is based on

[1]This essay is part of a larger study of the Ngoni which deals with the persistence of chiefship among them. I am grateful to Roland Oliver, John Iliffe, and Michael Twaddle for their constant advice and assistance, to the Commonwealth Association and Canada Council for their financial help in the course of my research, and to L. Larson for checking some of the references used here.

[2]For example, John Iliffe, "The Organization of the Maji Maji Rebellion," *Journal of African History,* VIII, 3 (1967).

[3]Archives of the Benedictine Abbey, Peramiho (Songea area) [hereafter Peramiho Archives], "Kigonsera Cnronicles," 23 Aug. 1905, 21 Sept. 1906; P.H. Gulliver, "An Administrative Survey of the Ngoni and Ndendeuli of Songea District" (unpublished manuscript, 1954), Cory Papers, University of Dar es Salaam Library, Dar es Salaam, 16; E. Ebner, "History of the Wangoni" (unpublished manuscript, Peramiho, 1959), 167; James J. Komba, "God and Man" (unpublished Ph.D. dissertation, University of the Propagation of the Faith, Rome, 1959), 13; O.B. Mapunda and G.P. Mpangara, *The Maji Maji War in Ungoni* (Dar es Salaam, 1969); O.B. Mapunda and G.P. Mpangara, "The Maji Maji War in Ungoni," *Maji Maji Research Project Collected Papers* (Dar es Salaam, 1968) [hereafter MMP] 6/68/4/1, 10-11; R.M. Bell, "The Maji Maji Rebellion in Liwala District," *Tanganyika Notes and Records,* 28 (1950); Iliffe, "Organization," 495; G.C.K.

the supposition that the attitudes of different groups among the Ngoni toward both the Germans and the advantages of independence were variable. Not all felt either severely oppressed under German dominance or looked forward to a better life without them. Moreover, where possible this variability determined commitment to rebellion. The Maji Maji among the Ngoni was not a united struggle against a hated enemy, but a conflict fomented by those whom its successful outcome stood to benefit.

The argument lies in an analysis of the political, economic, and social life in Ungoni, the country of the Ngoni, prior to colonial rule and of the German impact on it. Two factors in particular are important: the influence of social rank on the Ngoni reaction to the Germans, and the role of the internal political situation in determining who was willing to fight.

The Background

The Ngoni presence in Songea district was an offshoot of the Mfecane, the dispersion which followed Shaka's rise to power and the growth of the Zulu nation in southern Africa. Of those who migrated, one group, the Maseko Ngoni, reached Songea in the 1840s, while another, the Njelu and Mshope Ngoni, came there in the 1850s. The two groups fought for control over the region and its peoples, and the earlier arrivals were defeated and driven from the area. The victors then set up two kingdoms and began a period of remarkably successful state building. Better organized politically and more sophisticated militarily than their neighbors, they had little trouble in expanding their numbers. From the early 1850s until the end of the century their population increased from less than a thousand[4] to what has been conservatively estimated at 36,000.[5]

In the process of building their kingdoms the Ngoni created new societies in eastern Africa whose characteristics in part reflected those of their forebears in southern Africa. Political structure and organization continued to be centralized and based on royal families—the Gama

---

Gwassa, "Kinjikitile and the Ideology of Maji Maji," in T.O. Ranger and I.N. Kimambo, eds., *The Historical Study of African Religion* (London, 1972).

[4]P.M. Redmond, "A Political History of the Songea Ngoni from the Mid-Nineteenth Century to the Rise of the Tanganyika African National Union" (unpublished Ph.D. dissertation, University of London, 1972), 93-94. This estimate is a rough one based on Booth's 1905 analysis of their numbers. See John Booth, "Die Nachkommen der Sulukaffern (Wangoni) in Deutsch Ostafrika," *Globus*, LXXXVIII (1905).

[5]Frederick Fülleborn, *Das Deutsche Njassa und Ruvuma Gebiet* (Berlin, 1906), 132, quoting *Jahresbericht über die Entwicklung der Deutschen Schutzgebiete in Afrika und in der Südsee im Jahre 1903/04* (Berlin, 1905).

in Njelu and the Tawete in Mshope—whose chosen head, called the *nkosi*,[6] was the single most powerful person in the kingdom. He controlled the military organization with the assistance of senior members of the royal household and senior military commanders, called *manduna*. He directed national administration, assisted once again by leading relatives, called *wantwana*. Differences in political organization developed in some matters. For example, in one kingdom a few military *manduna* became extremely powerful and quite independent. Military tactics, weapons, and much of the organization of the fighting force also continued the way they had in southern Africa. However, numerous changes also occurred, and it was these which gradually produced new societies.

Most of these changes were the result of adaptation to the East African environment. Militarily, the system was not as refined as it had been in southern Africa. The overwhelming numbers of local people in the army had meant the general abandonment of such things as age regiments, separate military villages, and some social practices. Socially, the Ngoni adopted much of the culture of their East African adherents. For example, the language of the migrants was gradually replaced by a local language.[7]

Successful in forging a new society, the migrants took care to preserve their preeminent role in it. This was done through a careful emphasis on the distinction between them and their East African captives and the allocation of rights and responsibilities based on the differences. The migrants were known as the true Ngoni, while those who were captured and integrated after the newcomers arrived were called *sutu*. Everyone knew to which class he belonged, and the implications of this hierarchy were reflected on most levels of organization within the two kingdoms. For example, on the political level the true Ngoni held all the senior administrative posts. The *sutu* held junior posts, and very few of them could pose any challenge to true Ngoni control. In the military, the *manduna* were chosen from among the true Ngoni. The *sutu* could become lieutenants, although usually they had to be satisfied with positions as ordinary soldiers. In economic life, the true Ngoni controlled raiding and any benefits it brought; it was they who received

[6]For this variation in spelling from the southern African Nguni equivalent, see Redmond, "Political History," 100, which is based on Ebner to Redmond, personal correspondence, 17 Dec. 1970.

[7]For some details on assimilation, see Ebner, "Wangoni," 37; E. Ebner, "History of the Wangoni: Revised Edition" (unpublished manuscript, Archiv der Erzabtei St. Ottilien, St. Ottilien, Bavaria), 83-84, 92-93; Gulliver, "Administrative Survey," 114; Redmond, "Political History," 97-100, 159-165.

tribute from satellite villages. The largest farms and the greatest number of people to work them were theirs. In trade, they decided which contacts to allow, and when these developed, as for example in the coastal trade, they were the ones who profited. Socially, the true Ngoni enjoyed many privileges denied to the *sutu*. For example, they alone could wear any clothing or choose any wife.[8]

Either willingly or under force, the *sutu* accepted these arrangements. Many acquiesced because they benefited from their status as Ngoni. They participated in military campaigns and received a part of the spoils. Some gained in prestige after proving themselves successful warriors or administrators. Many were proud to belong to the strongest state in the region and to share much of its life style. But even those unwilling to accept Ngoni status were forced to endure it, since they were too weak militarily to free themselves.

These two successful and rapidly expanding kingdoms encountered the Germans in the 1890s, and submitted to them in 1897. Their surrender was a reluctant but nonviolent one, the result of three factors. First, the Ngoni feared and respected the Germans, who had defeated the powerful Hehe nation to the north. In addition, Njelu, the more powerful of the two kingdoms, was rent with internal strife.[9] Finally, the Ngoni leaders were deceived. Twice previously German expeditions had entered Ungoni, talked with Ngoni leaders, demanded and received tribute and the rectification of grievances, and left. The third time they invited the leaders to talk, then held them hostage until they accepted their terms.

The Varying Impact of German Rule

Submission brought many changes to Ngoni society. Of critical importance to understanding them is an awareness of their selective effect on the Ngoni. In most cases, the true Ngoni suffered the most.

The Germans hoped to take over effective political control for the eventual purpose of economic hegemony.[10] However, the kind of con-

---

[8]Ebner, "Revised History," 83-84, 92-93.

[9]Tom Von Prince, "Geschichte der Magwangwara nach Erzahlung des Arabers Raschid bin Masaud und des Fussi, Bruders des vor drei Jahren verstorbenen Sultans der Magwangwara Mharuli," *Mitteilungen von Forchungsreisenden und Gelehrten aus den Deutschen Schutzgebieten*, VII (1894), 221-222, n. 3; Ebner, "Wangoni," 105-106, 134-139, 141-142; Mapunda and Mpangara, *Maji Maji*, 112.

[10]For comments on German rule, see T.O. Ranger, "African Reactions to the Imposition of Colonial Rule in East and Central Africa," in L.H. Gann and Peter Duignan, eds., *Colonialism in Africa, 1870-1960*, I (London, 1969); John Iliffe, "The Effects of the Maji Maji Rebellion on German Occupation Policy in East Africa," in P. Gifford and R. Louis, eds., *Britain and Germany in Africa* (London and New Haven, 1967); R.A. Austen,

trol that had been established on the coast, through *liwalis* and akidates, was impossible inland, since the Germans lacked the resources in men and money to implement it, particularly if the existing leadership resisted total removal. Instead, they manipulated the existing Ngoni administrative system. Ultimate power was withdrawn from the Ngoni and placed in the hands of the German representative in the district, who had the final say in all local administrative matters. In the political arena this allowed him to determine the allocation of power on subordinate levels by appointing and dismissing chiefs and altering the basis of their authority through, for example, removing sections of their following. He could also mobilize the population for desired ends, such as the building of roads and general construction. In financial matters, he and his superiors decided how Ngoni resources would be used. Accordingly, he could demand the tribute that formerly had gone to other groups in Ngoni society, as well as determine Ngoni activity in economic fields such as agriculture and trade. In judicial matters, he became the ultimate guarantor of law and order. This gave him the power to make his own laws and to ensure that they were enforced by his police and his system of courts.

The appropriation of these powers brought fundamental changes to the Ngoni political system. The former division of leadership among the *mankosi, wantwana,* and *manduna* was replaced by a relative standardizing of control among all three. The more important leaders were now classified as *sultans,* the lesser ones as *jumbes;* both were given specific rights and responsibilities. They were required to receive and pass on orders, to call up labor, and to run their local administration efficiently.[11] They insured that tribute or taxes were collected,[12] and they handled civil court cases using customary law.[13] To represent the Ngoni leaders before the administration the Germans appointed a man they felt entitled to the position: Songea, the most powerful of the military *manduna* in Njelu.[14]

Within the Ngoni hierarchy, those at the top were the most adversely

---

Northwest Tanzania under German and British Rule: Colonial Policy and Tribal Politics, 1889-1939 (London and New Haven, 1968).

[11] *Deutsches Kolonialblatt,* XII, 11 (1 June 1901), 389-390, notes that some leaders offered labor to the Germans.

[12] Chiefs did not collect taxes in all areas. Marcia Wright, *German Missions in Tanganyika, 1891-1941* (London, 1971), 75-76, notes dissatisfaction at *askari,* or soldiers, collecting taxes.

[13] *Deutsches Kolonialblatt,* XII, 11 (1 June 1901), 390.

[14] Evidence of B.K. Mpangala, a resident of Songea's town, MMP 6/68/4/3/13; evidence of L. Moyo, MMP 6/68/4/3/14, 6; Ebner to Redmond, personal communication, 17-21 Oct. 1971.

affected by the system of administration the Germans imposed. Some were forced to relinquish all the senior powers they had once enjoyed. For example, each *nkosi* no longer had final control over matters in his kingdom. The *wantwana* no longer influenced political policy. The senior *manduna* no longer decided military and most administrative questions in their regions. Some lost important segments of their following. Nkosi Chabruma of Mshope, for instance, lost almost half his kingdom when the Germans removed large blocks of territory from his control.[15] All lost the financial benefits they once had enjoyed; tribute, regular supplies of captives, the unrestricted use of subject labor, and the profits of trade in slaves and ivory passed from their hands. Senior leaders relinquished their considerable judicial powers. Almost to a man, they were unable to find in the responsibilities the Germans were now allocating an adequate alternative to those they had given up. This was so even for Nduna Songea, who although allowed greater rights than his compatriots, exercised much less authority in all spheres of political activity than he had previously done.

While the leaders, all true Ngoni, were adversely affected by the German takeover, most *sutu* were not. None had held senior political power before 1897, and so may have experienced only limited changes in the replacement of their true Ngoni superiors by Germans. In fact, some of them appear to have benefited. For example, some groups apparently were able to select their own leaders under the Germans.[16] To groups such as the Matengo, this change must have been a welcome one. And in legal matters, they now had the option of appealing to a neutral force. To a few this was particularly useful.[17] Financially, they suffered the loss of what they formerly had gained from warfare. However, some aspects of economic life improved. They could sell their labor and keep the earnings. They could participate in trade by collecting the wild rubber then in demand; some people, such as the Ngindo, seem to have done well in this enterprise.[18] In agriculture, it is likely that many were freer to produce what they wanted and dispose of it as they wished. In fact, the German appearance most probably brought a gradual diffusion of wealth in Ngoni society, a diffusion that was most noticeable to and appreciated by those members who had had little before 1897. In social

---

[15]See "The Story of the Likuyu Area," Mss. Afr. s. 585, Rhodes House, Oxford University, Oxford, for information on its administration.

[16]"Tanganyika District Book" (unpublished manuscript, Library of the School of Oriental and African Studies, London), IV, 237.

[17]For one example, see Mapunda and Mpangara, *Maji Maji,* 14.

[18]Alfons Adams, *Im Dienste des Kreuzes* (St. Ottilien, 1899), 132; "Bericht über den Bezirk und die Militärstation Ssongea," *Deutsches Kolonialblatt,* XV, 18 (1904), 565.

life, the preeminence of the true Ngoni life style was beginning to give way to that of the Europeans and coastal peoples. In religion, respect for the elders lost meaning as its purpose was withdrawn. Replacing it were the religions of the newcomers—Christianity, brought in with the Roman Catholic Benedictines of St. Ottilien, and Islam, disseminated by traders and colonial officials. Education that prepared an individual for a military life was replaced with one stressing an administrative life under German rule. Attitudes were changing; it seemed likely that a new class would emerge.

Reaction to German Rule

The response of the true Ngoni to these events seems to have passed through two stages. At first they were tolerant of German rule; after a time, however, their feeling grew into a much stronger commitment, either in favor of or against it. The initial acquiescence apparently was due to uncertainty over the implications of submission, and was reflected in a general openness toward cooperation. Contemporary government sources suggest a willingness to discuss problems.[19] Mission sources indicate a comparable receptiveness in, for example, the Ngoni's ready acceptance of missionaries to the area,[20] the more specific result of curiosity and a desire for the prestige they could bring, the hope of material benefit,[21] and an interest in their culture.[22]

While the Europeans remained a novelty more than an oppressor, the true Ngoni continued to preoccupy themselves with matters of traditional importance. This is most poignantly evident in the Njelu kingdom, where a disputed succession to the nkosiship showed that internal political life remained critically important. In 1898 Mlamilo died. The difficulties which arose over determining his successor brought to the fore Njelu rivalries which had been building up for more than a decade over matters half a century old. In the late 1850s, before the Njelu helped to overthrow the Maseko, their leadership had suffered severe reversals at Maseko hands. Some of the senior leaders had been killed, and a number of the Gama royal family were forced to flee west of the lake. Among those who left was the recently installed *nkosi*, Gwazerapasi. After the Maseko defeat, men from junior branches of the royal family—Hawai (c. 1864-1874) and Mharule (1874-1889)—

---

[19] *Deutsches Kolonialblatt*, IX, 12 (15 June 1898), 350.
[20] See, for example, C. Spiss, "Peramiho Chronicle," *Missionsblätter: Organ der St. Benediktus—Missionsgenossenschaft zu St. Ottilien* [hereafter *Missionsblätter*] (1899), 119.
[21] *Ibid.*
[22] Komba, "God and Man," 11.

took control of the kingdom. In the 1880s, when Njelu was at the height of power, Nkosi Mharule invited his kinsmen to come back from exile and a number did. But after Mharule died, the electors disagreed on their choice for a successor. According to Tom Von Prince, the most important source of information on the conflict,[23] Mharule's brother Mlamilo was the legitimate heir but he declined to serve, apparently due to ill health. The only other brothers were those who had returned from west of the lake, and their flight made them ineligible. Accordingly, sons of Hawai and Mharule were considered, as was a third possibility, Zamchaya, a son of Gwazerapasi. Zamchaya was from the senior family and, unlike his father's generation, was eligible to succeed, or so Prince says. Zamchaya returned to receive the nkosiship, but a number of electors rejected him because, again according to Prince, he was unsatisfactory.[24] Yet Prince fails to mention the very important reason why he should be considered legitimate when the older generation had not been. Based on their subsequent behavior, the sons of Hawai and Mharule clearly were unwilling to accept him or any of his family. In any case, the succession remained unresolved. Mlamilo chose to rule one part of the kingdom, while Zamchaya claimed another. At the same time, some of the leading *manduna* took advantage of the situation to assert their independence of either overlord, and dissension within the kingdom grew strong. By the time Mlamilo died in 1898, Zamchaya's older brother Mputa had returned and claimed the throne. Though little information on the succession remains—the Germans ignored it after officially abolishing the office—it appears that Mputa was opposed by Usangila, a son of Mharule.[25] According to E. Ebner, Mputa became the de facto leader; he enjoyed considerable power and simply took the title of *nkosi*.[26] Mputa's accession subsequently influenced the attitudes of dissident members of the royal family toward the Germans.

Among some true Ngoni, initial tolerance toward the foreigners gradually gave way to fuller cooperation and receptiveness. One of Njelu's senior leaders, Putire Gama, became very friendly with the missionaries. While this may suggest an openness to the new order, it probably merely reflects one stage in Gama's growing independence of the traditional power center.[27] Usangila Gama seems to have established cordial

[23]Prince, "Geschichte der Magwangwara."

[24]*Ibid.,* 217-218.

[25]Ebner, "Wangoni," 130, 158; Ebner to Redmond, personal communication, 17-21 Oct. 1971.

[26]*Ibid.*

[27]Ebner, "Wangoni," 121, notes Putire disputing with Mharule.

contacts with the Germans at the administrative headquarters or fort,[28] apparently in an attempt to gain support for his faction. He may also have wished to counteract the benefits Mputa gained from his relations with the missionaries. A few true Ngoni took advantage of the opportunities the Germans made available. For example, some worked for them. One, Kaziburre, a son of the Njelu military *nduna* Mpambalioto, became an interpreter.[29] Some sons of true Ngoni leaders attended mission and government schools. They probably did so initially through force, then continued out of genuine interest. Among their numbers were Dominikus Missoro Tawete and Ali Songea, sons of the two most powerful leaders of Ungoni.

Although some true Ngoni began to cooperate with the Germans, most came to oppose them as their attitude of tolerance proved inadequate under the circumstances. Occasionally the response turned to despair. For example, after being summoned repeatedly to the fort to answer for his apparently unfriendly attitude, Fusa Gama hanged himself.[30] Sometimes the response was confrontation. Philip Gulliver notes Chabruma Tawete, *nkosi* of Mshope, as being strongly belligerent: "[He] was far more truculent [than Mputa, *nkosi* of Njelu] and had several brushes with the German officers at the Songea boma . . . in the tradition of the high autocracy of the Mshope Ngoni [he] was far less ready to give way to the whiteman."[31] On one occasion he ignored the limits the Germans had placed on his judicial powers and sentenced to death a subject who had interfered with one of his wives. The man escaped and reported the leader, who was admonished.[32]

But confrontation had its limits; it fostered rebellion, and this the Germans were not prepared to tolerate. When a former subject, a Matengo chief, rebelled against German taxation policies, he was promptly and severely repressed.[33] And others were made to realize that rebellion would not be taken lightly. Accordingly the Ngoni pursued a policy of noncooperation only as far as they could safely do so. Mputa Gama spurned the missionaries after 1904 when one burned the *mahoka* hut where he prayed to his ancestors,[34] but otherwise they had

---

[28]T.W. Turuka, "Maji Maji Rebellion in Njelu," MMP 6/68/3/1.

[29]Tanzania National Archives, Dar es Salaam [hereafter TNA]/155, Songea District Book, vol. 4, 87.

[30]C. Spiss, correspondence, *Missionsblätter* (March, 1901); Ebner, "Wangoni," 158-159.

[31]Gulliver, "Administrative Survey," 17.

[32]MMP 6/68/2/13/1 and MMP 6/68/4/1 contain details on this.

[33]Peramiho Archives, "Kigonsera Chronicles," 1901, 1902, *passim*.

[34]TNA/G9/6, Albinus to Government, no. 68 of 15 Feb. 1904; *Missionsblätter* (1903-1904), 33-35.

to content themselves with lamenting their lot. Many must have longed to return to the free and successful life of the past,[35] when they held firm control over wealth and power. Presumably they hoped for some means to restore it.

Although most of the true Ngoni found little satisfaction in the German presence, the same cannot be said of the *sutu*. We already have seen a few ways in which the German impact on the *sutu* varied from that on their leaders. Numerous contemporary references clearly suggest considerable adaptation to the new political situation, commenting on their willingness to give up raiding in favor of peaceful farming[36] and to participate in porterage and other German economic activities.[37] More recent works have also noted the openness of many *sutu* to the Germans. One student, remarking on oral evidence collected on their response to the newcomers, wrote: "We the Wahamba [Wandenduli] somehow appreciated a number of the German rules because they directly opposed the Ngoni rules, especially of using us as unpaid servants."[38] Certainly the reaction was not uniformly positive. Many were unhappy with taxes, forced labor, and the general mistreatment they suffered at German hands.[39] Undoubtedly these reasons were sufficient justification for rebellion for some, but certainly not for all.

By 1905 the Ngoni had reacted to German domination in varied and complex ways. Some of the true Ngoni were adapting to and benefiting from the German presence, although most were chafing under ever increasing restrictions. Some among the *sutu* were dissatisfied with the harshness of German rule and the losses they had suffered, but many had improved their lot under the new masters. Into this society a powerful religious movement with strong political overtones spread in the summer of 1905.

The Spread of the Maji in Ungoni

In July 1905 some Matumbi, a people living to the east of Songea district, took courage from a powerful *maji* given to them by their religious

---

[35]Booth, "Nachkommen der Sulukaffern," 197, comments on the decline.

[36]Walter Busse, *Bericht über eine im Antrage des kaiserliche Gouvernements von Deutsch-Ostafrika ausgeführte Forschungsreise durch den südlichen Theil dieser Kolonie* (Berlin, 1902). During 1902 this work was published serially in the Dar es Salaam newspaper *Deutsch-Ostafrikanische Zeitung* [hereafter DOAZ]. The source used here is DOAZ, 5 July 1902.

[37]C. Spiss, correspondence, *Missionsblätter* (1898), 103; *Deutsches Kolonialblatt*, X, 2 (15 Jan. 1899), 54-55.

[38]Evidence of Kawahili, MMP R/S/1/69.

[39]Many traditions in the MMP 6/68 series make this clear.

leader and began uprooting cotton plants at Nandete.[40] Shortly afterward they forced the local administrator to leave the district. Then on 15 August a neighboring people, fortified as well by the medicine, attacked the German boma at Liwale. On 30 August, Ngindo and eastern Pogoro stormed the German boma at Mahenge,[41] and the Maji Maji rebellion was in full swing.

While the rebellion was beginning elsewhere, the Ngoni encountered Kinjala, an emissary of the man who was spreading the *maji* cult. Kinjala first came into contact with a subchief of Chabruma, through whom he met the great leader. According to the evidence of a British colonial officer given in the 1930s, Chabruma was at first reluctant to accept the *maji*, but after consulting the ancestors and his advisers he decided to use the medicine to regain Ngoni independence.[42] He ordered everyone in the Mshope kingdom to do likewise, and almost all complied—even those whom the Germans had removed from his control—because they were afraid of displeasing him. Then Chabruma invited the Njelu Ngoni to participate. Mputa was receptive, and after visiting a Mshope center where the *maji* was being distributed he returned to Njelu to enlist the support of other leaders. Not all were willing to join—Putire Gama, Usangila Gama, and Chabruma Gama were among those who refused—but most other leaders received the water, as did the *sutu*. Like their counterparts in Mshope, the latter had little choice in the matter. The stage was now set for the Ngoni uprising, the most protracted and vicious part of Maji Maji.

A Reinterpretation of Participation

As noted above, most analyses of the Ngoni rebellion claim that the Ngoni fought to free themselves from European control and to restore their former state to greatness. In reports to the government written shortly after the conflict occurred and in his book published in 1909,[43] Graf von Götzen listed a variety of causes, including annoyance at taxation and other economic measures, a desire for independence, and the

[40]Gwassa, "Kinjikitile."

[41]Iliffe, "Organization." I am grateful to L. Larson for information on Maji Maji in Mahenge.

[42]Noted in Mapunda and Mpangara, *Maji Maji,* 15.

[43]Deutsches Zentralarchiv (Potsdam) Reichskolonialamt [hereafter RKA], file 723, Götzen to Foreign Office, 10 Nov. 1905; Graf von Götzen, *Deutsch-Ostafrika im Aufstand 1905/06* (Berlin, 1909); "Denkschrift über die Ursachen des Aufstandes in D.O.A. 1905," in Stenographische Berichte über die Verhandlung des Reichstages, Anlagen, 1905-1906 session, Vierter Anlageband: Aktenstuck, no. 194. I am grateful to John Iliffe for this reference.

influence of superstition. The Colonial Economic Committee offered another analysis, and one of its members, John Booth, was well acquainted with the Ngoni. He considered the rebellion the result both of an attempt by Ngoni leaders to regain their power and of a spreading of the *maji*.[44] A third group to offer their views were the Benedictine missionaries. In a report of late 1906, one of their converts described the rebels' desire to expel the Europeans from their country.[45] A more official Benedictine report came from the Bishop of Dar es Salaam; he suggested that nationalism was an important cause, comparing the rebellion to the struggles of the Tirol people in 1809 and the Germans in 1813 against Napoleon.[46]

John Iliffe has analyzed the views of these and other Germans[47] and divided them into two opposing schools of thought: the witchcraft group, which held that the *maji* gave the Africans their cohesion and fanatical courage, and those holding an abuses theory, that the rebellion was a popular protest against specific injustices. Until the 1950s, most subsequent studies were composed by British colonial officials, who usually saw the rebellion as an expression of grievances against unjust German rule. That by R.M. Bell on Liwale District is one of the most revealing. After analyzing many oral traditions, Bell concluded that Maji Maji was a "national war of independence—a fanatical and desperate fight for freedom."[48] In the 1950s, sociologists, missionaries, and converts published further work on the Ngoni. The first of these was by government sociologist P.H. Gulliver. In 1954 he wrote that Maji Maji had been a purely political effort which had used the *maji* for specific purposes:

> It seems clear that the Rebellion was primarily a military one in the Ngoni warlike tradition and in an attempt to regain the old mastery by this tribe of soldiers and marauders. It cannot be said that there was a really unified Maji Maji movement, or that the Ngoni allied themselves with the Ngindo and others—those other tribes were thoroughly despised by the arrogant Ngoni who had plundered them so easily for so long. The Ngoni merely seized the opportunity afforded by the "magical

[44]RKA, file 728, Colonial Economic Committee to Foreign Office, 23 Jan. 1906.

[45]Peramiho Archives, "Kigonsera Chronicles," 23 Aug. 1905, 21 Sept. 1906.

[46]Peramiho Archives, "Die Benediktinermission und der Aufstand in DOA vom Jahre 1905 oder Stellungnahme der Benediktinermission zur Denkschrift über die Ursachen des Aufstandes in DOA und Anderes," Thomas Spreiter (manuscript in unmarked blue file, n. d.). I am grateful to John Iliffe for showing me a copy of this document.

[47]Iliffe, "Effects of the Maji Maji Rebellion," 561.

[48]Bell, "Liwala District."

waters" to rise against the white man and to resume their independence and their old way of life and war.[49]

In 1959 missionary Father Elzear Ebner published his major "History of the Wangoni." He argued that the prime motivation had been the desire for independence: "They hoped to regain their independence by this war and to re-establish their former glory and greatness. The main reason for the participation of the Wangoni in the Majimaji war was a revival of Ngoni nationalism."[50] The same year an African priest from the district, Father James Komba, wrote a thesis on religion among the Ngoni in which he reiterated Ebner:

> The proud Ngoni, once the sole masters of the land, could not bear the humiliation of having masters over them. The medicine-men, who went about at this time advertising their newly discovered medicine which would turn bullets into water (maji), offered a welcome opportunity to the bellicose Ngoni to rise against their European masters.[51]

Since 1961 some important new contributions have been made. In 1967 John Iliffe synthesized existing interpretations of the Maji Maji rebellion. In his view, participation among the Ngoni was a delayed resistance to German rule. Elsewhere he noted that rebellion had been undertaken to reunite societies that were breaking up.[52] And more recently, students supervised by Iliffe have researched motivations behind the struggle. They discovered several general complaints, as well as various particular ones, underlying Ngoni resistance. In general, the Ngoni resented being forced to donate labor to the building of the new Songea fort around 1900; they were unhappy with taxation and the demands it made on food and other resources, and were opposed to the cruelty of the German regime. Individual complaints included their disillusionment with the new system of justice. Iliffe's students also found that the Ngoni responded to the rebellion in a variety of ways.

The library of the University of Dar es Salaam subsequently made the accumulated data available in a bound work entitled *Maji Maji Research Project Collected Papers*. In 1969, two of the researchers, O.B. Mapunda and G.P. Mpangara, analyzed a selection of this data and published it as a research paper entitled *The Maji Maji War in Ungoni*. According to them, the rebellion was the result of grievances over taxation, unpaid

[49]Gulliver, "Administrative Survey," 16-17.
[50]Ebner, "Wangoni," 167.
[51]Komba, "God and Man," 13.
[52]Iliffe, "Organization," 495; Iliffe, "The Effects of the Maji Maji Rebellion," 561; Iliffe, "The Age of Improvement and Differentiation (1907-45)," in I.N. Kimambo and A.J. Temu, eds., *A History of Tanzania* (Nairobi, 1969), 130-131.

labor, the decline of Ngoni political power, and the dislocation of the traditional economy and culture. They doubted the importance of the *maji* itself; rather they felt that political considerations were primary. They noted the internal disunity in Njelu and the varied reactions to the *maji*, but drew no conclusions from these.[53]

Common to most interpretations—Booth's being the noted exception—is a description of the rebellion as the action of a single united people. Those like Iliffe, Mapunda, and Mpangara, who have acknowledged that not all the leaders participated or that many *sutu* did so under force, have not used this evidence to reinterpret the nature of the conflict, instead setting it apart as an anomaly to the main body of data. However, the nature of Ngoni society, the variable impact of German rule, and the internal political situation in Ungoni before 1905 all suggest that these instances of forced and nonparticipation point to a different hypothesis.

Because the social distance between the *sutu* and the true Ngoni made the impact of German rule a varied one having a much greater effect on the latter group, no mass grievance could have motivated all the Ngoni. The distinction between the true Ngoni and the *sutu* was not an absolutely rigid one; some *sutu* felt and acted much the same as the true Ngoni. In general, however, a successful overthrow of German control stood to benefit most *sutu* politically, economically, and socially much less than most true Ngoni. This has been shown clearly in the above analysis; the true Ngoni suffered most from the obligation to give rather than receive tribute and forced labor, from the loss of political and economic power, and from the dislocation of traditional culture. Accepting this fact gives new meaning to the argument that the Ngoni were fighting for independence. The evidence of Booth and some recent informants makes it quite clear that the leadership hoped to free themselves. One of the latter comes from a true Ngoni, who stated:

> The main reason why the Ngoni leaders accepted the Maji Maji movement was that they wanted to get rid of German domination and thus retrieve their former political position. Before the coming of the Germans, the Ngoni leaders had been enjoying a great deal of power and authority and the privilege of power such as getting a lot of animals and human captives. But under German rule all these privileges were abolished and their sovereign power suppressed.[54]

On the other hand, the *sutu* were less committed to independence under Ngoni control. Indeed, most *sutu* might not have rebelled had

---

[53] Mapunda and Mpangara, *Maji Maji*.
[54] Evidence of L. Moyo, MMP 6/68/4/3/14.

they been given a choice. This is supported by various facts. First, many former subjects freed from Ngoni control by the Germans refused to participate. Their numbers included the Ruvuma Yao,[55] the Nyasa,[56] and many Matengo.[57] Furthermore, many of those who did participate knew they had no alternative. In one source, a mission convert described clearly how strong the pressure to take the *maji* was.[58]

Forcing people to participate was insufficient, however. Essential to a German defeat was determination. Here the *maji* was of crucial importance. People who had little to gain but much to lose had to be convinced that victory was inevitable, and the *maji* appears to have served this purpose.[59] How durable the fighting spirit was is not clear. Some *sutu* seem to have fought only once. For example, many Ndendeuli apparently were mobilized only for the battle at Lumecha. Certainly once the warriors suffered military setbacks, saw the Germans taking their food, dispersing their families, and killing their friends, they lost faith in the *maji*. After four months the rebellion ended in the Njelu kingdom because the *sutu* stopped fighting. Only in Mshope, where Chabruma controlled his people with an iron grip, did fighting continue for some while longer.

The lack of commitment among some Ngoni was one factor weakening the struggle. But it was not the only one. In addition, those who advocated the rebellion were unable to unite, although it seems reasonable to assume that they made an attempt to do so. Unity had proved an asset against the Maseko around 1863 and the Hehe in 1878 and 1881; they must have been aware that challenging the Germans required the same achievement. Yet they failed, apparently for the following reasons. In the first place, opinion seems to have divided on how the benefits of success should be allocated. Odd traditions suggest this. One states that Mputa did not fight with other generals because he "feared that if he succeeded in defeating the Germans with help of the other Ngoni generals they would share his reign . . . this was the general feeling of most of the Ngoni leaders at the time."[60] Also suggestive is the

[55]RKA, file 700, Kurt Johannes, "Bericht über die Tätigkeit des Expeditions-Korps Major Johannes in der Zeit vom II Marz bis 3 Mai 1906," 18 June 1906, notes Ruvuma Yao support.

[56]Peramiho Archives, "Kigonsera Chronicles," 29 Sept. 1905, notes the Nyasa as friendly to the Germans.

[57]*Missionsblätter* (1905-1906), 87-91, states that the Matengo stayed neutral. Other reports indicate that some joined the rebellion.

[58]G.C.K. Gwassa and John Iliffe, *Records of the Maji Maji Rising. Part I* (Dar es Salaam, 1967), 20.

[59]For example, the evidence of M. Luoga, MMP 6/68/2/3/2.

[60]Evidence of Luambano, MMP 6/68/1/3/4.

fact that not all the leaders participated in the rebellion; among those who did not fight were Putire Gama, Usangila Gama, and Chabruma Gama. Putire may have been influenced by the missionaries, but it seems clear that the other two were discouraged by the outcome of the recent succession issue. Losers, they were unwilling to support a cause in which the victor, Mputa, would reap most of the benefits. In fact, Usangila and Chabruma were in the German fort during the rebellion. Although a few traditions say that Usangila was studying there at the time,[61] this seems not to have been the case. His son states that he had earlier taken refuge in the fort during a quarrel with Mputa, when Mputa threatened to assassinate him.[62] Another informant agrees that Mputa planned to kill his rival after defeating the Germans.[63] The refusal to support competition occurs at other times in Ngoni history with disastrous results,[64] and could easily have happened in 1905.

Lack of time and a strong tradition of military independence also affected the move toward unity. Freedom of action among the military was particularly noticeable in Njelu during the 1890s and apparently continued in 1905. Only once do Mapunda, Mpangara, and others describe the Ngoni as united—at the battle at Lumecha.[65] However, evidence from German historians, including the forces there, and Ndendeuli traditions say that only Chabruma's Mshope warriors took part in the encounter.[66] No traditions indicate that Songea's, Mpambalioto's, and Kapungu's forces participated. Finally, while some claim that Mputa's men were there, this is doubtful in light of the fact that he was fresh·enough to fight three further battles in another region shortly

[61] Evidence of S. Usangila, son of Usangila, MMP 6/68/4/3/16.

[62] Ibid.

[63] T.W. Turuka, "Maji Maji Rebellion in Njelu," MMP 6/68/3/1.

[64] For example, in the succession dispute that took place in Mshope between 1952 and 1954. For information on this dispute, see TNA/16/37/105; Redmond, "Political History," ch. 7.

[65] Mapunda and Mpangara, Maji Maji.

[66] Götzen, Aufstand, 124-125, 206; Ebner, "Wangoni," 178. MMP R/S/1/69/lb, among others, notes the Germans fighting the Mshope Ngoni. This and other sources refer to this battle as the Namabengo or Lumecha battle. This is in contrast to Mapunda and Mpangara, Maji Maji, 23-24, who claim that there were two battles, one at Namabengo, the other at Lumecha, in late 1905. I do not follow their suggestion, as other sources do not support it. In particular, the Maji Maji records collected in 1968, which Mapunda and Mpangara use as their main source of information, do not substantiate their claim. Of the forty traditions collected, none confirms that two battles took place. Although two note a battle at Namabengo, one says that it was at "Lumecha, or what we may regard as old Namabengo" (evidence of M. Ngonyani, MMP 6/68/4/3/2), while eight describe a battle at Lumecha. Of the other sources, Gulliver, "Administrative Survey," 15-16, refers to the Lumecha battle. I call it the Lumecha battle to facilitate discussion of the claims Mapunda, Mpangara, and others make concerning it.

after Lumecha, while Chabruma took a considerable time to reorganize.

Indeed, the battles which took place suggest that the rebellion was
almost exclusively of a local nature. In early September 1905, Palangu
(Mshope) killed a tax collector. Shortly afterward, military leaders in
various parts of the two kingdoms killed itinerant traders in their areas.
In September and October, Mputa, Songea, and Kapungu (all Njelu)
made a number of attacks on the town of Kikole. During the same
months, Songea (Njelu) harassed the Germans and their associates who
had taken refuge in the fort. In September, Mputa and Mpambalioto
(both Njelu) attacked the mission settlements at Peramiho and Kigonsera, and by December had destroyed both. In late October the Mshope
combined forces at Lumecha. In early November, Mputa and possibly
others (Njelu) fought three separate battles against German troops. In
early 1906, Masese Mbano (Njelu) encountered the Germans in
southern Njelu. In late January and early February 1906, Chabruma
(Mshope) engaged them. In mid-March, Magewa, a Mshope elephant
hunter, fought a German contingent, and shortly after that Palangu
(Mshope) did the same. Then on 27 May and 25 June, Chabruma and
Palangu (Mshope) met them again.[67] Almost all who fought either surrendered or fled independently or in small groups and at different times.

In conclusion, the Maji Maji rebellion seems to have been the complex outcome of the existing political structure in Ungoni, and as such
lacked both the full commitment and the unity such a struggle needed
from its people.

The Outcome of the Maji Maji Rebellion

The Maji Maji rebellion in Songea was a disastrous failure. Although
the Ngoni enjoyed the upper hand for two months, they were unable to
eradicate the German presence from the district. Then the foreigners
began to succeed.[68] By the time Major Kurt Johannes led the Eighth
and Thirteenth Field Companies of the defense forces into Songea in
late November 1905, the end was in sight. Johannes intended to smash
the Ngoni military state. Everywhere villages were burned, planting
crops was forbidden, and men were ruthlessly murdered. In December
1906, Njelu Ngoni leaders began surrendering, and by February 1906
all but a few had given themselves up, been caught, or died. Those who
had surrendered or been captured were hanged. In Mshope, Nkosi

[67]For details, see Redmond, "Political History," 251-270.
[68]*Ibid.*

Chabruma forbade capitulation and continued fighting until late June 1906, when he and a number of leaders retreated into Portuguese East Africa.

The Ngoni were devastated by the rebellion. The true Ngoni leadership had been decimated and any possibility that those remaining could establish an independent military empire was gone forever. The *sutu* also paid a heavy price. Thousands died in the war and in the severe famine which followed in 1906 and 1907. By 1908 life was returning to normal in Songea. Rehabilitation brought political and economic life and activity back to what it had been before the conflict. The Germans retained the traditional political leadership, although in considerably weakened form,[69] headed by true Ngoni who had remained neutral or allied with the foreigners or who had been too young to fight. They were supplemented by outsiders and some local leaders from among the *sutu*. Economic life changed as German interest swung toward the northern parts of their colony. In Songea people turned to migrant labor to alleviate increasing poverty. Social life changed. Many traditional Ngoni practices and customs began giving way to European ones. The distinction between true Ngoni and *sutu* gradually ended. The Ngoni reluctantly adapted to colonial rule, although they have never forgotten the past and the great nation that once was theirs. The Maji Maji rebellion in Songea had been a heroic struggle, but one whose slight chance of success was circumvented by its position in the larger structure of contemporary Ngoni political life.

[69]I refer here to the retention of families noted in Mapunda and Mpangara, *Maji Maji,* 29; Ebner, "Wangoni," 183; *Deutsch Ostafrikanische Rundschau,* III, 14 (19 Feb. 1910).

Journal of African History, XII, 4 (1971), pp. 629–651
Printed in Great Britain

JOHN CHILEMBWE AND THE NEW JERUSALEM

BY JANE AND IAN LINDEN

War in Europe, war here against the Germans, a religious war, persecution almost. You might think that we were close to the end of the world.

Nzama Montfort Mission Diary, 30 January 1915.[1]

IN THE search for the progenitors of modern mass nationalism, intertribal
movements which culminated in armed resistance to colonial rule have
been studied in some depth. The intertribal Nyasaland rising of 1915,
which seriously threatened white rule in the southern region of the protectorate for a brief period of three days, is no exception. Although less than
900 Africans were actively involved, it bears with the much larger scale
Maji-Maji war in Tanganyika an inordinate weight of hagiography and
historical analysis. That its leader, John Chilembwe, would come to occupy
pride of place in the pantheon of Malawi's nationalist heroes, and so become shrouded in mythology,[2] was already predicted by Shepperson and
Price in their now classic biography, *Independent African*.[3]

The desire to demonstrate a continuity in African aspirations, from the
early resistance movements of the beginning of the twentieth century to
later secular nationalism,[4] has meant that the political goals of rebellions
have been stressed. Religious elements, when they have been given emphasis, as in Ranger's treatment of the Ndebele and Shona risings[5] and
Gwassa's discussion of the religious ideology of Maji-Maji,[6] have been
fitted into a Weberian framework. Traditional religion has been treated as
an integrative force bringing together disparate tribal groups, and Christianity, far from being an opiate, has been shown to have provided radical
apocalyptic themes through which Africans articulated opposition to
colonial rule. The authority of the Bible legitimized the use of force by
both charismatic prophets and leaders of Christian sects.

Nonetheless, the ideological content of Africans' religious beliefs has
been given short shrift. In contrast to the detailed consideration of the
theological niceties involved in the politico-religious movements of Europe,

---

[1] Trans. French Montfort Archives, Rome.

[2] G. Shepperson, *Myth and Reality in Malawi*, Fourth Herskovits Memorial Lecture,
Northwestern (1966), 13–18.

[3] G. Shepperson and T. Price, *Independent African* (Edinburgh, 1958), 416.

[4] T. O. Ranger, 'Connexions between "primary resistance" movements and modern
mass nationalism in East and Central Africa', *J. Afr. Hist.*, IX, no. 3 (1968), 437–53.

[5] T. O. Ranger, *Revolt in Southern Rhodesia 1896–7*, London, 1967.

[6] G. C. K. Gwassa, 'The Role of Religious and Other Traditional Beliefs during the
Maji-Maji War 1905–7', *Dar/U.C.L.A. Conf. on the history of african religious systems*,
University College, Dar-es-Salaam, June 1970.

such as the English Puritan revolution,[7] those of African Christians are labelled *en bloc* 'Christian revolutions'. The heuristic value of such broad categories is debatable. In Nyasaland, Protestantism was a religion of the Book. Biblical piety provided the reader with a Jewish concept of linear time and with images of oppression that stimulated the growth of political and historical consciousness. Catholic piety, eucharistic devotion, was centred in the synchronic duality of Christ's immanence and transcendence, in Sacred Host and Church. Its missionary manifestation was profoundly ahistorical. And, of course, within Protestantism itself the distinction between the institutional churches and Troeltsch's sect type proved as fundamental in colonial Malawi as in Europe.[8] A full understanding of the political postures adopted by the different churches during the critical period 1958–64 in Malawi demands insights into the ideology of Calvinism and Catholicism.[9]

Another danger in a simplistic treatment of Christianity and its denominations is that the actual beliefs and religious behaviour of African Christians are either assumed or ignored. Yet the equation of the credal formulas and confessional statements of mission societies and churches with the beliefs of individual African Christians is mere wishful thinking.[10] The leading officials of rain shrines in Malawi today do not disguise their allegiance to the major churches in the country. Furthermore, European missionaries visiting their African pastors were for ever complaining that they were preaching a private and idiosyncratic version of the scriptures. The relationship between Christian thought and African political consciousness will only be elucidated when the difficult task of analysing the interaction between social position in colonial society, religious beliefs and political behaviour is undertaken.

Accounts of the Nyasaland rising shed little light on this interaction. In *Independent African*, religious ideology is a theme secondary to the presentation of the radical political influences on Chilembwe, especially those of Booth and American blacks. Within Nyasaland the development

[7] C. H. George, 'Puritanism as History and Historiography', *Past and Present*, no. 41 (December 1968), 77–105.

[8] E. Troeltsch, *The Social Teaching of the Christian Churches*, London, 1931, I. 241–6 and G. Shepperson, 'Church and Sect in Central Africa', *Rhodes–Livingstone Journal*, XXIII (1958), 12–46.

[9] For example the formation of a Christian Democrat party under the patronage of the Archbishop of Blantyre by Chester Katsonga, see *Malawi News*, 22 Oct. 1960, vol. 2, no. 21, an unsigned article 'Vatican Imperialism by Archbishop Theunissen and Katsonga'. The formation of the party was not supported gy the White Fathers' Bishops, however, nor by many of the clergy who lacked a Dutch Catholic political background. For the influence of Calvinism, see the preamble to Rev. A. Ross, 'Origins and Development of the Church of Scotland Mission, Blantyre Nyasaland 1875–1926', Ph.D. thesis, Edinburgh, 1968, which gives a fascinating insight into the way the C.C.A.P. had cast itself in the role of the future state church of independent Malawi.

[10] This was particularly true of Watchtower in the 1920s, when its African version in Nyasaland and Northern Rhodesia was disowned by the Watchtower Bible and Tract Society in South Africa. T. Walder to Zomba secretariat, 21 Aug. 1926. NN 1/20/3. National Archives, Zomba.

of religious radicalism is referred to with Booth as *fons*, if not *origo*, and discussed as a succession of individuals. Chanjiri, the traditional Kunda prophetess, 'Daughter of God',[11] gives way to Kamwana and Watchtower. The time between Kamwana's deportation and the rising is filled by Charles Domingo.[12] It is impossible to assess the religious beliefs of their followers and the rest of the population. Whether they change in step with the individuals who broadcast them is not clear. The inference is that they do, since the hiatus between such chiliasts as Kamwana and Chilembwe's supposed southern Baptist orthodoxy is positively underlined.

One of the most colourful additions to the European legend of Chilembwe is the persistent assertion that he was an adherent of the Watchtower movement ... but the demonstrable fact is that Chilembwe had no more connection with Watchtower than was imposed on him by the adherence of *the few Africans* who may have been influenced at some point by millenarian teaching.[13]

With limited data, it is easy to show connexions between movements, but it is methodologically impossible to prove the contrary. One piece of positive evidence destroys the argument. That Shepperson and Price are willing to take this risk, and unwilling to leave the influence of millenarianism an open question in an otherwise cautious discussion of motives, signifies that some pre-judgment has been made. Chilembwe, it can be inferred, is to be placed, not against a background of revolutionary chiliasm, but in the future perspective of proto-nationalism.

What thanks to Shepperson's Bultmann-like pre-occupation with demythologization is only a tendency, becomes in Rotberg's *The Rise of Nationalism in Central Africa*, and his later *Protest and Power in Black Africa*,[14] an unquestioned premise. The Nyasaland rising has become one man, an asthmatic, charismatic nationalist martyr with qualities of Padraig Pearse and John Brown. The view that Chilembwe may have been planning to 'set up an independent government in the Shire Highlands', and that 'unlike Kamwana and Domingo, he eschewed millennial teachings'[15] has given way to a portrait of a leader who 'radiated (newly discovered?) sources of incandescent illumination'.[16] It was, of course, Rotberg and not Chilembwe who newly discovered the 'incandescent illumination' as the

---

[11] Chanjiri is one of four Chewa names for the deity. Her movement seems to have been not unlike that of the Bisa '*mfumu ya pansi*' who toured the northern Ngoni with great success in the nineteenth century. W. A. Elmslie, *Among the Wild Ngoni* (Edinburgh, 1899), 64. For Chanjiri's prophecies see *Nzama Mission Diary*, 23 June 1907.

[12] Shepperson and Price, *Independent African*, 159–65 and R. I. Rotberg, *The Rise of Nationalism in Central Africa* (Harvard, 1965), 70–72. In 1916 Domingo was sent to Chinde as an army clerk but was transferred to Zomba in 1917. In 1919 Moggridge accepted him at Mzimba as a tax kapitao, where he appears to have stayed until 1927, when he was being offered some promotion classes to rise from the level of a third grade clerk. S1/927/19 and NN 1/23. National Archives, Zomba.

[13] Shepperson and Price, *Independent African*, 417. Our italics.

[14] R. I. Rotberg, 'Psychological Stress and the Question of Identity: Chilembwe's revolt reconsidered', in *Protest and Power in Black Africa*, ed. R. I. Rotberg and A. A. Mazrui, (Oxford, 1970), 337–77.   [15] Rotberg, *The Rise*, 77, 85.

[16] Rotberg, *Protest and Power*, 372.

only way to transform an apparently ineffectual pastor into the leader of several hundred Africans.

Tangri, with access to new material in the Zomba archives that was unavailable to Price, keeps well within orthodoxy:

> Though some of Chilembwe's following may have been swayed by Watchtower, there is no direct evidence to suggest that he himself was *in any way* influenced by such doctrines.[17]

When Kamwana's successes in Tongaland in 1909 are remembered, and the strength of Watchtower in colonial Zambia and Malawi from 1919 onwards,[18] it seems reasonable to ask what became of millenarianism in the First World War? In fact the reports of the rebels' trials and their unpublished, confiscated correspondence, which were unavailable to Shepperson and Price, now make it clear that millennial expectations were held by many of the Africans involved in the rising.

Rotberg's analysis of the rising rests on George Simeon Mwase's second-hand version in 'A Dialogue of Nyasaland, Record of Past Events, Environments, and the Present Outlook within the Protectorate',[19] written in 1932. According to Mwase:

> John said this case stands the same as that of Mr. John Brown. . . . Let us then 'strike a blow and die' for our blood will surely mean something at last.[20]

Rotberg assures the sceptic that 'Mwase's circumstantial account can hardly have been manufactured'.[21] But, since the rest of Mwase's account is interspersed with literary flourishes, and Mwase is known to have entered a literary competition in the 1930s,[22] it is difficult to see why not. Mwase was the leader of a predominantly Chewa Native Association in the 1920s, and was strongly opposed to the influence of Christian mission teachers in the Central Region.[23] He certainly received Garveyite literature from America.[24] It would be consistent that the head of a secularly orientated association of tobacco growers, with his own literary interests and a knowledge of black history, should create a Chilembwe in the image of John Brown. When Mwase is taken seriously as an interpreter, rather than a chronicler of the events of 1915, he becomes an important source for understanding 'The Present Outlook'—in 1932—but thoroughly unreliable as a 'Record of Past Events'. His account will therefore be given little weight here.

[17] R. Tangri, 'African Reaction and Resistance to the Early Colonial Situation in Malawi: 1891–1915', *Fifth History Conference of Central Africa* (September 1968), Salisbury, Historical Association, no. 25, 13.

[18] J. R. Hooker, 'Witnesses and Watchtower in the Rhodesias and Nyasaland', *J. Afr. Hist.*, VI, no. 1 (1965), 91–106.

[19] Published as *Strike a Blow and Die*, ed. R. I. Rotberg (Harvard, 1967).

[20] Rotberg, *The Rise*, 84 and *Protest and Power*, 357–9.   [21] Rotberg, *The Rise*, 84.

[22] B. Pachai, *Transafrican Journal of History*, I, no. 1 (January 1971), 131–4.

[23] M. Chanock, 'The New Men Revisited. An essay on the development of political consciousness in colonial Malawi', to be published.

[24] For example, *Negro World*, 28 July 1926, NC 1/23/1.

The conditions in colonial Malawi which produced the rush into Kamwana's Church in 1909 had deteriorated further by 1914. Although pressure from a Liberal government in England had resulted in labour recruitment being officially forbidden in 1907, recruiting posts merely moved across the border to resume business as usual. There were an estimated 20,000 Nyasaland workers in Rhodesia alone in 1910,[25] and a conservative estimate put the total number of workers out of the country by 1913 as 25,000.[26] The pressure of tax collection, with its attendant burnt huts and massive migration of labour, induced social changes in village life. While the Ngoni lamented an increase in divorce,[27] the uxorilocal Chewa husbands brought their wives to the village of their matriclan so that their family could watch them in their absence.[28]

In the Shire Highlands, with a large African population increasing by the immigration of Alomwe labourers from Portuguese East Africa, a high density of European planters generated tensions over land and labour. Conditions on the Bruce estates, the focus of the southern side of the rising, were not appreciably worse than on many other plantations in the Highlands.[29] A combination of famine and an increase in the hut tax in 1912 further aggravated African feeling in the protectorate. The District Administration Ordinance of that year only came into force in 1914—and then only in two districts—so it did nothing to shore up the fast disappearing authority of chiefs and headmen.

The period 1909–14 was one of growing alienation from European rule. Recruitment into the western institutional churches slumped[30] as solutions to social ills were sought in traditional remedies,[31] or in millennial dreams preached in the proliferating semi-independent churches. For the 'new men', the African pastors, businessmen or government employees, excluded from traditional offices, unable to obtain capital for business, and

[25] F. E. Sanderson, 'Nyasaland Migrant Labour in British Central Africa', M.A. thesis, University of London, 1956, 43.

[26] B. S. Krishnamurty, 'Land and Labour in Nyasaland: 1891–1914', Ph.D. thesis, University of London, 1964, 305. Casson's government estimate.

[27] J. A. Barnes, *Marriage in a Changing Society*, Rhodes–Livingstone Paper, no. 20 (Oxford, 1951), 121–5.

[28] M. Read, 'Migrant Labour in Africa and its Effects on Tribal Life', *International Labour Review*, XIV, no. 6 (June 1942), 628. For a different assessment of effects on the Tonga, see J. Van Velsen, 'Labour migration as a positive factor in the continuity of Tonga Tribal Society', in *Social Change in Modern Africa*, ed. A. Southall (Oxford, 1961), 230–41.

[29] Nzama Mission Diary 31 Jan. 1915. A letter from Nguludi from the Montfort Bishop suggests that it was another planter altogether, a Mr Dickie, who had 'fanatacisé les Angourous'. The Bruce Estate secretary claimed during the Commission of Enquiry that practices on the estate were normal. He pointed out that Magomero was the only estate with a proper hospital and free medical attention. Similarly Mrs Livingstone pointed out that all planters were targets for attack, not just her husband. This was certainly true. S1/3008/23. National Archives, Zomba.

[30] I. Linden and J. Linden, 'Eklesia Katholika: Roman Catholics in protestant Nyasaland 1889–1939', chapter III. Forthcoming publication.

[31] For example, *nyau* societies, witchcraft accusations and polygamy were recorded to be on the increase. Church attendances dropped away, see M. W. Retief, *William Murray of Nyasaland* (Lovedale, 1958), 117.

with no place in white society that did not carry with it daily humiliations, it was a period of profound social malaise. Cohn's description of the membership of chiliastic movements in the Middle Ages can be applied, with obvious reservations, to the 'new men' of Nyasaland:

These people lacked the material and emotional support afforded by traditional social groups . . . they were not effectively organised in village communities or in guilds; for them there existed no regular, institutionalised methods of voicing grievances or pressing their claims.[32]

The social changes that occurred at all levels of Nyasaland society before the First World War were a sufficient cause for the growth of revolutionary chiliasm. It remains to be shown to what extent millenarian expectations were widespread before the rising, and what role they played in stimulating armed revolt. Or, in more general terms, what role did religious ideology play in the rising?

The first of several rumours of impending trouble came from the north of the administrative capital, Zomba, in the beginning of 1914. It was only communicated to the government by the Roman Catholic Bishop, Louis Auneau, after the outbreak of the rising.

Some time ago I heard from our fathers of Namkunda Mission . . . that there was some agitation amongst Mahommedan people; they were all saying that the Arabs will come and we will kill all Europeans and natives who will refuse to accept our creed.[33]

The Yao had suffered heavily from Johnston's punitive raids and the end of the slave trade. More adapted to trading under the loose control of the Sultan of Zanzibar than to the enforced economic stagnation of the *Pax Britannica*, they were perhaps the most disaffected group in the protectorate. An Islamic renaissance reported by missionaries in 1912[34] was the first symptom of what might have become a tribal revolt.[35]

More news of seditious talk came from the Ncheu district as Catholic catechists returned in June 1914 from their harvesting.[36] A month later, Paulos Mwenye, a Catholic catechist teaching within a mile of Chilembwe's Providence Industrial Mission, reported that he had been warned by a P.I.M. member, Mawson, that:

[32] N. Cohn, *The Pursuit of the Millennium* (London, 1962), 314–15.
[33] Moggridge to Turnbull 3 Feb. 1915 with letter from Auneau S10/1/6. National Archives, Zomba.
[34] A. G. Blood, *The History of the Universities' Mission to Central Africa Vol. II 1907–1932* (London, 1957), 62.
[35] Although the Ngoni were strongly opposed to colonial rule, even by the early 1890s hundreds of Ngoni were working in the Shire Highlands. The raiding pattern of life was displaced by periodic 'raids on the cash economy'. On the other hand the Yao slave trade disappeared with nothing to take its place.
[36] Oral Testimony. Fr. Auguste Basle S.M.M. A Montfort missionary at Nankunda in 1914—arrived in Nyasaland 1908. Interviewed at Pirimiti mission, Zomba, Oct. 1970.

you are a scholar of a European mission but be ready this year, 1914, as the Europeans are going to try to destroy us, we must agree, all of us Natives, to be ready.[37]

This information was passed on to the assistant district commissioner for the sub-district of Chiradzulu, Mitchell, who confronted Paulos—'a very sanctimonious and typically mission youth and a thorough rascal from the look of him'—with Mawson. The result was hardly in doubt; Mawson denied everything and the resident believed him. However, Moggridge, the DC in Blantyre, received a report of the incident and put the P.I.M. under close surveillance. From October 1914 onwards, all letters in and out of Chilembwe's mission were censored at the Chiradzulu Boma.[38]

The government's attitude towards Chilembwe was one of caution tempered by the suspicion that the Catholic warnings were a product of inter-mission rivalry.[39] Auneau was French and ultramontane, and had recently outwitted the Blantyre Town Council in the purchase of land in the township for a mission.[40] Moggridge did not know the district well, respected the Scots after a spell near Livingstonia, and felt that Hetherwick, the head of the Church of Scotland Mission, was 'probably far better informed on subjects of this sort than anyone else in the District'.[41] Church of Scotland teachers were sent round the Chiradzulu district at the beginning of December 1914 to make a thorough investigation. Six weeks before the outbreak of the rising, Moggridge was able to report that after 'three weeks hostile and fairly close scrutiny, there is little to be feared from this man'.[42]

Intensive surveillance failed to uncover any preparations for a rebellion because, probably, no such preparations were being made. The Catholic catechists had more likely heard the result of discussions about the end of the world, the belief that there was to be a Final Battle in which many Africans would be killed. Several months after Kamwana's deportation, in a remote area several days journey from Tongaland, the passage of Halley's comet brought hundreds of villagers fleeing into the bush to confess their sins and prepare for the end of the world.[43] If an apocalyptic mood

[37] Copy of depositions taken by Milthorp in Aug. 1914, S10/1/6. National Archives, Zomba.

[38] By early Nov. more than twenty letters in and out of the P.I.M. had been censored without any incriminating material being found. Moggridge to Zomba secretariat, 3 Nov. 1914. S10/1/6.

[39] The fields of evangelization of Nguludi and the P.I.M. overlapped. Further, since the arrival of the Catholics in 1901, the government had been faced with repeated squabbles between Catholics and the rest over spheres of influence. This was especially acute in the Central Region where Dutch Reformed Afrikaaners faced French, Canadian and Dutch White Fathers.

[40] Blantyre Mission Diary. Preamble to foundation 20 Aug. 1913. Diary kept at Blantyre Mission. [41] Moggridge to Hetherwick, 14 Nov. 1914. S10/1/6.

[42] Moggridge to Zomba secretariat, 11 Dec. 1914. S10/1/6.

[43] *Rapports annuels de la Société des Missionnaires de Notre Dame d'Afrique.* Report for Ntaka-taka, 1910–11. A bound copy of cuttings from the Nyasa vicariate in the White Fathers' Archives, Via Aurelia, Rome.

prevailed in 1910, it would be even more likely in 1914, the year Kamwana prophesied would bring the millennium.

Small Watchtower groups with centres at Limbe[44] and near Ncheu had survived Kamwana's deportation. Letters from Kamwana in Chinde came into the protectorate by diverse routes, and his brother, Eliot Yohan Achirwa, visited Watchtower supporters in several districts. Another Tonga, Bennet Gospel Siyasiya, was the main distributor of Watchtower literature in the Ncheu district, and was found after the rising with a certain Beswick Kangaulenda in possession of several tracts in ChiTonga, evidently from Kamwana.[45] Apart from this faithful remnant, Watchtower literature and Bibles reached a number of the semi-independent church pastors like David Shirt Chikakude, who was later found with the Watchtower book *Millions now living will never die*.[46] Another Church of Christ pastor, Fred Singano in Likabula, acted as a secret mailing address for Kamwana after the latter had moved from Chinde to Mlanje in September 1914; he was caught with a considerable volume of Watchtower literature after the rising.[47]

When rumours of war between the great powers became widespread in Nyasaland during July 1914, interest in Watchtower was rekindled. In villages the mood of impending doom gave rise to a rash of witchcraft accusations,[48] but amongst the more sophisticated mission élite in Blantyre it increased the interest in the apocalyptic books of the Bible. On 7 July 1914, Haya Edward Mlelembe, alias Peters, one of Chilembwe's closest associates, wrote to America for Watchtower books for his school.[49] Peters was no simpleton. He had been a past associate of Domingo and the founder and secretary of a 'Negro Industrial Union' that had an ephemeral existence in 1909 under Chilembwe's patronage.[50] He was, moreover, an admirer of the conservative politics of Booker T. Washington,[51] and an obsessive imitator of European ways.[52] His business interests included timber and tobacco, and Chilembwe was heavily in his debt by 1914.

[44] Limbe railway station was their mailing address. The group was led by J. R. Aphiri of Ndirande. NCN 4/1/1, NCN 4/1/2.

[45] Affidavit of H. Silberrand, Ncheu DC, 17 June 1915. S2/68/19.

[46] NC 1/23/2. A government report on Watchtower compiled after the rising stated that Watchtower literature was circulated to Seventh Day Baptists, Church of Christ, Native Church of Christ and other 'independent native religious teachers'. S2/68/19.

[47] See Eliot Yohan Achirwa to Lot Collection Chiwembe, 6 Oct. 1914. NCN 4/1/1.

[48] Utale Convent Diary 7 Aug. 1914. A witchfinder from Mbalaze village had considerable success. We are indebted to Sister Marie-Terese, Providence Teachers' Training College, Mlanje, for allowing us to read this diary.   [49] S10/1/8/3.

[50] Chilembwe to Peters 20 Oct. 1908. The first meeting of the Union was on 24 Apr. 1909 and the last scheduled meeting in December that year. S10/1/8/3.

[51] Peter's opening speech drew heavily on Washington's writing, e.g. 'I have never met one who had learnt a trade and regretted it in manhood'. Blacks had to work 'quietly, patiently, doggedly' to create 'visible, tangible, indisputable . . . products and signs of civilisation'. 'Truck-farms', i.e. market gardens are also mentioned. Many of the words carried over them a dictionary definition where Peters had looked them up. For Washington's influence see Rotberg, *Protest and Power*, 364.

[52] Rotberg, *Protest and Power*, 361.

A few weeks later, Gordon Mataka, who had travelled to Natal with Chilembwe and Booth in 1896 and was in business with Duncan Njilima, one of the leading rebels, wrote to Chilembwe:

The European war will I think put matter into a shape and people will see that our local ministers were quite right.[54]

On being questioned at his trial what he meant by this, Mataka replied:

I meant only according to the Bible. John Chilembwe came to Duncan's village either in June or July 1914. I was there. Duncan said to me: 'Did you not know that 1914 is the end of the world?' I said I did not know. Then he (Duncan) said to me: 'You had better repent and take the land (i.e. our estate) and be one denomination and build a church. I never agreed to this and did not repent.'[55]

It is interesting to note that both Peters and Mataka were far from the centres of revolt when the rising began, the former on a hunting expedition on the P.E.A. border and the latter at his store in Fort Jameson.

That Chilembwe also was thinking about the Final Battle can be inferred from a letter sent to him by Eliot Yohan Achirwa in the middle of 1914. There had evidently been some discussion of Armageddon, with Chilembwe advocating that the Elect should be prepared.

Reference to our *conversation* I will call your attention to what Paul says, 'let every soul be subject unto the higher powers'. . . . From these you will see we are not thinking about war so far as we know that God is to our side and He said to us 'avenge not yourselves but rather give place unto wrath for it is written that Vengeance is mine and I will repay'. . . . It is our duty to say to the household of the faith, 'Fear ye not, stand still and see Salvation of the Lord'.[56]

As Shepperson and Price point out,[57] this is the orthodox pacifist position of Charles Taze Russell, President of the Watchtower Bible and Tract Society, and reveals Kamwana's brother as a strict Watchtower adherent.

The news of the outbreak of war reached Nyasaland in the first week of August and put the Kamwana–Chilembwe debate on to a new footing. By October rumours abounded in the Blantyre area. A group of women told Moggridge that:

a Church of Christ teacher near Limbe and John Chilembwe had received messages that the end of the world was coming within the week.[58]

Hetherwick's scouts came back with news of a widespread belief that the Americans were fighting at Karonga against the British, and that the name of Chilembwe's church was 'Noah's Ark'.[59] Mitchell's replacement, Milthorp, collected a number of rumours that Europeans were about to kill

---

[53] Shepperson and Price, *Independent African*, 69–72.
[54] Extract of a letter read at Mataka's trial. S10/1/3.　　　　　[55] S10/1/3.
[56] E. Y. Achirwa to John Chilembwe 26 July 1914, c/o Richard Zuze, Limbe. NCN 4/1/1.
[57] Shepperson and Price, *Independent African*, 232.
[58] Moggridge to secretariat 11 Dec. 1914.
[59] Mitchell to Moggridge 18 Aug. 1914. S10/1/6.

all the Africans.[60] This fear was sufficiently general for the *askaris* in the Chiradzulu district to refuse to sleep away from the Boma.[61] These rumours clearly stemmed from apocalyptic themes: the battle of Armageddon and the Karonga war, the saved remnant and Chilembwe's sect, the war between the Just and the Unjust, the fear of an attack by the Europeans on the Africans.[62]

Again, this heightening of millenarian expectations was not limited to illiterate villagers. Two of Chilembwe's teachers, Damson Buloweza and Wilson Kusita, Ngoni elders of the P.I.M., became full-time Watchtower preachers at about this time and preached in the Ncheu district where Kusita formerly directed a P.I.M. school.[63] Duncan Njilima, the richest businessman in Nyasaland with three stores and a timber business, who had been prominent in Chilembwe's second attempt at an industrial union in 1911 and whose son, Richard, attended the P.I.M. school,[64] was later reported to have made mysterious references to the fact that 'the bugle was ready to sound'.[65] Johnston Zolongola, a P.I.M. elder, told villagers during the rising that; 'We are the people on Noah's Ark and know the real truth'.[66] All of these men were in Chilembwe's inner circle of conspirators.

When Moggridge questioned Yotan Bango, alias Saiti, in October 1914, he admitted that Chilembwe expected the second coming at the end of the month.[67] Bango was later Chilembwe's emissary to the Germans. Another

[60] Milthorp to Moggridge 19 Oct. 1914. The testimony of Lupiya Zalela, alias Kettleo, was that Johnston Zilongola rallied his group in the attack on Ferguson and Robertson by telling them that the Europeans would attack the Africans on 25 Jan. 19 Feb. 1915. S10/1/6, S10/1/3. [61] Milthorp to Moggridge, 19 Oct. 1914. S10/1/6.

[62] Revelation 20: 7–10 'Satan will be released from prison and . . . deceive all the nations in the four quarters of the earth, Gog and Magog, and mobilise them for war. . . . They will come swarming over the entire country and besiege the camp of the saints which is the city that God loves.' Cf. a ChiTonga Watchtower tract found at Ncheu: 'The Europeans are Magog because they are of the tribe of Japhet and the people of Ham, the natives, are crying because the people of Magog are stealing all their possessions.' S2/68/19.

[63] Turnbull to Moggridge, 23 Feb. 1915: 'Wilson Daniel Kusita, Ngoni, resided for about ten years at John Chilembwe's village. Closely identified with Chilembwe's Church. Recently a preacher of the Watchtower Society at Maganga's village, Mphezi, Liwonde sub-division and in Ncheu division.' S10/1/6. Cardew and Turnbull, unlike Moggridge, were far more aware of differences between the churches. Kusita appears in a photograph taken *c.* 1912 of P.I.M. members, see Shepperson and Price, *Independent African*, 294. Turnbull to Moggridge, 15 Feb. 1915, describes Boloweza as 'nominally' a teacher of the Watchtower Society at the same villages as Kusita. He appears with Kusita on the 1912 photograph. S10/1/6.

[64] Oral Testimony. Pio Ntwere, Catholic catechist at Nguludi 1910–71. Interviewed at Nguludi mission, Mar. 1971. S2/18/22.

[65] Evidence given by Betty, wife of Gordon, Mataka in Blantyre 1 Feb. 1915: 'One such occasion was Saturday January 16th 1915.' It is not improbable that she could recall something said by Njilima only two weeks earlier. S10/1/5.

[66] Statement made by Moffat Kuchandika, cattle kapitao at Ferguson's for eighteen years. Not a suspect. S10/1/5.

[67] Moggridge to Secretariat 24 Oct. 1914. 'Chilembwe by the way, although he apparently holds the belief in a 2nd advent due this month has nothing to do with the Church of Christ.' Moggridge invariably confused Church of Christ with Watchtower, some measure of the penetration of the smaller Protestant sects by Watchtower literature. S10/1/6.

witness after the rising said that Chilembwe had told him that: 'God would come and all except John Chilembwe's christians would be killed.' 'And I believed it.'[68] To what extent such statements were projections on to Chilembwe of beliefs held by the rank-and-file is difficult to assess. He might easily have interpreted his debilitating asthma, bereavement, failing sight, heavy debts, government surveillance and probable coming deportation as the suffering foretold in the Book of Revelation before the exaltation of the Just. World War I, with its multi-national ramifications of which educated Nyasalanders were well aware,[69] was easily seen as the war prophecied in the Book of Daniel that was to precede the arrival of the Archangel.[70]

The period from December 1914 to January 1915 provide more telling evidence. A 'Christians' Roll Book during the war', only half completed and in the handwriting of Stephen Mkulichi, secretary to the inner circle of conspirators, was discovered by government troops at the P.I.M.[71] It enabled the government to round up many participants in the rising who might not otherwise have been suspected, and is difficult to explain in anything other than an eschatological context. The 'Book of the Predestinate' is a theme running through many apocalyptic passages in the Bible,[72] and Chilembwe would certainly have been aware of it. The link between phrases used by Chilembwe and P.I.M. elders and the 'Christians' Roll Book during the war' is provided in the Books of Daniel and Isaiah.

There is going to be a time of distress unparalleled since nations first came into existence. When that time comes, your own people will be spared, all those whose names are found written in the Book.[73]

This was to occur after the Final Battle between the nations, and it is not difficult to appreciate how, in January 1915, Chilembwe might take it literally.[74]

The last extant letter from Chilembwe does nothing to dispel the impression that Chilembwe thought he was in the last times. It was sent to Wilson Kusita and Jordan Njirajaffa in the Ncheu district[75] and dated 22 December 1914, thus written after Chilembwe had become aware that

[68] Statement of P.I.M. member, Amon Mankaule, 24 Mar. 1915. S10/1/3.
[69] An open letter to his 'Dear Brothers and Co-Labourers in the harvest' was sent by Kamwana from Chinde as soon as he heard about the war. He informed them that Germany, Austria, Hungary and Turkey were fighting against France and England. 9 Aug. 1914. S10/1/8/2.
[70] Daniel, chapters 10, 11 and 12.
[71] Turnbull to Moggridge, 14 Feb. 1915: 'I shall send you and Milthorp a copy of the P.I. Mission "Christians' Roll Book during the war" written on January 25th 1915. It contains 175 names.' 'was not completed as a number of important rebels are not entered'. S10/1/6.
[72] Exodus 32: 32–3; Psalms 69: 28 and 139: 16; Isaiah 4: 3; Luke 10: 20; Revelation 20: 12.
[73] Daniel 12: 1–2.
[74] For example Isaiah 4: 3 has a very similar passage: 'Those who are left of Zion and remain of Jerusalem shall be called holy and those left in Jerusalem noted down for survival.'
[75] See appendix for details of Njirayaffa.

his mail was being censored.[76] Chilembwe had been bypassing the Boma by using runners since mid-November, so he would not have been likely to write in biblical code.[77]

> We are not yet in prison. . . . It is true that I have written a letter to ask the government for the rights of my people. Brother Chinyama will tell you all about it as he has read the copy of the letter. My dear brethren be strong, preach the true Gospel trusting that our Heavenly Father will help us. Strengthen all weak brethren. *Preach the Kingdom of God is at hand.*[78]

It is difficult to reconcile such an undisguised escatological proclamation with portraits of a nationalist martyr. By the beginning of 1915 Chilembwe was moving towards a messianic consciousness that he would inaugurate the 'New Jerusalem'.

The strong circumstantial evidence that Chilembwe was profoundly influenced by millenarian expectations does not explain, however, why almost nine hundred Africans rose in armed rebellion. To answer this more important question it is necessary to return to Kamwana and Watchtower, and the spectrum of belief about the coming of the millennium.

Something of the feeling after the outbreak of war amongst hard-core Watchtower adherents can be gauged from a letter sent to the Watchtower magazine from Nyasaland in August:

> Surely we are living in the Time of the End, according to the Scriptures. . . . In Nyassaland we see many things which have been preached in our churches, and what we are learning the Volumes[79] and Watchtower—all these things are now being fulfilled.[80]

But when the parousia failed to dawn in October the excitement began to turn to frustration. In the middle of November, a Seventh Day Baptist supporter of Watchtower wrote to Bennet Gospel Siyasiya to reassure him:

> But we will believe that Brother Eliot is a wise man. He would not mislead you because he is a man of understanding. You tell people that this is not the time to learn English as the time has now passed.[81]

By December recent converts to Watchtower like Kusita began to fall by the wayside.

[76] A treasury clerk wrote to Stephen Mkulichi, Chilembwe's brother-in-law, on 11 Nov. to tell him that it would be safer to send letters by runners. On 17 Nov. Milthorp wrote to Moggridge that Chilembwe was no longer sending for his letters at the Boma. S10/1/6.

[77] Chilembwe was not an over-cautious personality, and surprised a number of the Ncheu pastors by his letter to the *Nyasaland Times*, 'in behalf of my countrymen'. Shepperson and Price, *Independent African*, 234–5.

[78] Chilembwe to Kusita, 22 Dec. 1914. NCN 4/2/1. Italics ours, but the same passage was underlined by a government source when the letter was later found at Ncheu.

[79] The Watchtower doctrines of Pastor Taze Russell contained in a series *Studies in the Scriptures*, no. 4, *The Battle of Armageddon* (Brooklyn, 1897) being the most important in this context. See Shepperson and Price, *Independent African*, 458.

[80] *The Watchtower*, Sept. 1914. Quoted in Shepperson and Price, *Independent African*, 230.

[81] Matthew Jadali to Bennet Gospel Siyasiya, 14 Nov. 1914. Trans. ChiChewa. NCN 4/3/1.

I am going to let you know about our sayings please I am try to think or thought it, then I find best way that it is impossibility to be in Watchtower. I will not be as one of you in business I am return back my own old place as P.I. Mission.[82]

From Achirwa's letter to Chilembwe it is clear that the critical issue was pacifism v. activism. Kamwana and his disciples preached Pastor Russell's passivity, while at the other end of the spectrum were men like David Kaduya, an extreme activist. Kaduya, who effectively took command of the southern side of the rising, was the son of an Mpotola chief near Phalombe and travelled widely as Chilembwe's school inspector.[83] He had signed on at Fort Lister and gone to Somaliland with the Nyasaland troops to fight in the campaign against the 'Mad Mullah'.[84] His experiences of an Islamic religious war in Somaliland seem to have made a deep impression on him. It was reported after the rising that as early as February 1914 he travelled around the Zomba district elaborating on Isaiah, Chapter 52: 'Awake, awake.'[85] He explained that it meant Africans should 'fight for their own nation' and told people:

Jesus! You believe that he is the Saviour of all people? He is not the saviour of all people but he is the Saviour of the Jews. He fought on the hill of Calvary with the Romans to save Israel.[86]

Chilembwe's plans for rebellion at this time may be judged from the letter he wrote to Peters in which he said that he was thinking of leaving Nyasaland for Europe or America.[87]

Kaduya's unorthodox and singularly martial doctrine of salvation did not go unheeded. In June 1914, Daniel Mungalama, a clerk and typist at Port Herald and a P.I.M. member, wrote significantly—to Kaduya and not to Chilembwe—that four *askaris* at the Boma 'had expressed themselves as willing to destroy Europeans'.[88] If the origin of the idea of an armed nationalist uprising is to be sought, then it should perhaps be in Africa and Islamic nationalism,[89] rather than in American slave revolts.

[82] Kusita to E. Y. Achirwa, 16 Dec. 1914. NCN 4/1/1.

[83] Oral Testimony. Pio Ntwere and Ben Mononga, Alomwe, plantation worker from Mkanga's village. Employed on Bruce estates at time of rising. He described Kaduya as 'in charge of school affairs'. Interviewed Mar. 1969 at Chiradzulu Boma. Ntwere's and Mononga's information was confirmed by Kosamu Mpotola, Mpotola's village, Chiradzulu, in an interview at P.I.M. in Aug. 1969. Mpotola fought in the defence of the P.I.M. under Kaduya's command.

[84] Shepperson and Price, *Independent African*, 406.

[85] Evidence of George Masangano taken by E. Costley-White on 26 Jan. 1915. S10/1/2.

[86] Ibid.

[87] Chilembwe to Peters, 26 Mar. 1914: 'Believe I will square before I leave this country for Europe or America.' Chilembwe was referring to his debts. S10/1/8/3.

[88] Turnbull to Resident, Port Herald 19/2/15. The four *askaris* were Corporal Chidawale, Lance-Corporal Chikoko, Private Achille and Private Marekebu Njala, alias Joseph, bugler. Chidawale and Achille were Muslim Yao. NSP 1/2/2.

[89] Chilembwe was certainly interested in Islam and had several books on the topic in his library—Turnbull to Moggridge, 3 Feb. 1915. S10/1/6. Similarly two out of the three headmen detained after the rising, Majawa and Fundi, were Muslim Yao—Turnbull to

The conduct of the rising lends itself to the interpretation that Chilembwe's forces saw themselves as the Just and assumed they would be afforded supernatural protection. After the abortive attack on the Mandala stores on Saturday night, groups were still moving towards Blantyre in broad daylight at 7 a.m. on Sunday morning. A priest on his way from Blantyre mission to say mass at Limbe was lucky enough to be mistaken for a Protestant minister.

> I had got to within a mile of Mandala stores on the Zomba road when I was stopped by a band of about 60 men armed with spears, axes, sticks and a few rifles. . . . Finally after I had told them I neither made war nor carried any arms, they hesitated and, handing me back my breviary—my 'bibulo' they called it— said 'If it is true you are not a man of war strike your Bible'. This I did. Then they let me go.[90]

The same pre-occupation with the 'men of war' marked the whole rising. Women were to be spared and sent to the Chiradzulu Boma after their husbands had been killed.[91]

The Ncheu side of the rising was even more quixotic and confused. Cardew, the local D.C., a veteran of the Rhodesian Pioneer Column, had been stationed in the district since 1902 and knew it well.[92] When a relative of James Kamwamba, a local Ngoni chief who was friendly with Philipo Chinyama, informed the Boma of seditious meetings, Cardew immediately rounded up all pastors in the area with known Watchtower sympathies.[93] Chinyama, a Seventh Day Baptist pastor, had visited the P.I.M. in the last two weeks of December[94] and then tried to win over local pastors and headmen to the idea of rebellion.[95] On 23 January 1915, as the

---

Moggridge, 22 Feb. 1915. S10/1/6 and S1/46/19. Auneau, in some notes prepared for an article on the rising, recorded that several of the rebels when caught were wearing amulets as war-medicine, a typical Yao practice from the nineteenth century. L. Auneau, *Brouillons* Montfort Archives, Rome. These must have been Kaduya's recruits.

[90] Blantyre Mission Diary, 25 Jan. 1915. The priest was Fr. Guimard.

[91] Statement of Mrs Roach confirmed by Mrs Stanton and Mrs Livingstone. S10/1/2. It is interesting that in the Final Battle of Isaiah 4:1 there is the same selectivity. 'Your men will fall by the sword, your heroes in the fight. . . . And seven women will fight over a single man that day.'

[92] Claud Ambrose Cardew was born at Sandhurst in 1870, the third son of Sir Frederick Cardew, former governor of Sierra Leone. He joined the British South Africa Police and guarded the Limpopo drifts against Boer incursions. He arrived in Nyasaland with a letter of introduction from Rhodes for Johnston. A. S. Hickman, *Men who made Rhodesia*, B.S.A. Co., S. Rhodesia, 1960.

[93] Nzama Mission Diary, 4 Feb. 1915: 'Kamwamba has been given a £4 reward.' In Jan. 1915 James Kamwamba wrote to Chinyama: 'You mean about the war, but I cannot try to do so. . . . I cannot try to speak this to which I have heard.' Nonetheless, Chinyama wrote again on 18 Jan. 1915 pleading with him to keep quiet, obviously too late. NCN 4/1/2.

[94] The timing of the visit can be guessed from a number of letters. On 14 Dec. 1914 Chinyama wrote from his own village to Njirajaffa with 'Rev. Chilembwe' as a forwarding address. On 8 Jan. 1915 James Poya Malangui wrote to Chinyama from Ncheu district: 'Glad to hear that you have come back all right.' Chilembwe to Kusita 22 Dec. 1914 indicates that 'Brother Chinyama' is at the P.I.M. It was then approximately from 17 Dec. 1914—7 Jan. 1915 that the Ncheu side of the rising was planned. NCN 4/2/1 and 2.

[95] NCN 4/2/1.

rising was beginning in the south, a very worried Chinyama wrote to his American patron, Walter Cockerill:

Now regret is this Brethren B. Siyasiya and Jordan[96] and David[97] they has caughted by Resident yesterday but even myself I am very near to catching by the hands of Resident.[98]

After Chilembwe's runners had reached Dzunje during the night, on Monday morning, 25 January, Boma police arrived at Chinyama's village to confiscate his papers.[99] Despite protests from his chief, Makwangwala,[100] Chinyama had assembled 200 spearmen and now moved south towards the Shire to link up with the other rebels.[101] It was, of course, two days too late.

The confusion that characterized the rising can easily be dismissed as a result of hurried planning; by mid-January Smith, the Governor of Nyasaland, had plans to deport Chilembwe and some of the P.I.M. elders.[102] And there were P.I.M. members in government service who could have, and doubtless did, warn Chilembwe.[103] But after the initial attacks on Blantyre, there was more than confusion; the rebels simply did not know what to do. Survivors of the rising can give no coherent account of

[96] Jordan Njirajaffa. See Appendix.
[97] David Shirt Chikakude. See Appendix.
[98] Chinyama to Brother W. B. Cockerill, 23 Jan. 1915. Letter forwarded by Cockerill to Moggridge, 31 Jan. 1915. S10/1/6.
[99] Oral Testimony. Griven Chinkasi, teacher at Nthinda at the time, and Tom Kabanga-Ndau, chief *nduna* to present chief Makwangwala. Interviewed at Malondo village, Dzunje, June 1969. Makwangwala 'beat them with a stick to stop them going'. These oral testimonies are confirmed in case 91 of Philipo Chinyama in the Ncheu District Magistrate's Book, National Archives, Zomba.
[100] Makwangwala was a product of the Baptist Industrial Mission at Gowa and went to Blantyre *c.* 1905 for further schooling. He was known at Chiradzulu by P.I.M. members and Pio Ntwere, who had no difficulty in distinguishing him from Barton Makwangwala, a Zomba headman, involved in the rising. According to Kabanga-Ndau, Makwangwala went to Durban in 1903, hoping to go on to the coronation of Edward, but never left South Africa. His trip to South Africa would coincide with that of Kamwana and provides an interesting parallel with other important politico-religious figures in the pre-war period. A Ngoni chief, he belonged to the same war division, Mvimbo, as Chinyama, whose father had been an *nduna* of Makwangwala's father, Kabanga-Ndau. Personal Communication, Inkosi Willard Gomani III. Makwangwala was described in a handbook for DCs produced *c.* 1912 as 'of some education and requires watching'. *Chiefs and Headmen of Nyasaland,* Society of Malawi Library, Blantyre.
[101] Shepperson and Price, *Independent African,* 293.
[102] Governor G. Smith to Governor of Mauritius, 14 Aug. 1916: 'I regret I did not follow up the telegraphic communication which passed with Sir John Chancellor at the beginning of 1915 with a fuller statement of the situation. There was at the time grave reasons for believing that under the cloak of a missionary movement certain natives were preaching a seditious propaganda and I had in view the deportation of the leaders of the movement.' Before action could be taken, the matter culminated in the rising of 23 Jan. 1915, led by John Chilembwe. S2/68[11]/19.
[103] For example, Moses Chikwanje, the government clerk who warned Mkulichi, later tried and convicted of unlawful assembly. S10/1/3. B. Pachai also records an oral testimony that Chilembwe was warned of deportation—see 'The Nyasaland rising of 1915; an assessment of events leading to it', unpublished paper. Chancellor College Library, University of Malawi.

Chilembwe's movements.[104] From Rotberg's story of meditation on a hill[105] to the government report that he watched the raids on Mandala from the 'old road railway bridge',[106] Chilembwe does not appear to have played a prominent part in the rising.[107] It may have been that after the initial raids there was a general expectation that some supernatural intervention would occur.

Another enigmatic feature of the rising which finds explanation in a chiliastic interpretation is the selection of Roman Catholics, alone amongst missionaries, as targets for attack. The Ngoni chief, Njobvualema[108] at Kaloga, next to the Montfort mission of Nzama, received a letter from Chinyama with orders to kill the priests. They were only saved by the coincidence that the chief had already left for Ncheu to defend the Boma, and the letter was handed over to one of the only literate members of his entourage to read; this was the head catechist from the mission.[109] The letter was immediately burnt, and Njobvualema razed and looted Makwangwala's village to prove his loyalty to the Boma.[110]

The Montforts in the south were not so fortunate. Nguludi mission, only four miles from the P.I.M., was burnt to the ground in the early hours of Tuesday, 26 January. The attackers, led by Kaduya, left a priest who had stayed to defend the mission for dead in the cemetery.[111] Fr. Swelsen, a tough six-foot Dutch carpenter, survived, but a coloured orphan inadvertently left behind by the sisters perished in the blaze.[112] Onlookers say that the raiders stayed from about 3.30 a.m. until almost daybreak singing hymns in the half-built shell of the cathedral.[113] Kaduya was shot in the

[104] All accounts given in interviews were strongly Biblicized, e.g. Chilembwe was for ever disappearing for periods of three days and then appearing suddenly to his followers as they prayed. 'Major' Kaduya, on the other hand, could be traced from his direction of the defence of the P.I.M. to his death as his *machila* carriers left him to flee. Interviews at P.I.M., Aug. 1969 and a collection of interviews with old P.I.M. members, kindly lent to us by a Peace Corps worker, Lee Higdin, teacher at Chiradzulu Secondary School.

[105] Rotberg, *The Rise*, 87. Possibly also a Biblicization.

[106] Moggridge to Turnbull, 6 Feb. 1915. He was with Morris Chilembwe and Stephen Mkulichi, S10/15.   [107] Oral testimonies: Ntwere, Monoga, Mpotola.

[108] Njobvualema, who had accepted a Montfort mission in 1901, was by 1914 thoroughly opposed to the Catholic missionaries. See I. Linden and J. Linden, *Eklesia Katholika*, chapters II and III.

[109] Njobvualema had left Kaloga on 27 Jan. The letter was taken to Ncheu by a catechist, Montfort, and read by the head catechist as the chief was illiterate. Nzama Mission Diary, 27 Jan. 1915 and 21 June 1915 and Oral Testimony of Maurillo Karvalo, Ngoni, Catholic catechist, interviewed at Nzama Mission, June 1969.

[110] Nzama Mission Diary, 30 Jan. 1915. Makwangwala then put a rifle to his throat and committed suicide. Oral Testimony: Griven Chinkasi. According to Karvalo, Njobvualema was known to have been jealous of Makwangwala's education and the *machila* he used to travel in. An enormous brick monument to Makwangwala is to be found at Malondo village, an obvious act of defiance to the colonial authorities. See also Shepperson and Price, *Independent African*, 295.

[111] Oral Testimony: Valentino Mwasika. Eye-witness and mission cook at the time, interviewed at Nguludi mission, Mar. 1970.

[112] L. Auneau, 'Report on the burning of Nguludi Mission', handwritten MS. and a letter of 5 Feb. 1915 to *La Règne de Jesus par Marie*, Feb. 1915, 111–15, Montfort Archives, Rome.

[113] Oral Testimony. Mwasika and Augusto Liboti, house servant at the mission, George village, Chiradzulu. Higdin interviews. Feb. 1969.

leg by a local Catholic headman, Sumani, and left carried in a *machila*; he was later killed by government troops near the P.E.A. border.[114]

Rotberg presents the attack on Nguludi as a probable accident when Chilembwe had lost control of his forces.[115] Shepperson, on the other hand, makes the more perceptive suggestion that it was a deliberate attack on the mission that had first informed the government.[116] The priests would have agreed to neither view. For them the rising was a deliberate act of religious persecution carried out by a fanatical Protestant sect against the Catholic Church.[117] Their intemperate verdict contained some insight. Auneau, with a training in Church History that concentrated on the glorious Middle Ages, saw Chilembwe as an *'illuminé'* against a backdrop of Hussites and Anabaptists.[118] Eken, who wrote a short book on the revolt after discussions with the Nguludi priests, Dutch fathers who had visited Chilembwe for tea on a number of occasions, suggested that the war and expectations of the end of the world had precipitated the rising. It comes as something of a suprise to find an insignificant Dutch Montfort, writing in 1924, suggesting that Chilembwe's problem was that he, and his associates, were *'gedeclasseerden'*—marginal men.[119]

The Catholic view was not just a symptom of a ghetto mentality. The smaller Protestant sects were virulently anti-Catholic. An example of this is Cardew's translation of one of the ChiTonga tracts found at Ncheu:

The Kingdom of Great Britain is increasing itself, like the church of Rome, because Great Britain collects together all the churches of Babylon that they may pray for their chief, the Pope. . . . such churches are in agreement with the Church of Rome, and whoever refuses to adhere to their teachings will be persecuted and perhaps banished.[120]

It is not hard to understand how Christians, interpreting Chilembwe's possible deportation and their experience of school disputes[121] with the

---

[114] Auneau, *Brouillons*. The *machila* belonged to Auneau and was later returned.

[115] Rotberg, *The Rise*, 90.

[116] Shepperson and Price, *Independent African*, 300–1. The authors proffer a number of suggestions as to why the attack was made.

[117] Fr. Brung in a letter to *Messager de Marie-Reine des Coeurs*, Feb. 1915. The Montfort magazine for their Canadian province. 'Ce fameux John Cilembur (*sic*) fier, orgueilleux et quelque peu illuminé', and L. Auneau, 'Christenvervolging in Shire', *Onze Missionarissen* (our missionaries), May 1915. In a letter sent before the rising to the Montfort magazine of the Dutch province he wrote: 'Under the pretext of driving out the Europeans his main aim seems to be to attack the Catholic Religion and deal it a mortal blow', trans. Dutch.

[118] Brung and Auneau, ibid.

[119] P. W. Eken, *Een Afrikaansch Oproermaker* (An African Rebel), Meersen (*c.* 1925), 14, 15. This book is in the possession of Rev. Dr J. M. Schoffeleers, Likulesi Catachetical Institute, Phalombe. We are very grateful for his directing us to, and helping to obtain, Dutch material on the rising.

[120] In an affidavit of H. Silberrand, DC Ncheu, 29 June 1915, Government Trans. S2/68/19.

[121] Pio Ntwere: Hostility grew up because Chilembwe thought Bruce was allowing Catholic schools on the estates. Ben Mononga: Chilembwe was annoyed at the collusion of Catholics in the burning down of P.I.M. prayer houses on the estates. Ntwere confirmed that on one occasion Chilembwe had warned Swelsen about one such incident.

Catholics through the distorting prism of this style of teaching, could come to see the Catholics as the 'Beast' of the Apocalypse. Bennet Gospel Siyasiya does use the expression 'chirombo popa of the Roman Chalolika' (the Beast, Pope of the Roman Catholics) in one letter.[122] When 'Babylon' was attacked, the 'Beast' could not be spared.

The development from a passive waiting for the millennium to active rebellion, from Kamwana to Kaduya, took place between October 1914 and January 1915. By November, the prophet's mantle had begun to slip from Kamwana as it became apparent that the parousia would not dawn without resort to arms. Although Kamwana seems to have pushed the date back to April 1915,[123] the tremendous upsurge of millennial expectation caused by the world war could not be dammed. Wilson Kusita, a useful barometer of the change from passivity to activity, was writing to Eliot Yohan Achirwa in December; 'I know that you are Great Pastor in the Lord',[124] but sometime between 9–23 January he wrote again:

The people will not be saved by you but here it is possible that we will be saved (because) that John Chilembwe is really American. Here I am with people that I know and we are not afraid.[125]

Although it was Kamwana who had focused hopes on October 1914, and had been supported by the apparent accord between the biblical apocalyptic prophecies and events in the world, Watchtower teaching could not provide a legitimization for violence.[126] None of Kamwana's close followers joined in the rising. Only Chilembwe, with the prestige of his foreign travels to America and black helpers, like Cheek, and his pre-eminent knowledge of the Bible, could produce the supernatural mandate for revolt. By bringing together the images of oppression in the Babylonian captivity and the two great eschatological themes of the Final Battle and the saved remnant, he was able to lead himself and his followers from passivity to revolt.

Why then has this chiliastic interpretation been shunned, or overlooked, by former writers?[127] The most important reason seems to be the dissociation of religious ideology from the beliefs and social consciousness of Africans in the rebellion. The Europeans whose 'legend' Shepperson

[122] B. G. Siyasiya to D. S. Chikakude, 27 Dec. 1913. A letter sent by Siyasiya from the North Rand. NCN 4/3/1.

[123] Mwenda to Governor of Nyasaland, 19 Feb. 1926. S2/8/26, quoted in Rotberg, *The Rise*, 69. Auneau gave a first date as 2 Nov., when an attack was due. 'The hostilities were due to begin on the night of November 2nd 1914. We do not know what the future holds in store for us.' *Onze Missionarissen*, May 1915. This would fit Kamwana's earlier prophecies of the parousia at the end of Oct. well.

[124] Kusita to Achirwa, 16 Dec. 1914. NCN 4/1/1.

[125] Letter 'E' (Letter D was 9 Jan. 1915). Kusita to Achirwa Trans. Chichewa NCN 4/1/1. Siyasiya then wrote to Zuze 15 Jan. 1915, 'Wilson Kusita has left the truth because he wants to be as those people in that place (P.I.M.)'. NCN 4/3/1.

[126] For example, a typical Watchtower response was that of Achirwa to Kusita's defection: 'Although we are suffering in the flesh we are rich in spirit and in hope and our true treasure is in heaven.' Trans. ChiChewa. NCN 4/1/1.

[127] Even in G. Shepperson, 'Nyasaland and the Millennium' in *Millennial Dreams in Action*, ed. S. Thrupp (The Hague, 1962), 144–59.

mocks, and Shepperson himself, never get beyond the obfuscating abstraction 'Watchtower' to the beliefs of men in the Nyasaland of 1914-15. The Europeans, aware of the millennial overtones of the rising and of Chilembwe's planned 'theocracy',[128] concluded 'Watchtower' was to blame. Shepperson, without the material that showed the extent of millenarian beliefs in the protectorate, emphasized the hiatus between 'Watchtower' and the rising. That Kamwana's views were merely the articulate expression of a widespread, more inchoate sense of impending catastrophe could only be discovered when the focus of analysis moved from the elite to the crowd.

The failure of the rising to reach the scale of the Maji-Maji war, in which the critical role was played by traditional religious beliefs, seems to lie as much in the nature of Christianity as a religious system as in the social conditions in colonial Malawi. The different missions with their varied theologies split Chilembwe's potential Christian support. None of the Catholic peasants on the Bruce estates joined the rising. They had access only to collections of Bible stories, 'Mulungu Yekha' and 'Za Mpulumutsi',[129] which, of course, lacked the apocalyptic passages of the Bible. More importantly, they would have been unlikely to have heard sermons on the Second Coming from their priests at Nguludi. On the other hand, the Churches of Christ, with whom Chilembwe appears to have attempted to unite on 12 January 1915,[130] while having millennial expectations, were strongly influenced by Watchtower pacifism.

The problem of enlisting the support of the Yao was even more acute. Despite Kaduya's efforts to recruit chiefs and headmen in the Zomba and Mlanje districts, the attacks planned in these areas were a fiasco.[131] However great Chilembwe's prestige, he could not produce a Biblical legitimization for revolt that would be acknowledged by readers of the Koran. This absence of concerted tribal support from the Yao was more serious than the indifference of the Ngoni chiefs. The Yao had many grievances, and a successful attack on Zomba from neighbouring Yao chiefs might have prolonged the rising and thus encouraged more widespread support.

While it may be agreed with Worsley[132] that the important criterion for assessing religious movements is not 'millenarian v. non-millenarian' but 'passivism v. activism', it is plain that members of pacifist movements with millennial expectations can experience intense deprivation, social and religious, driving them to realize their frustrated hopes by violence.[133]

[128] Report of the Commission of Enquiry into the Nyasaland Native Rising, *Nyasaland Government Gazette*, Supplement, 31 Jan. 1916. Zomba, paragraph 14.

[129] 'God alone' and 'About the Saviour'.

[130] Report on Hollis and Churches of Christ. Undated. S1/486/19.

[131] Moggridge to Milthorp, 14 Feb. 1915: 'I think many of them were sitting on the fence'—in reference to Yao chiefs and headmen. S10/1/5.

[132] P. Worsley, *The Trumpet shall sound* (London, 1957), 236.

[133] Another example comes from the Middle Ages. A mystic, Melchior Hoffman predicted that the end of the world would come in Strasbourg in 1533. He was imprisoned for life but his followers in Muntzer awaited the millennium with calm and confidence. By the beginning of 1534 a Dutch anabaptist, Jan Matthys, was able to direct their frustration at

Neither did Christian ideology provide an integrative, legitimizing force in the Chilembwe rising. Quite the reverse. Just as the Bible separated Chilembwe from his own Yao, the inherent divisiveness of Christianity further split his already fragmented Christian support. The essential dualism of Christianity, its grace and works, passion and action, cross and sword, provided a formulation of the latent needs of Africans in the protectorate, but an ambivalent one. Ideally a dialectic, this duality never seems to have been solved by Chilembwe. As Rotberg recognizes, Chilembwe never appears to have resolved whether his role was that of the suffering servant or the prophet armed; in this sense he did personify the African response to revolt. As praxis, his Christianity integrated neither himself, it seems, nor Nyasaland Africans. The Nyasaland rising of 1915 provides a paradigm of the divisiveness of missionary Christianity as an ideology of political action in the colonial period.

SUMMARY

The Nyasaland rising of 1915 has been dealt with previously within the perspective of proto-nationalism, and a hiatus has been emphasized between *prophetae* like Kamwana and the Baptist orthodoxy of Chilembwe. An analysis of the beliefs of many of the lesser lights in the rising, however, shows that millennial expectations were rife at the outbreak of the rising. Kamwana's prophecies of the advent of the millennium in October 1914 were provided with support by the outbreak of the First World War. The rising is analysed within the context of millennial belief in an attempt to show how a development from passivism to activism from October 1914 to January 1915 was the proximate cause of open revolt. The failure of the rising is discussed in terms of the religious ideology used to legitimize it, and the role of Watchtower beliefs is clarified. Evidence of millennial hopes is taken from trial reports of rebels and from correspondence confiscated after the rising at Ncheu and Chiradzulu.

APPENDIX

A list of Africans with some connexion with the rising for
whom there is a body of information concerning social
position, religious belief and degree of involvement.

ELIOT KENAN KAMWANA. Tonga. Resident at Chinde 1910–14 where he conducted a wide-ranging correspondence. Moved to Mlanje at his own request in September 1914. Received visits at Mlanje from Watchtower pastors from Port-Herald and Limbe and conducted services contrary to government instructions. Maintained contact through his brother Eliot Yohan Achirwa with Watchtower representatives in Nyasaland. Refused to join the rising. Lyall-Grant, Attorney-

---

the failure of the millennium to dawn into active preparation for its inauguration by the sword. On 27 Feb. 1534 an armed uprising expelled Lutherans and Catholics from the town of Muntazer. Cohn, *Pursuit of the Millennium*, 279–86.

General, in 1915 opposed his deportation on the grounds that he preached submission and pacifism. He was deported for attempting to escape, not for Watchtower views. S2/68/19.

ELIOT YOHAN ACHIRWA. Tonga. Came to Nyasaland c. 1914 to organize Watchtower groups. He was at Bennet Gospel Siyasiya's village when the rising broke out and was given six months imprisonment for seditious words. In correspondence with Chilembwe, he took a pacifist line like his brother, Kamwana. Deported in 1916 to Mauritius. S10/1/8/5, S2/68/19 and NCN 4/1/1.

LOT COLLECTION CHIMWEMBE. A relation of Kamwana. Convicted of seditious words after arrest at Siyasiya's. Sentenced to six months and afterwards detained. Tonga. NCN 4/3/1, S10/1/8/5, S2/68/19, S1/218/19.

BESWICK KANGAULENDA. Ngoni. Sentenced to six months at Ncheu for seditious words. A committed Kamwanaite. While in detention at Kota-kota baptized four people and preached that Europeans were 'hirelings' and not 'true shepherds'. He was in possession of numerous Watchtower tracts. After release given three month sentence again at Ncheu for failure to notify village headman of meetings. Similar cases: Esau Sinos Chadza and Jackson Banda. Ngoni. S1/46/19, S2/68/19, NN 1/20/22.

JAMES RAMSAY APHIRI. Resident of Ndirande from South Nyasa District. Full time head of Limbe Watchtower group. In correspondence with Siyasiya and made official reports to Achirwa. On Sunday, 24 January, he conducted his usual morning service in Limbe. No evidence of any complicity. Similarly JAMES ASAFAITI known to have visited Kamwana at Mlanje, and RICHARD ZUZE, cook to a Goan who worked on Limbe railway. S10/1/8/5, NCN 4/1/1, S10/1/6.

WILSON FOSTER MALUNGA. Church of Scotland adherent in Mlanje district especially working amongst Alomwe, where he made many converts. Member of the Negro Industrial Union of 1909 but no apparent business interests. Under strongest suspicion of complicity in the Midima conspiracy. At Nkanda's, Mlanje, during rising. His house was razed by Midima volunteers and his gun never found. He refused to speak while under arrest. Released. Together with Kufa he was thought to have been unable to reconcile fighting with his Christian principles. S10/1/8/3, S10/1/6. Oral Testimony: Pio Ntwere.

BENNET GOSPEL SIYASIYA. Worked in the North Rand in 1913. Virulently antiCatholic and an active Watchtower pastor. A close contact of Jordan Njirayaffa and Philipo Chinyama. A note found on him when arrested on 22 January 1915: 'Please send your boy every day for letters. P. Chinyama.' He was only sentenced for seditious words and given six months. Later detained. He called his church at Msakambewa's village both 'the Watchtower Church of Christ' and 'the Watchtower Bible Society'. NCN 4/1/1, S2/68/19, S1/46/19, S10/1/8/5, S10/1/6.

JORDAN NJIRAYAFFA. Ngoni. Disciple of Hollis (Church of Christ) and attended the Negro Industrial Union in 1909. Close associate of Siyasiya. Appears to have been a Seventh Day Baptist at one time and became a Watchtower adherent in

1911. He was linked by Chilembwe with Wilson Kusita. Strong connexions with Chinyama. Life imprisonment and recommended for removal from Nyasaland because of political influence on other convicts. S10/1/8/3, NCN 4/2/1, S10/1/8/2, S2/68/19, S2/102/23.

DAVID SHIRT CHIKAKUDE. Ngoni. Corresponded with Siyasiya who was on the Rand. Sentenced to ten years but released on ticket of leave in 1921. Brought before resident at Ncheu for holding night meetings without permission, upon which he explained that he was teaching the doctrines of the Church of Christ as expounded by Njirayaffa and Hollis. Also had Watchtower literature. S1/168/22, S2/68/19, S2/102/23, NC 1/23/2, S10/1/6.

WILSON KUSITA and DAMSON BOLOWEZA. See text. Escaped into P.E.A. S10/1/3.

ANDERSON CHIMUTU. Teacher at Tambala's village for the Nyasa Industrial Mission but allowed Chinyama to establish a Seventh Day Baptist school in his home village. By 1915 said by the government to be a Seventh Day Baptist. Executed. NCN/4/2/1, S2/68/19.

MATTHEW JADALI. A letter sent to Siyasiya in November 1914 on behalf of Achirwa, although Jadali was, according to the government, a Seventh Day Baptist. Address 'Seventh Day Baptist Church of Christ, Dzunje' i.e. Chinyama's. Executed. S2/68/19, NCN 4/3/1.

FREDERICK SINGANO. Church of Christ teacher who received Watchtower literature and acted as a mailing address for Kamwana. According to government closely identified with Hollis. After release from a sentence of seven years returned to Church of Christ as a teacher and received funds from Mary Bannister in Glasgow. He gave evidence against Chikakude that the latter was a Watchtower adherent. S1/486/19, S2/85/23, NCN 4/1/1, NN 1/20/22.

GEORGE MASANGANO. Began his career as an interpreter in the resident magistrate's office, Zomba. Then became a Church of Christ teacher at 3 shillings per month. Went on a preaching expedition to Bandawe, Kamwana's district, in 1911 and then joined an independent Church of Christ led by Barton Makwangwala at Zomba (executed). Worked as a cotton kapitao in government agriculture department and was contacted by David Kaduya. Given seven year sentence. S1/468/19, S2/85/23. Shepperson and Price, *Independant African*, pp. 352, 489.

RONALD KAUNDO. Accompanied Masangano to Tongaland in 1911. He was contacted by Kaduya whilst a teacher with the independent Church of Christ at Zomba. Given a five-year sentence and later rejoined Church of Christ on release. S1/486/19, S2/85/23.

JOHNSTON ZOLONGOLA. Alias James Stone. Nyanja, ex-kapitao of Magomero but a resident on the Bruce Estates. P.I.M. elder, said to have attended church in the village of Chimbia. Leader of the smaller gang that killed Ferguson and said 'We are the people of Noah's Ark. . . .' Fled to Likabula with Kaduya where he was caught. S10/1/3. Other Kapitaos: WILSON MZIMBA, ex-kapitao of Ferguson in the attack on Livingstone, probably the leader. S10/1/3. Also LIFEYU, ex-kapitao of Robertson in the gang that attacked Magomero and according to A. L. Bruce had led a deputation for a P.I.M. school/prayer-house. Dismissed for attending P.I.M. services instead of working. S10/1/3. Similarly two cotton kapitaos FRED MAGANGA and JAMES SAMUTI were in the Magomero attacks. S10/1/3.

ABRAHAM CHIMBIA. Yao. P.I.M. pastor and ex-cook of a local planter, Anderson. A leader in the attack on Livingstone, possibly the one who cut off his head. He took with him many followers from his village. S10/1/3. Other house servants involved: 'Faithful' Hinges (cf. Shepperson and Price, *Independent African*, p. 283). Shot by court martial. Let attackers into the house. S10/1/5. Oral Testimony: P.I.M. survivors of raid. Also Graham, C. S. Ingall's cook attempted to kill Ingall but attack unsuccessful. S10/1/5, and Robin Edward a cook and Z.I.M. member. Executed. S10/1/5.

DUNCAN NJILIMA. Originally a Church of Scotland member but close connexions with P.I.M. where his adopted son Richard Njilima was educated. He owned an estate, three stores and a timber business, the most prosperous African business-man in Nyasaland. His two sons were in America where they had been taken by the Rev. Cheek. Worked at one time as a house servant for a U.M.C.A. mission-ary. His connexions with the Ncheu district were a store and business run by his brother, Clair, a Church of Scotland elder, who was cleared of all complicity in the rising. According to Mataka, Njilima believed in the imminence of the Second Coming and was reported to have said on several occasions, 'the bugle was ready to sound'. Believed by the government to have been in charge of bribing the Blantyre police. Msalule, a relative of Njilima, killed the one *askari* to die in the rising. Like Kufa he may have lost heart at the last minute. Mang'anja. Executed. S2/68/22, S10/1/6, S10/1/5. Oral Testimony; Pio Ntwere.

GORDON MATAKA. Yao. Partner of Njilima on the Nsoni Estate. Rejected mil-lenarianism before the war but became interested by August 1914. Travelled with Chilembwe and Booth to Natal in 1896. Church of Scotland teacher. Tried but found innocent. S10/1/3 and see text.

WILLIAM MULAGHA MWENDA. Mentioned here because of his statements to the effect that Kamwana had become Chilembwe's pawn by the beginning of the rising. Worked in the office of the superintendent engineer for the A.L.C. at Chinde. Appears to have been Kamwana's Watchtower general secretary. Keen Watchtower supporter. Not, however, in Nyasaland during the rising, so any of his accounts about Kamwana at this time are, at best, second-hand, at worst lies to get himself out of detention in Mauritius and to dissociate himself from Kamwana. S10/1/8/2, NCN 4/1/1, S2/68/19 and Mulagha to Governor of Nyasaland 19/9/26. S2/8/26 quoted in Rotberg *The Rise*, p. 69, footnote 34.

Journal of African History, 20, 3 (1979), pp. 395–420
Printed in Great Britain

'CHIMURENGA': THE SHONA RISING OF 1896–97

BY D. N. BEACH

IN October 1896 H. M. Hole attempted to explain to his superiors how the great rising of the central Shona, which had begun in June of that year and which was still in progress, had come about. Hole's report dodged the entire issue of Company maladministration and placed the blame squarely upon the ingratitude of the Shona themselves:

> With true Kaffir deceit they have beguiled the Administration into the idea that they were content with the government of the country…but at a given signal they cast all pretence aside and simultaneously set in motion the whole of the machinery which they had been preparing.[1]

Although Hole conceded that the Shona had shown more ability to organize then he had thought possible, he could not credit the Shona rulers themselves with the ability to 'set in motion the whole of the machinery'. He claimed that, although the Ndebele who were in rebellion in Matabeleland had played a part, the prime mover of the rising was Mkwati, 'the high priest of the M'Limo' who sought to offset his defeats in the south-west by bringing in the evil influence of the '"Mondoros" or local witchdoctors'.[2] Hole's report was to be elaborated upon in the months and years that followed, as arguments about Company misrule flourished and more evidence about such other leaders as the medium of the Kaguvi *mhondoro* spirit became available,[3] but one part of his argument became entrenched in local historiography. This was the suggestion that in the politically divided Shona countryside a preconceived and co-ordinated plan of resistance had been agreed upon by the people and kept secret for weeks or months until the signal came for a simultaneous assault upon the Europeans. Hole gave a vivid and imaginative description of this in 1897: 'In almost every kraal the natives, even the women and children, put on the black beads, which were the badge of the Mondoro, while their fighting men, with Kaffir cunning, waited quietly for the signal to strike down the whites at one blow. So cleverly was their secret kept, and so well laid the plans of the witchdoctors, that when the time came the rising was almost simultaneous and in five days over one hundred white men, women and children were massacred in the outlying districts of Mashonaland.'[4]

This picture of a 'night of the long knives'[5] became part of the stock-in-trade not only of popular novelists and journalists but of historians as well. It is not difficult to see why. In the first place, it was one of the nightmares of white

[1] Unless otherwise stated, all archival and historical manuscript references are to the National Archives of Rhodesia: A 1/12/26, H. M. Hole, Civil Commissioner Salisbury, to Secretary, BSA Company, London, 29 October 1896, printed in BSA Company, *Reports on the Native Disturbances in Rhodesia 1896–97* (London, 1898), reprinted as *The '96 Rebellions* (Bulawayo, 1975), 69.

[2] *The '96 Rebellions*, 55.

[3] In October 1896 the Company had not yet identified the Kaguvi medium as a factor in the rising, but by December his influence in the Hartley and Salisbury districts had become apparent, and his role was mentioned in the report by P. Inskipp, Under-secretary to the Administrator, Salisbury, 1897. (*The '96 Rebellions*, 79.)

[4] H. M. Hole, 'Witch-craft in Rhodesia', *The African Review*, 6 November 1897.

[5] R. Hodder-Williams, 'Marandellas and the Mashona Rebellion', *Rhodesiana*, XVI (1967), 32.

0021-8537/79/2828-1290 $02.00 © Cambridge University Press

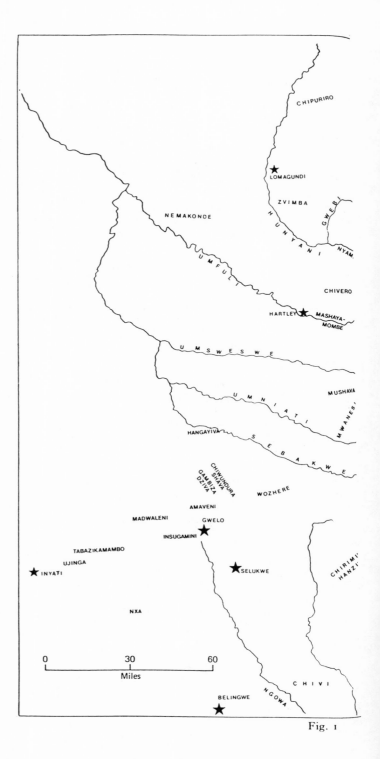

Fig. 1

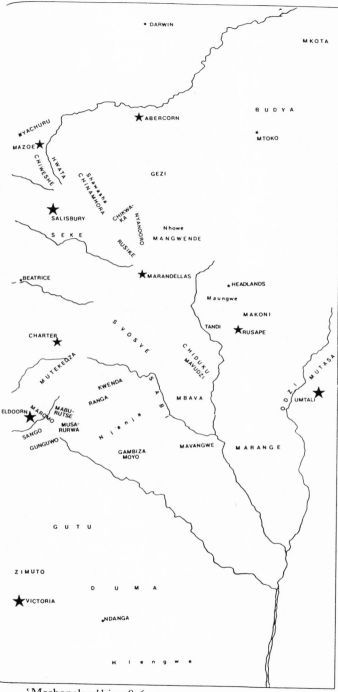

'Mashonaland' in 1896–97.

Rhodesians even before the Shona rising and it remained so afterwards.[6] In the second place, in the regimented existence of the African people under Rhodesian rule after 1897 it became increasingly difficult to think of radical change other than in terms of conspiracy, and as time passed this attitude began to affect the way in which the people thought about the 1896 risings.[7] Consequently the 'night of the long knives' became a matter of horrified or delighted memory and anticipation, depending upon the point of view assumed. Yet for the historian of the Shona in the 1890s it posed some peculiar problems. The rising of the Ndebele in March 1896 was much easier to understand in terms of such organization, for the Ndebele had had their own state in the southwest since the 1840s and, as has recently been convincingly shown, that state had not been destroyed in 1893–4 and was still very much alive in 1896.[8] The Shona outside the Ndebele state, however, had enjoyed no such political unity since the 1840s or, it seems, before then.[9] How, then, had they achieved such a feat of political organization in June 1896?

The first serious attempt to explain this was made at the Lusaka history conference in 1963 by Professor T. O. Ranger, whose *Revolt in Southern Rhodesia 1896–7* was published in 1967.[10] His work remains the standard book on the risings and has led to a considerable body of 'resistance' writing.[11] Since the rest of this paper relates to it, Ranger's arguments must be made clear in summary. His view of the Shona past before 1896 was as different from that of Hole as could be imagined,[12] and a devastating, well-documented account of Rhodesian misrule of the Shona gave ample explanation of why they should have risen,[13] but in his account of how they did so there were some curious resemblances to Hole's report, though very different conclusions were drawn. In the first place, Ranger agreed with Hole that the rising was a 'sudden and co-ordinated attack',[14] a 'co-ordinated force of arms'[15] 'concerted action'[16] 'almost simultaneous'[17] and preceded by a 'period of apparent calm [in which, in early 1896] preparations

[6] A1/12/27, L. H. Gabriel to Sir Thomas Scanlen, Salisbury, 27 March 1896, passed on a rumour of an Ndebele presence around Salisbury and a long-planned rising. From then on 'scares' were legion.

[7] C. G. Chivanda, 'The Mashona rebellion in oral tradition. Mazoe District', unpubl. University College of Rhodesia Honours Seminar Paper (1966), 8. Chivanda's criticism of traditions included the observation that the exact sequence of events was not always preserved accurately, a point that my own research confirms.

[8] J. R. D. Cobbing, 'The absent priesthood: another look at the Rhodesian risings of 1896–1897', *Journal of African History*, xviii, 1, (1977).

[9] The prime contender for pan-Shona political unity before 1896 was the Changamire Rozvi state, but this had finally surrendered to the Ndebele in 1866. It is argued in D. N. Beach, *The Shona and Zimbabwe 900–1850* (Gwelo and London, in press), that the state had not achieved the degree of political unity previously assumed.

[10] Subtitled *A Study in African Resistance* (London, 1967).

[11] T. O. Ranger, 'Primary resistance movements and modern mass nationalism in East and Central Africa', *J. Afr. Hist.* IX, 3–4 (1968); T. O. Ranger, 'African reactions to the imposition of colonial rule in East and Central Africa', *Colonialism in Africa 1870–1960*, I, ed. L. H. Gann and P. Duignan (Cambridge, 1969); T. O. Ranger, 'The people in African resistance: a review', *Journal of Southern African Studies*, IV, i (1977), 125–46; A. F. and B. Isaacman, 'Resistance and collaboration in Southern and Central Africa, c. 1850–1920', *International Journal of African Historical Studies*, x, i (1977); A. F. Isaacman, 'Social Banditry in Zimbabwe (Rhodesia) and Mozambique, 1894–1907: an expression of early peasant protest', *J. S. Afr. Studies*, IV, i (1977), 1–30.

[12] Ranger, *Revolt*, 1–45.   [13] *Ibid*. 46–88.   [14] *Ibid*. 1.
[15] *Ibid*. 81.   [16] *Ibid*. 196.   [17] *Ibid*. 200, 225.

for revolt were being made.'[18] The way in which it came about was, in Ranger's view, on the following lines – lines that must be described in some detail in order to make the *dramatis personae* and Ranger's argument clear.

Although there had been localized resistance to individual Europeans and to Company rule from 1891 to 1896, and the resistance of Nyandoro in the east of the Salisbury district in April 1896 'was in fact the first intimation of the Shona rising'[19] the real initiative came from the area of the Ndebele rising which had broken out in late March. There, the effective leader of the Ndebele was Mkwati, a Leya ex-slave and priest of the Mwari religious cult. Assisted by the woman Tenkela-Wamponga and Siginyamatshe, he had forged an alliance of the kingless Ndebele and their Shona subjects against the Europeans.[20]

After limited Rhodesian successes in early April, 'Mkwati's counterstroke, on the other hand, was very much more effective. The Shona rising, in the planning of which he was deeply involved', followed his initiative.[21] In April he sent Tshihwa, a Rozvi Mwari-cult officer from Madwaleni in the Gwelo district, to contact Bonda, another Rozvi Mwari-cult officer who lived under the Rozvi ruler Musarurwa in the Charter district, and Mashayamombe, a ruler on the Umfuli river in the Hartley district. Bonda and Mashayamombe's representatives went back with Tshihwa to Mkwati's headquarters at the old Rozvi centre of Taba zika Mambo in the Inyati district, this being before 24 May. There, they were encouraged to spread the rising into the central Shona country.[22] Tshihwa and Bonda stayed at Taba zika Mambo for the time being, but Mashayamombe's men went back to their ruler, who promptly – still in April – contacted Gumboreshumba, the medium of the Kaguvi *mhondoro* spirit. Gumboreshumba, who was related to the Chivero dynasty of the Hartley district and possibly to Pasipamire (the great medium of the Chaminuka *mhondoro* spirit who had been killed in 1883 while co-ordinating Shona resistance to the Ndebele), was then living in the eastern Salisbury district in the territory of the Chikwaka ruler, near the Chinamhora, Rusike and Nyandoro rulers. His spirit Kaguvi had been of little importance before 1896, but under the pressures of the times it was to assume superiority over other *mhondoro*, such as the famous Nehanda of the Mazoe district.[23] The Kaguvi medium had been chosen by Mashayamombe 'when there was need for a man to link the planned rising in the west [Hartley and Charter] with the paramounts of central Mashonaland',[24] and he fulfilled this role by moving to Mashayamombe's, which became practically a 'powerhouse of the Shona rising' from then on.[25]

At the end of May or the beginning of June 1896 the Kagubi medium summoned representatives of the central Shona paramounts to his new headquarters, using the same pretext as Mashiangombi had advanced [of seeking anti-locust medicine] for sending his messengers to Mkwati... It was a distinguished assembly, or rather series of assemblies. The central Shona chiefs sent trusted headmen or close relatives, in many cases their sons: Chief Chiquaqua, for instance, sent Zhanta, his best warrior and commander of his *impis* before 1890 and again after the outbreak of the rising; Chief Zwimba sent his son; Chief M'sonthi sent his younger brother; Chief Garamombe sent his son. These we know to have been there; others, in view of their later close collaboration with Kagubi we may guess to have been there: men like Panashe, bandit son of Chief Kunzwi-Nyandoro, or Mchemwa [son of Mangwende], or the turbulent sons of Makoni.

[18] *Ibid.* 191.   [19] *Ibid.* 86.   [20] *Ibid.* 127–90.
[21] *Ibid.* 190.   [22] *Ibid.* 202–4.   [23] *Ibid.* 212–18.
[24] *Ibid.* 218.   [25] *Ibid.* 282.

At these meetings the progress of the Ndebele rising was given; at this time, it will be remembered, Mkwati was bringing his picked *impi* back to the Umgusa. Assurances of the support of Mkwati and his Ndebele allies were also given and the Kagubi medium urged the central Shona peoples to join the west in a movement against the whites. Plans for an outbreak as simultaneous as possible were laid; it was to wait until the arrival at Mashiangombi's of Bonda and Tshihwa with the Ndebele warriors; and once it had begun the news was to be carried to central Mashonaland by messengers and passed from hill to hill there by the signal fires....[26]

These conferences held by the Kaguvi medium influenced the Hartley, Lomagundi, Mazoe, Umvukwes, Marandellas and Gutu districts – 'a spread covering virtually the whole area of the Shona rebellion'[27] – and were reinforced by most of the local *mhondoro* mediums, including Nehanda in Mazoe and Goronga in Lomagundi.[28] Finally, Tshihwa, Bonda and the Ndebele arrived from Mkwati's headquarters in June, and the signal for the rising was given.[29] Tshihwa went south to raise the Selukwe district,[30] and Bonda went back to Charter.[31] Ranger suggests that, apart from personal contacts made by these two and others[32] with the rulers in these areas, the Charter district was the 'nursery of the Mashona rebellion',[33] 'we may legitimately draw upon some later evidence' from 1913–15, when 'chain-letter' messages of the Mwari cult were passed from village to village.[34] In the rest of the area of the rising, the signal was given by messengers from the *mhondoro* mediums and rulers, and by prearranged signal fires.[35]

Once the rising had begun, Ranger points out, a feature of the religious organizers was their ability to react and re-plan their strategy in response to the changing military situation. Bonda became a liaison officer for the headquarters at Mashayamombe's and 'we catch constant glimpses of him in the next few months [after June]' carrying messages, raiding loyalists and generally playing a most significant role.[36] Mkwati, forced out of the Ndebele area, arrived at Mashayamombe's with Wamponga determined to carry on the fight and reinforced the Shona headquarters.[37] At the end of 1896 a new strategy was planned: not only had the Kaguvi medium persuaded the eastern Salisbury rulers not to surrender,[38] but he and Mkwati prepared to move into that area – over the protests of Mashayamombe who objected to their departure[39] – as part of their plan to revive the 'Rozvi Empire'.[40] This plan misfired on the arrest of the Rozvi Mambo-elect, but it led to a strengthening of the power of the religious authorities northeast of Salisbury: the Kaguvi medium was able to appoint a new Seke ruler,[41] and the *mhondoro* mediums of the Budya of the Mtoko district achieved a 'triumph of the pan-Shona teachings...over the raiding policy of a chief' of the Budya, Gurupira, when on his death they persuaded the Budya to turn against Native Commissioner Armstrong's patrol and force it to flee to Umtali, almost starving to death in the process.[42] In the end, however, the rising was gradually worn down by the superior force of the Europeans.

This, in brief, was Ranger's picture of the organization of the Shona rising. 'This supra-paramountcy co-ordination was not achieved through the paramounts alone...*We have to*[43] look once again to the traditional religious

[26] *Ibid.* 219–220.
[29] *Ibid.* 203.
[32] *Ibid.* 205.
[35] *Ibid.* 209–220.
[38] *Ibid.* 289–92, 285–6.
[41] *Ibid.* 291–2, 300.

[27] *Ibid.* 222.
[30] *Ibid.* 203.
[33] *Ibid.* 202.
[36] *Ibid.* 205.
[39] *Ibid.* 292–4.
[42] *Ibid.* 303–4.

[28] *Ibid.* 210–12.
[31] *Ibid.* 203–4.
[34] *Ibid.* 204–5.
[37] *Ibid.* 266–7.
[40] *Ibid.* 289–92.
[43] My emphasis.

authorities of the Shona to understand the co-ordination of the rising above the paramountcy level – and also to understand the commitment of the people to the rising at the paramountcy level, a commitment so complete and even fanatical that it cannot be explained simply in terms of loyalty to the paramount chief.'[44] This picture, and Ranger's view of the 'new society', of which more later, remained substantially unmodified for ten years. My own thesis of 1971 dealt with the Hartley, Charter and southern Shona districts. It added to Ranger's picture of Shona society before 1896 and the nature of Company rule, and pointed out the existence of important Shona groups that fought on the Company's side in 1896 for various reasons. It also pointed out that the actual areas in which the Mwari-cult officers and the Kaguvi medium operated were much more limited than Ranger suggested. Nevertheless, it did not seriously question the Hole-Ranger view of the 'night of the long knives' and the organization that led to it. It did, however, look back into Shona politics in an attempt to seek a political explanation for the unity of the central Shona in 1896, since the influence of the Mwari-cult officers and the Kaguvi medium did not extend far enough in terms of territory. It found the political factor in the growing resistance of the central Shona to the Ndebele in the 1880s, and especially in the Shona–Portuguese treaties of 1889, in which an unprecedented number of central Shona rulers committed themselves to an anti-Ndebele stance. This commitment was not tested against the Ndebele because the BSA Company arrived in 1890, but it served to give the central Shona the degree of unity they needed in 1896, with the religious organizations as a reinforcing factor.[45]

Since 1971 the main published revision of the historical picture of 1896 has been J. R. D. Cobbing's re-examination of the Ndebele rising, in which the influence of the religious factor was shown to have been far less than Ranger stated, and in which the prime mover behind the organization of the rising was shown to have been that of the old Ndebele state, substantially unaffected by its defeat in 1893.[46]

This paper seeks to summarize my own gradual reconsideration of the evidence on 1896, made during the years since 1971 when my own attention was primarily on pre-1850 Shona history. Essentially, it argues that all analyses of the rising made since 1896, including my own thesis, were wrong on two important points: the rising was not 'simultaneous' or 'almost simultaneous' even within the limitations of Shona communications and technology, and it had not been predetermined and co-ordinated in the way that had been previously assumed. Consequently, the need for a 'religious' or 'political' overall organization falls away, and our understanding of the social and political situation among the central Shona in 1896 must undergo a sharp revision. This paper relies upon the same basic documents used by Ranger, with some support from fieldwork carried out in Hartley and Charter in 1969–70, and involves a close examination of the picture given by Ranger, giving an alternative chronological account of the rising with the differences from Ranger's picture being pointed out *inter alia*. First, however, it is necessary to re-examine the background to the rising and to redefine the nature of Shona resistance to the economy and rule of the Europeans.

In the first place, no analysis of nineteenth-century Shona history can be

[44] Ranger, *Revolt*, 200.

[45] D. N. Beach, 'The rising in South-western Mashonaland 1896–7', unpubl. Ph.D. thesis, University of London, 1971.

[46] Cobbing, 'Absent priesthood'.

complete or accurate without a consideration of the workings of the Shona economy. This has been described and analysed elsewhere,[47] and can be very briefly summarized as follows: the Shona had an economy with an agricultural base, with supporting branches of production based on herding, hunting/gathering, manufacturing and mining. By the late nineteenth century the manufacturing and mining branches and external trade were in most areas in a depressed state relative to earlier centuries, though a certain amount of peasant production in agriculture and migrant labour had emerged as a response to the rise of capitalism in southern Africa after *c.* 1870. The agricultural base remained of paramount importance. It depended upon the preparation of fields and the sowing of grain crops at the beginning of summer – October through to December – and their reaping at the onset of winter, approximately from March to June. Problems of storage restricted the amount of food available at any one time, and consequently the maintenance of the crop cycle from year to year was vital. The danger of *shangwa* (disaster) due to drought or locusts was ever present. These factors were intimately linked to the 1896 rising in almost every significant way – its causes, timing, organization and its ultimate defeat.

The remarkable success of the Shona in extracting most of the upper-level gold from the reef mines between about 950 and 1800 accelerated the impact of colonial rule because the BSA Company, unable to make money from mining, encouraged and organized forced labour for very low wages, legitimized stock-raiding in the name of taxation and allowed oppressive methods of labour control, though obviously these were implicit in the South African brand of capitalism that it imported. Space forbids detailing these here, but the scale of colonial operations can be divided into two periods. From 1890 to 1894 the operations were at a relatively low level, essentially because Company activities were focused on the vain hope of finding payable upper reefs in different parts of the Shona country and, ultimately, the Ndebele state. There was a tendency for the emphasis on mining to shift from area to area, and although cases of forced labour certainly occurred the scale of mining activity was well below that of the period 1894–6, so that the impact of labour enforcement upon the Shona was partly cushioned by the Shona and foreign voluntary labour sector. Moreover, there was no permanent labour-coercion force during this period. Taxation was planned, but not implemented until 1894, and European farming activity was at a low level. After 1894 mining activity increased sharply, European farming settlements increased in some areas and a Native Department was created in order to coerce labour and collect tax. Consisting of one or two European officers and a body of African 'police' in each district, it rendered the Shona much more liable to labour and tax exactions. Often labour coercion took place during the agricultural work-season, and tax exactions involved the removal of valuable livestock accumulated and prevented as an insurance against crop failure.[48]

---

[47] D. N. Beach, 'The Shona economy: branches of production', *The Roots of Rural Poverty in Central and Southern Africa*, ed. R. H. Palmer and Q. N. Parsons (London, 1977), 37–65; D. N. Beach, 'Second thoughts on the Shona economy', *Rhodesian History*, VII (1976), 1–11; R. M. G. Mtetwa, 'The "political" and economic history of the Duma people of South-eastern Rhodesia from the early eighteenth century to 1945', unpubl. D.Phil thesis, University of Rhodesia (1976), 209–294.

[48] Ranger, *Revolt*, 46–88; Beach, 'South-western Mashonaland', 247–94; R. H. Palmer, 'War and land in Rhodesia in the 1890s', *War and Society in Africa*, ed. B. A. Ogot (London, 1972), 85–108; I. R. Phimister, 'Rhodes, Rhodesia and the Rand', *J. S. Afr. Studies*, I, i (1974), 74–90.

Apart from the relatively lower level of pressure upon the Shona before 1894, there were other reasons why no rising took place before that date. There seems to be little doubt that during this period many Shona believed that the European presence was temporary, like that of the Portuguese between 1629 and 1693 – a presence whose duration was underestimated in Shona traditions.[49] Secondly, many Shona rulers had found the Europeans useful in local politics, and it is remarkable how many of the clashes between the Europeans and the Shona in 1890–4 were engineered by other Shona groups to their own advantage.[50] From 1894 onwards resistance to Company rule became more noticeable, but it took the form of isolated and unconnected incidents. One of the reasons why there was no major rising in 1894–5 was probably the number and location of the police force being assembled by the Company for the attack upon the Transvaal: they were placed in small groups across the country, probably to escape interested observers, and provided a police presence to back up the Native Department. From October 1895 they were gradually concentrated upon Bulawayo, leaving only the Native Department, a much reduced police force and the part-time volunteers.[51] October, however, was the beginning of the intensive agricultural season, which in many areas was the more important because 1895 had been a bad year for locusts.[52] When the main Shona rising did break out in June 1896 it was at an optimum time from an agricultural point of view.

Nevertheless, the armed resistance carried out by the Shona before June 1896 is of crucial importance if the 1896–7 rising is to be understood. Shona resistance to colonial rule in the 1890s took a number of forms, including desertion from underpaid labour, abandonment of settlements in the face of tax and labour demands, theft,[53] cattle-maiming and other responses, but here we are concerned with actual violence. This took place across the country at different times in 1894–6, but the remarkable feature it showed when compared with the 1896–7 *hondo* (war) was its restricted nature. In every case it was limited to the enforcers of labour or tax collection – the police or the Native Department – or to actual employers of labour,[54] and did not develop into a general attack upon all local Europeans, who were allowed to carry on prospecting, mining, farming, trading and transporting. This contrasts strongly with the 1896–7 *hondo* when, once a Shona group had decided to rise, the attack was extended to almost all Europeans and foreign Africans and included travellers, women and small children who could have had no direct connection with local grievances. Moreover, after this 'preliminary resistance' had taken place, the districts reverted to normal and even the Native Department was allowed to function as usual, whereas in the full *hondo* resistance was more or less continuous up to the moment of defeat.

Examples of this can be seen in many districts. In the Charter district in February 1895 Native Department police collecting tax were fired upon and

---

[49] E.g. N3/33/8 NC (Native Commissioner) Marandellas to CNC, *c.* 1 Jan. 1904; Chivanda, 'Mazoe', 5 and N1/1/9 NC Salisbury to CNC, 21 Jan. 1896.

[50] E.g. the Gomwe ('Ngomo'), Mutekedza, Maromo, Gutu, Mugabe and Chirogwe incidents of 1892–3.

[51] S. 183, vol. 1, BSA Police Regimental Orders, 1 Jan. 1896 to 14 May 1897.

[52] N1/1/5 NC Lomagundi to Sec. Nat. Dept. 26 Sept. 1895; N1/1/3, NC Hartley to CNC 29 Dec. 1895; N1/1/9, NC Salisbury to Sec. Nat. Dept. 22 July 1895; EC 4/2/1, CNC to Administrator, 31 Jan. 1896.

[53] It is not suggested that all theft was classifiable as resistance.

[54] Similarly, not all cases of murder can be definitely linked to aggrieved employees, for lack of evidence.

sjambokked by the Njanja, and in July a farmer near Enkeldoorn was murdered.[55]
In Lomagundi district in August 1894 a policeman collecting labour was killed,[56]
and in May 1896 a miner was murdered in his own mine.[57] In the Mtoko district,
NC Armstrong was threatened by the Budya in April 1895; two of his police were
shot by February 1896; his patrols were fired upon by Mkota's Tonga shortly
afterwards; NC Ruping's patrol was attacked in late May by the Budya; fighting
occurred again on 7 June and the district remained tense until the news of the
main Shona rising arrived.[58] In the Umtali district in April 1896 Marange turned
out an armed force to recover his cattle, taken by the Native Department.[59] In
1894 an African policeman was killed at Makoni's[60] and on 9 June 1896 Makoni
held a meeting to propose the recovery of his tax cattle from ex-Hut Tax Collector
O'Reilly's farm and the killing of the Native Department personnel. On 16 June
this was proposed again, and the cattle-recovery began, but as late as the 18th
a Native Department policeman was allowed to bring a message to Makoni and
to depart alive.[61] In September 1894 in the Salisbury district Nyandoro's men
pursued policemen who were trying to arrest his son Panashe; in October 1895
police were fired upon by the same people, and in April 1896 Nyandoro openly
threatened the police and local Europeans as well.[62] In the Marandellas district
Gezi's people attacked police in December 1895 and March 1896.[63] It is clear
that those cases of preliminary resistance that occurred before the outbreak of
the Ndebele rising of March 1896 were not part of any general Shona rising, and
although Ranger saw Nyandoro's threats in April 1896 as 'the first intimation
of the Shona rising' the fact remains that in those Shona areas that resisted
between March and the spread of the main *hondo* in June the resistance
corresponded to that of before March: even in Mtoko those prospectors outside
the NC's camp were not touched until 25 June when news of the main rising
reached the local Budya, while in Nyandoro's, Makoni's and Marange's areas
the same was true. Nyandoro did not start fighting until 20 June, nor Makoni
until some time after 23 June, while Marange remained neutral.

There is, however, a danger in drawing too neat a line between this preliminary
resistance and the full *hondo* of June: whereas such rulers as Makoni did confine
themselves to preliminary resistance until a relatively late date, and whereas it
will be shown that there was no widespread concerted planning of the main rising
in advance of its outbreak, it is equally clear that between March and June the
central Shona country was in an exceptionally tense state, and that the possibility
of a full war was being discussed by the more militant personalities in several
areas, independently of each other. Nyandoro's threat to attack all local Europeans
was significant even if it was not carried out, and some time between 14 and 24

---

[55] N 1/1/2, NC Charter to CNC, 19 Feb. 1895; J 1/9/1, Ferreira to RM Salisbury, 14 July 1895.
[56] CT 1/56/6, MC Lomagundi to Acting Ad. Salisbury, 14 Aug. 1894.
[57] N 1/1/5, A. J. Jameson to MacGlashan, Lomagundi, 30 May 1895.
[58] N 1/1/6, W. L. Armstrong to H. M. Taberer, 17 July 1898, encl. 'Report on Mtoko's district or Budjla'; *The '96 Rebellions*, 53–4, 59; N 1/1/9, NC Salisbury to CNC, 22 April 1895.
[59] N 1/1/11, NC Umtali to CNC 15 Apr. and 4 May 1896.
[60] A2/1/6 Acting Ad. to NC Brabant, 8 Oct. 1894; A2/1/5, G. C. Candler to RM Umtali, 13 Aug. 1894.
[61] A 1/12/36, CNC to Acting Ad., 17 and 19 June 1896.
[62] W. Edwards, 'Wiri, 2', *NADA* 38, 1961, 8; EC 1/1/1 Acting Sec. to Council, Salisbury to CNC, 20 Apr. 1896.
[63] Edwards, 'Wiri, 3', *NADA* 39, 1962, 19–21; Rusike's people fired on police in April 1895, N 1/1/9 NC Salisbury to CNC 6 Apr. 1895.

May a similar plan to kill the police and local traders and to attack Hartley had been considered by Mashayamombe's people and rejected as inadequate.[64] In Marandellas district Mangwende's son Muchemwa had been considering a rising for some time, and although NC Edwards later connected such hints as a pair of sandals laid at his door and talk of a bird from 'Mwari' with a deep-laid plot involving all the Shona, they more probably reflected the discussions held by Muchemwa on his own initiative.[65] It seems highly likely that even if there had not been interaction between the Ndebele rising and the Shona of Hartley and Charter, in such an environment a major rising would have broken out somewhere else and spread, producing a very different pattern of resistance but a similar effect.

Another important distinction that must be made is between the different activities of the Shona during the rising itself: not all activities were related to the rising, even though in many cases they were made possible by the Company's preoccupation with the Shona *hondo*. Normal Shona politics continued, for example, and sometimes involved violence: in April 1896 longstanding political tensions in the Mutasa dynasty led to the emigration of the Chimbadzwa house to Barwe,[66] while in November the Pako people allied themselves with the Ngowa and took advantage of the situation to try to recover their ancestral hill Chirogwe from Chivi's Mhari who had seized it earlier in the century.[67] Neither Chimbadzwa nor the Pako appear to have acted as part of any overall commitment to the risings. Similarly, not all clashes between the Europeans and the Shona indicated Shona commitment to the rising, though the Europeans often thought that they did: in April 1896 a rumour that Mutasa was going to attack Umtali led to armed men parading the streets threatening to kill him, and another rumour occurred in November: in fact, Mutasa eventually joined the Company.[68] In October 1896 an attack was made upon Negovano of the Duma by the Victoria forces as the result of a rumour fabricated by a Cape African rapist and thief: again, the Duma were at no time in the rising.[69] Thefts from deserted stores took place in otherwise neutral areas,[70] and several attacks upon Europeans and foreign Africans appear to have been made by groups which did not intend at that time to join the rising or which did not do so, and which were simply taking advantage of the times to carry out robbery. Thus, Chingoma's people attacked Carruthers south of Belingwe, but did not join the rising,[71] while Chipuriro's people killed their ruler's son-in-law Box, Box's brother and also some migrant labourers from the Zambezi.[72] In each case the motive was apparently robbery. Another similar

[64] N 1/1/3, NC Hartley to CNC 24 May 1896.

[65] J. Farrant, *Mashonaland Martyr, Bernard Mizeki and the Pioneer Church* (Cape Town, 1966), 202–4; Edwards, 'Wiri, 3', 24.

[66] N 1/1/11 NC Umtali to CNC 21 Dec. 1896.

[67] NVC 1/1/1 NC Chibi to CNC 11 Sept. 1897 and NC Chibi to NC Belingwe 17 Oct. 1897.

[68] N 1/1/11 NC Umtali to CNC 6 Apr. 1896.

[69] A 1/15/4, OC Victoria to CSO Salisbury 26 Oct. and 6 Nov. 1896; N 1/1/12 NC Victoria to CNC 28 Dec. 1896.

[70] A 1/12/31 RM Victoria to Sec. Ad. 30 Mar. 1896; A 1/12/34 Strickland, Charter to Ad. 24 Apr. 1896.

[71] A. St Clair, 'On the white man's trail', *African Monthly*, v, 5 (Dec. 1908), 42–5, 48–50; D. Tyrie Laing, *The Matabele Rebellion* (London, 1897), 131–4, and NC Belingwe reports.

[72] S.401, 338, Regina vs. Kanzanga, Sakara, Kugushu and Tsimota, 30 Aug. 1898, evidence of Kanyenze, Sipolilo, Makori, 2 June 1898; A 1/12/27, evidence of Masiewo, 8 July 1896; a similar killing of labour migrants took place in the same area in 1901, N 3/1/9 Acting NC Lomagundi to CNC 8 June 1901.

case involved Matowa of Mbava's Rozvi, whose pregnant daughter was taken from him by the trader Basson, who caused her to abort her baby. While guiding Basson to safety on Mbava's orders, Matowa decided to take revenge and killed him.[73] Such actions could have varying results: the village whose people attacked Carruthers was destroyed later by Laing's column,[74] Chipuriro was largely unaffected by the rising after the killing of the Box brothers until the defeated leaders of the Shona rising reached his territory in late 1897 and he advised them to surrender.[75] Mbava's people, on the other hand, remained isolated until late 1897, but then seem to have assumed that Basson's death had implicated all of them and so fled over the Sabi to escape the police.[76] This 'peripheral violence' demonstrates that contemporary European assessments of Shona activity were not always correct, a fact of relevance to the so-called revival of the 'Rozvi empire' in 1896–7.

We now come to the central point of this paper, the reconstruction of the exact sequence of events that brought the central Shona country into a state of war. The Ndebele rose in the last half of March 1896 and most of the Shona members of their state joined them. On the edges of the south-eastern lowveld and across the southern Shona territory the Matibi, Chivi, Chirimuhanzu, Gutu and Zimuto dynasties blocked the spread of the rising by joining in on the side of the Company, as they had in 1893, basically because they feared an Ndebele victory in spite of the fact that they had suffered severely from Company misrule. The implications of their collaboration have been discussed elsewhere.[77] On the north-eastern frontiers of the old Ndebele state, beyond the collaborating dynasty of Chirimuhanzu and the resisting territories of Wozhere, Gambiza *dziva* and Chiwundura *shava*, was a relatively thinly populated zone comprising most of the Umniati and Sebakwe valleys.[78] Although the few Shona in these areas did not join the rising, Ndebele patrols reached as far as the Umfuli,[79] and in May some Ndebele from Amaveni raided Payne's farm in the Mwanesi range.[80] (This led Hole to call the Charter district the 'nursery' of the rising, but there is no evidence that this was anything more than an attempt to recover cattle lifted by Payne since 1893).[81] An important feature of this thinly populated zone was that it allowed good long-distance communications between the central Shona and the Ndebele.[82]

One of the dangers of having a keen appreciation of the part played by religious leaders in politics is that their purely religious role is sometimes underestimated:

[73] S. 401, 379, Reg. vs. Chikwaba and Matowa, 22 Nov. 1898, evidence of Chikwaba, 24 Aug. 1898, Matowa, 24 Aug. 1898 and Zirewo 19 July 1898.

[74] Laing, *Matabele Rebellion*, 134.

[75] N 1/1/6 NC Mazoe to CNC 30 Oct. 1897; LO 5/4/6 Under-Sec. Ad. to London Board, 5 Nov. 1897.

[76] LO 5/4/6 Report of NC Marandellas 30 June 1897; LO 5/4/8 Report of NC Marandellas 31 Dec. 1897.

[77] Cobbing, 'Absent priesthood', 77–9.

[78] It is not certain why this area should have been so thinly populated, apart from its being a high sodic-soil area. The Ngezi dynasty between the Umsweswe and the Rutala hills had been fragmented by raiding in the 1860s, but there is no evidence for intensive settlement before the *mfecane* for a considerable distance south of the Umsweswe.

[79] N 1/1/3 NC Hartley to CNC 11 Apr. 1896.

[80] A 1/12/35 Strickland, Charter, to Ad. 11 May 1896.

[81] S. 401, 1-40 Reg. vs. F. D. A. Payne, 20 May 1895.

[82] An apparent anomaly also to be seen in the south-eastern lowveld, caused by the necessity for the people to travel long distances between settlements.

this is particularly true of those involved in the train of events that loosely connected the Ndebele and Shona risings. In the first place it must be remembered that there was a very close connection between religion and the economy: religious leaders, of whatever particular cult, were expected to be able to use their connections with the high-god and senior *mhondoro* spirits to produce rainfall and to avert *shangwa*, disaster. Like the economy itself, this aspect of religion could not be suspended in wartime. As late as 1897 the religious leader Siginyamatshe was distributing anti-locust medicine in Belingwe while on the run from the police.[83] Such activities were, of course, taken by such officials as Hole to be a cunning cover for a political plot, and Ranger's *Revolt* tends to make the same assumption, yet the evidence for the contact between the Ndebele and Shona risings indicates that it was in the beginning a purely religious–economic contact and only later assumed a political significance. Whatever role Mkwati played in the Ndebele rising, and he was clearly not the supremo that Ranger thought, it is still true that he had been an important local religious figure in the Inyati–Ujinga area.[84] The summer of 1895–6 in the central Shona country had seen renewed attacks on the crops by locusts, and at some time before 24 May Mashayamombe sent some of his people – probably those of Muzhuzha house who had recently returned home after having been forcibly incorporated into the Ndebele state for some time and who still wore Ndebele ear-marks – across the thinly populated zone to Mkwati near Inyati, to get anti-locust medicine.[85] The first initiative for contact was therefore not Mkwati's, nor did he send his aide Tshihwa out at this point.[86] When the medicine arrived at Mashayamombe's, the ruler's village became a distribution point: 'I remember the people assembling at Mashangombi's kraal to get medicine for the locusts. *This had nothing to do with the rebellion*', recalled a witness later.[87] Mashayamombe then decided to make a small profit from this, and sent a message to Gumboreshumba, medium of the Kaguvi *mhondoro* spirit.

Gumboreshumba was of the Chivero dynasty and had the advantage of being the grandson of Kawodza, a previous medium of the Kaguvi spirit. Kawodza had lived in the territory of Chivero, but Gumboreshumba lived in that part of the eastern Salisbury district where the Chikwaka, Nyandoro, Seke, Rusike, Chinamhora and Mangwende dynasties bordered upon each other.[88] His spirit

---

[83] NB6/3/1 Report of NC Belingwe 30 June 1897; NB1/1/2 ANC Filabusi to CNC 21 Mar. 1898.

[84] Cobbing, 'Absent Priesthood', 76.

[85] N1/1/3 NC Hartley to CNC 24 May 1896; N1/1/6 NC Mazoe to CNC 30 Oct. 1897. On the confusion caused by Muzhuzha house in the identification of 'Ndebele' near Hartley, see D. N. Beach, 'Kaguvi and Fort Mhondoro', *Rhodesiana*, xxvii (1972), 38 n, 45. Ranger noted NC Hartley's reference to Mashayamombe's contact with Mkwati for the purpose of getting locust medicine, but read a political significance into it because it also reported the plan to attack the Hartley police and traders. In *Revolt*, 202, he omits the statement that this plan has been abandoned, though he had mentioned it in 'The organization of the rebellions of 1896 and 1897, Part Two, The rebellion in Mashonaland', *History of Central African Peoples Conference* (Lusaka, 1963), 5.

[86] Ranger, *Revolt*, 202–3, traces Tshihwa's movements through LO5/4/1 NC Chilimanzi to CNC 7 and 10 January 1897, and assumes that Tshihwa visited Mashayamombe's three times, on Mkwati's orders in April and June, and with Mkwati in October. Tshihwa in fact made no reference to any journey there in April, only to the 'second' and 'third' journeys.

[87] S.401, 391, Reg. vs. Zuba and Umtiva 20 Feb. 1899, evidence of Marowa, 6 Dec. 1898. Italicized words omitted in Ranger, *Revolt*, 220.

[88] Pasipamire, the famous Chaminuka *mhondoro* medium killed in 1883, was of the Rwizi dynasty, and his only connexion with Chivero was a common totem, *shava*. On his actual role in

was thought to have been the spirit husband of the Nehanda spirit, and was also thought to have had special rain-making abilities, but Gumboreshumba made the Kaguvi spirit more famous for his ability to find game, an attribute that was especially useful in the famine of the late 1880s in the Chikwaka area.[89] In short, like most Shona religious leaders, the Kaguvi medium had a strong interest in the Shona economy. Mashayamombe's message to him was that he had anti-locust medicine from Mkwati available for distribution, but when an envoy from the Kaguvi medium went to investigate he found that Mashayamombe would not supply the medicine unless a payment of one cow was made. The Kaguvi medium refused to pay this, and sent his own messengers to Mkwati, while Mashayamombe sent messengers at the same time. It was probably about this time that the Kaguvi medium moved from the Chikwaka area back to the area where his grandfather had been famous. It was significant, however, that he did not go to Mashaya- mombe's but to a village in Chivero's country: from the very beginning, there was a division between him and Mashayamombe.[90]

Meanwhile, another religious leader had made contact with Mkwati, but we have no information as to how, when or why this occurred. Bonda was a Rozvi, born in the Selukwe area of the Ndebele state,[91] which would explain why some Charter traditions refer to him as an Ndebele,[92] but from 1894 he lived in the Charter district, probably in the hills to the west.[93] There, he appears to have founded a small religious centre, and was reputed to be able to make plates of food appear by magic.[94] We do not know how he came to be there, but in early June he was at Mkwati's centre at Ujinga; possibly he had the same need for medicine as Mashayamombe and the Kaguvi medium, possibly he was making normal contact with Mkwati.[95]

Thus, in late May or early June, Bonda and messengers from Mashayamombe and the Kaguvi medium arrived independently at Mkwati's, and all the evidence is that at this stage the religious–economic factor was paramount: they had come for locust medicine. Once there, however, they heard news and received encouragement that was to precipitate the main Shona rising. As mentioned earlier, from late 1895 the main Company forces in the central Shona country had been a small force of police and the Volunteers. In April a major force of 150 Volunteers left Salisbury to join the Company forces in action against the Ndebele. To the Shona, it must have seemed as though the Europeans had committed their main strength into the struggle with the Ndebele, especially as they recruited 200 Shona auxiliaries, mostly from the Mutekedza territory on the road to the south.[96] This force fought actions at Makalaka Kop on 30 April, at

Ndebele–Shona politics, see D. N. Beach, 'Ndebele raiders and Shona power', *J. Afr. Hist.* xv 4 (1974), 647.

[89] N 1/1/6 NC Mazoe to CNC 30 Oct. 1897; Beach, 'Kaguvi and Fort Mhondoro', 33–4; N 1/1/9 NC Salisbury to CNC 3 Mar. 1898.

[90] N 1/1/6 NC Mazoe to CNC 30 Oct. 1897. Ranger, *Revolt*, 218, omits all reference to this haggling over the medicine price, and to the separate contact with Mkwati made by the Kaguvi medium. On the location of Kaguvi's first base, see this reference and White's map in Hist. MSS WH 1/1/2.

[91] NSE 2/1/1 NC Hartley to NC Gwelo 28 Sept. 1897.

[92] University of Rhodesia History Department Texts 35, 40–1 Ctr.

[93] L 2/3/43, Brabant to Ad. 27 Aug. 94; A 1/12/27 Evidence of Tshenombi *et al.* 13 July 1896.

[94] URHD Text 35 Ctr.

[95] LO 5/4/1 NC Chilimanzi to CNC 10 Jan. 1897.

[96] A 1/12/10 NC Charter to Ad. 3 Apr. 1896; A 1/12/13 Beal to Vintcent 12 July 1896.

Amaveni on 9 May and Nxa on 22 May,[97] and the news carried back to the central Shona country by Bonda was that this force had been destroyed.[98] This was repeated as far away as the Mazoe valley,[99] and it seems that these actions against the Ndebele mentioned above had far more impact upon the situation amongst the central Shona than any actions on the Umgusa, as Ranger suggested.[100]

So far, it will have been noted, 'Mkwati's counterstroke' had not been very much in evidence. The contacts between the Ndebele and the central Shona had been confined to the question of locust medicine. Now the political element emerged, though it is difficult to see Mkwati rather than the Ndebele leadership in general as the prime mover. He did sent out one of his aides – Tshihwa the Rozvi from Madwaleni – but the Ndebele secular leadership was even more heavily involved, for it sent some men of the 'Mangoba' *ibutho* to Mashaya-mombe's and the Kaguvi medium's bases and a force, reputedly led by the influential Manondwana of Insugamini to back up Bonda in Charter, though only six Ndebele were definitely identified.[101] These forces, then, set out with Bonda and Mashayamombe's and the Kaguvi medium's messengers in the second week of June to precipitate the rising in Hartley and Charter. The 'counterstroke' of the Ndebele – rather than of the religious leadership especially – had finally emerged, though as has been seen it had involved a strong element of the fortuitous in the shape of the locust medicine and the actions of the Salisbury Column, but here the resemblance to Ranger's model of the Shona rising breaks down.

Ranger's major assumption had always been that the political element of contact between the central Shona and Mkwati had been there from the beginning, since April, and that preconcerted planning at what he thought was the joint headquarters of Mashayamombe and the Kaguvi medium had preceded the arrival of Tshihwa and the Ndebele. In fact, there was no preconcerted planning. Not only was there no joint headquarters, not only was there abundant evidence from each district that the rulers and their people had not known of the rising more than a day in advance in every case, but there were no conferences at the Kaguvi medium's village before the rising. Ranger's main evidence that these took place comes from a misreading of the documents. Zhanta, war-leader of the Kaguvi medium's old ruler Chikwaka, was one of the few actually to visit the medium in his new base, but this was *after* the rising had broken out in the Chivero territory: 'Kukubi sent two messengers to Mashonganyika's, they went on to Gonda's and told the people they were to come to Kukubi at once. I went with them. I thought he would give us something to kill the locusts. When I got there *I found he had a lot of whitemen's loot.* He ordered me to kill the white men. He said he had orders from the gods. *Some Matabele who were there said watch all the police wives. I returned and gave Chiquaqua Kukubi's orders.*' Since there is no evidence for major thefts around Hartley before the rising, and since Ndebele had already arrived at the medium's village, it follows that this

[97] A 1/12/35 Beal to Vintcent 1 May and 6 May 1896; LO 5/6/1 Grey to Kershaw 12 May 1896; Cobbing, 'Absent priesthood', 78.

[98] A 1/12/27 Evidence of Tshenombi 12 July 1896.

[99] A 1/12/27 Evidence of Machine, 4 July 1896 and later statement.

[100] Ranger, *Revolt*, 182, 190.

[101] LO 5/4/1 NC Chilimanzi to CNC 10 Jan. 1897; A 1/12/27 Evidence of Tshenombi *et al.* 12 July 1896. Tshihwa stated that he and Bonda had been told to 'accompany' the 'Mangoba', not that the latter were an escort for them.

'conference' took place after 14 June.[102] The evidence of Zhanta's neighbour Zawara son of Garamombe only confirms that the Kaguvi medium told Chikwaka's people to visit him, and does not suggest that this was any earlier than 14 June.[103] The evidence from the Zvimba ruler, his brother Musonti and the people of Lomagundi district is only that a message reached the Zvimba ruler from the Kaguvi medium and was then passed on, not that anyone from Lomagundi went to Kaguvi's beforehand.[104] The evidence for the presence of Panashe the son of Nyandoro, Muchemwa the son of Mangwende and the 'turbulent sons of Makoni' at the medium's village either before or after the rising began remains where it originated, in Ranger's guesswork.

How, then, was the news of the rising spread if it was not preconcerted beforehand? The answer is that since it was nowhere near simultaneous, preplanning was not needed and the different Shona dynasties simply joined the rising, opposed it or stayed neutral as the news reached them.[105] The Shona certainly could have carried out a simultaneous or nearly simultaneous rising if they had preplanned one: they had a lunar calendar, and it would have been easy to start the rising on a previously agreed day after a certain phase of the moon; or the *chiwara* signal-fire system could have been used, for visibility is usually fair to good in June and a line-of-sight system of signals could have carried the signal very rapidly indeed. *Chiwara* fires were used in the Mazoe and Marandellas districts, but apparently only within territories of single rulers, following a political decision by the ruler himself.[106] But the word travelled relatively slowly, taking about five days to cover the 75 miles between Mashayamombe and Mangwende, for example – a painfully slow speed for a pre-arranged *chiwara* system, but a fair rate for a message to pass by messenger from territory to territory, allowing for a night's discussion in the process. In fact, the word of the rising spread gradually from Mashayamombe's, from Sunday 14 June, and had covered most of the central Shona country by the following Sunday, though some north-eastern areas were not affected until Thursday 25 June. Ranger's *Revolt* obscures the timing issue by starting with the Marandellas district, which rose on 19–20 June and only later reverting to the rising's beginning in Hartley.[107]

This brings us back to the situation in the Umfuli valley, with the returning messengers and the Ndebele coming to give news of Ndebele victories at Maveni

---

[102] S. 401, 213, Reg. vs. Zhanta, evidence of Zhanta. Italicized words omitted in Ranger, *Revolt*, 221. Evidence for robbery in Hartley was very slight from March to June: N1/1/3 NC Hartley to CNC 29 Mar., 11 Apr., 26 Apr., 26 Apr. and 14 May 1896.

[103] S. 401, 215, Reg. vs. Zawara, evidence of Zawara 23 Nov. 1897.

[104] The evidence for the southern Lomagundi district shows clearly that a message from the Kaguvi medium arrived in Zvimba's area and was given to the medium of the recently dead Zvimba Musundi, Zvimba and his brother Musonti. A son of Zvimba went with a force to spread the word to Nemakonde. S. 401, 256 and 301, Reg. vs. Mangojo *et al.* 27 May 1898, S. 401, 260 and 341, Reg. vs. Msonti, Aug. 1898, S. 401, 378, Reg. vs. Samkanga 22 Nov. 1898. There was a man from Zvimba's at Kaguvi's, but he was only involved with the death of the African policeman Charlie some time after the first killings, S. 401, 253, Reg. vs. Kargubi *et al.* 8 Mar. 1898.

[105] The 'ripple' effect was originally considered by Ranger and rejected because it clashed with the opinion of the Company 'experts' of 1896, 'The rebellion in Mashonaland', 2. Significantly, the word *Chindunduma* often used to describe the 1896 *hondo* means 'ripple' as well as 'rage'.

[106] A1/12/27 re-examination of Machine, 4 July 1896. Edwards noted that fires were seen on the hills near Marandellas on the evening of 19 June ('Wiri, 3', 25–6) and much later wrote that they were seen on the previous night and also far to the west at Goromonzi and Jeta (W. Edwards, 'The Wanoe', *NADA*, IV (1926), 21).

[107] *Revolt*, 191–3, 225–6. Ranger dates the Mashayamombe outbreak five days too late.

and Nxa. The evidence would appear to indicate that Mashayamombe had actually decided to rise *before* his messengers returned, or at least that their return tipped the balance in what was already a very tense situation. On about Thursday 11 June, a clash had developed between the wives of Muzhuzha Gobvu, Mashayamombe's nephew, and those of the police of NC Moony, who lived very close by. This clash escalated, and Moony flogged Muzhuzha. The recollections and traditions of Mashayamombe's people are adamant that this was what caused the rising, and Moony's surviving policeman agreed with this in 1897, making no mention of messengers from Mkwati. It is possible that they had not arrived by then. In any event, Moony's men began to desert on 13 June, and the rising began on the next day with the killing of some Indian traders and Moony himself.[108].

The way in which Mashayamombe organized this rising emerges clearly from the evidence concerning the killing of Hepworth on the Umsweswe. Dekwende, medium of the local Choshata *mhondoro* of Mashayamombe, declared: 'The day they were going to murder the white men my eldest brother the live Mashayamombe sent for me and told me we must kill the white men. I only sent out the impi to murder the men I did not go myself.' Dekwende sent his son to call house-head Kakono and others to a conference, and became possessed by his spirit: 'I heard Dekwende order the men to kill the white man...He said this about 8 p.m. in the night before the man was killed.' 'The next morning, Mgangwi, since dead, said I was to come with him to help carry the blankets of Kakono and the others, who were going hunting to the Zwe Zwe....' As they approached Hepworth's 'Kagono...told us that the eland hunt was a blind and that our real orders from Mashayagombi were to kill the white man.' 'The older men shouted "Ndunduma, the axe is red".' It is clear from this that even Mashayamombe's brothers did not know of the rising until the night before it broke out and that although the mood of the people was quite ready for a *hondo* nevertheless even Kakono's raiders did not know their real mission until very late.[109]

An indication of the general unpreparedness of the people is given by the man who actually killed Moony, Rusere: he had just come from the Kaguvi medium's village and found Moony being pursued, but was so unready that he had to borrow a gun from his uncle before he could join in.[110] This would suggest that at this early stage the medium himself had not known of the rising – it is noticeable that none of Mashayamombe's people claimed that they had had any leadership from him in the carrying out of the killings, and it was the Mashayamombe medium of the Choshata *mhondoro*, Dekwende, who gave the religious sanction there. Mashayamombe's forces struck east to kill the Europeans at the Beatrice mine on 15 June,[111] west to the Umsweswe[112] and on the evening of 18 June they began the siege of Hartley.[113] By then, however, the rising had spread.

From Mashayamombe's word was carried south-east to the Mushava ruler, in

[108] Beach, 'Kaguvi and Fort Mhondoro', 36–8. None of Mashayamombe's people mentioned Tshihwa, Bonda or Ndebele at their trials.
[109] S. 401, 334, Reg. vs. Dekwende, 26 Aug. 1898, evidence of Dekwende, Pemimwa, Sipanga; N1/1/3, NC Hartley to CNC 19 Apr. 1898, evidence of Mandaza.
[110] S. 401, 246, Reg. vs. Rusere and Gonye, 24 Feb. 1898, evidence of Rusere 3 Feb. 1898.
[111] A1/12/27 Evidence of Jan, 16 June 1896.
[112] N1/1/3 NC Hartley to CNC 19 Apr. 1898.
[113] *The '96 Rebellions*, 62.

the only case where the Kaguvi medium's name was mentioned outside the Hartley, eastern Salisbury and Lomagundi districts: 'I remember the beginning of the rebellion, a messenger came from Mashangombi saying that Kagubi had given orders for the white men to be killed so the three prisoners and I and two others started early in the morning.'[114] This took place on about 16 June,[115] and by 18–19 June the Charter district was coming into the rising. Here, however, the leading influences varied. Some unnamed messengers came from Mashaya-mombe, who had close ties with the Maromo ruler of Charter,[116] but there was also Bonda. Although Tshihwa claimed in January 1897 that he had set out from Mkwati's for Mashayamombe's with Bonda,[117] it is curious that neither the Hartley nor the Charter sources from June 1896 to the present mentioned Bonda being at Mashayamombe's until after the collapse of the Charter rising in September 1896. It seems possible that he went directly to Charter and was not connected with the so-called powerhouse on the Umfuli until he was forced to flee there in about October, and that his arrival and that of Mashayamombe's messengers in Charter was therefore partly coincidental. Once there, Bonda and his Ndebele helped to bring in the Sango, Maromo and Mutekedza dynasties, but this was the limit of his influence.[118] (It was an indication of the unexpected nature of the rising that Mutekedza Chiwashira, who from 1893 had relied upon the Company and his son-in-law Short for support and who had allowed his men to join the Salisbury Column in April, joined in; this left him with men on both sides, which would hardly have happened if he had known of the rising in advance. His daughter was able to hide Short from her father's men until 25 June, but had had no time to help him get into safety.)[119] Bonda's impact was therefore

---

[114] D3/5/1 Reg. vs. Marubini, 12 July 1898, evidence of Urebwa, see also S. 401, 380, Reg. vs. Mahughlu et al. 27 Nov. 1898. The evidence for a very short interval between the first arrival of the news of the rising and the decision by the people to rise also emerges in: D3/5/1 Reg. vs. Kondo and Matungwa, evidence of Biri, 18 April 1898: 'Billy [a Xhosa trader near Charter] had been warned he was going to be killed – he knew he could not get away as there were Mashonas living all round.' S. 401, 213, evidence of Wampi, 'Zhanta was Kagubi's postman, he brought a message that day that the Mashonas must kill the whites.' S. 401, 241, Reg. vs. Mutuma, 27 Feb. 1898, evidence of Chinyanga: 'I remember the word coming to kill all the whites in June two years ago. Next day Joe [Norton] and his driver came to our kraal [and were killed]'; S. 401, 243, Reg. vs. Chizengeni et al., 23 Feb. 1898, evidence of Tagamania: 'I never heard of killing the whites till Chizengeni called for his impi to kill him'; S. 401, 295, Reg. vs. Mzilingeni and Mtshenge, 21 May 1898, evidence of Mafunga and Mlele: William and Hendrick, Cape Africans, had been at a beer party, started for home 'and just then Kagubi's *impi* came up...' and people from the party joined it, followed them and killed them; S. 401, 381, Reg. vs. Tshinwada and Tshisaka 23 Nov. 1898, evidence of Chikuni, 'At the beginning of the rebellion a messenger from Mashangombe came to our kraal and gave orders to kill all whites and their native servants...so at daybreak the prisoners and I took our kerries and went to kill him'; S. 401, 255, Reg. vs. Mashonganyika, evidence of Mashonganyika, 'Mr Campbell came the day the god said kill all the white people.' These are the cases that give an indication of the time involved. *None* claim that there was a pre-arranged rising or that there was a long interval between the decision to rise and the actual killings.
[115] A1/12/36, Firm to Ad. 19 June 1896.
[116] S. 401, 381, evidence of Chikuni; URHD Texts 41 Ctr.
[117] LO5/4/1 NC Chilimanzi to CNC 10 Jan. 1897.
[118] A1/12/27 evidence of Tshenombi et al.; URHD Texts 34–52 Ctr. The rising in the Charter district appears to have spread rather more slowly than in other districts, which tends to support the idea that Bonda's group and messengers from Mashayamombe influenced the three local resistance rulers independently, A1/12/36 Firm to Acting Sec. 16 June 1896, Firm to Ad. 18 June 1896, 19 June 1896, 22 June 1896.
[119] Hist. MSS WE3/2/6, reminiscences of M. E. Weale; A2/14/1 Acting Ad. to Short, 25 Oct. 1893; A1/12/36 Firm to Scanlen 26 June 1896 and Ref. 96 above.

limited to a small area. Tshihwa went straight back to Mkwati, and only helped reinforce the rising in the Selukwe district in July, long after it had started there.[120] No 'chain-letter' methods of passing messages were recorded in 1896, which is not surprising because this was a ritual used to dispel fever and colds and the only person in 1913–15 who thought it had anything to do with 1896 was a rather naive African messenger from Hartley.[121]

The evidence for the spread of the rising north and east from Mashayamombe's not only shows how the 'ripple' effect engulfed areas of preliminary resistance such as Mtoko and Makoni, but gives us a clearer idea of the extent and nature of the Kaguvi medium's influence. If he had not known of the rising on the morning of 14 June, he had certainly thrown his weight behind it by the evening of 16 June, when his messenger arrived at Nyamweda's village on the Hunyani. Norton's cattle were stolen, and the next day he was killed, though the Kaguvi medium was not always obeyed unquestioningly: 'It was said by Kagubi that the whites must be killed so Mija my father told his people that it was the order *so we said you are wrong father, why should we kill whitemen when we work in the town so I killed the Bushman* [servant of Norton].[122] From Nyamweda's the word went north: on 18 June Shona on the Gwebi had joined in.[123] By this time the Company's own system of communications was beginning to run faster than that of the Shona, and although outlying Europeans were surprised and killed north and east of Salisbury, in many cases the telegraph warned people before the Shona started fighting. Thus, Salisbury was already on guard by the night of 17 June,[124] and many of the Mazoe Europeans were warned before fighting broke out on 18 June.[125] In the eastern Salisbury district, sixty miles from Kaguvi's village, the word was brought by Zhanta on the night of 19 June, and the shooting started the next day.[126] The rising also reached the Mangwende area on the night of 19 June, and again the fighting started on the 20th. (The statement by Farrant that the missionary Mizeki was killed on the night of 17 June appears to rely upon Hole's and Edwards' theories and assumes that the *chiwara* fires seen by Mizeki before his death burned for two nights before anyone else noticed them.)[127] In the Makoni territory the preliminary resistance that had been going on since 16

[120] LO 5/4/1 NC Chilimanzi to CNC 10 Jan. 1897; Hist. MSS. WE 3/2/6, Reminiscences of M. E. Weale; BA 2/9/2 Hurrell to GOC 2 Aug. 1896.

[121] N 3/14/5 NC Hartley to CNC 29 Mar. 1915 and linked documents.

[122] S. 401, 241, Reg. vs. Mutuma, 22 February 1898, evidence of Mutuma, italicized words omitted in Ranger, *Revolt*, 221.

[123] A 1/12/27 Report of Jim Matabele, 19 June 1896; *The '96 Rebellions*, 81.

[124] *The '96 Rebellions*, 82.   [125] *Ibid.* 83–95.

[126] P. S. Garlake, 'The Mashona rebellion east of Salisbury', *Rhodesiana*, XIV (1966), 2–3; S. 401, 255, Reg. vs. Mashonganyika 3 Mar. 1898, evidence of A. D. Campbell. The timing of Zhanta's movements would appear to have been as follows: two unnamed messengers from the Kaguvi medium travelled to Chikwaka's and summoned Zhanta and a few others to Kaguvi's. Zhanta arrived there and saw the loot gathered and the Ndebele from Mkwati's. The loot probably came from Thurgood's agent George's station nearby. Zhanta then returned to Chikwaka's on 19 June and gave the news of the rising. Assuming that each man travelled only 30 miles a day over the 60 miles between these places, and that each slept a night on the road and at each end of the journey, the first messengers need have left Kaguvi's only on 14 June. But it is unnecessary to assume such a tight schedule: as Zhanta pointed out, when he started he thought he was going to get locust medicine, so the first messengers could well have started before 14 June.

[127] Edwards, 'Wiri 3', 24–31; Hodder-Williams, 'Marandellas', 29–40. The 19th would appear to be the decisive date: Edwards's police deserted that afternoon and the fires were seen that night. Farrant, *Mashonaland Martyr*, 188–217. Farrant adopted a pre-Rangerian stance and assumed a general Ndebele presence in each district.

June, and the news coming down the telegraph wire, had led the Native Department to concentrate all available Europeans at Headlands, just east of the Makoni–Mangwende border. When an attack was made on Headlands on 22 June, however, it was made by Mangwende's and Svosve's people following the retreat from Marandellas, and the Headlands party was to retreat all the way through Makoni's territory to the Odzi without being attacked. Makoni can therefore be counted as one of the rising only after 23 June.[128] Of the outlying areas, the Lomagundi and Abercorn districts came into the rising on 21 June, on 24–25 June the news reached Mtoko, and on 25 June it reached the Darwin district.[129]

This 'ripple effect' covered a very wide area in those crucial twelve days in June, but the area affected by the Kaguvi medium was relatively small. Apart from the single rather ambiguous reference in the Mushava area cited above, and about four references from the Zvimba and Nemakonde areas of Lomagundi where the Kaguvi medium sent a messenger, all the references to his role in leading people into the rising come from only two areas, whereas Ranger mistook the location of events and thought that the Kaguvi references extended to Mazoe and Gutu and thus 'virtually the whole area of the Shona rebellion'.[130] In fact, the Kaguvi medium was mainly influential in the Chivero–Nyamweda area of Hartley where the previous medium of Kaguvi, Gumboreshumba's grandfather Kawodza had been active, and his own previous area of operations in the 1880s and early 1890s, the border country between the Salisbury and Marandellas districts.[131] Consequently, though there is no doubt that the Kaguvi medium played a powerful role in these areas, there is nothing surprising about it. Nor, in view of the opinion, which was probably held by the medium himself, that the Kaguvi spirit had been the husband of the Nehanda spirit, is it surprising that Gumboreshumba was for a while more influential than Charwe, the Nehanda medium.[132] In short, the Kaguvi medium was not a supreme co-ordinating figure in the Shona rising, but since the Shona evidently did not need such a figure in 1896 this is of less significance than it might have been.

The lack of co-ordination continued after the initial phase of the rising. In an incautious phrase in my thesis I referred to the Shona conduct of their wars as 'almost incurably defensive-minded',[133] which was obviously not precisely true in view of certain long-distance raids made by Mashayamombe in 1896–7,[134] but broadly it was true that the Shona rulers fought almost exclusively within their territories and very rarely combined to attack targets.[135] Where rulers and leaders did combine later, it was usually as a result of having been driven out of their own areas by superior force. Thus Bonda and Maromo joined refugees from Charter at Mashayamombe's after the rising collapsed in their area in September

[128] A 1/12/36 Scanlen to Firm, 23 June 1896; Edwards, 'Wiri 3', 31.
[129] *The '96 Rebellions*, 59–60, 63–4, 98–101; A 1/12/22, note by MacGlashan, Jan. 1897.
[130] Ranger located the Nyamweda–Norton area in Mazoe, and confused house-head Gutu *soko* of the Shawasha with the Gutu *gumbo* dynasty of the south.
[131] See files S. 401 and D 3/5/1 in general.
[132] Beach, 'Kaguvi and Fort Mhondoro', 33.
[133] Beach, 'The rising in South-western Mashonaland', 146.
[134] Beach, 'Kaguvi and Fort Mhondoro', 38. Other long-distance raids by Mashayamombe and Bonda in 1897 were on refugee camps in Charter and the neutral Ndebele settlement at Hangayiva, 45 and 65 miles away, respectively, N 1/1/2 NC Charter to CNC 24 Jan. 1897, N 1/1/3 NC Hartley to CNC 12 Sept. 1897. These raids, which were essentially for supplies for the beleaguered Mashayamombe stronghold, involved the killing of several women and children.
[135] The joint attack on the Alice mine in June 1896 may have been partly due to its location near the junction of the Hwata–Chiweshe and Nyachuru territories.

1896,[136] and when the Kaguvi medium was driven out of his first base in Chivero's country in July, he re-established himself at Kaguvi hill just south of Mashayamombe's. This base, however, was in an enclave of Chivero territory,[137] and although he did co-operate with Mashayamombe's medium Dekwende[138] his establishment remained separate from that of Mashayamombe and in January 1897 a fatal split developed between them. Mkwati and Tenkela, too, eventually reached Mashayamombe's area in early October, but not as part of any pre-conceived plan. They had gradually retreated eastwards from point to point across the thinly populated zone and had tried to reorganize Ndebele resistance from Hangayiva hill near the Sebakwe–Kwe Kwe confluence, but divisions between their followers prevented this, and only then did they move to Mashayamombe's.[139]

Ranger's picture of Mkwati and the Kaguvi medium forging a new plan to revitalize the rising by reviving the 'Rozvi empire' in late 1896 and early 1897 falls down when the evidence is examined. The Kaguvi medium had been successful in encouraging the eastern Salisbury rulers not to surrender during that summer,[140] but the 'Rozvi empire' idea was a product of the fears of the Native Department, whose officers had in effect undergone a crash course in the significance of Shona history. One incredible rumour of a pan-Rozvi plot had already circulated in the Ndebele state, and Native Commissioners – notably W. L. Armstrong – were all too ready to give credence to rumours. In late December 1896 three senior Rozvi rulers from the upper Sabi valley where the Changamire dynasty had made its last stand in the Mavangwe hills, namely Chiduku, Mbava and Mavudzi and the son of the Gambiza *moyo* ruler whose lands bordered Mavangwe, went to Ndanga and called Chikohore Chingombe the leader of the Mutinhima Rozvi house to come back to Mavangwe and be their Mambo.[141] The Changamire leadership had previously been in the hands of the so-called Gumunyu faction, and this selection of a Mutinhima leader as Mambo was significant, but only within Rozvi politics.[142] What alarmed the Native Department was a series of unconnected reports: one from eastern Salisbury that the Kaguvi medium intended to collect reinforcements from 'Chiduku's Rozvi' on the upper Sabi; a report from Charter that in March 1897 Bonda had gone down to the Rozvi area of the upper Sabi;[143] a report that Mwari-cult messengers had been in the Hlengwe country in southern Ndanga district, and that, from the upper Sabi, Rozvi had returned to Ndanga 'and told the Makalakas that it was no use working their lands as the Mlimo *had gone to get the assistance of Mudsitu Mpanga Mtshetstunjani and Govia to help him* wipe out all whites and friendlies'.[144] This looked most sinister, and Ranger assumed that only

---

[136] N 1/1/3 NC Hartley to CNC 6 Aug. 1897.
[137] Beach, 'Kaguvi and Fort Mhondoro', 39–40.
[138] A 1/12/14 Nesbitt to Vintcent, 5 Aug. 1896. See ref. 90.
[139] LO 5/4/1 NC Chilimanzi to CNC 10 Jan. 1897.
[140] Ranger, *Revolt*, 286–7. The Company officials were partly led to exaggerate the influence of the Kaguvi medium because their base in Salisbury lay between the two areas where he did play a great part.
[141] Ranger, *Revolt*, 158–9; N 1/1/8 NC Ndanga to CNC 2 Mar. 1897.
[142] I would now revise my opinion, stated in my thesis, that Muposi Chikore had been an undisputed Mambo before *c.* 1893.
[143] N 1/1/2 NC Charter to CNC 11 Mar. 1897; LO 5/4/2 Report of CNC Mashonaland, 19 Mar. 1897; LO 5/4/2 Armstrong to CNC 20 Feb. 1897.
[144] N 1/1/8 NC Ndanga to CNC 2 Mar. and 30 Mar. 1897. Italicized words omitted by Ranger in *Revolt*, 291. Mpanga and Mtshetstunjani (Masesenyana) are identifiable as *mfecane* Ngoni from

14   AFH 20

Chingombe's arrest stopped the full plan from coming into effect.[145] In practice, however, the Rozvi were too scattered to form a cohesive fighting force;[146] Bonda did not in any case go to Ndanga or Mavangwe where Chingombe had been installed, but went towards Maungwe where the Rozvi leader Tandi had recently surrendered;[147] and the story that the *madzviti* (Ngoni) leaders Mpanga and Ngwana Maseko of the 1830s and Manoel António de Sousa (who died in 1892) were going to join the rising was simply false.[148] The whole episode was evidently just another example of ordinary Shona politics being carried on in wartime.

Nor was the departure of Mkwati and the Kaguvi medium part of any master-plan: Mkwati's movements in December–January were probably part of an abortive attempt to join an intransigent band of Ndebele under Gwayabana on the lower Umfuli,[149] and when he did arrive in the country north-east of Salisbury the evidence that he did much to keep the rising going is very thin.[150] As for the Kaguvi medium, he left his hill near Mashayamombe's not as part of a grand plan but as a consequence of his having stolen two women from Mashayamombe and a minor war having broken out between them. Mashayamombe informed the police, and a temporary truce between them lasted while the police tried to capture the medium, with Mashayamombe supplying intelligence. When the medium finally fled back to his old area it was because it was impossible for him to remain.[151]

Resistance continued in 1897, but it remained, as it always had been, a local war fought by each ruler in his territory – until he was driven out of it. The Kaguvi medium continued to be influential in the eastern Salisbury area, but then lost influence. When he was driven out of it into the Nehanda medium's area his power was much reduced. Even in his home area, his influence had its limitations: in the Seke territory in December 1896, for example, in the abortive ceasefire negotiations the Company had supported the Zhakata house in its bid for the Seke title, and when the Kaguvi medium became involved in this internal dispute all he did was to endorse the Company's nominee.[152] Another notable failure of the religious factor to influence events – assuming any such attempt was made – occurred when NC Armstrong led a force of Budya under Gurupira to join a police attack on the Mangwende–eastern Salisbury resistance strongholds: Gurupira was fatally wounded on 23 April, but far from turning against Armstrong as Ranger has it, the Budya did not lift a finger against him. They

G. Fortune, 'A Rozvi text with translation and notes', *NADA* xxxiii (1956), 72, 80, and K. R. Robinson, 'A history of the Bikita district', *NADA* xxxiv (1957), 78–9.

[145] Ranger, *Revolt*, 289–92.

[146] Most Rozvi groups of any size had committed themselves to the rising long before, and many had been defeated.

[147] N 1/1/2 NC Charter to CNC 19 Mar. 1897; LO 5/4/2 NC Makoni to CNC *c*. February 1897. It is possible that the Kaguvi medium and Bonda did try to get help from Chiduku's Rozvi, though nothing came of it, but the Mavangwe Rozvi 35 miles away were not involved.

[148] N 1/1/8 NC Ndanga to CNC 30 Mar. 1897.

[149] LO 5/6/7 NC Gwelo to CNC 1 Dec. 1896 and 13 Jan. 1897; LO 5/6/8 NC Gwelo to CNC 2 Feb. 1897; N 1/1/3 NC Hartley to CNC 9 Nov. 1897.

[150] N 1/1/2 NC Charter to CNC 14 Mar. 1897. The evidence that Mkwati started a shrine north-east of Salisbury is thin, and depends upon the correctness of officials' assumptions that a screened cave was a cult centre, N 1/1/9 NC Salisbury to CNC 19 Aug. 1897.

[151] Beach, 'Kaguvi and Fort Mhondoro', 43–4. This uses the same documents as Ranger, who omits mention of this quarrel

[152] LO 5/4/1 Harding to CNC 3 Dec. 1896 and 19 Jan. 1897; N 1/1/9 NC Salisbury to CNC 22 July and 1 Aug. 1897. This uses the same sources as Ranger.

remained with the main force until 29 April, when it set out for Salisbury. Armstrong's party of 13 then started back to contact the telegraph party near Mount Darwin, and accompanied the Budya war-party who had been paid off and were on their way home. Because the Budya had briefly risen in June the previous year Armstrong was in a highly nervous state, and in his melodramatic account he repeated the details of a *mhondoro*-inspired plot to kill him that he claimed he had overheard. But the Budya did not show any hostility whatsoever, but went on into their territory when asked to do so by Armstrong, leaving him to run for Umtali; if he nearly starved to death in the process, it was his own fault for ignoring supply points nearer at hand. When the next patrol came into the area its reception was perfectly friendly. Armstrong's reports had always been rather excited, and it seems that he had simply panicked.[153]

The central Shona lost their war in 1896–7 for three main reasons. In the first place, the extent of the rising was checked by a number of dynasties that collaborated with the Europeans. Their motives varied: we have already noted that the Gutu, Chirimuhanzu, Zimuto, Chivi and Matibi dynasties in the south collaborated early, in order to avoid the consequences of an Ndebele victory. The western rulers of the Njanja confederacy also collaborated, thus preventing the three resisting rulers Sango, Maromo and Mutekedza from spreading the rising farther east, but it was characteristic of the Njanja at that stage of their political fragmentation that they did so for different reasons. Gunguwo, for example, had been at war with Maromo in 1892, while his neighbour Maburutse *dziva* apparently had a land dispute with Maromo.[154] The north-western Njanja rulers Ranga and Kwenda, on the other hand, refused to kill the African missionaries living with them when asked to do so by Mutekedza and Svosve, and later came in on the Company side.[155] The Budya, as we have seen, did join in the rising in its initial stage after a period of preliminary resistance, but then they remained neutral and collaborated later. They had feuds with the central Shona going back to 1887. And, in the east, the important Mutasa dynasty remained neutral at first and later collaborated. Not only did the collaborators prevent the rising from spreading farther, but they enabled Umtali and Victoria to be used as staging points for the Company counter-offensive, and supplied food and auxiliary troops.

The second reason for the failure of the rising was a purely military one. Although the Company deliberately played down the role of the Imperial troops that came into the war, they did help shorten it. On the other hand, the pattern of the European victory had already become apparent in the first two months of the rising. By withdrawing from all untenable positions, even abandoning whole

[153] LO 5/4/2 Howard to Grey, 12 and 20 Mar. 1897, Armstrong to CNC 20 Mar. 1897; LO 5/4/3 Armstrong to Grey 29 Apr. 1897, CNC to Grey, 10 May 1897; LO 5/4/4 Armstrong to CNC 26 May 1897; LO 5/4/5 Harding to Moleyns, 21 Sept. 1897; LO 5/4/6 Harding to Moleyns 9 Oct. 1897; N 1/1/6 Armstrong to Taberer 17 July 1898; N 1/1/7 Armstrong to CNC 27 Feb. 1897, 19 and 20 Mar. 1897, 14 and 26 May 1897; N 1/1/9 Armstrong to CNC 20 Mar. 1897. This uses the same sources as Ranger.

[154] A 1/9/1 Brabant to RM Victoria 26 Apr. 1892; URHD Texts 34–5, 38, 41 Ctr; A 1/12/27 evidence of Tshenombi *et al.*, 13 July 1896; URHD Texts 41 Ctr, 68 Bha.

[155] URHD Text 44 Ctr; H. E. Sumner, 'The Kwenda story', *NADA*, ix, 4 (1967), 4; J. White, 'The Mashona rebellion', *Work and Workers in the Mission Field*, April 1897, 151. For reasons why the Njanja would have wanted to preserve their missionaries, see D. N. Beach, 'The initial impact of Christianity upon the Shona: the Protestants and the southern Shona', *Christianity South of the Zambezi*, 1, ed. A. J. Dachs (Gwelo, 1973), 25–40.

14-2

townships when necessary, they were able to concentrate on a few impregnable points. From there, they were able to concentrate their manpower and put more men into the field than any single Shona ruler; they won many of their battles because they outnumbered the Shona. The third reason was economic: the Shona rulers were committed to the defence of their fields, without which Shona society could not continue, but they could not prevent Company columns from removing foodstuffs to feed the towns or, later, calculatedly destroying crops. The war ended in late 1897 not so much because of the fighting but because it was vital for the people to start the 1897–8 summer crop.

At this point a few conclusions can be drawn. It has been shown that the 'night of the long knives' theory did not apply to the central Shona in 1896, though it may very well have been true of the Ndebele. In retrospect, it is surprising that such a view should have ruled unchallenged for so long. The fact was that Shona society at that time was too disunited to mount such a vast operation in the total secrecy required for its success. There were too many rulers who were prepared to collaborate. As Maburutse's son remarked in July 1896, 'The reason he did not report the trouble to the white men was that they did not know it was coming and when it came they ran away.'[156] Not surprisingly, the question of collaboration has remained a sensitive issue among the Shona ever since. For years the Nhowe spat when a Budya passed, and as recently as 1973 a Shona student suggested that 'studies in ethnic origins of these collaborators should be carried out. One should really determine whether they were real Shonas or not. This should be done because the 1896–7 Shona rebellion was a reaction against the white rule by the Shona people. If they are found not to be true or real Shonas, then this may explain the reason why they acted as they did.'[157] Another reason why the 'long knives' theory was impracticable was because there were too many marriages between the Shona and the newcomers. Wives of such men as Short or Billy the Xhosa were loyal to their husbands, and were regarded as a security risk. As the Ndebele at Kaguvi's told Zhanta in June, the wives of the policemen had to be watched.

This brings us to the ideology of the rising. Ranger suggested that the Kaguvi medium had started to build a new society that looked to the future, just as the 'Rozvi empire' plan had looked to the past. He offered the fighters a war medicine that made them invulnerable, received war-loot from many areas and thus 'brought thousands of Shona into membership of a new society, the true believers in the M'Lenga, with their own distinguishing symbols and obligations and their own promises of divine favour. This loyalty to a supra-tribal society and this belief in the millenarian transformation of colonial society helps to account for the fervour of the Shona rising.'[158] In fact, this is reading a lot into the evidence; even allowing for the fact that the Kaguvi medium was not influential over such a wide area as Ranger thought, much of this is commonplace. The medium's name *murenga* meant simply 'rebel, fighter' and was an ideophone of resistance and violence like *chindunduma* rather than an aspect of a high-god trinity, as Ranger tentatively suggested;[159] his promises of immunity from bullets were typical of

[156] A1/12/27, evidence of Marandowri, 13 July 1896.

[157] Edwards, 'Wanoe', 24; W. Mangwende, 'To understand the Shona rebellion one has to understand the Shona past', URHD Honours Paper (1973), 6. As a footnote, I might add that as a result of my 1969 paper on collaborators circulating among scholars at St Augustine's Penhalonga, a boy named Chivi has apparently been victimized, by his fellow-pupils. (Private information.)

[158] Ranger, *Revolt*, 214–17, 219, 224–5.   [159] Ranger, *Revolt*, 219.

African warfare at that time, though it was noticeable that the Shona did not rely upon them but continued to make good use of cover, and it was hardly surprising that he should have been offered loot and women – though sometimes he took them anyway. In the end, the Kaguvi medium himself showed that he saw the rising more in terms of a traditional war, in which the loser could pay compensation: '*I have heard what these women say but it is not true. I only want a place where I can live. If the government want me to pay for these things I will pay with a young girl.* I want Nyanda, Goronga and Wamponga brought in, they started the rebellion.'[160] In short, the ideology of the Shona rising seems to have been strictly traditionalist, and it is difficult to see more than a desire to return to the pre-colonial situation as it was: 'They were sick of having the white men in their country and wanted to drive them back to the Diamond Fields, they said.'[161]

To conclude, this article shows how the 1896 Shona *chimurenga* was not organized, rather than the way in which it was. After the breakdown of the Rangerian model of a tightly knit Ndebele–Shona religious high command organizing a pre-planned, simultaneous rising, there is no space to show how in fact the rising was organized at the local level, but the example of the Mashaya-mombe dynasty mentioned here gives some idea of what will be involved in future articles on the subject: a portrait of a complex set of personality and interest-groups in each area reacting with remarkable swiftness and decision to the events and opportunities and pressures of the 1890s, but doing so according to their conception of their own territory as an independent, undefeated entity, rather than as part of a larger organization that solved 'the problem of scale'. In short, the history of the 1896 central Shona *chimurenga* promises to be the history of many local *zvimurenga* with their similarities, differences and con-nexions – or lack of them.[162]

SUMMARY

There was a basic similarity between the way in which Rhodesian colonial historians looked at the central Shona *chimurenga* (rising) of 1896 and T. O. Ranger's seminal *Revolt in Southern Rhodesia 1896–7*: both thought in terms of a pre-planned conspiracy led by religious authorities and a simultaneous outbreak on a given signal. Ranger's recon-struction of the organization of the *chimurenga*, however, depended partly upon the misreading and misquotation of the sources. In fact, the rising was neither pre-planned nor simultaneous. In the second quarter of 1896 limited resistance to European rule was being carried on in separate, unconnected outbreaks and some communities were thinking of starting a full-scale *hondo* (war); the threat of famine caused by locusts led certain central Shona leaders to contact the religious leader Mkwati in the Ndebele area, then in revolt against the Europeans, in search of locust medicine. News of European defeats

[160] S. 401, 253, Reg. vs. Kargubi *et al.*, 8 Mar. 1898, evidence of Kargubi. Italicized words omitted in Ranger, *Revolt*, 212, where the statement is taken as a serious comment on the religious organization of the rising. It looks a lot more like an attempt to transfer the blame; of all the prisoners tried, those in the Kaguvi medium's group were possibly the most unstoic.
[161] LO5/4/4, Van Niekerk to CSO 8 June 1897.
[162] Ranger's *Revolt* picture of 1896 was so attractive to Zimbabwean nationalists in the 1960s (Cobbing, 'Absent priesthood', 61, 82–4) that for a long time it was looked upon as the last word, rather than the first, on the *chimurenga*. Later, it began to encounter criticism: in Maputo in 1977 resistance studies stressing the roles of rulers and spirit mediums were considered as 'élitist' (Ranger, 'The people in African resistance', 140) while M. Tsomondo presaged some of the points made here in 'Shona reaction and resistance to the European colonization of Zimbabwe, 1890–8, a case against colonial and revisionist historiography', *J. S. Afr. Affairs*, II, 1 (1977), 11–32.

transmitted by these contacts led to a full *hondo* in the Umfuli valley, which triggered a 'ripple effect' in which Shona communities resisted or collaborated as the news reached them. The element of religious leadership was limited and the element of central pre-planning non-existent. This makes the success and commitment of the local Shona communities all the more impressive, even though it was a traditionalist rather than a proto-nationalist rising.

This article was republished in a slightly revised form in D.N. Beach, *War and Politics in Zimbabwe 1840-1900*, (Mambo, Gweru, 1986), pp. 119-56 and the author published a review article on *Revolt in Southern Rhodesia 1896-7* in the *International Journal of African Historical Studies*, xiii, 1, 1980.

Journal of African History, 31, (1990), pp. 217-244
Printed in Great Britain

REVOLUTIONARY MAHDISM AND RESISTANCE TO COLONIAL RULE IN THE SOKOTO CALIPHATE, 1905-6[1]

BY PAUL E. LOVEJOY

York University, Ontario

AND J. S. HOGENDORN

Colby College, Maine

A WAVE of revolutionary Mahdism swept through the western emirates of the Sokoto Caliphate during the years of the colonial conquest (1897–1903).[2] It culminated in an insurrection that began at Kobkitanda in French Niger late in the year 1905 and spread to Satiru, about 220 kilometres away in British Northern Nigeria, early in 1906. The revolutionary Mahdists sought the overthrow of all established authority, including the colonial regimes and local officials who collaborated with the Europeans.

The uprising of 1905–6 revealed strong divisions on the basis of class, an insight first made by A. S. Mohammad in his study of Satiru.[3] This movement received virtually no support from the Fulbe aristocracy of the Caliphate. Instead it attracted radical clerics, disgruntled peasants and fugitive slaves. The absence of aristocratic involvement distinguishes revolutionary Mahdism from all other forms of contemporary Mahdism.

Mahdism has usually challenged established authority, and consequently its revolutionary potential in the context of the colonial conquest has been widely recognized. A suggestive study by Thomas Hodgkin first compared Mahdism, messianism and Marxism as expressions of anti-colonialism.[4] Hodgkin contended that Mahdism was one type of revolutionary ideology, but he did not distinguish among the various strands of Mahdism. He did accurately note, however, that Mahdism could be revolutionary to the degree that it provided a universal ideology that transcended kinship, locality, ethnicity and pre-colonial state structures. Mahdism could appeal to Islamic

[1] This study is part of a larger project on the economic and social impact of the colonial conquest on the Sokoto Caliphate. We wish to thank Abubakar Sokoto Mohammed, Kimba Idrissa, Andrew Roberts and David Robinson for their comments, and A. H. M. Kirk-Greene and Colin Newbury for their advice and encouragement. The research was funded by grants from the Social Science and Humanities Research Council of Canada (for Lovejoy) and the Guggenheim Foundation (for Hogendorn). The authors also wish to thank York University and Colby College for their generous support.

[2] For details of the conquest, see D. J. M. Muffett, *Concerning Brave Captains. A History of Lord Lugard's Conquest of Hausaland* (London, 1964); Richard H. Dusgate, *The Conquest of Northern Nigeria* (London, 1985); Kimba Idrissa, 'La formation de la colonie du Niger, 1880–1922: des mythes à la politique du "mal nécessaire"' (thèse pour le doctorat d'état, Université de Paris, VII, 1987).

[3] Abubakar Sokoto Mohammad, 'A social interpretation of the Satiru Revolt of c. 1894–1906' (M.Sc. thesis, Ahmadu Bello University, 1983), 164, 172–3. Also see Kimba Idrissa, *Guerres et Sociétés. Les populations du Niger occidental au XIXe siècle et leurs réactions face à la colonisation (1896–1906)* (Niamey, 1981), 171–2.

[4] Thomas Hodgkin, 'Mahdism, messianism and Marxism in the African setting', in Yusuf Fadl Hasan, ed., *Sudan in Africa* (Khartoum, 1971), 109–27.

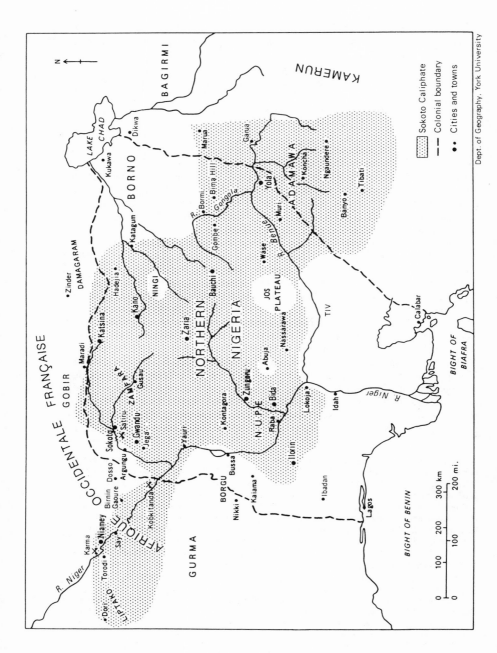

Fig. 1. Sokoto Caliphate: French, British and German spheres (1906).

tradition to justify the transformation of society, and it could provide a structure of ideas and institutions that drew the masses into a more active political role. We advance a new interpretation here because the evidence of class divisions among Mahdists shows that it is confusing, indeed inaccurate, to refer to Mahdism in and of itself as 'revolutionary'.[5]

Mahdism has not always been revolutionary. Adherents have advocated a range of political positions from (1) tolerance of established authority, despite a belief that the Mahdi would eventually appear, through (2) severe criticism of existing Islamic regimes which was often expressed through emigration (*hijra*) in expectation of meeting the Mahdi, to (3) the replacement of incumbent Muslim officials by Mahdist critics, often through violent means, and finally to (4) revolutionary action with the intention of destroying the Muslim state and the class structure on which it was based.[6]

All these forms of Mahdism were in evidence in the years immediately before and after the conquest of the Sokoto Caliphate. Our purpose is to identify carefully 'revolutionary Mahdism' within the larger context of the colonial conquest and to show how the 'revolutionary' character of the uprising of 1905–6 differed from other forms of Mahdism.[7]

The uprising of 1905–6 was a turning point in the consolidation of colonial rule in Niger and Northern Nigeria. Until then, the French and British

[5] For example, Muhammad A. Al-Hajj labelled Hayatu b. Sa'id a 'revolutionary Mahdist', but without explanation; see 'Hayatu b. Sa'id: a revolutionary Mahdist in the Western Sudan', in Hasan, ed., *Sudan in Africa*, 128–41.

[6] Asmau G. Saeed has recognized three groups of anti-colonial Mahdists in the Caliphate: first, the local followers of Mahdi Muhammad Ahmad of the Nilotic Sudan; second, 'revisionist Mahdists' who awaited the coming of the Mahdi but did not emigrate or emigrated only reluctantly; and third, 'spontaneous Mahdists' who followed self-styled Mahdis. Saeed has made an important contribution in recognizing distinctions among Mahdists. This article clarifies her category of 'spontaneous Mahdists'. See Asmau Saeed, 'British fears over Mahdism in Northern Nigeria: a look at Bormi 1903, Satiru 1906 and Dumbulwa 1923', unpublished paper presented at the School of Oriental and African Studies, London, 1986; and 'The British policy towards the Mahdiyya in Northern Nigeria: a study of the arrest, detention and deportation of Shaykh Said b. Hayat, 1923–1959', *Kano Studies*, II, 3 (1982–5), 95–119.

[7] Our reconstruction is based on a re-examination of available archival materials in Nigeria, Niger, France and Great Britain, including previously unused files in the Shillingford Papers, Mss. Afr. s.547, Rhodes House, Oxford. It is worth noting that the file on Satiru in the Shillingford Papers contains a large collection of official reports and telegrams on the uprising, many otherwise unavailable and previously unused by scholars to the best of our knowledge. A. A. Shillingford held an education portfolio, and the presence of this file in his papers, presumably a transfer made at some point from other files at headquarters, is unusual. We have attempted to balance the colonial materials, with their inevitable biases, through a reading of contemporary Hausa documents on Satiru and through a critical assessment of the scholarly literature, some of which is based on oral sources. Finally, Lovejoy, accompanied by Kimba Idrissa, conducted interviews at Kobkitanda and Karma in October 1988. These interviews confirmed and supplemented Idrissa's earlier work. Lovejoy wishes to thank Idrissa for his collaboration, without which the interviews could not have been undertaken.

[8] R. A. Adeleye, 'Mahdist triumph and British revenge in Northern Nigeria: Satiru 1906', *J. Hist. Soc. Nigeria*, VI (1972), 193–214; A. H. M. Kirk-Greene, 'Crisis and choice in the Nigerian Emirates: the decisive decade, 1897–1906', forthcoming; and Dusgate, *Conquest*, 242–9. Also see T. Büttner, 'Social aims and earlier anti-colonial struggles: the Satiru rising of 1906', in T. Büttner and G. Brehme, eds., *African Studies* (Berlin, 1973), 1–18; Muhammad Al-Hajj, 'The Mahdist tradition in Northern Nigeria'

presence was fragile. As many scholars have shown, the British were successful in obtaining the collaboration of the Sokoto aristocracy in defeating the rebels at Satiru,[8] while the French secured similar aristocratic support in overcoming the Mahdists at Kobkitanda and Karma.[9] Most scholars agree that the suppression of the revolt re-enforced the alliance between the colonial authorities and the Muslim aristocracy. Kimba Idrissa and A. S. Mohammed have recognized that the revolt crossed the colonial frontier between Niger and Northern Nigeria, but most scholars only mention this fact in passing. J.-P. Rothiot even disputes Idrissa's claim of a coordinated uprising within Niger.[10] It is our contention that the pan-colonial dimension of the 1905-6 uprising provides essential evidence for establishing the revolutionary significance of this movement.

THE 1905-6 UPRISING

The revolt was supposed to begin on the Id al-Kabir, which fell on 5 February 1906, but in fact it began on 8 December 1905 at Kobkitanda, 150 kilometres south of Niamey in French Niger, when local villagers killed two gardes-cercles from Dosso. The leader of the revolt was a blind Zarma cleric, Saybu dan Makafo. The attempt to arrest Saybu and his supporters spread the revolt through much of the region between Dallol Mawri and Dallol Bosso.[11]

The first sizeable action in the French zone occurred at Kobkitanda on 4 January 1906. The Mahdists lost an estimated 30 men, the French 12, including one French officer. Saybu's followers retreated to Sambera, 15 kilometres to the south. In subsequent battles, another twenty Mahdists

---

(Ph.D. thesis, Ahmadu Bello University, 1973), 194-9; Idrissa, *Guerres et Sociétés*, 171-5; Peter Kazenga Tibenderana, 'The administration of Sokoto, Gwandu and Argungu Emirates under British rule, 1900-1946' (Ph.D. thesis, University of Ibadan, 1974), 164-72; Modibbo Tukur, 'The imposition of British colonial domination on the Sokoto Caliphate, Borno and neighbouring states' (Ph.D. thesis, Ahmadu Bello University, 1979), 283-330.

[9] Idrissa, *Guerres et Sociétés*, 151-68; Y. Rash, 'Un établissement colonial sans histoire, les premières années françaises au Niger' (thèse de 3e cycle, Université de Paris I, 1972); also see A. Le Grip, 'Le Mahdisme en Afrique Noire', *L'Afrique et l'Asie*, XVIII (1952), 3-16.

[10] Jean-Paul Rothiot, *L'ascension d'un chef Africain au début de la colonisation : Aouta le conquérant (Dosso-Niger)* (Paris, 1988), 167-72.

[11] Rapport politique du Commandant de Région de Niamey, Dec. 1905, Archives Nationales du Niger, Niamey (hereafter ANN) 15.2.6; Rapport politique mensuel, Région de Niamey, Jan. 1906, ANN 15.2.7; Ponty, Rapport no. 132, Kayes, 26 Mar. 1906, Service de Microfilm, Paris (hereafter SMP) microfilm 11G4; Mission Robert Arnaud, Rapport sur les mobiles islamiques des troubles de janvier à mars 1906 dans le territoire militaire, Kandy, 22 Nov. 1906, SMP microfilm 11G4; Lofler, Rapport sur le tournée de police executée dans la région troublée de Kobkitanda (28 Dec. 1905-15 Jan. 1906), 10 Feb. 1906, SMP microfilm 1D200. Also see Idrissa, *Guerres et Sociétés*, 150-1.

[12] Idrissa, *Guerres et Sociétés*, 148, 152-3; Rapport politique du Commandant de Région de Niamey, Dec. 1905, ANN 15.2.6; Rapport politique mensuel, Région de Niamey, Jan. 1906 ANN 15.2.7; Rapport politique mensuel, Région de Niamey, Feb. 1906, ANN 15.2.7; Rapport politique, Mar. 1906, Cercle du Djerma, ANN 15.2.9; Rapport politique et administratif, Région de Niamey, second trimestre, 1906, ANN 15.2.8; Bouverot, Rapport au sujet du rattachement des villages de Sambira et Koba Kitanda, Dosso, 5 Nov. 1907, ANN 5.2.3; Boutig, Monographie du Cercle du Djerma, 15 Nov. 1909, ANN 15.1.2.

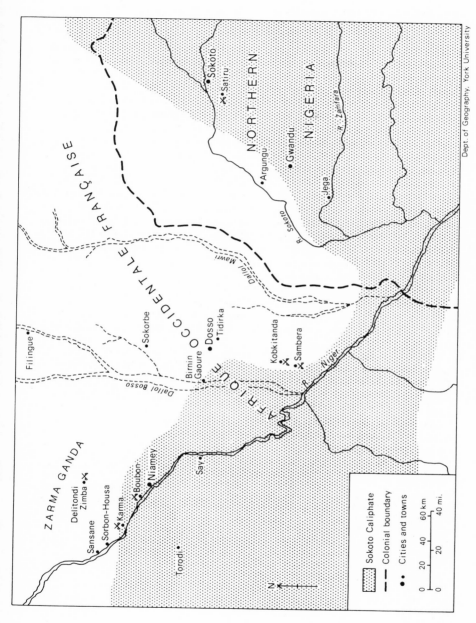

Fig. 2. The Mahdist revolt, 1905–6.

Dept. of Geography, York University

died. Saybu and many of the survivors then fled east across the nearby colonial boundary and made their way to Satiru, which they reached sometime after mid-January.[12]

A second centre of revolt erupted at Karma, a Songhay town and sub-emirate of Say that was located on the Niger north of Niamey. Emir Umaru, a loyal supporter of Saybu Dan Makafo, had resisted the imposition of French colonialism in 1904, only to suffer the inevitable subjugation. In December 1905, Saybu sent an emissary to inform Umaru of the skirmish with the *gardes-cercle*. Umaru decided to join the Mahdists in an attempt to reverse the defeat of 1904; he was the only accredited ruler within the Caliphate who would do so.[13]

The revolt extended along the left bank of the Niger 400 kilometres from Sorbo Haoussa in the north to the border with Nigeria in the south. Boubon, a mere ten kilometres from Niamey, was lost. The revolt spread westward across the river to Say, Torodi and Tera and northward among the Tuareg. The French posts at Sandire and Filingue had to be abandoned, and troops from Dori had to fight their way to Niamey. On 17 January the French attacked Boubon, which was taken despite two vigorous Mahdist counter-attacks. Karma, 25 kilometres from Niamey, was taken the next day, and Umaru retreated 65 kilometres north-eastward to Delitondi Zimba, in the semi-desert region of Zarma Ganda.

Elsewhere conditions were volatile. In some cases there was open rebellion; in others there was danger that there would be. Trouble spread southward to Bariba and Dendi country and westward to Fadan Gurma. French reports also suspected that the emirates of Say and Birnin Gaoure would rise, but in fact they did not. While some Tuareg joined Umaru, many others waited to see what would happen.[14]

The end of the revolt in French territory came quickly in early March. A combined force of French troops and cavalry from Dosso, Filingue and other places loyal to the French attacked Umaru at Delitondi Zimba on 3 March.[15] The battle lasted all day, but in the end the revolt was crushed. The next two days were spent destroying villages that had supported the revolt. Umaru and many of his troops were killed, and the survivors were taken to Niamey.[16] Thereafter the French re-established an uneasy presence through-out the rebellious zone.

Across the frontier in British territory, the centre of resistance was Satiru, where Saybu Dan Makafo found refuge late in January. Satiru's location southwest of Sokoto in the direction of Gwandu placed it between the twin capitals of the Caliphate, a position dangerously close to the centres of

[13] Interview, Amirou Tinni Nouhou, chef de canton de Karma, 1 Oct. 1988. Also see Rapport politique mensuel, Région de Niamey, Jan.–Mar. 1906, ANN 15.2.7; and Idrissa, *Guerres et Sociétés*, 155–70.

[14] Idrissa, *Guerres et Sociétés*, 156, 176–7.

[15] His forces reportedly suffered 30 killed and five wounded.

[16] Ponty, Rapport no. 132, Kayes, 26 Mar. 1906; Bouchez, Rapport sur le detachment de marche sur les operations dans le Djermaganda, Niamey, 13 Mar. 1906, SMP microfilm 1D200; Idrissa, *Guerres et Sociétés*, 167–9.

[17] Mohammad ('Social interpretation') has estimated that the population of the town was 10,000. We believe this estimate to be exaggerated, although the influx of supporters certainly swelled the ranks; see H. S. Goldsmith, Annual Report, Sokoto Province 1906, SNP 7 2001/1907, Nigerian National Archives, Kaduna (hereafter NNAK).

political power.[17] The revolt in French territory had engulfed the whole region surrounding French headquarters at Niamey; now the revolt in the British zone threatened the capitals of the Caliphate itself, with a potential to undermine British authority elsewhere.[18]

The revolt at Satiru was also scheduled to begin on the Id al-Kabir, 5 February, but it was postponed, apparently because of a dispute in the Mahdist community.[19] The dispute centred on the necessity of a revolt and the recognition of Isa, the village head of Satiru, as a messianic leader who would accompany the Mahdi.[20] The Satiru Mahdists (Satirawa) decided the issue on 13 February, eight days after the Id, when they attacked the neighbouring village of Tsomau. A number of people were killed.[21]

On the next day, 14 February, a unit of the West African Frontier Force (WAFF), Company C of Mounted Infantry under Acting Resident H. R. Preston-Hillary, moved quickly to deal with this rural unrest. The reasons for the violence were not known to Hillary and were clearly misinterpreted. The British were apparently unaware of the rising in French territory. Though Hillary was not exactly walking into a trap, his misjudgement of the situation was monumental. The Mahdists attacked the WAFF column; Hillary and his escort were killed, and in the ensuing battle the WAFF suffered heavy losses and was forced to retreat in disarray.[22] In the words of

[18] Lt.Gov. Ponty's comments (Extract of report of W. Ponty, Lt.-Gov. Haut-Sénégal-Niger, p. 348, enclosed in C. F. Cromie, British Consul-General, Dakar, to Sir Edward Grey, 18 Sept. 1906, no. 34903, CO 446/57) on the apparent disunity of the Mahdists are perhaps ironic, considering the extent to which resistance crossed colonial boundaries, and the failure of the British and French to co-operate in crushing the 1905–6 uprising: 'Fortunately for us these events have once again proved that when left to themselves the natives are incapable of the combination and union necessary to carry out a preconceived plan. Otherwise the situation might have been very serious'.

[19] Malam Isa and Saybu Dan Makafo had sent letters to Caliphate officials calling on them to join the revolt. Malam, son of the emir of Gwandu, was reported to have enquired whether or not a revolt had begun the day before the Id al-Kabir festival and was told by one of his followers that the revolt would begin the next day. British reports later credited the delay to strategy; Resident Burdon was scheduled to go on leave, and the Satirawa are said to have been waiting for his departure. See Burdon to Lugard, 5 Mar. and 15 Mar. 1906, Shillingford Papers.

[20] The people of neighbouring Tsomau failed to appear at Satiru for the Id al-Kabir, which was interpreted as lack of support for the revolt. In previous years the Tsomau Mahdists had attended the Id ceremonies. The village head of Tsomau, Yahaya had been a student of Maikafo, Isa's father, and Isa and Yahaya were related by marriage. Yahaya refused to recognize Isa's leadership and particularly his claim to be the successor to the Mahdi, as in Mahdist tradition. H. A. F. Johnston's compilation of Satiru traditions ('Dan Makafo and the Satiru rising', in Johnston, ed., *A Selection of Hausa Stories* (Oxford, 1966), 164) quotes Yahaya as saying: 'How can we believe that you are the Prophet Jesus [Isa]...when we have known you ever since we were all children?' The importance of the Isa tradition is examined later in the article.

[21] Malam Yahaya, twelve other townsmen, and one woman were killed. Burdon to Lugard, 15 Mar. 1906.

[22] Total deaths included three white officers and 27 African soldiers and carriers; see Goldsmith, Sokoto Province Annual Report, 1906. Lugard to Onslow, 28 Feb. 1906, Shillingford Papers, says three white officers and 25 African soldiers. Four of the wounded were able to make their escape. For a contemporary account of the reasons behind the British fiasco, see Charles Orr, *The Making of Northern Nigeria* (London, 1911), 173–4. Also see Dusgate, *Conquest*, 242–9; Adeleye, 'Mahdist triumph', 200–14; Mohammad, 'Social interpretation'.

High Commissioner Frederick Lugard, this defeat was the 'first serious
reverse suffered by the West African Frontier Force since it was raised [in
1898]'.[23]

The Satiru Mahdists also suffered heavy losses in the initial encounter:
30–40 were dead and wounded. Their leader, Malam Isa, was severely
wounded.[24] According to later reports, Isa had planned to announce a *jihād*
at the Friday prayer, 16 February, two days after the defeat of Hillary's
expedition, and raise a green flag. Isa's wound proved mortal, and he died on
the day he was supposed to unfurl the standard of revolt. But the revolt was
now firmly established in British territory, despite the death of one of its
leaders.[25]

The British feared that a tremendous upheaval would ensue from this
'Sokoto Rising', as the London *Times* headlined it.[26] The regime was thinly
spread over Northern Nigeria, and a major detachment of the WAFF was far
to the southeast, engaged in a protracted campaign to subdue the Tiv. The
situation appeared grave.

The Satiru Mahdists quickly regrouped, and in the aftermath of their
initial victory they wreaked havoc on neighbouring towns and villages.
Danchadi was burned on 6 March and Dange on 8 March 1906. Resident
Alder Burdon reported that 'all the thickly populated country between these
two was devastated'.[27] The Satirawa attempted to intimidate reluctant
Mahdist sympathizers into joining the revolt, and they specifically attacked
slave plantations, apparently to liberate slaves.[28] What worried the British
were expressions of support for the uprising. Officials reported signs of
disaffection in Katsina and Zamfara. The loyalty of the emir of Gwandu was
in doubt, and there were rumblings even in Sokoto town itself.[29]

Despite the gravity of the situation, the Sokoto aristocracy proved loyal to
the British. Marafa Maiturare of Gwadabawa, the Sokoto official in charge

[23] Lugard to Onslow, 21 Feb. 1906, in Northern Nigeria, Correspondence Relating to
Sokoto, Hadejia and the Munshi Country, 1907, Parliamentary Papers [Cd. 3620]. In fact
it proved to be the only serious reverse.

[24] Burdon to Lugard, 21 Feb. 1906.

[25] Burdon to Lugard, 26 May 1906, Shillingford Papers. Also see Frederick D.
Lugard, Annual Report, Northern Nigeria, 1905–6, 371.

[26] *Times* (London), 21, 22, 23, 26 Feb., 6 Mar. 1906.

[27] Burdon to Lugard, telegram, 11 Mar. 1906, Shillingford Papers.

[28] Among the places burned between 16 February and early March were Runjin
Kwarai, Runjin Gawo, Rudu Makera, Jaredi, Dandin Mahe, Zangalawa, Bunazawa,
Hausawan Maiwa, and Kindiru. The towns of Shuni, Bodinga and Sifawa were
evacuated. See A. S. Mohammed, 'The songs and poems of the Satiru revolt, c.
1894–1906', unpublished seminar paper, Department of Sociology, Ahmadu Bello
University, 1985. *Runji* (*rinji*) signifies plantation. Many of the other settlements appear
to have been slave estates, too. For a discussion of the terminology of Caliphate slave
estates, see Paul E. Lovejoy, 'The characteristics of plantations in the Sokoto Caliphate
(Islamic West Africa)', *Amer. Hist. Rev.*, LXXXIV (1979), 1267–92.

[29] Burdon to Lugard, telegram, 28 Feb. 1906; Lugard to Secretary of State, 9 May
1906, Shillingford Papers. As one Sokoto cleric wrote at the time, 'We have been
conquered. We have been asked to pay poll tax and *jangali* [cattle tax]. We have been made
to do various things, and now they want us to fight their wars for them. Let them go and
fight themselves'. Malam Bako to Malam Jafaru of Argungu, Feb. 1906; manuscript in
the Nigerian National Archives, Kaduna and quoted here as cited in Al-Hajj, 'Mahdist
tradition', 199. The capital districts of Sokoto and Gwandu had not been subject either
to *jizya* (poll tax) or *jangali* before the conquest, and their imposition under colonialism
was clearly a major grievance.

of the Sarkin Musulmi's levies, who later became Sarkin Musulmi himself (1915–24), marched on Satiru with a force of 3,000 horse and infantry on the morning of 17 February. But the Marafa's troops refused to attack and retreated in disarray.[30] It became necessary to await reinforcements who soon arrived from other parts of Northern Nigeria. On 10 March, a combined force of WAFF troops and Sokoto levies approached Satiru.[31] Although the rebels had dug trenches, they did not stay behind them. Nor did they use the Maxim gun and rifles that had been captured in the first encounter.[32] Instead, the Satirawa repeatedly charged the WAFF square, even though they already were aware of what modern weapons could do. Destructive volleys from the square, together with the rapid fire of the Maxims, struck down hundreds of rebels. Attack gave way to flight, and slaughter followed as charging Sokoto cavalry hacked to death many of the defeated survivors. The outcome was difficult to justify even from an imperialist perspective. At least 2,000 Satirawa were killed. An estimated 3,000 women and children were herded to Sokoto, many into servitude.[33]

Defying the odds, blind Saybu Dan Makafo survived the slaughter, although he had been wounded in the final attack. He was captured by the local levies from Dange, whose *sarki* took him to Sokoto. Even then the authorities were apprehensive.[34] Dan Makafo's boy guide supposedly shouted out at the trial, when Dan Makafo asked for water, 'Don't let him have it or he'll vanish into thin air and then I shall be the only one left for you to execute'.[35] The report, accurate or not, captures the tension surrounding the trial.

[30] Burdon to Lugard, 21 Feb. 1906.

[31] Goldsmith, Sokoto Province Annual Report, 1906.

[32] It was not for lack of ammunition; also captured were two cases of machine gun bullets in belts, and the rifle cartridges found on the slain mounted infantrymen. The machine gun and the rifles could conceivably have caused considerable damage if they had been employed. (See Lugard to Onslow, 21 Mar. 1906, and Burdon to Lugard, 22 Mar. 1906.) Ironically, it was lack of water that prevented the captured Maxim from being put into action. Its jacket, through which water circulated to cool the hot gun barrel, had been ruptured during the first battle. Why the rifles were not employed by the Satirawa is unknown. The operation of a breech-loader would no doubt be difficult for people who, so it appears, did not even possess flintlocks. Yet the organization and carrying through of this revolt shows plenty of initiative, arguably more than sufficient to overcome the rather minor technological barrier of loading and firing a rifle. We have come across no evidence to explain this absence of military enterprise among the Satirawa and their commanders. Had the British been met by rifle volleys and supporting fire from a Maxim, which presumably would have worked until it overheated, they would undoubtedly have prevailed anyway given their overwhelming strength, but the effect on public opinion might have been electrifying.

[33] Edwardes Diaries, 17 Mar. 1906, Rhodes House, Mss. Afr. r.106; Lugard to CO, 19 Jul. 1906 [Cd. 3620]; Goldsmith, Sokoto Province Annual Report, 1906.

[34] According to Tukur, 'Colonial domination', 478–9, the *alkali* was al-Mustafa Modibbo. According to oral testimony reported by Tukur, Burdon instructed the *alkali* to issue a death sentence for the killing of the British personnel. The *alkali* is reported to have objected on the grounds that the dead were not Muslims, so that it was not possible to impose a death sentence. The issue was resolved because Muslims had also been killed by the Satirawa; consequently al-Mustafa is said to have guaranteed to Burdon that a death sentence would follow.

[35] See Johnston, 'Dan Makafo and the Satiru rising', 166. Johnston compiled this story from a number of sources. The portion about the trial is attributed to Malam Nagwamatse, whose father was present.

The public executioner decapitated the hero of Satiru and Kobkitanda on 22 March. His head was mounted on a stake in the market to serve as a dire warning to would-be Mahdists and revolutionaries. Four subordinates suffered a similar fate. The Sokoto citizenry dutifully participated in the public humiliation of the Mahdists. As Burdon telegraphed to Lugard:

All Sokoto went out yesterday [11 March] to inspect battlefield and raze Satiru to ground. No wall or tree left standing. Sarikin Muslim [Musulmi] has pronounced curse on anyone building or farming on site.[36]

Thus ended the Mahdist rebellion. Today the deserted site of Satiru is on the edge of a forest reserve. It has not been inhabited since its destruction and the official curse.[37] Kobkitanda remains a remote and tiny village, far from any motorable road. Karma has fared better because of its proximity to the main highway along the Niger, but it too is far from thriving.

MAHDISM IN THE SOKOTO CALIPHATE

The religious overtones of the 1905–6 uprising drew upon a common tradition of Mahdism that was current in the Sokoto Caliphate, and indeed in many other parts of Muslim Africa in the nineteenth and early twentieth centuries. Mahdists predicted the arrival of a messianic figure, 'the rightly-guided one', who would purge the world of unbelief. As Muhammad Al-Hajj and other scholars have demonstrated, the thirteenth century of the Muslim era, which ended in 1883, was a period of particularly high Mahdist expectations.[38]

Thousands of Mahdists demonstrated their discontent with the Caliphate through emigration (hijra) towards the east, the direction from which the Mahdi was supposed to appear. Many Mahdists expected the Mahdi to appear on a mountain, which was sometimes interpreted as Bima Hill in Gombe Emirate, and this may explain why Bormi, a few kilometres up the Gongola River valley from Bima Hill, became a Mahdist settlement.[39] Implicitly hijra meant the rejection of the Caliphate government. Furthermore, the travels of Mahdists had the effect of spreading their unsettling doctrines throughout the western and central Sudan and, indeed, through the regions to the east as far as the Nilotic Sudan.[40]

[36] Burdon to Lugard, 22 Mar. 1906.

[37] Evidence that the curse is still being taken seriously can also be found in the recent paper by Habib Alhassan, 'Rashin Jituwa Tsakanin Malaman Satiru da Turawan Mulkin Mallaka (1906)', paper presented at Usmanu Danfodiyo University, Sokoto, June, 1988. We wish to thank Ibrahim Jumare for drawing our attention to this paper, which reiterates the official Sokoto version of the revolt.

[38] Al-Hajj, 'Mahdist tradition', and Al-Hajj, 'The thirteenth century in Muslim eschatology: mahdist expectations in the Sokoto Caliphate', Research Bulletin, Centre of Arabic Documentation, Ibadan, III, 2 (1967), 100–13.

[39] Al-Hajj, 'Mahdist tradition', 169–70.

[40] R. A. Adeleye, Power and Diplomacy in Northern Nigeria, 1804–1906 (New York, 1971), 321–7; Adeleye, 'Mahdist triumph', 193–9; Saburi Biobaku and Muhammad Al-Hajj, 'The Sudanese Mahdiyya and the Niger–Chad region', in I. M. Lewis, ed., Islam in Tropical Africa (Oxford, 1966), 425–39; Al-Naqar, Pilgrimage Tradition in West Africa (Khartoum, 1972); Murray Last, 'Administration and discontent in Northern Nigeria', Africa, XL (1970), 351–2; Mark R. Duffield, 'Hausa and Fulani settlement and the development of capitalism in Sudan: with special reference to Maiurno, Blue Nile Province' (Ph.D. thesis, University of Birmingham, 1978), 9–32.

The culmination of much of this Mahdist activity was the creation of a Mahdist state in the Nilotic Sudan in the 1880s. At that time, Muhammad Ahmad declared himself Mahdi and gathered sufficient support to oust the Egyptian colonial regime, together with its European allies, from the Sudan.[41] Mahdism emerged on the world stage as an anti-colonial movement, capturing the attention of Europe after the dramatic death of General 'Chinese' Gordon at Khartoum in 1884.

This Mahdist movement reverberated westward to the Sokoto Caliphate. Muhammad Ahmad and his officials established formal links with representatives in the Caliphate and thereby reinforced Mahdist sympathies there. Those Mahdists who pledged their loyalty to Muhammad Ahmad became identified as his *ansar* (followers). He received considerable support in the Caliphate and on the eastern frontier of the Caliphate, as the careers of Rabih b. Fadallah, Hayatu b. Sa'id and Jibril Gaini demonstrate.[42]

The Mahdist uprising of 1905–6 had no direct connection with this Nilotic tradition. Because many of the *ansar* had emigrated eastward, the supporters of Muhammad Ahmad became concentrated in the eastern portions of the Caliphate and beyond. They were especially numerous in northern Adamawa and Gombe emirates. In this article, we deal with other Mahdists who were located in the central and western portions of the Caliphate.

These other Mahdists, who did not recognize the legitimacy of Muhammad Ahmad, included many clerics, aristocrats and common people, not just those who became associated with the revolutionary cause. The colonial conquest after 1897 heightened the expectations of all these Mahdists, and numerous messengers appeared to announce the imminent arrival of the Mahdi. Sometimes colonial officials, who failed to appreciate the finer distinctions of Mahdist eschatology, thought that these messengers were claiming to be the Mahdi, when in fact they were only heralding his arrival.

One important leader in this new phase of Mahdist activism was Sarkin Musulmi Attahiru I.[43] The British occupation of Kano and Sokoto in 1903

[41] The discussion that follows is based on Biobaku and Al-Hajj, 'Sudanese Mahdiyya'; Al-Hajj, 'Mahdist tradition'; Umar Al-Naqar, *The Pilgrimage Tradition*; Duffield, 'Hausa and Fulani settlement' and Martin Z. Njeuma, 'Adamawa and Mahdism: the career of Hayatu ibn Said in Adamawa, 1878–1898', *J. Afr. Hist.* XII, 1 (1971), 63–4. The classic study of the Mahdist state is P. M. Holt, *The Mahdist state in the Sudan* (Oxford, 1958).

[42] R. A. Adeleye, 'Rabih b. Fadlallah and the diplomacy of European imperial invasion in the Central Sudan, 1893–1902', *J. Hist. Soc. Nigeria*, V, 3 (1970), 399–418, and Adeleye, 'Rabih Fadlallah 1879–1893: exploits and impact on political relations in Central Sudan', *J. Hist. Soc. Nigeria*, V, 2 (1970), 223–42; W. K. R. Hallam, *The Life and Times of Rabih Fadl Allah* (Ilfracombe, Devon, 1977); Njeuma, 'Adamawa and Mahdism'; Al-Hajj, 'Hayatu b. Sa'id', 128–41; and J. E. Lavers, 'Jibril Gaini: a preliminary account of the career of a Mahdist leader in North-Eastern Nigeria', *Research Bulletin, Centre of Arabic Documentation*, Ibadan, III, 1 (1967), 16–38. The continuation of this tradition of Mahdism under colonial rule in Northern Nigeria has been the subject of further research. See C. N. Ubah, 'British measures against Mahdism at Dumbulwa in Northern Nigeria 1923: a case of colonial overreaction', *Islamic Culture*, L, 3 (1976), 169–83; Saeed, 'British policy', 95–110

[43] Even among many other Caliphate officials, such as Emir Zubeiru of Yola, who did not actually join Attahiru I, there were strong sentiments in favour of this brand of anti-colonial Mahdism. See Martin Z. Njeuma, *Fulani Hegemony in Yola (Old Adamawa) 1809–1902* (no place of publication indicated, 1978), 201. Some officials, such as the Emir of Gwandu, who acceded to office after the British conquest, wavered; their sympathies

8-2

convinced Attahiru I, who had become Caliph only the previous year, to emigrate to the east in search of the Mahdi.[44] Many officials and commoners joined his *hijra* as he moved eastward through Zamfara and Kano. As Burdon reported from Sokoto more than a month after the *hijra* began, 'The farmers are still trying to make their way to him [Attahiru I] in the belief that he would lead them to the Mahdi'.[45] In the end tens of thousands of people joined the exodus, according to the best estimates. On 27 July 1903, the British defeated these Mahdists at Bormi, the Mahdist stronghold in Gombe Emirate that had been taken only a year earlier. Attahiru I and many others died on the battlefield. The survivors continued the *hijra* eastward and eventually settled at Mai Wurno in Sudan.

Despite the disaster at Bormi, Mahdist expectations within the aristocracy did not subside. The Emir of Gwandu, installed by the British and hence not committed to Attahiru's emigration, is known to have harboured Mahdist beliefs.[46] Undoubtedly other aristocrats secretly discussed and probably encouraged Mahdist prophesies as well. The heightened expectations of 1906, including the exhortations of the revolutionary Mahdists, arose from a general malaise.[47]

Most of the ruling class accepted colonial rule, however reluctantly.[48] For those who acquiesced, the apologia of Muhammad al-Bukhari, the Waziri of Sokoto (1886–1910), addressed the dilemma of their submission to the Christian incursion. In his *Risālat al-wazīr ilā ahl al-'ilm wa'l-tadabbur*, the Waziri explained that the protection of Muslims depended upon accommodation with the Europeans; emigration would turn the land into one of unbelief. It was the duty of some Muslims to stay in office, despite the

---

were with those who resisted, and they too interpreted their actions, at least in part, in the context of Mahdist beliefs. On the Emir of Gwandu's Mahdist sympathies, see Tukur, 'Colonial domination', 233, 283–95; and Tibenderana, 'Sokoto, Gwandu and Argungu', 162–3, 169–70. Mahdist sympathies were widespread among the aristocracy at the time of the conquest; see the translation of Arabic letters referring to the Mahdi which were written in the last years of the independent Caliphate in H. F. Backwell, ed. and trans., *The Occupation of Hausaland, 1900–1904, Being a Translation of Arabic Letters found in the House of the Wazir of Sokoto, Bohari, in 1903* (Lagos, 1927). The letter of a royal slave of Sarkin Kudu (emir of Yola) Zubeiru to the Sarkin Musulmi, which was written at the time of the British conquest of Yola 'pledges allegiance to you by Allah and the Prophet and after you to the Imam Mahdi' (pp. 67–8). Zubeiru fled Yola upon the British conquest on 2 Sept. 1901 and informed the Sarkin Musulmi that Imam Mahdi commanded his attention (pp. 74–5). Muhammadau Alhaji, brother of the emir of Missau, was also a Mahdist and joined Attahiru I (letter to Sarkin Musulmi, p. 77).

[44] Report of F. Cargill, Resident of Kano, in Frederick D. Lugard, Annual Report, Northern Nigeria, 1903, 177; Al-Hajj, 'Mahdist Tradition', 166–84; R. A. Adeleye, 'The dilemma of the Waziri: the place of the *Risālat al-wazīr ilā ahl al'ilm wa'l-tadabbur* in the history of the Sokoto Caliphate', *J. Hist. Soc. Nigeria*, IV, 2 (1968), 292–4; Adeleye, *Power and Diplomacy*, 283–4, 291; and Tukur, 'British colonial domination', 137–45.

[45] A. Burdon, Report No. 2, Sokoto Province, 30 Apr. 1903, Sokprof 2/1 23/1903, (NNAK).

[46] Tibenderana, 'Sokoto, Gwandu and Argungu', 162–3, 169–70; Tukur, 'British colonial domination', 233, 283–95.

[47] Burdon to Lugard, 26 May 1906, Shillingford Papers; Lugard, Annual Report, Northern Nigeria, 1905–6, 371; Goldsmith, Sokoto Province Annual Report, 1906.

[48] On the extent of accommodation with colonial rule, see Adeleye, 'Dilemma of the Waziri', 285–98; and Idrissa, *Guerres et Sociétés*, 148, 179.

apparent treason involved in accepting colonial dictates.[49] This rationalization justified the accession to office of the colonial emirs and their subordinates, who soon found themselves in direct conflict with the anti-colonial stance of many Mahdists and their belief that the Mahdi was about to come.

REVOLUTIONARY MAHDISM

Revolutionary Mahdism shared many features with other forms of Mahdism. First, there was the primacy of religious conviction, especially the belief in the imminent arrival of the Expected Mahdi. Second, revolutionary Mahdists were decidedly anti-colonial and believed that the imposition of colonialism was an important indication that the millennium was fast approaching. Like all Mahdists, they were hostile to colonial rule, but unlike some Mahdists, they were not willing to accommodate themselves to the European occupation. Third, revolutionary Mahdists, like the *ansar*, opposed the government of the Caliphate, both before and after the colonial conquest, but these Mahdists did not recognize the political claims of the *ansar* either.

Revolutionary Mahdism can be distinguished from all other strands of Mahdism in four respects. First, it exhibited a dimension of class struggle in that it drew its support from peasants, fugitive slaves and subject populations; in contrast to other forms of Mahdism, few merchants and aristocrats joined the movement. Second, there was an ethnic dimension to revolutionary Mahdism that reflected the class division; few, if any Fulbe, from whom most of the aristocracy came, supported the movement. The lack of Fulbe support stands in sharp contrast to all other instances of Mahdism. Third, revolutionary Mahdism was associated with the expected appearance of Isa (Jesus) as well as the Mahdi Himself. Other Mahdists may have recognized Isa as a Prophet, but the revolutionaries highlighted his role. Finally, revolutionary Mahdists did not encourage emigration to the east. When emigration was necessary, people moved to the frontiers between emirates or the uninhabited areas between fiefs. These features of revolutionary Mahdism coalesced in the uprising of 1905–6.

First, the class dimension is unique. As Sokoto Mohammad has assessed the situation at Satiru, 'peasants, slaves and petty malams saw the new situation [of colonial rule] as a continuation of their struggle against oppression and exactions which they had been waging against the Sokoto Caliphate'.[50] At Kobkitanda, according to Idrissa, opposition to Dosso, which was not part of the Caliphate, was closely associated with resistance to the French.[51] Revolutionary Mahdism sought the expulsion of the colonial authorities and the overthrow of those officials who were collaborating with the colonial occupation.

The Mahdists in the region between Dallol Bosso and Dallol Mawri were mostly disgruntled peasants. The villages near Kobkitanda, founded in the later 1890s, swelled with the arrival of people seeking to avoid colonial exactions.[52] People along the Niger had been forced to provide labour and

---

[49] Adeleye, 'Dilemma of the Waziri', 285–311. The fullest account of the debate within the aristocracy and the best identification of the principal collaborators is in Tukur, 'British colonial domination', 248–334.

[50] Mohammad, 'Social interpretation', 173.

[51] Idrissa, *Guerres et Sociétés*, 175–9.   [52] Idrissa, *Guerres et Sociétés*, 146.

food for the march on the desert and Lake Chad. The severity of the conquest and heavy taxation laid the foundation for revolt.[53]

The Kobkitanda Mahdists were openly hostile to Dosso, which had co-operated willingly with the French intrusion and had used the French presence to expand its control in the region of the Dallols. In particular, Zarmakoy Awta, the ruler of Dosso after 1902, antagonized many Zarma because of what they believed to be his overt opportunism. Much of the exploitation associated with the French conquest was blamed on him.

Few, if any, slaves or fugitive slaves were apparently involved in the events at Kobkitanda. French reports and local oral traditions are largely silent on the subject of slavery.[54] Other than their opposition to Dosso, the villages near Kobkitanda were not very different from most Zarma communities, which had been in revolt against the Sokoto Caliphate for much of the nineteenth century.

The Mahdists may have tried to recruit slaves, however. A French army manual written at Dosso in 1910 provides instructions on how to deal with a Mahdist uprising and is clearly based on the 1905–6 revolt. There is specific mention of promises to liberate slaves as a method of recruitment.[55] Appeals to Karma, Say, Birnin Gaoure, Torodi and other parts of the Caliphate, implicitly at least, called for slaves to join the revolt. These emirates had heavy concentrations of slaves. Even though the French doubted the loyalty of the emirs, none of these emirates actually joined the Mahdists.[56] In the event only Karma rose, and at Karma, fugitive slaves were not a factor. Indeed the Karma nobles who fought the French were slave owners.

At Satiru, fugitive slaves found sanctuary with the Mahdists. As Moham-med has established, the Satirawa 'encouraged the emigration of slaves to Satiru'.[57] In fact its radical clerics believed that slavery was a prime example of the injustice of Caliphate society. According to Maidamma Mai Zari, Dutsen Assada ward, Sokoto, 'the leaders of Satiru abolished slavery and as a consequence...slaves flocked to them. The freedom of these fugitives was effectively and strenuously guarded'.[58] It should be noted that at this time neither the British nor the French colonial governments advocated, let alone enacted, the abolition of slavery.

Throughout the Muslim areas of West Africa, including the Sokoto Caliphate, slaves were leaving their masters in considerable numbers by the late 1890s.[59] Both the French and the British faced a fugitive crisis, although

[53] Rothiot, *Aouta*, 161–83.   [54] Interview at Kobkitanda, 2 Oct. 1988.
[55] Leblond, 'Rapport destiné à l'élaboration d'un manuel tactique', Journal de Poste de Dosso, 1910, quoted in Rash, 'Établissement colonial', 210.
[56] See, for example, Milot, Monographie du Cercle de Dosso, 1909, ANN 15.1.1, where the loyalty of Emir Bayero of Birnin Gaoure was questioned.
[57] Mohammad, 'Social interpretation', 171; and Mohammad, 'Songs and poems'.
[58] Cited in Mohammad, 'Social Interpretation', 171, and based on an interview given by Saleh Abubakar, 14 Aug. 1975.
[59] For the situation in the areas to the west of the Caliphate, see Richard Roberts and Martin Klein, 'The Banamba slave exodus of 1905 and the decline of slavery in the Western Sudan', *J. Afr. Hist.*, XXI, 3 (1981), 375–94. For the Caliphate, see Paul E. Lovejoy, 'Fugitive slaves: resistance to slavery in the Sokoto Caliphate', in G. Okihiro, ed., *In Resistance: Studies in African, Afro-American and Caribbean History* (Amherst, Mass., 1986), 71–95; J. S. Hogendorn and Paul E. Lovejoy, 'The reform of slavery in early colonial Northern Nigeria', in Suzanne Miers and Richard Roberts, eds., *The End of Slavery in Africa* (Madison, 1988), 391–414.

in the context of the Caliphate, there were more slaves in the British sphere, and hence the crisis was more severe there. By 1906 slaves were still running away, although by then the alliance between the new colonial regime and the Caliphate aristocracy had begun to take hold. Controlling slaves was high on the agenda of this alliance. The fact that fugitive slaves were a major component of revolutionary Mahdism comes as no surprise.

The first British reports concerning Satiru confirmed the importance of the slavery issue. In his despatch of 21 February 1906, Burdon stated: 'As far as I can learn the adherents who at one time flocked to it [the Satiru cause] were nearly all run away slaves'.[60] This interpretation made sense to Lugard at the time, and he therefore informed the Colonial Office that the Satirawa were 'mostly fugitive slaves, and I suppose some outlaws from French territory', a reference to Saybu Dan Makafo and his followers.[61] In his report of 7 March, Lugard still subscribed to this theory: 'it appears that the rising was instigated by an outlaw from French territory named Dan Makafo, who gathered together a band of malcontents and runaway slaves, and forced Malam Isa, the son of a man who had previously [in 1904] declared himself Mahdi, to head the rising'.[62] Since both Lugard and Burdon were aware of the seriousness of the fugitive crisis, their assessment should be given considerable weight.

The extent to which revolutionary Mahdism revealed ethnic friction, the second distinguishing feature of the movement, is particularly significant because of the close association between ethnicity and class in the Caliphate. As is generally accepted by scholars, there was a strong tradition of Mahdism among the aristocracy; much of the leadership of the *ansar* was aristocratic in origin, and of course the *hijra* of 1903 was led by Sarkin Musulmi Attahiru I himself. By contrast, the revolutionary Mahdists espoused anti-aristocratic sentiments. The opposition of these Mahdists was directed against the ruling class, and because the ruling class was comprised almost wholly of Fulbe and high-ranking slave officials loyal to them, revolutionary Mahdism took on the dimensions of a class struggle cast in ethnic terms.

There were no Fulbe among the revolutionary Mahdists on either side of the colonial frontier. In Niger, the rebels were mostly Songhay or Zarma, which are closely related ethnic groups whose languages are mutually understandable.[63] Karma was a Songhay town, while Kobkitanda was Zarma. At Satiru, Hausa from a variety of backgrounds were predominant. The fact that Saybu Dan Makafo could move easily between Kobkitanda and Satiru indicates that the Zarma and Hausa supporters of revolutionary Mahdism recognized a common enemy: the colonial regimes and those who collaborated with them, including the Caliphate aristocracy and the *zarma-koy* of Dosso. In the context of the Caliphate, the peasantry and assimilated slaves were identified as Hausa, while aristocrats were usually Fulbe. Zarma were classified as protected people, even though Dosso itself had maintained its independence since the middle of the nineteenth century. The Fulbe referred to both Hausa and Zarma as Habe.

It is striking that no Fulbe bodies were reported among the dead

---

[60] Burdon to Lugard, 21 Feb. 1906, CO 446/53.
[61] Conference of 28 Feb. 1906, no. 11115, CO 446/53.
[62] Lugard to C.O., 7 Mar. 1906, CO 446/53.
[63] Personal communication, Kimba Idrissa, 1 Oct. 1988.

Satirawa,[64] nor do there appear to have been any among the fallen rebels in French Niger on the battlefields at Kobkitanda, Sambera, Karma, and Zimba.[65] Burdon grasped the significance of the ethnic dimension in his report to Lugard:

Satiru was a Hausa village and only Hausas or their kindred races have joined them. All the faces on the battlefield had Gobir, Kebbi, Zanfara, Katsena and other such tribal marks. Not a single Fulani *talaka* [commoner] joined them.[66]

Mohammed, on the basis of oral sources, presents a similar picture, with some additions. The ethnic groups included Zamfarawa, Gobirawa, Gimbanawa, Kabawa (Kebbi), Azbinawa (Azben), Arawa (Arewa), and Katsinawa:

There might have been some non-Habe and non-Muslims among the Satirawa since quite a number of the slaves owned by the Sarakuna [i.e. title-holders] and Attajirai [wealthy merchants] were from other societies.[67]

It is significant that other non-Hausa identities are not remembered, despite the presence of fugitive slaves. By staying to fight, fugitive slaves in effect had renounced their other loyalties and were fighting as Hausa.

In fact the relationship between class and ethnicity was much more complicated. Many Fulbe were not aristocrats, while some Hausa were wealthy merchants, and Zarma/Songhay *wangari* (warlords) owned many slaves. It is also significant that the opposition of Mahdists at Kobkitanda was against Dosso, whose aristocracy was Zarma and not Fulbe. We are not attempting to simplify complex class and ethnic relationships, but attempting only to identify patterns in the resistance.

The third feature of revolutionary Mahdism was the importance of the Isa tradition. Isa was to accompany the Mahdi or to appear shortly after his arrival to combat Daggal, the enemy of the Mahdi. Prophecies concerning Isa were to have an important role in the uprising at Satiru in 1906.

The Isa tradition can be traced back to the 1840s in the Sokoto Caliphate, although the tradition is found in classical Islam and was probably widespread in the Caliphate throughout the nineteenth century. The earliest known Isa protagonist was Malam Hamza, a cleric who lived in Tsokuwa in southeastern Kano Emirate. He came to the attention of Kano authorities in 1848, when his followers refused to pay tax other than the *zakka* (tithe). After tax officials (*jakadu*) were beaten and sent back to Kano city in 1848, Hamza fled to the Ningi Hills. These Mahdists were known as Isawa (followers of Isa).[68] Isawa extremists were seized in Kano city in the 1850s

---

[64] Burdon to Lugard, telegram, 28 Feb. 1906; Burdon to Lugard, 15 Mar., 21 Mar. 1906, Shillingford Papers.   [65] Idrissa, *Guerres et Sociétés*, 147–69.
[66] Burdon to Lugard, 15 Mar. 1906.   [67] Mohammad, 'Social interpretation', 164.
[68] For a discussion of Hamza and the Ningawa resistance, see Adell Patton, Jr., 'The Ningi chiefdom and the African frontier: mountaineers and resistance to the Sokoto Caliphate' (Ph.D. thesis, University of Wisconsin, 1975); Patton, 'Ningi raids and slavery in the nineteenth-century Sokoto Caliphate', *Slavery and Abolition*, II (1981), 114–45; and Ian Linden, 'Between two religions of the book: the children of the Israelites (c. 1846–c. 1920)', in Elizabeth Isichei, ed., *Varieties of Christian experience in Nigeria* (London, 1982), 79–98; and Linden, 'The Isawa Mallams, c. 1850–1919: some problems in the religious history of Northern Nigeria', (unpublished seminar paper, Department of History, Ahmadu Bello University, 1975).

and impaled in the market, an action which demonstrates how seriously the
Caliphate authorities took these clerics and how brazen the clerics were.[69]

Stories collected at Lokoja in the early 1880s demonstrated that the Isa
tradition was widely believed. Reverend C. J. John (an African convert) of
the Church Missionary Society may have been surprised when he heard

> the news of the prophet Jesus which I heard from the mouth of the people at
> Lokojah who were mussulmen or Mahommedans. They said, He will come again
> at the resurrection of the world, and wage war with Duggal or Daggal [the anti-
> Christ of Mahdist tradition]. At that time the world will have peace, because he
> will slay the wicked people, but the good people will remain in the world.... Who
> is this Daggal? Daggal is a man who is doing all the wickedness in this world, who
> in the day of the appearance of Jesus Christ will make war with Him, but Jesus will
> slay him with all his followers.[70]

Jesus [Isa] would come with the Mahdi. Other stories of Isa were also
common.[71]

One Mahdist poet, in response to the West African Frontier Force march
on Zaria in 1901, equated the colonialists with Gog and Magog, the eternal
enemies of the Mahdi:

> Gog and Magog are coming, they approach,
> They are small people, with big ears,
> They are those who cause destruction at the ends of the earth,
> When they approach a town, its crops will not sprout....
> The fertility of the world will be taken away,
> The place that once gave seventy bushels will not give seven,
> Anti-Christ is coming,
> He will come and have authority over the world,
> The Mahdi and Jesus, they are coming
> In order to straigthen out the tangle [of the world].[72]

The Anti-Christ was none other than the Daggal of earlier teachings.

The belief in the second coming of Isa made emigration to the east
unnecessary for revolutionary Mahdists – the fourth feature that distinguishes this form of Mahdism. The revolutionaries, who sought sanctuary on
the frontiers of the Caliphate, interpreted emigration as *hijra*, but they
expressed the *hijra* in a very different way. Fulbe Mahdists and their
supporters moved east, congregating in Gombe, northern Adamawa and
areas further east still. The revolutionaries, who did not include Fulbe,
sometimes moved to the borders of the emirates but otherwise stayed close
to the centres of the Caliphate. Satiru, for example, was located between four
fiefs, Danchadi, Dange, Shuni and Bodinga, a mere twenty kilometres
southwest of Sokoto.[73]

[69] Paul E. Lovejoy, 'Problems of slave control in the Sokoto Caliphate', in Lovejoy,
ed., *Africans in Bondage; Studies in Slavery and the Slave Trade* (Madison, 1986), 263.
[70] See Jacob Friedrich Schön, *Magana Hausa, Native Literature, or Proverbs, Tales,
Fables and Historical Fragments in the Hausa Language. To which is added a translation in
English* (London, 1885), 161–2.
[71] 'The Prophet Jesus meeting with a skull to which he restored the power of speech',
in Schön, *Magana Hausa*, 162–3.   [72] Quoted in Hiskett, *Islam in West Africa*, 272.
[73] Mohammed, 'Songs and poems'. The location of Satiru has been the object of some
confusion. Various sources have placed the village haphazardly; see, for example, Robert
W. Shenton, *The Development of Capitalism in Northern Nigeria* (Toronto, 1986), 27;
Christopher Harrison, *France and Islam in West Africa, 1860–1960* (Cambridge, 1988),
45; and Idrissa, *Guerres et Sociétés*, map.

Kobkitanda was located to the south of Dosso, on the frontier with Birnin Ngaoure, one of the emirates in the Caliphate. Saybu's grandfather, Hangadumbo, had been the village head of Gulma, a village near Dosso. His decision to emigrate was an explicit statement of discontent, both with Dosso's territorial aggrandizement and the presence of the French.[74] Hangadumbo, together with his daughter, her husband, and blind Saybu, first moved to Mayakiday and then founded Kobkitanda in about 1902.[75] Several other villages, including Sambera, Toka, and Kofadey, were founded about this time as places of refuge for those Zarma who opposed both the French conquest and aristocratic cooperation with the French, as represented by the succession of Awta as *zarmakoy*.[76]

Karma was an exception to this pattern because it was not explicitly a Mahdist community but rather a sub-emirate under Say that had joined the Caliphate only in the last years of the nineteenth century.[77]

THE RADICAL CLERICS

The radical clerics who led the revolutionary Mahdist movement were humble in origin, in some cases perhaps of servile origin. From the perspective of the Caliphate, the more important and the most respectable Muslim clerics, the *'ulama*, were closely associated with aristocrats and merchants, often being of the same families. Wealthy merchants, clerics and aristocrats also intermarried.[78] As far as we know, none of the radical clerics was Fulbe or associated with the *'ulama*-merchant class.

Malam Siba, who founded Satiru, was of Nupe origin. A second cleric, Maikaho, who was accused of declaring himself Mahdi in 1904, came from Gobir, the country which Uthman dan Fodio had subjugated. A third cleric, Malam Bawa, was from Zamfara, which had been in revolt against Sokoto on several occasions in the nineteenth century.[79]

The antipathy of the radical clerics to the Fulbe aristocracy, even before the European conquest, is perhaps best revealed in the alleged statement of Malam Siba:

that he was fed up with the exactions of the ruling class [*sic*] and that he was not going to obey the instructions of anyone anymore...[but instead] was going to set up a new great regime.[80]

[74] Interview at Kobkitanda.
[75] Interview at Kobkitanda; Idrissa, *Guerres et Sociétés*, 147–9.
[76] Idrissa, *Guerres et Sociétés*, 148–9.   [77] Interview at Karma.
[78] For an excellent analysis of Caliphate class structure, see Ibrahim Tahir, 'Sufis, saints and capitalists in Kano, 1804–1974: pattern of a bourgeois revolution in an Islamic society' (Ph.D. thesis, Cambridge University, 1975), although his analysis should be amended in one respect: aristocrats and wealthy merchants did intermarry. We wish to thank A. S. Mohammed for his critique of Tahir's analysis. Mohammad points out that there is a common Hausa proverb: '*maikudi abokin Sarki*', i.e. 'the wealthy man is the friend of the *sarki*'. There were various alliances between wealthy merchants and the aristocracy, including political, commercial and marital.
[79] In addition to the oral traditions collected by Mohammad and Idrissa, there are several contemporary accounts of Satiru, including 'Asalin Gabar Satiru', in Frank Edgar, ed., *Litafi na Tatsuniyoyi na Hausa* (Belfast, 1911), I, 263–9, 431; and 'Labarin Farkon Gabar Satirawa', in Edgar, ed., *Litafi na Tatsuniyoyi na Hausa* (Belfast, 1913), III, 404. To these should be added the poems and songs collected by Mohammad ('Songs and poems of the Satiru rising') and the compilation of Johnston, 'Dan Makafo and the Satiru rising'.   [80] Mohammad, 'Social interpretation', 171.

Satiru did not pay taxes or contribute corvée labour to Sokoto either before or after the British conquest.[81] The reference to 'ruling class' refers in this context to the Fulbe aristocracy and high ranking slave officials.

By 1900, Mahdist agents were active in Nupe, Kontagora, Zaria, Sokoto, and Gwandu. In 1902, for example, Malam Mai Zanna responded to the British occupation of Bida by calling for the expulsion of the British and the Emir. It is reported that Mai Zanna claimed to be the Mahdi. As noted above, such reports must be treated with caution. None the less, he

collected numerous followers from the neighbouring villages of Bida and the lower classes in the town. This rabble was, however, unprepared for any action and the ringleaders were surprised and quietly arrested by the Emir's *dogarai* [police]. The Mahdi was tried and sentenced by the Native Court to six months imprisonment in the town dungeon and the followers were fined 25 bags of cowries each.[82]

It is likely that many of Mai Zanna's supporters were slaves.

In January 1904, Malam Maikaho was reported to have proclaimed himself Mahdi at Satiru. The authorities quickly summoned him to Sokoto.[83] At his trial he claimed that he was only a Mahdi of farming, not a Mahdi of war.[84] The significance of that distinction is not clear, but it is likely that Maikaho only claimed to be an agent, and not the true Mahdi Himself. As C. W. J. Orr, Acting Resident of Sokoto, reported to Lugard on 29 February,

During the month the Serikin Mussulmin reported that a Mallam was endeavouring to set himself up as a Mahdi in the south of the Province to induce the people to rise against the Whiteman, and that he had sent messages to that effect to the Serikin Kiawa of Kaura [Namoda]. The man was arrested and is now in custody in Sokoto, but is ill, so that investigation is delayed temporarily. The matter will be thoroughly gone into and the Mallam tried in the Native Court, but I have told the Serikin Mussulmin that he is to keep me informed and will not pass any sentence without previous reference to me for the consideration and information of your Excellency. I do not look upon the matter as serious, but it bears close watching.[85]

Orr's report establishes that Maikaho died on or shortly after 29 February, and while foul play is not indicated in the documents, it was certainly possible that he was killed, considering Sokoto's fears of Mahdism in the light of the disaster at Bormi seven months earlier. Lugard's marginal note on Orr's report approved of a trial before the Islamic (Native) court, 'if they will punish adequately'.[86] Maikaho's supporters were released 'after taking an oath on the Koran to keep the peace'.[87] Maikaho's son, Hassami, became

[81] Burdon and Lugard realized this situation but easily convinced the Colonial Office that taxation was not a factor. See Oliver's and Antrobus' minutes, Conference of 7 Mar. 1906, CO 446/53; Burdon to Lugard, 21 Mar. 1906.

[82] E. C. M. Dupigny, *Gazetteer of Nupe Province* (London, 1920), 25.

[83] There is some discrepancy over the events surrounding Satiru in 1904. Mohammad ('Social interpretation', 159) claims that Maikaho declared himself Mahdi in January, apparently relying on E. J. Arnett, *Gazetteer of Sokoto* (London, 1920), 45. Arnett is wrong on a number of points relating to Satiru, however, and it may be, as other sources suggest, that Maikaho only came to the attention of authorities in February. As noted above, he probably did not declare himself Mahdi, only his agent.

[84] 'Labarin Farkon Gabar Satirawa', 404.

[85] Orr, Sokoto Province Report no. 1, 29 Feb. 1904, Sokprof 2/2 51/1904 (NNAK).

[86] Lugard's marginal note on Orr's Sokoto Report no. 1.

[87] Burdon to Lugard, 21 Feb. 1906, CO 446/53; and Lugard, Annual Report, 1905–6, 369.

the new headman at Satiru, and when he died in the summer of 1905, another son, Isa, became headman.[88] Saybu Dan Makafo made much of Isa's name, claiming that Isa was the successor to the Mahdi in Mahdist eschatology.

The Mahdists at Satiru commanded significant local support. The citizenry of neighbouring towns and villages celebrated the Muslim festivals there, and some Muslims in the area had studied under Isa's father and had accepted his Mahdist leadership.[89] Hassami apparently respected the 1904 order that revolutionary Mahdism be curtailed, presumably under the threat that a local fiefholder, the Sarkin Kebbi of Danchadi, would send police to break up the town if militant Mahdism were being preached. The Sarkin Kebbi was informed when Hassami died in the summer of 1905, and may have approved the succession of Isa. By this time, however, Satiru once again was beyond control. The Sarkin Kebbi had not collected taxes, and after the rebellion

he confessed that he was afraid to do so. He knew it [Satiru] as a gathering of fanatical Malams, a hotbed of disaffection, and he neither took action nor made any report.[90]

The accession of Isa appears to have marked a shift towards militancy at Satiru.

Further west, there were a number of clerics in Dosso who appealed to Mahdists in Dosso and in the western emirates of the Caliphate. Two clerics, Aman Beri of Tidirka and especially Saybu Dan Makafo of Kobkitanda, stood out.[91] Initially, Aman Beri appears to have been the most important Dosso cleric. The French, who learned of his subversive activities from Zarmakoy Awta, accused him of fomenting revolt as early as April 1905. Aman Beri was arrested, taken to Niamey, and sentenced to three years in prison. He was later accused of complicity with Saybu, but at the time of Aman Beri's detention, the French were unaware of Saybu's existence. The arrest propelled Saybu into the role of leader, a role he filled with sufficient competence that Aman Beri's imprisonment did not have the desired effect of preventing an uprising.[92]

[88] It has been assumed wrongly that Isa become the leader at Satiru upon the death of his father in early 1904 (see, for example, Dusgate, *Conquest*, 242), but Burdon's report of 21 Mar. 1906 clarifies the situation.

[89] Johnston, 'Dan Makafo and the Satiru rising', 163–5.

[90] Burdon to Lugard, 21 Mar. 1906.

[91] One cleric from Kano, Malam Danba, came to the attention of French officials and apparently to British officials in the Gold Coast as well. Danba was predicting the imminent arrival of the Mahdi; see Idrissa, *Guerres et Sociétés*, 174, citing Robert Arnaud, Report no. 4, 11G4, Archives Nationales, Paris. He came via Sokoto and 'was said to be preaching a holy war against Europeans'. (Ponty, Extract of Report.) Other Mahdist agents included Omaru Paruki, about whom we know nothing more, and Mohammed Othman, who was arrested in Bonduku in May 1905 and exiled to Dakar. Mohammed Othman's activities in the areas west of the Caliphate suggest that he had joined the revolutionary Mahdist ranks; see Jack Goody, 'Reform, renewal and resistance: a Mahdi in Northern Ghana', in C. Allen and R. W. Johnson, eds., *African Perspectives: Papers Presented to Thomas Hodgkin* (Cambridge, 1970), 143–56, and Emmanuel Terray, 'Le Royaume abron du Gyaman de 1875 à 1910: de l'indépendance à l'établissement du pouvoir blanc', in Marc H. Piault, ed., *La Colonisation: rupture ou parenthèse?* (Paris, 1987), 296–7.

[92] This reconstruction is based on Enregistrement de la correspondance de route, 1906, Journal de Poste de Dosso, ANN 5.6.1. See especially the entries for 12 and 18 March and

As Idrissa has demonstrated, Saybu Dan Makafo played a key role in the uprising; he is the only cleric to be identified with all parts of the revolt.[93] Traditions at Karma clearly establish this leadership, even though Saybu was not present, while the revolt at Satiru did not occur until Saybu arrived, though the planning of it had probably already taken place. Both the French and the British independently confirmed his central role.[94]

Saybu Dan Makafo had leadership abilities that are unusual, considering his blindness. The French thought he was only about thirty years old in 1906; oral traditions remember him being about forty.[95] According to French reports, he had the gift of ventriloquism which may help explain his fame as a magician.[96] He reportedly had Tijani connections,[97] but the significance of this is unclear, since he was a self-proclaimed agent of the Mahdi. As Idrissa has noted, Dan Makafo was considered a *wali*, a saint.[98] His detractors considered him an agent of Satan, and his movement heretical.[99]

Saybu's call for a revolt was unequivocal. It was to occur on the Id al-Kabir, 5 February.[100] At that time the Mahdi Musa would arrive from the east.[101] In Saybu's earlier preaching, there is no known mention of Isa, but he stressed this feature of revolutionary Mahdism once he reached Satiru. He instructed his supporters not to pay tax or contribute corvée labour. They were not to obey local officials who supported the colonial regime. A great

---

5 April. Also see Rapport politique du mois d'avril 1906, Cercle du Djerma, ANN 15.2.9; Rapport politique mensuel, Apr. 1906, Région de Niamey, ANN 15.2.7. Rothiot (*Aouta*, 149–50) bases his information on oral sources and on Rapport politique de la Région de Niamey, Apr. 1905, and Rapport politique du commandant de la Région de Niamey, 1 Dec. 1905. Rothiot does not provide a source for the connection between Aman Beri and Saybu, but see Idrissa, *Guerres et Sociétés*, 148–9. According to Idrissa, Aman Beri was arrested in May 1905 and was released from prison on schedule in 1908, but he was immediately sent into exile, where he died only a month later.

[93] Idrissa, *Guerres et Sociétés*, 147–171.

[94] Rothiot, *Aouta*, 179–82, has concluded otherwise on the basis of oral material. A critique of Rothiot's interpretation cannot be presented here, but it should be noted that traditions collected at Karma and Kobkitanda in September–October 1988 and a reading of available archival materials in Niger confirm Idrissa's interpretation.

[95] Ponty, Extract of Report; Idrissa, *Guerres et Sociétés*, 148. Some reports claim that Saybu Dan Makafo was not totally blind but could see shapes. The extent of his blindness is not clear, but it was certainly sufficient that he was identified as such. Traditions at Kobkitanda, however, insist that he was totally blind from birth; oral information obtained from the elders of Kobkitanda on 2 Oct. 1988.

[96] Ponty, Extract of Report; Ponty, Rapport no. 132, Kayes, 26 Mar. 1906; Idrissa, *Guerres et Sociétés*, 148; Johnston, 'Dan Makafo and the Satiru rising', 163. Johnston's informants claimed that Dan Makafo could produce kola nuts at will and could levitate on his prayer mat.

[97] Ponty, Extract of Report.

[98] Idrissa, *Guerres et Sociétés*, 149.

[99] Idrissa, *Guerres et Sociétés*, 214–15.

[100] Idrissa, *Guerres et Sociétés*, 149; Burdon to Lugard, 5 Mar. 1906. Aman Beri as well was apparently preparing for revolt on the day of the Id.

[101] The Mahdist agent, Musa, arrested in the Northern Territories of the Gold Coast in 1905, may have been the Musa who was expected to appear. The connection between the Musa of the middle Volta basin and the Musa of the revolutionary Mahdist tradition at Satiru has yet to be explored fully. See Goody, 'Mahdi in Northern Ghana', 143–56; and Terray, 'Royaume abron du Gyaman', 296–7.

Muslim army would liberate the country from the Christian occupation. To protect his followers, he devised numerous supernatural preparations:

To achieve this he prepared magical charms which mixed animism and Islam. They involved a mixture of plant material (roots and leaves) and Coranic verses. The participants drank it in order to make themselves invulnerable to guns (or the bullets directed at them would be transformed into water) and stimulate their combativeness and courage.[102]

In fact, Saybu probably never learned to write because of his blindness.[103] Rather than basing his authority on the traditions of scholarship, he relied on mysticism alone, including the charms and the encouragement of belief in supernatural protection from bullets referred to in the quotation.

There were other clerics as well, although exactly how many is uncertain. Aman Beri and Saybu were in touch with agents in the Niger valley to the immediate north of Kontagora; there seem to have been contacts with the Satiru community, where Saybu eventually fled. Similar Mahdist agents were active further west as far as Gonja, Abron and adjacent areas.[104] By September 1905, Saybu's agents were known to have been at Anzuru, Sonay, Torodi and other places such as Dokimana and Boki in the Emirate of Say. A close associate and relative of Aman Beri, Yonkori Bontamni of Sokorbe, gathered support in the Zarma villages of Hilo, Tidirka and Kaina, but otherwise his role is not known.[105] Yonkori Bontamni was detained in April 1906, three months after the battle at Kobkitanda. Once the French realized the seriousness of the situation, they proceeded to round up as many clerics as possible, whether they were involved or not.[106]

The organization of Mahdist resistance was thus well established in 1905. There were serious problems of co-ordination, given the state of communications and the military superiority of the colonial armies and their allies. Travelling clerics, who spread the doctrines of Mahdist resistance widely, none the less overcame these difficulties to a considerable extent. The emergence of Saybu Dan Makafo as a charismatic leader provided the spark that touched off the uprising.

COLONIAL POLICY AND THE MAHDIST REVOLT

Richard Dusgate has called the culminating battle at Satiru 'the most bloodthirsty expedition in the history of British military operations in Northern Nigeria'.[107] Adeleye has concluded that British policy was characterized by 'misjudgments, panic and miscalculations', for which the British took 'revenge'.[108] Margery Perham, in her biography of Lugard, has noted that vengeance,

[102] Idrissa, *Guerres et Sociétés*, 149. Malams at Satiru utilized similar charms and spells.
[103] Interview at Kobkitanda.
[104] For a discussion of Mahdism in the middle Volta basin, see Goody, 'Mahdi in Northern Ghana', 143–56; and Terray, 'Royaume abron du Gyaman', 294–7.
[105] Journal du poste de Dosso, 12 and 18 Mar., 5 Apr. 1906. Rothiot, *Aouta*, 175–8, interprets these events differently.
[106] Rapport politique et administratif, Région de Niamey, second trimestre, 1906; Rapport politique du mois de mars 1906, Cercle du Djerma; Rapport politique mensuel, Région de Naimey, mois de octobre 1906, ANN 15.2.7.
[107] Dusgate, *Conquest*, 247.   [108] Adeleye, 'Mahdist triumph', 200.

it must be admitted, was what most of the white men in Northern Nigeria wanted [after the initial loss at Satiru], and with them in this were those Fulani [Fulbe] leaders who had accepted their rule.... It was a terrible vengeance, more terrible than Lugard knew at the time.[109]

Just how 'terrible' came out in subsequent reports which were kept secret. They found that the 'killing was *very* free, not to say slaughter [italics in original]'; 'they killed every living thing before them' so that the fields were 'running with blood', while the 'spitting of mallams on a stake' and the 'cutting off the breasts of women' were typical atrocities. These reports also make it clear that Perham was wrong in her assessment of Lugard's ignorance. Lugard not only knew the extent of the massacre; he sanctioned it.[110]

There were two reasons why the British permitted the brutality, and it should be noted that the results in French territory were as brutal as in the British sphere. First, there was the danger of Mahdism itself, which would continue to bother the colonial regimes for the next twenty years. Given the fact that Saybu's movement crossed the colonial boundaries of two European regimes and threatened to engulf the heartlands of British Northern Nigeria, Lugard made the decision, probably wise from an imperial perspective, to set a bloody example. He only learned that the uprising at Satiru was a continuation of the revolt in French Niger after the Hillary expedition. Despite French offers of assistance, the British chose to act alone, and events proved they possessed more than enough resources to crush the revolt. Still, both colonial governments had cause to be concerned.

Lugard was not sure how far the unrest might spread in British territory. Mahdist activity accelerated during the period of the Satiru revolt. Malam Siba actually escaped from the massacre, due to his magical powers so it was said. He might have been a source of further agitation, but his alleged powers failed to save him from later arrest and detention in the Sokoto prison. He did continue to write and sell Islamic tracts, and he retained a following as a *malam* until he died in detention, but without important consequences.[111] In Kontagora, a Mahdist cleric 'drew attention to the impending end of British rule and exhorted people to stop paying taxes to the British administration'.[112] Other agents were operating at Jebba, Yelwa, and Maradu.[113]

Yet another Mahdist agent, Malam Mai Layu, came to the notice of the authorities on 10 March, only days after the destruction of Satiru. At the

---

[109] Margery Perham, *Lugard: The Years of Authority, 1898–1912* (London, 1960), 259–60.

[110] Edward Lugard (Sir Frederick's brother and close confident) and William Wallace, Acting High Commissioner after Lugard was transferred to Hong Kong later in 1906, carried out the investigation in response to enquiries from Walter Miller, the C.M.S. missionary in Zaria. See Wallace to Lugard, 31 Oct. 1907, Lugard Papers, Mss. Brit. Emp. 62, Rhodes House; Edward Lugard to FDL, 7 Oct. 1907, Lugard Papers. Also see the embarrassing typographical error, or so we assume, by Goldsmith that 'all parts of stragglers were cut off'. Presumably he meant that all *parties* of stragglers were cut off; Sokoto Province Annual Report, 1906.

[111] Personal communication, A. S. Mohammed.

[112] Lugard, Annual Report, 1905–6, 367; Adeleye, *Power and Diplomacy*, 322.

[113] Hiskett, *Islam in West Africa*, 272; H. S. Goldsmith, Report no. 30, Sokoto Province, Quarter Ending June 1906, Sokprof 2/2 625/1906 (NNAK).

time, he was building a village in Dajin Gundumi, the great forest region southeast of Sokoto.[114] Burdon considered Mai Layu potentially more dangerous than Isa and Saybu Dan Makafo. He believed that Mai Layu was a rival to Saybu, but this may have been wishful thinking. As with the other revolutionary Mahdists, however, Mai Layu's followers were non-Fulbe; they appear to have been mostly Zamfarawa from Raba. No chances were taken, and Mai Layu was detained by the Sarkin Musulmi on 22 March,[115] which further confirmed Lugard's belief that most Caliphate officials had decided to support the British.[116]

Moreover, the French were worried about Mahdism further west. They were uncertain whether or not the activities of agents there were connected to Saybu.[117] Consequently, E. Roume, Governor General of French West Africa, took initiatives to prevent a similar crisis from spreading across colonial boundaries in the future. He proposed to the Governor of Southern Nigeria and the High Commissioner of Northern Nigeria mechanisms for policing the frontier, with a particular concern for restricting the movements of radical clerics.[118] Although the British and French had difficulty implementing some features of this proposal, in practice colonial officials did in fact work out an arrangement. Anything that might lead to Muslim agitation was treated seriously.[119]

The second reason for the brutality related to the issue of slavery. As noted above, both the British and the French were worried about the slave exodus. Slaves had to be kept in place in order to allow colonial policies on slavery to take effect.[120] In Northern Nigeria, slavery was not abolished, despite a legal fiction that the 'legal status' of slavery was. Because many slaves ran away, the issue of fugitives was very sensitive. Therefore, it was necessary to downplay the extent of the fugitive problem in official circles, at the same time that local slave owners were re-assured about the intention of British 'reforms'. In the French sphere, slavery was technically abolished in 1905, but in fact only the term changed; slaves were subsequently referred to as *captifs*.

The Colonial Office, later followed by Lugard, attempted to shift attention to other factors. While slavery was clearly mentioned as a contributing cause to the revolt in early reports, the issue was deliberately removed from later reports. Lugard's initial cable stated succinctly: 'The rebels are outlaw

[111] Adeleye, 'Mahdist triumph', 211.
[115] Burdon to Lugard, 22 Mar. 1906.
[116] Adeleye, 'Mahdist triumph', 211.
[117] Terray, 'Royaume abron du Gyaman', 194–297.
[118] Rapport de E. Roume, 15 August 1907. This document is reproduced as an appendix in Idrissa, 'Formation de la Colonie du Niger', vol. 6, 2223–31.
[119] Peter Kazenga Tibenderana, 'The role of the British Administration in the appointment of the Emirs of Northern Nigeria, 1901–1931: the case of Sokoto Province', *J. Afr. Hist.*, XXVIII, 2 (1987), 231–57. Also see Tibenderana, 'The making and unmaking of the Sultan of Sokoto, Muhammadu Tambari, 1922–31', *J. Hist. Soc. Nigeria*, IX, 1 (1977), 91–134. The British were so concerned about the connections between Mahdism in Northern Nigeria and Sudan that a full report was undertaken; see G. J. F. Tomlinson and G. J. Lethem, *Islamic Political Propaganda in Nigeria* (London, 1927).
[120] J. S. Hogendorn and Paul E. Lovejoy, 'The development and execution of Frederick Lugard's policies toward slavery in Northern Nigeria', *Slavery and Abolition*, X, 1 (1989), 1–43.

fugitive slaves'.[121] The Colonial Office announcement of the revolt stated something quite different: 'The rebels are outlaw fugitives'.[122] A marginal note next to Lugard's telegram indicates how the incident was to be handled: 'Better say nothing of slaves'.[123] By 9 May, Lugard incorporated this cleaned-up interpretation into his official reports. If there had been a cover-up with respect to the severity of the repression, there was equally one with respect to slavery. And the reasons were interrelated. The annihilation of the Satirawa was a lesson to slaves as well as the aristocracy. It demonstrated to the slave population that slavery was to continue, despite the introduction of reforms that gradually resulted in the demise of the institution, and it allowed the aristocracy one last sanguine warning to those slaves who had not already fled. The destruction of Satiru was the last time the British called upon Caliphate levies to quell a disorder. Given the number of fugitive slaves at Satiru and the extent of violence perpetrated by those troops, the message to slaves and masters alike elsewhere must have been particularly clear.[124]

There was still unrest among the slave population after the uprising, but the exodus of slaves peaked about that time. Many slaves in Say, Torodi and other western emirates under French rule fled during the rainy season of 1906,[125] while some slaves continued to move southward from Sokoto, Kano, Zaria and other emirates in British territory as well.[126] Whether or not the suppression of the 1905–6 uprising discouraged slaves from leaving, the extent of the suppression certainly prevented fugitive slaves from joining an organized resistance.

The collaboration between the colonial powers and the local aristocracies in confronting the uprising consolidated colonial rule. As noted above, both the British and the French received considerable support.[127] Because of superior technology, the colonial regimes did not need this assistance from a military perspective. The danger was that the Caliphate aristocracy would take advantage of the crisis to expel the British and French. Burdon fully realized this when he learned of Hillary's march on Satiru. At the time, he was only about twenty kilometres south of Satiru. In the evening he first received news of the Mahdist victory from Hassan, the Sarkin Baura of Dange. The significance of this fact was apparent to Burdon at the time, and the warmth with which Hassan greeted Burdon in the early hours of the morning only confirmed Burdon's belief that the aristocracy would stand by the British.[128] Revolutionary Mahdism provided the cement that solidified the alliance between the aristocracy and the British.

[121] Lugard to CO, telegram, 14 Feb. 1906, CO 446/52, PRO.
[122] CO 446/52, p. 567.
[123] Lugard to Secretary of State, 9 May 1906, CO 446/52.
[124] The implications of the Satiru revolt on the development of slavery policies is explored in Hogendorn and Lovejoy, 'Lugard's Slavery Policies', but will be examined in greater detail in a volume forthcoming from Cambridge University Press.
[125] Rapports d'ensemble, Feb., May, June, Aug. and Dec., 1906 Cercle de Say, 16.5.1, ANN.
[126] To be examined in our forthcoming study with Cambridge University Press.
[127] Lugard, Annual Report, 1905–6, 373, provides a convenient summary of these pledges of support in British territory. For the importance of local military levies in the French sphere, see Idrissa, Guerres et Sociétés, 148, 179.
[128] Burdon to Resident Sokoto, 11 Mar. 1932, SNP 15 Acc 312 (NNAK). Also see Burdon, 'Early Days in Nigeria', West African Review, Mar. 1932, 120.

After the uprising was suppressed, there was some mopping up to do. The emir of Gwandu had to be deposed, the emirate of Hadejia had to be brought to its knees, and the political situation at Kano had to be stabilized.[129] There was also trouble in French Zinder. None the less, the Fulbe aristocracy could now be relied upon, and the French alliance with Dosso was further strengthened. The policy enunciated in the famous treatise of Waziri al-Bukhari of Sokoto was firmly in place.[130] The aristocracy would co-operate with the colonial regimes in order to protect the Muslim community and, it should be added, maintain the privileged position of the Fulbe aristocracy itself.

For his role in the destruction of Satiru, Sarkin Musulmi Attahiru II received a most curious award for a Muslim ruler. King Edward VI bestowed upon him, for his indispensable co-operation, the Companionship of the Order of St Michael and St George.[131] Haliru, although not in the direct line of succession, became emir of Gwandu in 1906 because he provided horses and supplies in the campaign against Satiru. He replaced his father who had sympathized with Mahdism to the point that he wavered in supporting the British.[132] The role of Marafa Muhammadu Maiturare, the official in charge of the Sokoto levies, was also praised. In one official's assessment, 'it was his influence and authority which was in no small measure responsible for a local disaster not ending in a general rising'.[133] The Marafa subseqently became Sarkin Musulmi in 1915 and reigned until 1924.[134] Similarly, Hassan, the *sarki* of Dange, the fief near Satiru where Burdon first realized that the Sokoto aristocracy would remain loyal to the British and the very man responsible for delivering Saybu to the authorities, was to become Sarkin Musulmi in 1931.[135]

CONCLUSION

How 'revolutionary' were the Mahdists at Kobkitanda and Satiru? We have shown that there was a coordinated uprising that was organized by a network of radical clerics; that the movement revealed class tensions in Caliphate society; and that the uprising was aimed at all governments, including Dosso, the Caliphate and the colonial regimes. None the less, the movement was seriously flawed. Because the Mahdists believed in a millennial vision

---

[129] Tibenderana, 'Sokoto, Gwandu, and Argungu', 166–70; Lugard, Annual Report, 1905–6, 373; Lugard to Secretary of State, 9 May 1906, CO 446/52, PRO.; Adeleye, *Power and Diplomacy*, 325; Tukur, 'British colonial domination', 283–95. For a contemporary account of the deposition of the emir of Gwandu, and his subordinate the Sarkin Jega, see Goldsmith, Sokoto Province Annual Report, 1906, and his Report no. 31, Sokoto Province, quarter ending 30 Sept. 1906, Sokprof 2/2 977/1906 (NNAK). Goldsmith also dismissed the *alkali* of Jega for refusing to try the Dangima on the charge of preventing the arrest of two agents from Satiru. See Tukur, 'Colonial domination', 462–92, citing J. A. Burdon, Sokoto Provincial Report no. 29 for the quarter ending 31 Mar. 1906, Sokprof 758/1906.   [130] Adeleye, 'Dilemma of Waziri'.

[131] Lugard, Annual Report, 1905–6, 373. Other emirate officials were rewarded in various ways; see Goldsmith, Report no. 31, Sokoto Province, 30 September 1906.

[132] Tibenderana, 'Appointment of Emirs', 239–43.

[133] Backwell, *Occupation of Hausaland*, 78.

[134] Tibenderana, 'Appointment of Emirs', 241–2, 247, 250.

[135] Burdon to Resident, Sokoto, 11 Mar. 1932; Burdon, 'Early days in Nigeria', 120.

and relied on supernatural powers, they undermined their effectiveness on the battlefield. As noted above, the Mahdists made fanatical charges against large and well-armed colonial forces; they made no use of the Maxim gun and other weapons that they captured, and they did not engage in guerrilla tactics that might have made the situation much more difficult for their enemies. Had they been more adaptive, they would have prolonged the uprising, with indeterminate consequences.

Despite the military weakness of the revolt, revolutionary Mahdism seriously threatened the stability of the colonial occupation. Until 1906, the alliance between the colonial regimes and the aristocracy of the Sokoto Caliphate was uncertain. The French trusted the *zarmakoy* of Dosso, but they doubted the loyalty of the emirs. The British thought that they had installed reliable officials, and in most cases the revolt proved this to be true. None the less, in early 1906, there was the clear possibility that the Mahdist revolt would lead to a general rising. Instead, the colonial presence became more firmly established than before.

The significance of the revolt does not rest with the military threat, but rather with the impressive set of grievances that were shared over a wide area. Clerics were able to articulate these grievances in a form that many slaves and peasants could understand, despite the complexity of different aristocracies and two colonial regimes. For one brief period, slaves and peasants participated in a movement that could have altered the course of early colonial history. The belief in revolutionary action was held so strongly that people committed their lives.[136]

SUMMARY

The Mahdist uprising of 1905–6 was a revolutionary movement that attempted to overthrow British and French colonial rule, the aristocracy of the Sokoto Caliphate and the *zarmakoy* of Dosso. The Mahdist supporters of the revolt were disgruntled peasants, fugitive slaves and radical clerics who were hostile both to indigenous authorities and to the colonial regimes. There was no known support among aristocrats, wealthy merchants or the *'ulama*. Thus the revolt reflected strong divisions based on class and, as an extension, on ethnicity. The pan-colonial appeal of the movement and its class tensions highlight another important feature: revolutionary Mahdism differed from other forms of Mahdism that were common in the Sokoto Caliphate at the time of the colonial conquest. There appears to have been no connection with the Mahdists who were followers of Muhammad Ahmed of the Nilotic Sudan or with those who joined Sarkin Musulmi Attahiru I on his *hijra* of 1903.

[136] There would be later manifestations of Mahdism, but not revolutionary in their intent. The Germans faced a Mahdist uprising in Caliphate territory in northern Kamerun in 1907, but this had no connection with the 1905–6 revolt. See Ahmadou Bassoro and Eldridge Mohammadu, *Histoire de Garoua: Cité Peule du XIXe siècle* (Yaounde, 1977), 53–60, 275–7; reports by Zimmermann and K. Strumpell, in 'Die Unruhen in Deutsch-Adamaua 1907', *Deutsches Kolonialblatt*, CCXXX (1907), 167–73; 'Unruhen in Kamerun', *Deutsche Kolonialzeitung*, 31 (3 Aug. 1907), 306; 'Unruhen in Adamaua', *Deutsche Kolonialzeitung*, 33 (17 Aug. 1907), 337. Similarly, the resurgence of Mahdism at Dumbulwa in 1923 was unrelated; see Ubah, 'British measures against Mahdism'; and Saeed, 'British policy towards the Mahdiyya'. In both these cases, the Mahdist adherents were associated with the *ansar* and maintained a connection with the Nilotic Sudan, which we have demonstrated had no direct influence on revolutionary Mahdism.

The suppression of the revolt was important for three reasons. First, the British consolidated their alliance with the aristocracy of the Caliphate, while the French further strengthened their ties with the *zarmakoy* of Dosso and other indigenous rulers. The dangerous moment which Muslims might have seized to expel the Europeans quickly passed. Second, the brutality of the repression was a message to slave owners and slaves alike that the colonial regimes were committed to the continuation of slavery and opposed to any sudden emancipation of the slave population. Third, 1906 marked the end of revolutionary action against colonialism; the radical clerics were either killed or imprisoned. Other forms of Mahdism continued to haunt the colonial regimes, but without serious threat of a general rising.

THE NYANGIRE REBELLION OF 1907:
ANTI-COLONIAL PROTEST AND THE NATIONALIST MYTH
Edward I. Steinhart

The past two decades have seen the rise and triumph of African
nationalism in virtually the whole of the African continent north of
the Zambesi River. Paralleling this has been the triumph of African
nationalist historiography. Starting in the early 1960's, an interpretation of the history of modern Africa, which sees nationalism as
a deeply-rooted and powerful force, became a major "school" of
historical writing about Africa. This "school" has concentrated on
explaining the social and political changes which transformed African
societies during the colonial era, placing heavy emphasis on the continuity of certain pre-colonial African forms and on the role of African
initiative in the transformation. The culmination of this transformation
was the rush to African independence in the 1950's and 1960's led by
professedly nationalist parties and movements. This climactic era
provides the point from which earlier events have been viewed and interpreted by the "nationalist school."

However, after the first flush of nationalist triumph, there has
been a period of stock-taking.[1] Africa south of the Zambesi remains
white-ruled despite nationalist wars of liberation and speeches of
denunciation. Independent African states have often fallen prey to the
hawks of civil war, military coup and economic and social stagnation.
Is African nationalism proving a weak reed because its roots do not
penetrate so very far into the past? If nationalism is not the forceful
creature we saw struggling to emerge in the 1950's, perhaps our interpretations of the roots of nationalism in African history need to be

---

[1]See I. Wallerstein's personal stock-taking in "Looking Back at African
Independence Ten Years Later," Africa Today, Vol. 18, No. 2 (1971), pp. 2-5.

re-examined, to say nothing of our interpretation of the nature and strength of nationalism in contemporary Africa.

This is especially true of the history of early African resistance and protest movements, which have been a special concern of the "nationalist school." The failure of the nationalist interpretation in the post-independence era threatens to leave an interpretative void in the growing scholarship on protest. In the following essay, I hope to examine some of the failings of the nationalist interpretation of protest, first by examining the views of the school and second by a case study in anti-colonial protest: The Nyangire Rebellion of 1907 in Bunyoro, Uganda. From these I will attempt to suggest a new hypothesis on the nature of protest in colonial Africa to fill the threatened void.

*　　*　　*

The announcement of the theme of resistance and protest as a major concern of African historians[1] came as no surprise and found an immediate audience and warm response among scholars and the general public. 1970 in a sense saw the high water mark of the protest theme with the publication of a massive tome of protest studies edited by Dr. Mazrui and Dr. Rotberg.[2] This volume of diverse studies has collected both the nationalist and what we might call para-nationalist points of view in a collection which as Mazrui has suggested will be a "primary source of thought and illumination on protest as a social fact in Africa. . ."[3] for some time to come.

---

[1] "Introduction" to Emerging Themes in African History, edited by T.O. Ranger (Nairobi, East African Publishing House, 1968), xvii-xviii.

[2] R.I. Rotberg and A.A. Mazrui, eds., Protest and Power in Black Africa (New York, Oxford University Press, 1970).

[3] Ibid., p. 1195.

Nonetheless, even in this recent statement of the literature of protest,
we can discern some discomfort with details of the interpretative
apparatus of the "nationalist school." But, such criticisms as Mazrui
and Rotberg raise are indirect and tangential, leaving the body of nationalist thought intact.[1]

A direct challenge to the nationalist literature of protest has
been aimed at the so-called "Dar es Salaam school" by two South African
scholars, Dr. Donald Denoon and Dr. Adam Kuper. These authors have very
forcefully argued against what they believe to be "ideological history,"
which "has adopted the political philosophy of current African nationalism,
and has used it to inform the study of African history."[2] While I believe
their criticism is well aimed, it leaves us asking how distorted is our
view of African protest and what kind of corrective lens can we apply?

The attack on the "Dar es Salaam school" has been aimed at
several representatives of that school in a rather ad hominem fashion. The
targets included those who have worked on subjects other than anti-colonial
protest, such as archaeology and pre-colonial history.[3] In contrast, I
will·concentrate on making the argument that a major failing of the "nationalist school" has been its misinterpretation of anti-colonial manifestations
as nationalist or proto-nationalist in sentiment, while disregarding or
deflating other sources of anti-colonial feeling and ideology.

---

[1]Cf. my review in Ufahamu II, 1,

[2]D. Denoon and A. Kuper, "Nationalist Historians in Search of a Nation,"
African Affairs Vol. 69, No. 277 (1970), pp. 329-349.

[3]Cf. the attack on A. D. Roberts, ed., Tanzania Before 1900 (Nairobi, East
African Publishing House, 1968) and on A. Temu and I. Kimambo, eds., A
History of Tanzania (Evanston, Northwestern University Press, 1969). Cf.
M. Chanock, "Development and Change in the History of Malawi," Conference
on the Early History of Malawi, Limbe, 1970, for a general critique of
nationalist historiography in Malawi.

What is the view of the "nationalist school" on African protest movements? The first point to be made is that the nationalist historians insist upon a continuity of early protest through the colonial period, a continuity which connects early protest forms with later forms of agitation that we generally accept as mass nationalism.[1] Thus, the roots of nationalism are placed far in the past, at least coincidental with the first expressions of protest against colonial overrule. The emphasis is on the deepness of the roots of African nations and the growth of popular participation in movements of protest, which culminated in the organization and success of nationalist parties and movements.[2] Anti-colonial protest is thus equated with nascent feelings of nationhood and the creation of institutions of national scale and identification. It is this "myth of nationalism" which has come under attack by both politicians and scholars, who have upheld the ultimate utility of objective scholarship.[3] While objective scholarship is readily applauded, it is not in itself a substitute for an interpretation of the nature of protest which can accommodate the diverse empirical data without theoretical banality.

---

[1] T. O. Ranger, "Connexions between 'Primary Resistance' Movements and Modern Mass Nationalism in East and Central Africa," Journal of African History, IX, 3 and 4 (1968), pp. 437-53, 631-41.

[2] J. M. Lonsdale, "Some Origins of Nationalism in East Africa," Journal of African History IX, 1 (1968), pp. 119-46; "The Emergence of African Nations," in Emerging Themes, T. O. Ranger, ed., pp. 201-17.

[3] Cf. Denoon and Kuper, "Nationalist Historians," pp. 346-48.

There are two basic pitfalls of the nationalist interpretation of protest. One has already been anticipated by Dr. Ranger when he briefly recognized that "African resistance, in the sense of movements similar to those categorized as 'primary resistance' movements, has taken the form of protest against dominance or sub-imperialism by other African peoples."[1] Moreover, Ranger also notes that "traditions of resistance can sometimes be used <u>against</u> nationalist movements as well as <u>by</u> them." However, this somewhat embarrassing fact is dismissed in a call for further investigation of "the whole question of African resistance to <u>African</u> pressures."[2] The whole question not only deserves investigation, but it may well require that we rethink the problem of resistance and protest and its implications for later social and political movements. If protest and "primary resistance" can and are directed against not only aliens who have come to dominate, but even against "domestic" forms of oppression, then perhaps protest must be viewed as something other than the expression of national aspirations for "self-government and self-expression as groups."[3] To interpret protest as proto-nationalism when it is recognized to include protest against non-aliens for reasons which are generated independently of--or in hostility to--ideals of national solidarity may be an exercise in wishful hindsight and historically unjustifiable. In the case of Nyangire, incipient Ugandan nationalism seems to me to have played no part in sparking organized opposition to colonial power.[4] Moreover, while the sub-nationalism (particularism) of Bunyoro was a potent force, the motive force and cause of protest feelings is something more subtle still.

---

[1] Ranger, "Connexions, II," p. 639.

[2] Ibid., p. 638

[3] Rotberg and Mazrui, <u>Protest</u>, xvii.

[4] Contrast the hyper-nationalism of G.N. Uzoigwe, "The Kyanyangire, 1907," University of East Africa Social Science Council Conference, Nairobi, 1969, pp.l; 70. Uzoigwe explicitly cites the inspiration of Ranger for his own interpretatior p. 162.

There is yet a second pitfall of the "Dar es Salaam school:" a tendency to ignore or misrepresent responses to colonial intrusion which do not conform to the themes of resistance and protest. It has been suggested that the nationalist historians, in their enthusiasm for "the genuine importance and formidable energy"[1] of the nationalist movements, have tended to ignore the phenomena of collaboration with the establishment of colonial overrule.[2]

The contention that nationalist historiography ignores primary collaboration, i.e., collaboration with the establishment of colonial regimes by members of African societies under the pressures of imperial invasion, must be somewhat refined. It is, I believe, largely true that the "Dar es Salaam school" has systematically avoided considering the role of African collaboration in the establishment of colonial rule in East and Central Africa. This, it might be contended, stems from their legitimate concentration on the important movements of resistance and rebellion which have taken place, particularly the Maji-Maji uprising studied by Dr. Iliffe and Dr. Gwassa and the Shona-Ndebele revolt studied by Dr. Ranger.[3] Yet, even

---

[1] Ranger, ed., Emerging Themes, xxi.

[2] E. Steinhart, "Primary Collaboration in Ankole," University of East Africa Social Science Council Conference, 1968-69, History Papers (Kampala, Makerere Institute of Social Research, n.d.), pp. 191-97.

[3] J. Iliffe, Tanganyika under German Rule 1905-1912 (Cambridge, University Press, 1969); J. Iliffe and G. Gwassa, Records of the Maji-Maji Uprising, Historical Association of Tanzania Paper No. 4 (Nairobi, East African Publishing House, 1968); J. Iliffe, "The Organization of the Maji-Maji Rebellion," Journal of African History VIII, 3 (1957), pp. 495-512; G. Gwassa, "The German Intervention and African Resistance in Tanzania," in A. Temu and I. Kimambo, History of Tanzania (Nairobi, East African Publishing House, 1969); T. Ranger, Revolt in Southern Rhodesia 1896-1897 (London, Heinemann, 1967).

the treatment of defection and submission as aspects of these rebellions seems to have been minimized. Moreover, except for A. D. Roberts' early and singular article on Ganda sub-imperialism in Uganda,[1] and despite Ranger's call for the investigation of "African resistance to _African_ pressure," there have been no studies of collaboration or the African opposition to collaboration by affiliates of the "Dar school."

But, the major reason that collaboration has appeared as an ignored or submerged theme among the nationalist historians has been a tendency to avoid the use of collaboration as a descriptive term and to completely eschew the term collaborators for characterizing Africans engaged in cooperative action with the colonial regimes. The highly colored and political origins of that term in the European context of non-resistance to Fascism can be used to justify this systematic avoidance. But, the complementary tendency to describe collaboration in the African context as accommodation or even modernization and to describe the African actors as modernizers or communicators has served to distort the nature of the response of collaboration by using terms loaded in an opposite direction. Instead of the condemnatory term of collaboration with its overtones of moral corruption and political self-seeking, we are confronted with essentially laudatory terms which emphasize (not coincidentally) the contribution of the collaborators to developing the conditions for the emergence of "nationalist movements." Dr. Lonsdale's communicators are explicitly the precursors of the later colonial communicators, the "nationalist elite."[2] And the modernizers

---

[1] A. Roberts, "The Sub-Imperialism of Buganda," _Journal of African History_ III 3 (1962), pp. 435-50.

[2] Lonsdale, "Some Origins," pp. 121 ff. A useful contrast is I. Henderson, "The Origins of Nationalism in East and Central Africa: the Zambian Case," _Journal of African History_ XI, 4, (1970), pp. 591-603.

of the journal, _Tarikh_, even when they are simultaneously resisters, are portrayed as prophets of national independence through selective adaptation.[1] Again, "African nationalism" and its triumph have cast a long shadow back, darkening our understanding of African behavior in both the colonial and immediate pre-colonial eras.

To let some light fall upon the nature of African initiatives and responses in the early colonial context, we will have to develop a far more subtle understanding of the nature of protest and collaboration than is allowed if we accept the nationalist contentions about protest as proto-nationalism and collaboration as modernization. But, before we can proceed to suggest a framework for such a new understanding of African responses, we must attempt to bury the wounded, but still dangerous, nationalist hypothesis. In aid of this, we move now to a case study of a rebellion which fits few of the nationalist criteria for African responses and which may provoke some inkling of a subtler ingredient in the nature of early colonial protest.

*   *   *

"The conspiracy had been marked with such able organization and recusancy for a long period so quietly and persistently sustained as to stamp it with the suspicion of non-native guidance."[2] So wrote the British colonial administrator, George Wilson, shortly after the suppression of the Nyangire Rebellion and the arrest of 54 of its African

---

[1] "Modernisers in Africa," _Tarikh_ I, 4 (1967).

[2] Wilson to Elgin, 25 June 1907, E[ntebbe] S[ecretariat] A[rchives] SMP 710/07.

leaders.   Wilson's long experience with Nyoro and Uganda politics
makes it difficult to dismiss his suspicions of "outside agitators" as
mere racist and reactionary hallucinations. Yet there is no evidence
whatsoever to sustain the suspicion that non-Banyoro organized or promoted the protest movement against colonial and Baganda overrule. What
made Wilson suspicious and how in fact was this anti-colonial protest
movement really generated?

In February, 1907, various Nyoro chiefs began to plan to evict
their Ganda co-chiefs from the positions to which they had come in the
previous half decade.[1] By March, a public refusal of cooperation drove
the Baganda from the Nyoro villages to the protection of the British
officials at Hoima, the capital. Confronted with direct orders to allow
the Baganda chiefs to resettle, the Nyoro chiefs refused pointblank
to reinstate the Baganda. Nyangire Abaganda, as the manifestation is remembered, means, "I have refused the Baganda." The Nyoro chiefs and their
followers gathered at the capital and persisted in refusing to allow the
Baganda to return to their posts. Finally, on May 16, 1907, with police
reinforcements on hand and prompted by fears for the safety of the Ganda
chiefs, the decision was taken by Wilson himself to break up the "frenzied"
demonstrations and arrest those chiefs at the capital. No one was killed
during the "rebellion," and violence against property was restricted to the
outlying areas where the huts of Ganda chiefs were burned. A strictly
constitutional agitation by means of civil disobedience aimed at the re-
dress of specific grievances had pushed the colonial administration to the

---

[1]For vernacular accounts of the events of the rebellion, see J. Nyakatura,
Abakama ba Bunyoro-Kitara (Canada, St. Justin's Press, 1947), p. 219 and
L. A. Katyanku and S. Bulera Obwomezi Bw' Omukama Duhaga II (Kampala, Eagle
Press, 1950), cyclostyled translation by Andrew Kigere-Kavuma, pp. 18-20.

point of counter violence. What were the grievances of the Banyoro
which underlay the protest?

Bunyoro, unlike the three other kingdoms of the Uganda Protectorate,
was a conquered province. No treaty or agreement regulated or formalized
the relations between the government of Bunyoro and the Protectorate
Government of British officials. The conquest of Bunyoro was begun in
1891 when Captain Frederick Lugard, acting for the Imperial British East
Africa Company and in alliance with the ruling group in the Buganda kingdom, invaded western Uganda and succeeded in severing Bunyoro's southern-
most counties and establishing a puppet regime in what became the Toro
kingdom. In 1893 a major military campaign was launched against the Mukama
Kabarega by the new Protectorate regime in Buganda. Acting in the interest
of Buganda's security and with a view to gaining control of the Nile
headwaters, Colonel Colvile, the British commander, succeeded in capturing
Kabarega's capital and establishing a military occupation. Kabarega was
eventually driven from his kingdom to exile north of the Nile where he
organized and led a guerrilla resistance which ended only with the Mukama's
capture in 1899.[1] It was Uganda's most protracted and heroic resistance
and a likely subject of nationalist mythology and historical attention.

From 1895 a new regime of collaboration was emerging in the rump of the
Bunyoro kingdom coincident with Kabarega's resistance. The severance of
Toro in 1891 had been followed by the alienation of large tracts of central
Bunyoro to Ganda chiefs as a reward for their participation in Bunyoro's

---

[1]See E. Steinhart, "Transition in Western Uganda: 1891-1901," unpublished
doctoral dissertation, Northwestern University, Evanston, Illinois, pp. 116-73.

341

conquest and in the hopes of settling Buganda's own turbulent religious situation.[1] Only the northernmost counties of the old kingdom were left to be administered by Nyoro chiefs. A young son of Kabarega's was proclaimed Mukama by the British authorities in 1898 in the hope of gaining a semblance of legitimacy for the regime of collaboration. With Kabarega's capture and exile in 1899 the path lay open for the _de facto_ elaboration of a new regime with new personnel under British guidance and protection, a regime which _de jure_ was a British creation as the victor claiming the spoils.

The British conviction that the Banyoro were both hostile to progress and incapable of efficient government led to the introduction of Baganda chiefs as tutors to the regime of collaboration. Everywhere in Uganda "progress" in administration and Christian religion was linked to the arrival of the agents of Buganda's sub-imperialism. But in Bunyoro it took a unique and particularly irritating form. Not only were vast areas of Bunyoro territory lying between the two kingdoms simply annexed to Buganda in the wake of the conquest, but even within the rump of Nyoro territory Baganda chiefs were set over Banyoro chiefs in order to teach them the arts of administration, à la Buganda.

In 1901, upon petition from the Nyoro chiefs charged with running the local administration, the Ganda chief, James Miti, was established as a chief in Bunyoro.[2] Miti and his following had a profound impact on Nyoro government. At first, it would appear that these men, particularly Miti, were well received by the Banyoro, or at least by the Nyoro

---

[1] A. D. Roberts, "The 'Lost Counties' of Bunyoro," Uganda Journal xxvi, 2, (1962), pp. 194-99.

[2] P. Lwanga, Obulamu Bw'omutaka J.K. Miti Kabazzi (Kampala, Friends Press, n.d.) and Wilson to Jackson, 14 Aug. 1901, ESA, A12/1. Ms. translation by Wm. Mukasa pp. 1-11.

political elite. Miti assisted in drafting a new territorial arrangement which regularized the chiefly hierarchy and confirmed various Nyoro chiefs and sub-chiefs in their titles and positions. This arrangement very much resembled the division of responsibility enacted by the formal agreements with Bunyoro's lacustrine neighbors, Ankole and Toro, except for the absence of landed estates granted to the title holders. Bunyoro, as a conquered territory, was not privileged to have chiefly freehold tenure introduced at this point.[1]

However, the chiefs had little room for complaint as it was clear that they governed at the sufferance of the colonial authorities. This was even true of the Mukama, Kitahimbwa, the son of Kabarega who was enthroned by British fiat in 1898. Both Miti and the collaborating chiefs, led by the Nyoro chief of Bugahya county, Paulo Byabacwezi, found Kitahimbwe difficult to work with in the governing council. In 1902 the chiefs petitioned the colonial regime for his removal and were obliged by the appointment of a new Mukama, an older son of Kabarega's who became Andereye Duhaga II. Miti especially was quick to gain the confidence of the new monarch and become effective ruler of the council and the country. This in turn led to increasing numbers of Ganda agents entering service in Bunyoro hoping by that means to advance their careers as colonial administrators.[2]

---

[1] See Steinhart, thesis, pp. 192-208.

[2] Tomkins to Commissioner, 16 Oct. 1902, ESA A12/2 and Interviews B/34, Princess Alexandria Komukyeya, 11 November 1968, and B/3 Martin Mukidi, 13 October 1968.

As early as June, 1902, the district officer noted "the very bad feeling that exists between the Ynyoro [sic] chiefs, and those who have been brought from Uganda and elsewhere, and put in charge of some of the counties".[1] While the eruption was still five years away, the roots of the disturbance in the fears among the Banyoro that their kingdom would be taken from them by piecemeal annexation or expropriation by Baganda chiefs "as was the case in Bugangaidzi and Buyaga," the "lost counties," were already evident. Moreover, the condition of the peasantry in the "lost counties" had even in 1902 become the source of real grievance, with Nyoro cultivators attempting to move from under the Ganda chiefs to escape harsh treatment.[2] Thus, the basic grievance over the presence of the Ganda chiefs and the treatment they gave their Nyoro underlings was present virtually from the onset of Ganda sub-imperialism.

This grievance was intensified by the fears that the Ganda would eventually take over full authority in Bunyoro. And the notion was not as far fetched as it might appear. As late as December, 1904, the local colonial official recommended to his superiors "the employment of carefully selected Waganda" as chiefs. It was his contention that in matters of the cultivation of cash crops in particular that these Baganda would "give more favorable results than are at present obtained by the apathetic, unreliable and

---

[1] Tomkins to Commissioner 16 June 1902, ESA A12/2.

[2] Bagge to Commissioner 16 May 1902, ESA A12/2 and interview B/10, Metushera Katuramu, 21 October 1968.

untrustworthy Wanyoro."[1]   In this fear it is safe to recognize a
certain community of interest between the Nyoro chiefs and the Nyoro
cultivators. Thus, while the inarticulate bakopi (common man) was not
in the forefront of protest, his opposition to Ganda overrule can be
seen in the attempted migration from the "lost counties" and in a curious
crisis which developed in 1904.

At that time, a new district officer took it on his own authority
to cancel the labor services owed to the chiefs by the bakopi as he
felt it interfered with the bakopi cultivation of their own gardens. There
was an immediate outcry from among the chiefs, including the Mukama Duhaga.
Administrative action was necessary, argued the district officer, as the
"peasantry," who had "become little more than slaves ready to work for the
chiefs when ordered" feared that their complaints would be cause for further
prestations when they came before the governing council dominated as it was
by Miti. Despite the humanitarian impulse and the recognition of the
legitimacy of some of the bakopi grievances, the labor services were
quickly restored.[2] It was decided to uphold the "properly constituted
authority" of the chiefs. Although the chiefs were lacking in education,
he said, "the peasantry require discipline in even greater degree."[3] Some

---

[1] Fowler to Wilson, 31 December 1904, ESA A12/5.

[2] Prendergast to Commissioner, n.d., 10 January 1904 and 8 February 1904,
ESA A12/5.

[3] Wilson to Commissioner, 10 March 1904, ESA A12/5. These events are
described as a "rebellion" by Katyanku and Bulera, Obwomezi, p. 18.

adjustments were suggested such as the keeping of labor rolls by chiefs and the right of appeal from the council to the local colonial officer, but I think it can be agreed that "peasant" grievances against chiefly authority, particularly the authority of the alien chiefs, was a constant factor underlying the rebellion of 1907.

At the time of the dispute over labor services, the chiefs had intended to petition the colonial authority for salaries and estates like those obtained by the chiefs of Buganda. The dispute over labor prestations temporarily delayed their appeal.[1] However, by 1905 new arrangements on the rights and responsibilities of chiefs were being made and were promulgated in 1906 as the System of Chieftaincy in Unyoro, 1906.[2] While the Nyoro chiefs seem to have been satisfied with the arrangements at the time, they contained the seeds of some discord. First, no private estates were allotted under the new system. By this time the Nyoro chiefs were well aware of the differences between themselves and the chiefs of the neighboring kingdoms, but that did little to soften the resentment. By late 1906 the Nyoro chiefs had petitioned unsuccessfully for private lands.[3]

Secondly, there was a marked increase in the territorial authority of both James Miti and Mika Fataki, a Musoga by birth but allied to the Ganda influence in Bunyoro. This too seems to have exacerbated the fears of the Nyoro chiefs and possibly heightened the incipient rivalry between Byabacwezi, the leading Nyoro chief, and Miti, the leading alien chief within the governing council.

_____

[1] Wilson to Commissioner 10 May 1904, ESA A12/5.

[2] Unyoro Chiefs, Grant of Estates to, ESA SMP 1019/06, includes the correspondenc of land grants and the text of the "System of Chieftaincy in Unyoro, 1906."

[3] Minute by H. Bell, 31 October 1906, ESA SMP 1019/06.

Indeed, the growth of Miti's direct territorial authority and his growing influence over the monarch seem to be the main sources of grievance among the Nyoro ruling elite. It is this last phenomenon which, in addition to producing the rivalry between Miti and Byabacwezi as arch-collaborator, seems to have alienated a large number of the Royal Bito dynasty from the rule of Duhaga. Criticism of Duhaga for allowing the Ganda to gain a foothold (although Miti himself was invited to Bunyoro before Duhaga was made Mukama) and for granting too much power to his Ganda advisors was a prevalent theme among Duhaga's numerous Bito kinsmen. How much was sincere objection to Duhaga's failure to exercise royal authority and how much self-seeking opportunism among potential candidates for Duhaga's throne is difficult to say. But there is evidence to indicate that both forces were at work among the Bito clansmen.[1]

To this list of injuries must be added the insult of Ganda cultural imperialism. The use of Luganda as the official language of state and church may have rankled from the onset of Ganda influence. However, when the C.M.S. missionary in Bunyoro, A.B. Fisher, wrote a letter to the missionary in Toro, Henry Maddox, on the subject of encouraging the use of Luganda, he triggered off more than he knew. The letter, in arguing for the retention of Luganda in church affairs, pointed up the growth of

---

[1]Interviews B/3, Martin Mukidi, 13 October 1968 and B/24 Z.K. Winyi and Z. K. Mugenyi, 2 November 1968.

Ganda influence sponsored by the Ganda chiefs in Bunyoro.[1] Maddox,
a proponent of local language use, particularly in translating the Bible
to make it as widely available as possible to the agricultural classes,
read the letter aloud to the Toro Church Council. The council, composed
of many of the important Toro chiefs, had direct connections to the
Nyoro chiefly hierarchy. We can assume that word passed very quickly
from the Toro chiefs, who had fought a considerable struggle to secure
both their political and cultural independence from Buganda, to the Nyoro
chiefs, who were prompted to begin their own struggle to rid themselves
of Ganda influence.[2]

Thus, at every level of Bunyoro's political hierarchy -- from the bakopi
peasant cultivators suffering under the sting of new taxes and labor prestations through the Nyoro sub-chiefs and chiefs jealous of the growing influence of their Ganda co-chiefs to the royal dynasty itself -- grievances
against the colonial system which had introduced the Baganda to Nyoro politics were rampant. In February, 1907, the rebellion began when the Nyoro
chiefs came forward to express their protest at the unhappy state of
affairs in the kingdom.

*   *   *

---

[1] Fisher to Maddox, Christmas 1905, Fisher Correspondence, Microfilm Makerere
Library.

[2] Thanks to Dr. Louise Pirouet for suggesting this interpretation based on her
work in mission history, for the Department of Religions, Makerere University.
See Steinhart, thesis, pp. 103-08 for Toro's cultural resistance.

The rebellion itself can be said to have begun in early February, 1907, when in the absence of James Miti from the Lukiko or governing council, a new spirit of protest and defiance arose. Miti, through his "undue influence over the Mukama and thus over the Lukiko generally,"[1] had come to dominate the political life of the court. It is of some significance that the voice of protest was first raised while he was away in Buganda. Suspicion that Miti was recruiting more Baganda for service in Bunyoro may lie behind the talk of a Baganda conspiracy to oust the Nyoro title holders.[2] In any case, Miti's absence provided "a much desired opportunity to speak out." At this stage, the protest remained strictly verbal and confined to the Lukiko, but the major themes of the rebellion were clearly articulated: anti-alien and anti-authoritarian feelings began to be voiced.

According to the British officer, Cubitt:[3]

> . . . the chief reason for this burst of feeling against the Waganda lies in the fact that the Mukama and chiefs asked H. E. the Commissioner if they could be given official and private miles (estates) and the Wanyoro are afraid that a lot of their land will be handed over to the Waganda.

---

[1] Cubitt to Deputy Commissioner, 21 February 1907, ESA SMP 267/07.

[2] Nyakatura, Abakama, p. 219.

[3] Cubitt to Deputy Commissioner, 21 February 1907, ESA SMP 267/07. Cf. Interview B/3, Martin Mukidi, 13 October 1968.

While Cubitt tended to dismiss such fears as groundless, the fact that the leading chiefs, including the alien chiefs led by Miti, had petitioned the government for extensive grants of freehold land late in 1906 provided a major threat to the Nyoro cultivators and minor chiefs. It would be well to note that Cubitt's report speaks of the protestors as "Batongole," a Ganda term referring not only to the senior chiefs on the Lukiko, but to lesser chiefs who, while they were Lukiko councilors, would not have shared in the distribution of land grants. If freehold tenure had been introduced at this time as it had been earlier in Buganda, it might well have created a class of landed oligarchs whose economic control of land and political power reinforced each other. This would have created a monopoly of power from which the Nyoro populace and the minor chiefs would suffer. Thus, an anti-authoritarian element can be seen in the attempts to thwart the senior chiefs, including the alien chiefs, from gaining a permanent foothold in Bunyoro and vastly increasing their power by becoming landlords as well as chiefs.

But, it was the anti-alien theme which came to predominate in Nyoro motivation. Miti's position as a Muganda chief focused their anti-authoritarian complaints. Originally, he had been invited to Bunyoro to teach the Nyoro chiefs how to rule. In his wake had come an influx of Baganda into the country, who as friends and followers of Miti had found themselves comfortable and often lucrative positions in the conquered province. They came as petty traders, evangelists, and eventually as minor chiefs and headmen, bringing with them a cultural arrogance, commercial and religious attitudes, and a desire for authority which was not calculated to win friends among the Nyoro population. They began turning out the "rightful landholders" and assuming power at a grassroots level. Another complaint was "that the Waganda have brought nothing into the country, and that all the profits that they get they send over to (B)Uganda, thus impoverishing (B)Unyoro and enriching (B)Uganda. . ."[1] It is not difficult to see the formation of stereotyping of the alien exploiters which preceded the outburst of feeling against them. Both elements of anti-Ganda and anti-authoritarian protest were symbolically united in the protest against the twenty or so Baganda chiefs and in this Miti himself provided a perfect target.

But, the groundswell of resentment against the chiefs was quickly channeled. The chief reason for the protest, the fear of land grants, was reduced to the fear of alienation of land and loss of authority to the alien intruders. In this the Nyoro senior chiefs were able to join. While the minor chiefs started the manifestations, it was the senior chiefs, Paulo Byabacwezi, Leo Kaboha and Katalikawe, who began to organize the protest to bring it to the next stage: the explusion of the Ganda chiefs.[2] By siding with the dissidents, the senior chiefs were able to channel the anti-authoritarian resentment into more narrowly anti-alien protest, which still struck a responsive chord among the Nyoro populace. By early March, 1907, the Baganda were being driven out of the countryside by the threat of violence from the Nyoro "peasantry" and were seeking refuge at Hoima, the capital.[3]

The British response to the expulsion of the Baganda was remarkably unimaginative. While Cubitt initially felt that the protest might be

---

[1] Ibid.

[2] Nakiwafu to Jemusi (Miti) Kago, 6 February 1907, ESA SMP 267/07.

[3] Fataki to Apolo Kagwa Katikiro, 7 March 1907 (trans.) ESA SMP 267/07.

viewed as an opportunity for allowing the Nyoro chiefs to govern under threat that any "regressive movement" would be handled by bringing the Baganda back,[1] Wilson, as Deputy Commissioner, insisted on upholding the letter of the law. He advised the district officer "to nip in the bud any attempt to interfere with the scheme of chieftainships proposed by the Lukiko and confirmed by the Commissioner according to the book published. . ." in 1906[2]. Unhappy with the way Cubitt was handling the situation, Wilson dispatched another officer, Tomkins, who arrived in early April.[3] But, Tomkins arrived bearing instructions to strictly enforce the system of chieftaincy "according to the book." Despite the statements of Byabacwezi that he and Kaboha had only "signed as they feared to do otherwise, and the Mukama did what Jamusi [Miti] told him," Tomkins was unable to retreat to a flexible solution to the crisis.[4]

Tomkins called a Baraza of all the senior chiefs and reminded them of the system of chieftaincy which had been agreed to by the chiefs and the Protectorate government. To the Nyoro chiefs' pleas of duress in their signing the agreement were added the catalogue of complaints against the the Ganda chiefs and Miti in particular. Tomkins reported that the "great point with the Bunyoro chiefs is that they should be allowed to rule their own country as the chiefs of Toro, (B)Uganda, Ankole, etc., are allowed to do."[5] While this was not the great point of the Nyoro populace or of the

---

[1]Cubitt to Deputy Commissioner, 21 February 1907, ESA SMP 267/07.

[2]Wilson to Collector, Hoima (telegram) 13 March 1907, ESA SMP 267/07.

[3]Tomkins to Deputy Commissioner (telegram) 7 April 1907, ESA SMP 267/07.

[4]Tomkins to Deputy Commissioner, 15 April 1907, ESA SMP 267/07.

[5]Ibid.

lesser chiefs, it was a point which seems to have convinced Tomkins of
the justice of the Nyoro case.

By May there was no longer any time for continued protest. The
Ganda chiefs had been thoroughly driven out of the country and were waiting
in Hoima to be reinstated. Some huts had been burned, but no violence
against persons had taken place. Still Wilson insisted on a hard line and
Eden, the new district officer, called a Baraza and put it to the chiefs:
They must reinstate the Baganda or risk losing their own positions. Even
if the reinstatement were only temporary, subject to the government's review
of the Nyoro grievances, it was the only term the Protectorate government
would consider. On May 7 the order to reinstate the Baganda was read to
the assembled chiefs, who refused to cooperate, contending that even if they
were willing the bakopi or "peasants" could not be persuaded and wanted
the Baganda expelled.[1] This the government considered an excuse. Apparently
the absence of personal violence had convinced them already that this was
a well-organized and controlled demonstration out of keeping with European
stereotypes of African emotionalism and violent tendencies.[2]

Two more barazas on the 8th and 9th of May saw the Nyoro chiefs remain
adamant, but calm, in their refusal to allow the Baganda to return to their
villages even on a temporary basis. On the 9th Eden announced a four-day
ultimatum after which if the Nyoro chiefs persisted in refusing they would
jeopardize their positions. But, when Wilson's hard line was reiterated
after the four-day grace, the Nyoro chiefs who had been assembled at the

---

[1]Eden to Wilson, 11 May 1907, ESA SMP 710/07 and Lwanga, Miti, pp. 50-51.
[2]Wilson to Spires, 28 May 1907, and Wilson to Elgin, 25 June 1907, ESA SMP
710/07.

Post Office in Hoima not only refused but did so in loud and "passionate" terms. Two days later, May 16, the chiefs were again assembled, again refused, and this time, following the orders of Deputy Commissioner Wilson, fifty-four of the assembled rebels were arrested. This number included the names of senior and minor chiefs and important personages including many members of the royal Bito clan.[1]

Throughout the disturbances, the Mukama hewed to a neutral line. He insisted that he personally did not want the Baganda to leave, but that his chiefs were the motive force for expulsion. His failure to assume leadership in the protest has been laid to a weakness of character and the influence of his Baganda and missionary advisors. A more charitable view sees him in full support of the rebellion, but shrewdly avoiding a situation which would jeopardize his authority and his throne.[2] In support of this contention, it is not unlikely that the Baganda leadership in Kampala coveted an even more direct subjugation of Bunyoro and might well have aimed at placing a member of the Ganda royal family on the Nyoro throne. In that light, Duhaga's neutrality may well have served to preserve not only his own position, but it may have saved the Nyoro dynasty and the peace of the country as well.[3]

---

[1]Lwanga, Miti, pp. 51-52, and Eden to Wilson, 11 May 1907, and Wilson to Elgin, 25 June 1907, ESA SMP 710/07. Cf. Interview B/19, Isaya Bikundi, 30 October 1968. See Uzoigwe, "The Kyanyangire, 1907," pp. 149-59, for a detailed account of the events.

[2]Interviews B/3 Martin Mukidi, 13 October 1968, and B/34, Princess Alexandria Komukyeya, 11 November 1968.

[3]Ibid., and Katyanku and Bulera, Duhaga, pp. 19-20.

Of the senior chiefs, Byabacwezi, who was considered by Eden as the ringleader, managed to escape arrest. In fact, Byabacwezi appears to have wavered and to have been pushed into a hard line position by his co-chief, Leo Kaboha, and particularly by his sub-chiefs. Byabacwezi was prepared to surrender to the British pressure were it not for fear of loss of popular support. It was reported that Byabacwezi had verbally agreed to the ultimatum on the 14th day of May, but on telling his sub-chiefs this was derided into continued resistance. It was "better to suffer with the rest and have the good opinion of others. Byabacwezi is said to have cried and to have decided to be a martyr rather than a turn-coat. . ."[1]

It is the crucial role of the sub-chiefs that is deserving of note. Ibrahim Talyeba, the deputy (mumyoka) sub-chief under Miti, played a very prominent part in organizing the disturbances and in persuading Byabacwezi to persist. Daudi Bitaluli, the deputy to Byabacwezi, was also among the leaders arrested.[2] Pressure from the leading sub-chiefs may well have been motivated by jealousy at the growth of Baganda titleholding which excluded them from the senior positions. The large number of Babito among the sub-chiefs raises the question of the role of dynastic intrigue, possibly against Duhaga and favoring a restoration of Kabarega, then in his eighth year of exile. In any case, it was believed by the district officer, Eden,[3] and would appear from the numbers of sub-chiefs arrested,

---

[1] Haddon to Collector, Unyoro, 19 May 1907, ESA SMP 710/07.

[2] Interviews B/44, Yesse T. Kinimi, 3 December 1968, and B/12, Nebayosi Tibangwa, 22 October 1968. These men are the sons of Talyeba and Bitatuli respectively

[3] Eden to Wilson, 11 May 1907, ESA SMP 710/07.

that it was the second rank of Nyoro chiefs who initiated, organized and sustained the constitutional agitation and protest which Wilson could not believe was of local African authorship. While the British officials discounted the allegation by the chiefs that the bakopi were hostile to the Baganda and would kill them if they returned to the villages, the role of both Bito and commoner sub-chiefs in the agitation lends credence to the contention that popular discontent with the growth of alien influence and the resulting social uncertainty was a powerful force in sustaining the "rebellion" by the chiefs.

As a side note, the highly politically conscious nature of the rebellion as a constitutional protest can be illustrated by a unique maneuver by the Nyoro chiefs. During the disturbances envoys were sent to the neighboring kingdoms of Toro and Ankole and to Busoga and the "lost counties" in the hopes of finding allies there who might extend the anti-Ganda rebellion throughout the Ganda dominated provinces.[1] Such an attempt to increase the pressure on the British to remove the Baganda chiefs by seeking a multi-tribal, albeit single issue, organization shows a political wisdom which we tend to identify with only the more modern of the African protest movements. The agitation for the return of the "lost counties," which Wilson for one believed was the object of the entire exercise, spread to that district and required the presence of a police force under Apolo Kagwa, the Prime Minister of Buganda, to insure the "Pax Brittanica."[2]

---

[1]Isemonger to Wilson, 18 June 1907, ESA SMP 267/07. Cf. Haddon to Collector, Unyoro, 19 May 1907, ESA SMP 267/07.

[2]Lwanga, Miti, p. 53. Kagwa before being diverted to the "lost counties" had been en route to Bunyoro in the company of a Ganda prince lending credibility to the suspicion of a Ganda conspiracy to undermine Nyoro "sovereignty." Cf. Katyanku and Bulera, Duhaga. p. 19.

Deputy Commissioner Wilson arrived at Hoima on May 22, 1907, with police and military reinforcements. Unhappy at the handling of the disturbances by the local officers, he felt that prolonged confrontation even after the arrest of over fifty agitators might well lead to violence against the Baganda still at Hoima. It was his purpose to put a quick finish to the spirit of rebellion. A new round of barazas was begun with Wilson presiding.[1]

On the 27th day of May judgment was handed down by Wilson. His awards reflect his prejudices and the element of necessity in colonial efforts to secure peaceful subordination. The four Nyoro senior chiefs implicated in the rebellion were most unevenly punished. Leo Kaboha was deposed from his chieftaincy and exiled to Buganda.[2] Katalikawe was deposed and forfeited one-third of his land holdings. Daudi Katongole lost one-third of his estates and two years of tax revenues.[3] Byabacwezi, who most of the British believed was the prime mover in the rebellion, lost a third of his estates and was fined 500 to be paid within two years. The fine was later reduced. Moreover, whatever debts were due to him from the Protectorate government for a decade of service in establishing the regime of collaboration were considered as wiped out.[4] All in all, his penalties were not harsh. One wonders if leniency flowed from Wilson's merciful qualities and from the recognition of past services or if it

---

[1] Lwanga, Miti, pp. 53-54, and Wilson to Elgin, 25 June, 1907, ESA SMP 710/07.

[2] Wilson, "Award," 27 May 1907, ESA SMP 710/07 and Interviews B/4., Pancras Kaboha, 25 November 1968 and B/42, William Kaboha, 26 November 1968.

[3] Wilson, "Award," 27 May 1907, ESA SMP 710/07 and Interview B/19, Isaya Bikundi, 30 October 1968.

[4] Ibid.

resulted from a calculated realization of the importance of Byabacwezi to the functioning of any system of indirect rule and collaboration in Bunyoro.

All those arrested on May 16 when the baraza threatened to erupt into violence were to be removed to Buganda.[1] Twelve of these fifty-four were eventually deported from Uganda entirely. This number included Leo Kaboha, but was made up essentially of the most vocal agitators among the sub-chiefs. It was on these men that the penalties fell most heavily, complaints being received that their property was being confiscated and their wives and children were being driven off their estates.[2]

A word of sympathy was appended to the Award for the bakopi, whom Wilson felt had "not been deeply implicated." Even after the events, a realistic assessment of the role of popular support for the anti-Ganda and anti-authoritarian movement was not possible for the architects of British colonial overrule. The myth of a quiescent peasantry had to be preserved.[3]

The last section of the award reads:[4]

> The Unyoro chiefs, who are Baganda, are to be
> at once installed by a Government officer with proper
> impressiveness and with a fitting force. They will
> not be installed as Baganda but as Unyoro chiefs,
> who were removed from their posts in violation of
> the law.

---

[1] Ibid., and Manara to Wilson, 7 June 1907, ESA SMP 710/07.

[2] Various entries in "Deportation of Unyoro Chiefs," ESA SMP 1367/07.

[3] Cf. M. Weisser, personal communication, 24 March 1971, regarding a forth-coming paper on peasant crime in Spain.

[4] Wilson, "Award," 27 May 1907, ESA SMP 710/07 and Lwanga, Miti, pp. 54-56.

The Baganda were indeed restored and in that sense the rebellion was
a failure and the losses to the Nyoro organizers were suffered for
nought. The huts of two Ganda chiefs were burned the following year
and tensions continued to be high for several years. As a result, no
additional Ganda chiefs were appointed to positions in Bunyoro and
those in office were eventually retired in favor of Nyoro successors.[1]
Thus, a delayed and disguised success did attend this early protest
movement against a form of colonial overrule. Nyangire, along with
Kaberega's guerilla struggle of the previous decade, became a focus
of Nyoro pride in the courage and defiance of their leaders. But, the
"nationalist" pride of later generations does not establish the proto-
nationalist motives of the early resisters and protesters. We must try
to establish the nature of protest-generating sentiments without benefit
of such hindsight and see where such sentiments might lead.

*   *   *

That the Nyangire Rebellion was not proto-nationalist in its
motivation or organization seems evident from the events described. While
the anti-Ganda strain, which came to dominate the protest movement, can be
seen as particularist or "tribalist," that, too, would be an over-simpli-
fication. Traditional antipathies were certainly present, but to emphasize
them at the price of ignoring the real and pressing grievances against
the facts of colonial oppression is to flatten the texture of Nyoro society
in transition.[2] The fear of Ganda expropriation of land by the sub-chiefs,

---

[1] Leakey to Deputy Commissioner, 31 January 1908 and 24 April 1908, ESA SMP
C10/08; Eden, "Annual Report for 1911-12," p. 56, ESA SMP 2135.

[2] See Uzoigwe; "The Kyanyangire, 1907," while very richly documented, tends to
treat the anti-alien sentiments and appeal to history as uniform among the
various Nyoro classes, thus homogenizing Nyoro society for nationalist purposes.

the resentment against Ganda office holding by the senior chiefs, and the beginnings of hostility by the agricultural population against the agents of "modernization" (i.e., against bureaucratic and capitalist intervention into "traditional" social and political life) all fed the protest movement. Popular anti-authoritarianism and elite fear of social disruption fused with the protest against alien domination to propel the Nyoro people toward rebellion.

But, how can a rebellion by the Nyoro chiefs be called anti-authoritarian? Here we see the peculiar contradiction of the collaborating chiefs writ large. They were under pressure from below to champion the anti-colonial struggle and countervailing pressure to administer the colonial state. These cross pressures were most evident in the arch-collaborator Byabacwezi's ambivalence toward the struggle. But, the contradiction is also evidenced by the efforts of the collaborating Nyoro leadership to organize and direct the protest not against alien authority in general but against the Baganda aliens in particular. By identifying the exercise of illegitimate authority with the Ganda chiefs, the Nyoro chiefs were able to appear as the champions of popular anti-colonial sentiment without stirring anti-authoritarian feelings against themselves as colonial agents. They were thus able to harness popular revolutionary impulses to self-seeking and particularist programs which at base contradicted the impulses which propelled them.

If this is our interpretation of Nyangire, how can we relate it to other movements of anti-colonial protest or resistance? The answer, I believe, is that we must reinterpret the entire tradition of anti-colonial

protest from a perspective which allows us to see beyond the "nationalist"
flowering of later anti-colonial movements to a profounder understanding
of the roots of revolt.

Let me illustrate what must be done with an example from late colonial
history in Kenya. Two reinterpretations of the Mau-Mau movement were
published in the mid-1960's. By far the most influential is that of Rosberg
and Nottingham in their The Myth of "Mau Mau," subtitled "Nationalism in
Kenya."[1] Here we have made explicit the nationalist interpretation of anti-
colonial uprisings. Mau-Mau is related to the development of nationalism
in Kenya right back to the first resistance wars against the British invaders.[2] Thwarted politically, nationalist sentiment turns violent, but
remains fundamentally nationalist. This view, which is infinitely preferable
to the previous view of Mau-Mau as tribal atavism and savage frenzy, was
quickly applauded by the nationalist historians of the "Dar es Salaam
School."[3]

But, nationalism is not the only interpretation possible, nor, to
my mind, the most useful. The same year which saw the publication of
The Myth of "Mau Mau" also saw the release of Barnett and Njama's Mau-Mau

---

[1]C. Rosberg and J. Nottingham, The Myth of "Mau Mau" (New York, Praeger, 1966).

[2]Ibid., pp. 7-16.

[3]J. Lonsdale, "New Perspectives in Kenya History," African Affairs Vol. 66,
no. 265, pp. 348-53.

from Within.[1] As the title indicates, the perspective is what matters.
For Barnett's interpretation of Njama's autobiography emphasized another
element in the rebellion. Instead of the nationalist "communicators" as
the focus of the rebellion, Barnett emphasizes the peasant partisans, the
actual militants of the forest and mountains. From that perspective, i.e.,
from the bottom up, the roots of Mau-Mau lie not in nationalist organization
but in the revolutionary, anti-authoritarian impulses of the African
"peasantry." Such a view accords far better with the interpretation of
the Nyangire Rebellion presented here.

Instead of examining anti-colonial resistance, protest and liberation movements through the distorting lens of nationalist mythology, we
must create a better "myth," one better suited to interpreting the reality
of African protest. The meaning of nationalism must be stretched too far to
accommodate protests such as Nyangire (or Mau Mau).[2] By focusing on the
leadership, the communicators, be they chiefs or political party leaders,
we have accepted an interpretation of anti-colonialism as "African nationalism,'
a movement to expel the aliens and restore "national" independence. If
instead we look within the protest movements, at leaders and followers alike,
we are apt to discover that the impulses which the leaders organize and
interpret are profoundly anti-authoritarian and revolutionary rather than
anti-foreign and "nationalist." A "myth of popular insurrection" may

---

[1] D. Barnett and K. Njama, Mau Mau from Within (London, MacGibbon and Kee,
1966).

[2] Even Thomas Hodgkin's flexible definition seems too broad to be of much use,
as it covers too many non-national sources of anti-colonial sentiment.
Cf. T. Hodgkin, Nationalism in Colonial Africa (New York, New York University
Press, 1957), p. 23.

lead us further and deeper in our understanding of twentieth century movements of protest and liberation than the failing "myth of nationalism" has brought us.[1] Working out this interpretation in detail is the arduous task facing historians and students of Africa who have found nationalism a "false start."

---

[1] For those offended by the advocacy of a substitute "myth" instead of a call for objectivity, let me first apologize by indicating that the concept of interpretation can be substituted for that of myth and second recommend the chapter on "Myth and Society" in F. Welbourn and B. Ogot, A Place to Feel at Home (London, Oxford University Press, 1966) for an illuminating discussion of the role of myth in African societies under western impact.

ACKNOWLEDGMENTS

Ranger, T.O. "Connections Between 'Primary Resistance' Movements and Modern Mass Nationalism in East and Central Africa, Parts I & II." *Journal of African History* 9 (1968): 437-53, 631-41. Reprinted with the permission of Cambridge University Press. Courtesy of Yale University Sterling Memorial Library.

Obichere, Boniface I. "African Critics of Victorian Imperialism: An Analysis." *Journal of African Studies* 4 (1977): 1-20. Reprinted with the permission of Heldref Publications. Courtesy of Yale University Sterling Memorial Library.

Ram, K.V. "The Survival of Ethiopian Independence." *Journal of the Historical Society of Nigeria* 8 (1977): 131-41. Courtesy of Yale University Sterling Memorial Library.

Afigbo, A.E. "Patterns of Igbo Resistance to British Conquest." *Tarikh* 4 (1973): 14-23. Courtesy of Yale University Sterling Memorial Library.

O'Sullivan, John M. "The Franco-Baoulé War, 1891-1911: The Struggle against the French Conquest of Central Ivory Coast." *Journal of African Studies* 5 (1978): 329-56. Reprinted with the permission of Heldref Publications. Courtesy of Yale University Sterling Memorial Library.

Oloruntimehin, B. Olatunji. "French Colonisation and African Resistance in West Africa up to the First World War." *Tarikh* 4 (1973): 24-34. Courtesy of Yale University Sterling Memorial Library.

Isaacman, Allen and Barbara Isaacman. "Resistance and Collaboration in Southern and Central Africa, c. 1850-1920." *International Journal of African Historical Studies* 10 (1977): 31-62. Reprinted with the permission of the African Studies Center. Courtesy of Yale University Sterling Memorial Library.

Ahmed, Christine Choi. "God, Anti-Colonialism and Dance: Sheekh Uways and the Uwaysiyya." *Ufahamu* 17 (1989): 96-117. (Revised Edition) Reprinted with the permission of the African Activist Association. Courtesy of Christine Choi Ahmed.

Kakwenzire, Patrick. "Resistance, Revenue and Development in Northern Somalia, 1905-1939." *International Journal of African Historical Studies* 19 (1986): 659-77. Reprinted with the permission of the African Studies Center. Courtesy of Yale University Sterling Memorial Library.

Holt, P.M. "The Place in History of the Sudanese Mahdia." *Sudan Notes and Records* 40 (1959): 107-12. Reprinted with the permission of the Sudan Notes and Records. Courtesy of Yale University Sterling Memorial Library.

Giblin, James. "Famine and Social Change During the Transition to Colonial Rule in Northeastern Tanzania, 1880-1896." *African Economic History* 15 (1986): 85-105. Reprinted with the permission of the African Studies Center. Courtesy of Yale University Sterling Memorial Library.

Iliffe, John. "The Organization of the Maji Maji Rebellion." Journal of African History 8 (1967): 495-512. Reprinted with the permission of Cambridge University Press. Courtesy of Yale University Sterling Memorial Library.

Redmond, Patrick M. "Maji Maji in Ungoni: A Reappraisal of Existing Historiography." International Journal of African Historical Studies 8 (1975): 407-24. Reprinted with the permission of the African Studies Center. Courtesy of Yale University Sterling Memorial Library.

Linden, Jane and Ian Linden. "John Chilembwe and the New Jerusalem." *Journal of African History 12 (1971): 629-51.* Reprinted with the permission of Cambridge University Press. Courtesy of Yale University Sterling Memorial Library.

Beach, D.N. "'Chimurenga': The Shona Rising of 1896-97." *Journal of African History* 20 (1979): 395-420. Reprinted with the permission of Cambridge University Press. Courtesy of Yale University Sterling Memorial Library.

Lovejoy, Paul E. and J.S. Hogendorn. "Revolutionary Mahdism and Resistance to Colonial Rule in the Sokoto Caliphate, 1905-6." *Journal of African History* 31 (1990): 217-44. Reprinted with the permission of Cambridge University Press. Courtesy of Yale University Sterling Memorial Library.

Steinhart, Edward I. "The Nyangire Rebellion of 1907: Anti-Colonial Protest and the Nationalist Myth." *East African Studies* 12 (1973): 38-69. Reprinted with the permission of the Institute of Social Research, Makerere University. Courtesy of Gregory Maddox.

S